MATTHEW,
Disciple and Scribe

MATTHEW, Disciple and Scribe

The First Gospel and Its Portrait of Jesus

Patrick Schreiner

Baker Academic

a division of Baker Publishing Group
Grand Rapids, Michigan

© 2019 by Patrick Schreiner

Published by Baker Academic
a division of Baker Publishing Group
PO Box 6287, Grand Rapids, MI 49516-6287
www.bakeracademic.com

Printed in the United States of America

Library of Congress Cataloging-in-Publication Data
Names: Schreiner, Patrick, author.
Title: Matthew, disciple and scribe : the first Gospel and its portrait of Jesus / Patrick Schreiner.
Description: Grand Rapids : Baker Academic, a division of Baker Publishing Group, 2019. |
    Includes bibliographical references and index.
Identifiers: LCCN 2018053552 | ISBN 9780801099489 (pbk.)
Subjects: LCSH: Bible. Matthew—Criticism, interpretation, etc.
Classification: LCC BS2575.52 .S37 2019 | DDC 226.2/06—dc23
LC record available at https://lccn.loc.gov/2018053552

ISBN 978-1-5409-6217-1 (casebound)

19   20   21   22   23   24   25   7   6   5   4   3   2   1

To Jonathan Pennington
and my teachers at Southern Seminary,
who taught me the wisdom of the Scriptures

Contents

Preface   ix

Abbreviations   xi

Introduction   1

Part 1: The Scribe Described   5

1. Matthew, the Discipled Scribe   7
2. The Scribe's Convictions and Methods   37

Part 2: The Scribe at Work   63

3. Jesus and the Journey of the Davidic King   65
4. Jesus as the Ideal and Wise King   101
5. Jesus and the Mosaic Exodus   131
6. Jesus and Abraham's New Family   169
7. Jesus and Israel's Destiny   207
   Conclusion   241

   Bibliography   255
   Index of Authors   268
   Index of Scripture and Other Ancient
      Sources   271
   Index of Subjects   281

Preface

Expectations are key. Though the title of this book might compel you to think this is a work on authorship or even Matthean priority, that is not the case. The pages before you focus more on the theology and narrative of Matthew. Though I do think it was Matthew—the disciple and scribe—who wrote the First Gospel, my argument does not depend on Matthean authorship, nor will I spend time arguing for Matthean authorship. My aims are broader than this.

Two brief notes should be made before I begin. First, the work before you is more constructive than deconstructive. Though it undoubtedly has elements that work against certain tendencies, the aim of this work is not to take a theory and overturn it. Rather, I present one way to view Matthew's narrative. This means I don't begin by identifying a problem nor developing tension and then spend the rest of the work trying to solve it. Rather, I put forward my argument, hoping that it will bring some light to Matthew's narrative.

Second, though I do support my assertions with footnotes, I have tried to limit repeated references and not to log what each commentator says about each passage. Therefore, some statements stand without a reference at all, even when I make statements like "many commentators" or "most scholars." I realize that this is an academic *faux paux*, but it has helped keep it at a manageable length. In addition, the initial plan was to be more introductory, but it quickly took an academic turn, and therefore the book at times straddles both worlds. I realize that this could be a stumbling block for readers, so I hope you are the type who reads the preface.

This book was birthed out of a love for the Gospels and an affinity for Matthew more specifically—a love that has continued from the days of my seminary course work and doctoral thesis. In many ways, the book does not feel complete, because I discover something new each time I read and study the Gospel. I recognize that the editing, organizing, and clarifying of this work could continue *ad infinitum*. In many ways, no book is ever done; it is simply due.

Many helped me improve this work. Jonathan Pennington read an early and later version and provided both structural and more detailed comments. My father, Thomas Schreiner, also read many chapters as I finished them and enhanced the project on many levels. My colleagues Josh Mathews and Todd Miles also read parts of the book and pointed out areas that could be strengthened. Nathan Ridlehoover read sections and pointed me to other parts of Matthew that aligned with my argument. Peter Gurry helped me on the chapter concerning scribes, and Chris Bruno gave me some structural suggestions and noted places where I needed more clarity. Adam Christian read a section of the book with the oral tradition (rather than written) in mind. Chad Ashby gave me feedback in the initial stages, and Katlyn Richards completed the Scripture and author indexes. Bryan Dyer was instrumental in getting this project off the ground and provided good feedback along the way. The editors at Baker also improved the work, especially Wells Turner, who provided an editorial eye and double-checked my cross-references. I would be remiss not to mention my wife and children as they endured many late nights and coffee shop trips as I worked through this material. I could not have completed any of this if my wife were not such a stabilizing force at home.

My prayer as you read this book is that you too will follow the teacher of wisdom by paying close attention to the scribe's recounting of Jesus's life. Matthew, as the disciple and scribe, wrote about Jesus in a unique way to make disciples of future generations (Matt. 28:18–20).

Abbreviations

Bibliographic and General

ANE	ancient Near East
ANF	*The Ante-Nicene Fathers: Translations of the Writings of the Fathers down to A.D. 325*, ed. Alexander Roberts and James Donaldson, rev. A. Cleveland Coxe, 10 vols. (New York: Christian Literature, 1885–87; repr., Peabody, MA: Hendrickson, 1994)
AT	author translation
BBR	*Bulletin for Biblical Research*
BDAG	W. Bauer, F. W. Danker, W. F. Arndt, and F. W. Gingrich, *A Greek-English Lexicon of New Testament and Other Early Christian Literature*, 3rd ed. (Chicago: University of Chicago Press, 2000)
BECNT	Baker Exegetical Commentary on the New Testament
BETL	Bibliotheca Ephemeridum Theologicarum Lovaniensium
Bib	*Biblica*
BTB	*Biblical Theology Bulletin*
BWANT	Beiträge zur Wissenschaft vom Alten und Neuen Testament
BZNW	Beihefte zur Zeitschrift für die neutestamentliche Wissenschaft
ca.	*circa*, about
CBQ	*Catholic Biblical Quarterly*
cf.	*confer*, compare
chap(s).	chapter(s)
ConBNT	Coniectanea Biblica: New Testament Series
DSSSE	*The Dead Sea Scrolls Study Edition*, ed. Florentino García Martínez and Eibert J. C. Tigchelaar, 2 vols. (Leiden: Brill, 1997–98)
ed(s).	editor(s), edited by, edition
Eng.	English versions/versification
esp.	especially
ESV	English Standard Version
et al.	*et alii*, and others

ETL	*Ephemerides Theologicae Lovanienses*
ExpTim	*Expository Times*
FOTL	Forms of the Old Testament Literature
frag(s).	fragment(s)
GCS	Die griechischen christlichen Schriftsteller der ersten [drei] Jahrhunderte (Leipzig: Hinrichs, 1897–)
HALOT	*The Hebrew and Aramaic Lexicon of the Old Testament*, by Ludwig Koehler, Walter Baumgartner, and Johann J. Stamm, trans. and ed. under the supervision of Mervyn E. J. Richardson. 4 vols. (Leiden: Brill, 1994–99)
HBT	*Horizons in Biblical Theology*
HTR	*Harvard Theological Review*
IBS	*Irish Biblical Studies*
ICC	International Critical Commentary
Int	*Interpretation*
JBL	*Journal of Biblical Literature*
JETS	*Journal of the Evangelical Theological Society*
JGRChJ	*Journal of Greco-Roman Christianity and Judaism*
JMT	*Journal of Moral Theology*
JSNT	*Journal for the Study of the New Testament*
JSNTSup	Journal for the Study of the New Testament Supplement Series
JSOTSup	Journal for the Study of the Old Testament Supplement Series
JSP	*Journal for the Study of the Pseudepigrapha*
KJV	King James Version
LCL	Loeb Classical Library
LNTS	Library of New Testament Studies
LXX	Septuagint
MT	Masoretic Text
NA[28]	Novum Testamentum Graece, ed. Eberhard Nestle, Erwin Nestle, B. Aland, K. Aland, J. Karavidopoulos, C. M. Martini, and B. M. Metzger, 28th rev. ed. (Stuttgart: Deutsche Bibelgesellschaft, 2012)
NABRE	New American Bible, Revised Edition
NAC	New American Commentary
NASB	New American Standard Bible
Neot	*Neotestamentica*
NETS	New English Translation of the Septuagint
NICNT	New International Commentary on the New Testament
NIDNTTE	*New International Dictionary of New Testament Theology and Exegesis*, ed. Moisés Silva, 2nd ed., 5 vols. (Grand Rapids: Zondervan, 2014)
NIGTC	New International Greek Testament Commentary
NIV	New International Version
NovT	*Novum Testamentum*
NovTSup	Supplements to Novum Testamentum
NRSV	New Revised Standard Version
NSBT	New Studies in Biblical Theology
NT	New Testament
NTS	*New Testament Studies*

OBO	Orbis Biblicus et Orientalis
OT	Old Testament
PG	Patrologia Graeca [= *Patrologiae Cursus Completus. Series Graeca*]. Edited by Jacques-Paul Migne. 161 vols. (Paris, 1857–86)
PNTC	Pillar New Testament Commentary
RBL	*Review of Biblical Literature*
repr.	reprinted
SBLSP	Society of Biblical Literature Seminar Papers
SBT	Studies in Biblical Theology
SJT	*Scottish Journal of Theology*
SNTSMS	Society for New Testament Studies Monograph Series
STDJ	Studies on the Texts of the Desert of Judah
Them	*Themelios*
TJ	*Trinity Journal*
trans.	translator, translated by
TynBul	*Tyndale Bulletin*
v(v).	verse(s)
WBC	Word Biblical Commentary
WTJ	*Westminster Theological Journal*
ZAW	*Zeitschrift für die alttestamentliche Wissenschaft*
ZNW	*Zeitschrift für die neutestamentliche Wissenschaft und die Kunde der älteren Kirche*

Old Testament

Gen.	Genesis	2 Chron.	2 Chronicles	Dan.	Daniel
Exod.	Exodus	Ezra	Ezra	Hosea	Hosea
Lev.	Leviticus	Neh.	Nehemiah	Joel	Joel
Num.	Numbers	Esther	Esther	Amos	Amos
Deut.	Deuteronomy	Job	Job	Obad.	Obadiah
Josh.	Joshua	Ps(s).	Psalm(s)	Jon.	Jonah
Judg.	Judges	Prov.	Proverbs	Mic.	Micah
Ruth	Ruth	Eccles.	Ecclesiastes	Nah.	Nahum
1 Sam.	1 Samuel	Song	Song of Songs	Hab.	Habakkuk
2 Sam.	2 Samuel	Isa.	Isaiah	Zeph.	Zephaniah
1 Kings	1 Kings	Jer.	Jeremiah	Hag.	Haggai
2 Kings	2 Kings	Lam.	Lamentations	Zech.	Zechariah
1 Chron.	1 Chronicles	Ezek.	Ezekiel	Mal.	Malachi

New Testament

Matt.	Matthew	Acts	Acts	Gal.	Galatians
Mark	Mark	Rom.	Romans	Eph.	Ephesians
Luke	Luke	1 Cor.	1 Corinthians	Phil.	Philippians
John	John	2 Cor.	2 Corinthians	Col.	Colossians

1 Thess.	1 Thessalonians	Philem.	Philemon	1 John	1 John
2 Thess.	2 Thessalonians	Heb.	Hebrews	2 John	2 John
1 Tim.	1 Timothy	James	James	3 John	3 John
2 Tim.	2 Timothy	1 Pet.	1 Peter	Jude	Jude
Titus	Titus	2 Pet.	2 Peter	Rev.	Revelation

Old Testament Apocrypha

Bar.	Baruch	Sir.	Sirach
2 Esd.	2 Esdras	Wis.	Wisdom of Solomon
2 Macc.	2 Maccabees		

Old Testament Pseudepigrapha

2 Bar.	2 Baruch	Pss. Sol.	Psalms of Solomon
1 En.	1 Enoch	Sib. Or.	Sibylline Oracles
2 En.	2 Enoch	T. Jud.	Testament of Judah
Ezek. Trag.	Ezekiel the Tragedian	T. Levi	Testament of Levi
Jub.	Jubilees	T. Sol.	Testament of Solomon

Other Ancient Sources

Abr.	Philo, *On Abraham*
Ant.	Josephus, *Jewish Antiquities*
1 Apol.	Justin Martyr, *First Apology*
CD	Cairo Genizah copy of the Damascus Document
Dem. ev.	Eusebius, *Demonstration of the Gospel*
Exp. Ps.	Chrysostom, *Expositiones in Psalmos*
Haer.	Irenaeus, *Adversus haereses* (*Against Heresies*)
Inst.	Quintilian, *Institutes of Oratory*
Mos.	Philo, *On the Life of Moses*
Progym.	Aelius Theon or Hermogenes, *Progymnasmata* (*Preliminary Exercises*)
1QSb	Rule of the Blessings (Appendix b to 1QS)
4QFlor	Florilegium
4QpIsaª	Isaiah Pesherª
11QMelch	Melchizedek
11QPsª	Psalms Scrollª
Sel. Ps.	Origen, *Selecta in Psalmos*
Spec. Laws	Philo, *On the Special Laws*
Strom.	Clement of Alexandria, *Stromateis* (*Miscellanies*)
Virt.	Philo, *On the Virtues*

Introduction

I don't think I quite understood the beauty of the Gospels until I grasped that they were laced with the Jewish Scriptures. Don't get me wrong. It was not that I had been reading them in isolation from the OT, for I understood that the Gospels continued the story of Israel. I read them as answering the hopes of the Jewish people. I comprehended that the evangelists presented Jesus as the solution to Israel's plight, and I sought to read Jesus in light of his historical and ethnic background.

What I had failed to see was that Jesus was presented as the continuation of the story in the *form* the story was written. The truth of a story is often carried in its arrangement, in the inspired world it evokes. It was not merely Matthew's words, but also the placement of those words, the portraits the evangelists painted, the *way* they told their stories that revealed their convictions about him. If we can compare the First Gospel to an oil painting, earlier I understood that I was looking at a Jewish painting through which the author expressed certain convictions about Jesus of Nazareth, but I neglected to step closer and concentrate on the brushstrokes to see that each drop of paint was chosen with care and had certain resemblances to previous portraits.[1] The artist had put together a portrait that made sense if you stepped back, but treasures could be brought forth if one moved a little closer and lingered for a moment.

This book is simply an attempt to step closer to the First Gospel's portrait. My claim is that a close analysis of Matt. 13:52 reveals that Matthew becomes

---

1. Paul Ricoeur describes a text not as a reproduction of reality but a re-presentation of it. Thus texts are like paintings rather than photographs. While a photograph holds everything in it, a painting focuses on essentials and eliminates uninterpreted material. Ricoeur and Klein, *Interpretation Theory*, 40–42.

a teacher in the style of Jesus:[2] "Therefore every scribe who has been trained for the kingdom of heaven is like a master of a house, who brings out of his treasure what is new and what is old." Luke 6:40 says, "A disciple is not above his teacher, but everyone when he is fully trained will be like his teacher." Matthew expounds the wisdom of Jesus by becoming a scribe and teacher to future generations, mediating the instruction of his sage. To put this in the First Gospel's terms, Matthew is a "discipled scribe" who learned to bring out treasures new and old from his teacher of wisdom (13:52).[3] Jesus formed an alternative scribal school; one of the main ways he instructed them in the paths of wisdom was to reveal the relationship between the new and the old, with himself at the center.[4] Matthew was one of these trained scribes who passed on Jesus's teaching to future generations. He wrote about Jesus's life in a rich and multilayered way, incorporating the new (found in Jesus), and the old (how Jesus's life fulfilled the story of Israel).

Person	Description	Task
Jesus	Teacher-Sage	Offers wisdom instruction concerning the new and the old (the secrets of the kingdom)
Matthew	Discipled Scribe	Learn, write, distribute, and teach the material from his sage

Though Jesus as a teacher of wisdom plus Matthew as a scribe is not the only lens through which we should look at the First Gospel, and these images certainly don't exhaust the content of Matthew, they do provide an entry point into Matthew's aims and theology.[5] This study could take many detours and turns, some of which I was tempted to explore, but my aim is specific and narrow: to focus on *how* Matthew as the scribe passes on the wisdom of Jesus—listening to his use of the new and the old.[6] I attempt to pay close attention to the OT echoes in Matthew's writing style and attend

2. Bauckham, *James*, 30.

3. There is debate about whether Jesus is better described as a "teacher of wisdom" or "wisdom incarnate." I will focus on the reality of Jesus as a teacher of wisdom, but I don't think the two ideas are mutually exclusive. See the argument of James Dunn, "Jesus: Teacher of Wisdom or Wisdom Incarnate?"

4. A *sage* or *teacher* is someone who offered various forms of teaching that could be called wisdom, while a *scribe* (though related) is someone who put such material in writing and so preserved it for later audiences. Sometimes the two categorizes do collide, since a sage can also be a scribe. Jesus ben Sira is described as a sage and scribe.

5. Jesus being a teacher-sage-rabbi is not opposed to Jesus being the Son of God, Son of Man, messiah, and king. Allison (*Constructing Jesus*, 31) is right to call one of his chapters on Jesus "More Than a Sage: The Eschatology of Jesus."

6. Admittedly, this book is not meant to be a full theology of Matthew. There are portions of Matthew not covered and topics significant to Matthew never broached.

to the development of the Jewish story in and around Jesus. In this sense, I am asking questions revolving around the topics of biblical theology and hermeneutics.

The first two chapters argue Matthew is the disciple and scribe following his teacher and sage of wisdom.[7] This becomes the metaphor I employ for the rest of my study of the Gospel. Through Jesus's life and teachings, he instructed his disciples on the nature of the relationship between the new and the old. I also explore Matthew's convictions and method in a more summative fashion because doing so allows for a more comprehensive summary and analysis than the later chapters will afford. The initial chapters also form the basis for the second half, giving some methodological parameters and a lens through which to view the rest of the study. The first part is therefore titled "The Scribe Described."

I extend the argument in part 2 (the bulk of the book), but in a different way. Rather than continuing to argue that Matthew is the scribe, or further supporting Jesus as a teacher of wisdom, I turn to "The Scribe at Work." If the first part "tells," then the second part "shows." Part 2 of the book thus demonstrates how Matthew brings out treasures new and old by examining some themes and characters in his writing. Therefore, it does not develop the argument in the same fashion, but attempts to argue by illustration. I examine Matthew's presentation of Jesus as David, Moses, Abraham, and Israel. Though I have separated these people (David, Moses, Abraham, Israel) and concepts (kingdom, exodus, family, exile), they ultimately interweave. In the ancient world, teaching through comparison (σύγκρισις) was ubiquitous.[8] This technique was even part of the preliminary exercises in rhetorical education. Each of these portraits will examine the new, while continually going back to the old to see the treasures of Matthew's literary style and the wisdom he gained from his teacher.

---

7. Jesus as a teacher for Matthew uniquely highlights his pedagogical function. He is also a sage in that he is the dispenser of wisdom (though sage as a distinct class of people is debated). He is also a rabbi, which technically means "my great one" but functions as an honorific for teachers. Thus John 1:38 transliterates rabbi as "teacher." See the short section on Jesus as teacher (rabbi) in Theissen and Merz, *Historical Jesus*, 354–55. The Gospels collectively affirm that Jesus is a rabbi (Matt. 26:25, 49; Mark 9:5; 11:21; 14:45; John 1:38, 49; 3:2; 4:31; 6:25; 9:2; 11:8) and teacher (Matt. 8:19; 9:11; 10:24, 25; 12:38; 17:24; 19:16; 22:16, 24, 36; 23:8; 26:18; Mark 4:38; 5:35; 9:17, 38; 10:17, 20, 35; 12:14, 19, 32; 13:1; 14:14; Luke 6:40; 7:40; 8:49; 9:38; 10:25; 11:45; 12:13; 18:18; 19:39; 20:21, 28, 39; 21:7; 22:11; John 1:38; 3:2, 10; 8:4; 11:28; 13:13, 14; 20:16). Keener (*Historical Jesus*, 187) says, "It is unlikely that Galilean Jews who saw themselves as faithful to God's law would have made a hard-and-fast distinction among the categories like charismatic sage, teacher of wisdom and teacher of Scripture."

8. Hermogenes, *Progym*. 8; Quintilian, *Inst*. 9.2.100–101.

While studies on Jesus as the new (fill in the blank) are accumulating as fast as apps on an iPhone, my analysis is distinctive in two respects. First, I enclose the study with the argument that Matthew is the *discipled scribe* instructed by his teacher of wisdom on how the new and the old interact. Looking at Matthew's style and form instructs readers about the nature of Jesus's teaching and the content of Matthew's discipleship. Matthew was forming a certain type of person through his narrative—or making disciples and thus fulfilling Jesus's command in the Great Commission. A study like this is not merely a search-and-find game or a study in parallelomania, but an attempt to view Jesus as his apprentices did, learn from their wisdom, and thereby appropriate this type of thinking into our intuitive processes.

Second, though I will examine titles and trace phrases, I will do so through the *narrative presentation* and connect figures to their great acts in redemptive history. To divorce a person from their great acts is to empty them of their importance. Who is Achilles without the Trojan War? Who is Odysseus without the odyssey? And who is Alexander the Great without his conquests? For Matthew, character and plot forge a close connection. Jesus's characterization is inherently tied to his participation in the plot. Or maybe better, Jesus's characterization is tied to character(s) and plot(s). And Matthew's canvas is larger than the first and last words of his book (and everything in between), for it both stretches backward, pulling from Israel's Scriptures, and points forward to the new creation. As Graham Stanton says, "The Old Testament is woven into the warp and woof of this Gospel; the evangelist uses Scripture to underline some of his most prominent and distinctive theological concerns."[9]

---

9. Stanton, *Gospel for a New People*, 346.

PART 1

The Scribe
DESCRIBED

*Scribes speculated about the beginning and
the end and thereby claimed to possess the
secrets of creation. Above all, they talked, they
memorized and remembered, they wrote.*

Jonathan Z. Smith

1

Matthew, the Discipled Scribe

Placing Matthew

Open your Bible and turn to the first page of the NT. There you will find the Gospel of Matthew speaking about the messiah in an unexpected form: a genealogy.[1] The Gospel's first words unveil Jesus through the prism of OT characters. Jesus is messiah, the son of David, the son of Abraham. In the genealogy, Matthew depicts Jesus not through the judgment of an ignorant disciple, an agnostic politician, or the questioning crowd but through the eyes of a Jewish scribe who is convinced Jesus is the messiah, the hope of his people. To read the Gospel of Matthew well is to read it with the Jewish story line—all twenty-four books that precede it—rumbling in the mind.[2] It

---

1. My argument in this book does not completely rest on Matthean authorship, though it will be assumed throughout. Certainly, Matthew as the author coheres with my thesis. Being a tax collector may imply he knew something of scribal techniques, though the amount of training is hard to know for sure (see Chris Keith's *Jesus' Literacy* for a literacy overview). It also fits to have someone who was an eyewitness of Jesus. Byrskog, Bauckham, and Hengel have all recently emphasized the role of eyewitnesses in their works. However, it could also be the case that the author was a disciple of a disciple of Jesus. If there is no relation to Jesus, then my argument is less convincing. For the sake of variety, I will use various ways of identifying the Gospel of Matthew, including some that imply Matthean authorship. Although the authorship of the First Gospel is disputed and the manuscript did not originally circulate with a formal title identifying who wrote it, very early in the church tradition this Gospel was associated with Matthew. On the basis of manuscript evidence from the second or early third century, Simon Gathercole ("Earliest Manuscript Title") has argued for an earlier use of titles than most assume. However, also see van der Toorn's chapter on authorship in antiquity, in van der Toorn, *Scribal Culture*.

2. The Tanak—the Hebrew Bible—has twenty-four books, which the OT of the Christian Bible counts as thirty-nine. The difference in number is because the Hebrew collection considers the twelve Minor Prophets as one book and does not divide some of the longer books into two parts.

is impossible to take two steps in Matthew's narrative without also taking a few steps back to see how each new tale interacts with a previous one.[3]

By beginning this way, Matthew tips his hat toward his method. Matthew functions as the scribe who learned from his teacher and sage how to make disciples by illuminating how Jesus fulfills the old. Without understanding the fluctuation between the new and the old, Matthew's narrative can be a confusing and curious piece. The database of a genealogy makes little sense unless one sees this as a historical *and* theological retelling. The temptation and baptism before Jesus's ministry warp into moralistic tales unless one relates these stories to Israel's past. The Sermon on the Mount is a beehive of misunderstanding unless one sees Jesus as the true and better Moses, David, and Solomon. And Jesus's death is merely a tragedy unless one sees that he fulfills all the Scriptures. Matthew's genealogical opening reveals that he is requesting his readers to engage his narrative through the lens of the new and the old.[4]

Matthew's persuasion is that "the shadows of the Old Covenant are not deceptive wraiths; they are 'fore-shadows' which enable readers to understand better that which comes in Christ."[5] The old system needed the moment of maturation, and that moment came in the messiah. The Gospel of Matthew is best understood with one eye looking back and the other eye attuned to the tectonic shifts from the old story. The form and content of the genealogy reminds readers of the old account while also introducing them to the new story. Like any good writer, Matthew depicts the familiar but with a twist; the Gospel, after all, is a furthering of the story, not a repackaging. To put this most simply, one can read Matthew's Gospel ably by asking three questions of the text: How does this echo Israel's story? How does Jesus fulfill Israel's story? How does it move the story of Israel forward?

Matthew reads both history and current events in a certain way, and any reading of this Gospel that neglects quotations from, allusions to, and echoes

3. Though this study largely examines Jewish backgrounds since this seems to fit the best with Matthew's emphasis, it would be interesting to write a book in a similar vein focusing on Greco-Roman backgrounds as a companion to this one.

4. The new and the old could be understood simply as what some call biblical theology. Carson ("Systematic Theology and Biblical Theology") asserts, "Everyone does that which is right in his or her own eyes and calls it biblical theology." By biblical theology, I mean what Geerhardus Vos ("Idea of Biblical Theology," 15) says when he describes it as "nothing else than the exhibition of the organic progress of supernatural revelation in its historic continuity and multiformity." More specifically, I am looking at redemptive history through a literary and canonical approach. See Klink and Lockett, *Understanding Biblical Theology*. While their work is helpful, its categories are too tight.

5. Clowney, *Church*, 55. Though Clowney refers here to the old covenant in contrast to the new covenant in Hebrews, I am not claiming that the old covenant equals the OT.

of Israel's Scriptures misses Matthew's lesson. The Gospel presents a figural reading of Jesus's life as the *master* discourse.[6] Through images and metaphors, he shows how Jesus walks in Israel's shoes while also bringing them to their destination. The genealogy instructs readers that the *content* of Matthew's Gospel is contained in its *form*. As Hans Urs von Balthasar argues, "The content [*Gehalt*] does not lie behind the form [*Gestalt*] but within it. Whoever is not capable of seeing and 'reading' the form will, by the same token, fail to perceive the content. Whoever is not illuminated by the form will see no light in the content either."[7]

Through his form, Matthew clarifies things about the Jewish narrative that were shadowy while also revealing new turns in the plotline. Matthew provides *explanation by emplotment*. His organization of the Jesus event explains the significance of the Jesus event. Events that are solitary and singular do not innately tell a story nor do they shape identity or culture. Yet when they are connected with other events and put into a plot, they then become intelligible and noteworthy. Narratives are stories that arrange and shape events into a coherent whole; they are like the numbering system in connect-the-dots children's books; if the numbers are removed, all that remains is a chaotic set of dots. However, if the numbers are followed, they will create a coherent picture.

For too long Gospel scholars have been prone to look away from the numbers rather than opening themselves up to the narrative itself. This appears in many forms: sometimes by comparing discrepancies between Gospel writers, other times by trying to figure out the "correct" order of historical events, and other times reaching for the community or tradition from which the stories sprang. Yet each of these methods peers *through* the narrative rather than *at* it. The beginning of Matthew's Gospel instructs us to look at the form and the content through the history of Israel. This book attempts to look *at* the narrative of Matthew as a whole through the numbering system Matthew himself provides: the new and the old.

Matthew, the Discipled Scribe

My argument is that *Matthew is the discipled scribe who narrates Jesus's life through the alternation of the new and the old*. The image I employ has its source in Matt. 13:52:

6. I use the term figural here because it seems to be a mediating term between typology, allegory, and inner-biblical exegesis. See chapter 2, where I also use the term "shadow stories."

7. Balthasar, *Seeing the Form*, 151.

Therefore every scribe who has been trained for the kingdom of heaven is like a master of a house, who brings out of his treasure what is new and what is old.

διὰ τοῦτο πᾶς γραμματεὺς μαθητευθεὶς τῇ βασιλείᾳ τῶν οὐρανῶν ὅμοιός ἐστιν ἀνθρώπῳ οἰκοδεσπότῃ, ὅστις ἐκβάλλει ἐκ τοῦ θησαυροῦ αὐτοῦ καινὰ καὶ παλαιά.

The word usually translated as *trained* (μαθητευθείς) is related to the Greek word for *disciple* (μαθητής). Matthew's verse could therefore be translated: "Therefore every *discipled scribe* for the kingdom of heaven is like a master of a house, who brings out his treasures new and old."[8] Jesus tells them that a *scribe* (someone who works with texts) who becomes a *disciple* (following Jesus as a teacher of wisdom) can produce great things for the kingdom of heaven.[9] The metaphor "master of a house who brings out treasures" is an image for interpretation, for the entire chapter is about right interpretation and understanding of Jesus's parables.[10] The word picture suggests strategic selection in what is new and old.[11] Treasures must be presented, stored, and organized in some sort of structure. In the words of one scholar, Matthew here betrays his method.[12] The Gospel itself demonstrates how Matthew accomplishes the scribal task mentioned in 13:52. Though this is not the only perspective through which one should view Matthew's writing, it does provide a helpful grid to lay over his presentation. Several indications suggest that Matthew presents his readers with the modus for his entire Gospel, but I will limit myself to two brief comments here.

8. The dative phrase τῇ βασιλείᾳ τῶν οὐρανῶν could be taken as sphere (in the kingdom of heaven), respect (concerning the kingdom of heaven), or dative of advantage (for the sake of the kingdom). I lean toward taking it as a dative of advantage or interest. Carson ("Matthew" [1984], 332), Orton (*Understanding Scribe*), and Luz (*Matthew 8–20*, 286) agree.

9. The verb employed in this verse is ἐκβάλλω, which more generally means expulsion: to "expel" or "send out" rather than "bring forth" or "bring out." Modern translations stem from a conflation of Luke 6:45, which uses προφέρω. In his commentary on Matthew, Origen even changed the verb to Luke's (*Commentarium in evangelium Matthaei* 10.15.1). Peter Phillips ("Casting Out the Treasure") capitalizes on the "expulsion" meaning of ἐκβάλλω and reinterprets the verse to mean that the discipled scribe expels the new and old in their storeroom to make way for the kingdom of heaven. However, ἐκβάλλω can have the more sedate meaning of "bring out" (see BDAG 299; Matt. 12:20, 35), and this meaning more closely aligns with Luke 6:45 and Matt. 12:35.

10. Jesus compares himself to a "master of a house" (οἰκοδεσπότης) in Matt. 10:25. In the same text he calls himself a teacher, and his followers disciples. They are slaves to him the master. The next two verses also reflect the tradition of wisdom by speaking of things hidden, revealed, and proclaimed on the housetops (10:26–27). Interestingly, in Prov. 9:1–6 Lady Wisdom is both a householder and a teacher.

11. Spellman, "Scribe Who Has Become a Disciple," 45.

12. Fuller, *New Testament in Current Study*, 83. Orton (*Understanding Scribe*, 166) says, "In any case, there is a great deal of evidence that the author has received a thorough training in Jewish exegesis and writing, the most tangible aspect of the traditional art of the scribe."

First, both early and modern interpreters have argued that γραμματεὺς μαθητευθείς (the discipled scribe) depicts Matthew. Origen, one of our earliest commentators on Matthew, viewed this verse as representing the disciples as scribes of the kingdom.[13] B. W. Bacon and Krister Stendahl also argue for a form of this theory, but from a redaction critical perspective.[14] In addition to Origen, Bacon, and Stendahl, many modern commentators also provide a passing comment to the same effect.[15] Second, a larger contextual hint also confirms my suspicion that Matthew is the scribe: the first word of his Gospel. Many argue that the beginnings of Matthew and Mark are actually their titles. Thus Mark's title would be "the beginning of the gospel of Jesus Christ the son of God." Matthew's would be "the book of the genealogy of Jesus Christ, the son of David, the son of Abraham" (Βίβλος γενέσεως Ἰησοῦ Χριστοῦ υἱοῦ Δαυὶδ υἱοῦ Ἀβραάμ, Matt. 1:1). The Greek word that Matthew begins with is βίβλος, which can also be translated as "scroll" or "record."

If this is the title for Matthew's Gospel, then he is describing his entire work as a scroll.[16] Even if one isn't convinced that the first eight words of Matthew's narrative contain the title, Matthew begins his description of the life of Jesus by speaking about his scroll. The scroll was a primary tool of the scribe. If anything defined what the scribe did, it was the surface on which the scribe wrote (βίβλος), the tool employed (σχοῖνος), and the action of writing itself (γράφω). Therefore, Matthew begins his narrative by referring to his work as a scroll. He lets his readers know that he is the scribe penning the life of Jesus. Before we explore Matthew's work under this banner, a few key

13. Origen questions how the disciples can be scribes when Acts 4:13 says that they are unlearned and ignorant. His solution is that one becomes a scribe when one receives the teaching of Christ, but on a deeper level when one, having received elementary knowledge through the letter of the Scriptures, ascends to things spiritual. *Commentary on Matthew* 10.15 (*ANF* 10:423; GCS 10:9–10).

14. Bacon (*Studies in Matthew*) asserts Matthew modified Mark in order to show the chief duty of the Twelve was to be scribes made disciples for the kingdom of heaven. Stendahl (*School of St. Matthew*) famously argues from the eclectic quotations that this practice was the product of a Jewish-Christian scribal school that searched for prooftexts. My proposal is not the same as Stendahl's, though there are some affinities.

15. Daniel Harrington (*Gospel of Matthew*, 208) comments that this "self-portrait of the evangelist" is a very widespread view, one might say almost the universal view. The majority view is that 13:52 describes Matthew, with many extending it to the disciples. See, e.g., Carson, "Matthew" (1984), 333; Blomberg, *Matthew*, 225; Morris, *Gospel according to Matthew*, 362; Nolland, *Gospel of Matthew*, 570. Yet Byrskog (*Jesus the Only Teacher*, 241) says there is no conclusive evidence for this, and the context speaks against this view.

16. One could argue that the word βίβλος covers only the genealogy. However, βίβλος can mean either a "brief written message" (cf. Matt. 19:7) or a "long written composition" (cf. Mark 12:26; Luke 3:4; 20:42; Acts 1:20; 7:42; Rev 20:15). I think the case I present in this chapter supports the idea that it covers his entire work. Allison ("Matthew's First Two Words") discusses the use of βίβλος.

concepts from 13:52 need more analysis if we are to move forward: disciple, scribe, and treasures new and old.

Discipled by the Teacher of Wisdom

Matthew is a disciple.[17] The term μαθητής (disciple) occurs only in the first five books of the NT and appears the most in Matthew and John. Seventy-eight times it appears in Matthew's work.[18] The term means that someone is an adherent, pupil, apprentice, or follower.[19] More specifically, a "disciple" is regularly defined in the realm of knowledge and learning. Jesus even said, "It is enough for the disciple [μαθητῇ] to be like his teacher [διδάσκαλος]" (10:25). According to BDAG (609), μαθητής is "one who engages in *learning* through *instruction* from another" or "one who is rather constantly associated with someone who has a *pedagogical* reputation." A disciple is thus someone who learns, who understands, who gains wisdom. This lines up with Matthew's presentation of the disciples as a whole, for as Markus Barth (and many others after him) has noted, Matthew omitted or interpreted differently all of the passages in Mark's Gospel that speak of the lack of understanding on the part of the disciples.[20] Barth even claims that the "faith" (πίστις) concept in Paul, John, and Mark is transferred to "understanding" (συνίημι) in Matthew.[21] Regardless of whether the entirety of Barth's claim is true, the characteriza-

17. Discipleship in Matthew has been viewed usually under two lenses: redaction criticism or narrative criticism. See Bornkamm, Barth, and Held, *Tradition and Interpretation in Matthew*; Luz, "Disciples in the Gospel according to Matthew"; Sheridan, "Disciples and Discipleship in Matthew"; J. Brown, *Disciples in Narrative Perspective*; Wilkins, *Discipleship in the Ancient World*; Kingsbury, *Matthew as Story*; Edwards, "Uncertain Faith"; Edwards, *Matthew's Narrative Portrait of Disciples*. Many of them note that the disciples' understanding functions to highlight Jesus as an effective teacher.

18. Wilkins (*Discipleship in the Ancient World*, 172) claims that Matthew has a special interest in the disciples as literary figures. "Matthew's gospel is at least in part a manual on discipleship. While all the major discourses directed at least in part to the μαθηταί, . . . and with the disciples called and trained and commissioned to carry out the climactic mandate to 'make disciples' in the conclusion of the gospel, Matthew has constructed a gospel that will equip the disciples in the making of disciples."

19. Wilkins (*Discipleship in the Ancient World*, 43–91) explicitly ties discipleship into the notion of scribes and wise men.

20. Barth, "Matthew's Understanding of the Law," 106. My claim is not that the disciples in Matthew are portrayed only in a positive light—they certainly have conflicting traits. As Verseput ("Faith of the Reader") notes, even at the end of the Gospel, Matthew speaks of their hesitation (28:17).

21. Though I am not convinced that this transfer can be substantiated, multiple scholars (Conzelmann, Byrskog) note the particular interest of Matthew in "understanding." Nine times Matthew employs συνίημι, but none of them occur before chap. 13, and six of the nine occur in chap. 13 itself (13:13, 14, 15, 19, 23, 51; 15:10; 16:12; 17:13).

tion of the Matthean disciples does uniquely highlight their *understanding* of Jesus's teaching.[22]

My proposal is Matthew is gifted in knowledge and wisdom by his teacher, Jesus.[23] Jesus's statement in Matt. 23:8, "You have one teacher," carries with it significance that goes far beyond the immediate context.[24] The idea of Jesus as a teacher of wisdom becomes an important concept for Matthew's presentation as a whole and also informs readers how to view Matthew's role.[25] Yet a brief survey of the titles of "rabbi" or "teacher" in the Gospels doesn't quite clarify what type of teacher Jesus is. Is he a teacher like those in the synagogues? Some scholars compare him to the Pharisees Hillel or Shammai. Others draw a correlation between Jesus and the Teacher of Righteousness or the eccentric John the Baptist. Should his pedagogical function be a subcategory of his prophetic role? Or is the best comparison with the Greco-Roman philosophers of the day? Is he a teacher and wise man primarily like the Jewish kings of the past? And if he is a teacher, then what wisdom did he pass on to his scribe? These are all legitimate questions, and while I won't address all of them, Matthew as a whole, and 13:52 more specifically, gives some assistance along these lines.[26]

Though no title or term can fully capture who Jesus is, and Matthew uses many descriptions, Jesus as the *teacher of wisdom* makes sense both in the context of Matthew and in chapter 13.[27] In fact, Matthew reserves the title of

22. See Byrskog (*Jesus the Only Teacher*, 221) for a similar suggestion. Sirach claims, "Every *understanding* person knows wisdom. . . . Those who are *understanding* in words become wise themselves, and pour forth precise parables" (Sir. 18:28–29 AT).

23. About referring to Jesus as a teacher, Riesner ("Jesus as Preacher and Teacher," 185) claims, "It seems not too risky to assume that this was quite the way in which many contemporaries could have looked at Jesus." All four times when Jesus uses "teacher," he speaks to his disciples (10:24, 25; 23:8; 26:17–18). Jesus never speaks of himself directly as a teacher except to the disciples. However, outsiders also identify Jesus as a teacher twice to his disciples (9:10–11; 17:24).

24. Josephus (*Ant.* 18.63) writes, "Now there was about this time Jesus, a wise man, . . . a teacher of such men as receive the truth with pleasure." Early church fathers also recognized the emphasis on teaching in Matthew's Gospel. Ignatius said in *To the Ephesians* 15.1, "There is then one teacher who spoke and it came to pass." Clement of Alexandria said, "God's first begotten Son, through whom God created all things and whom all prophets call Wisdom, is the teacher of all created beings" (*Strom.* 6.58.1).

25. Celia Deutsch ("Wisdom in Matthew," 46) argues that as wisdom is hidden and revealed, so too Jesus presents the secrets of the kingdom of heaven; as wisdom is a teacher who says her yoke is light, so too Jesus calls followers to discipleship; as wisdom is a prophet calling people to come to her and providing warnings, so does Jesus; as wisdom has agents through whom she works, so Jesus sends prophets, wise men, and scribes.

26. Many of these categories could even be combined. The error is to separate them.

27. See Dunn's fivefold argument for Jesus as a teacher of wisdom. Dunn, "Jesus: Teacher of Wisdom or Wisdom Incarnate?," 82–85.

"teacher" for Jesus alone in his Gospel.[28] But Jesus as a sapiential teacher has somewhat fallen out of use because of reactions to the Jesus Seminar's use of it. Yet a wisdom approach to Jesus (and Matthew) brings some clarity to Matthew's intentions.[29] By wisdom, I mean more than a genre—it is a skill *and* a concept.[30] As Raymond van Leeuwen claims, wisdom is a totalizing statement.[31] Maybe even more appropriately for this project, Barton puts wisdom under the lens of a hermeneutic: "Wisdom is not just a body of knowledge, it is also *a way of seeing* which attends to what lies hidden as well as to what lies on the surface."[32] Four arguments justify viewing Jesus as a teacher, and more specifically a teacher of wisdom, in Matt. 13 and the Gospel as a whole: (1) the Hebrew

28. For an overview of Jesus as teacher and sage, see Keener, *Historical Jesus of the Gospels*, 186–95. John Yieh (*One Teacher*, 327) says, "My literary critical study of the Gospel has shown that, while presenting Jesus as the Messiah, the Son of God, the Son of Man, and Lord, all such titles can be found in other Gospels, Matthew features his Jesus, most extensively and most distinctively, as an authoritative Teacher of God's will with eschatological significance." Yieh argues that this is supported by the narrative, plot, and characterization.

29. The Jesus Seminar and those associated with it describe Jesus as a cynic sage. A notable exception is Ben Witherington (*Jesus Quest*, 185–96).

30. The nature of "wisdom" and "Wisdom literature" is much debated. Pemberton (*Life That Is Good*, 10) speaks of wisdom as a skill or expertise on one level, the second level builds on the first and expands the first meaning to include living a life that is good. When I speak of Jesus as a teacher of wisdom, I am arguing that wisdom is more of a macrogenre that fits over the whole of the Scriptures and punches its way through every genre in the Scriptures. Though Jesus teaches on wisdom—like Proverbs, Ecclesiastes, and Job—in an explicit way, his entire ministry can and should be labeled as wisdom. In some sense this means wisdom should be understood not as a genre but more as a concept similar to holiness or righteousness. Wisdom is thus more of a skill, which Jesus passes on to his disciples. The genre of Wisdom literature is being questioned for a number of reasons. The literary form and content of Wisdom literature does not represent a clear genre distinction. Job, Ecclesiastes, and Proverbs have very little overlap in literary characteristics. They also fail to present unified teaching on the nature of wisdom. The only thing that brings the typically labeled "Wisdom books" together is that they "deal *explicitly* with wisdom questions and themes on a persistent basis" and have somewhat of a unique way of writing. See Jeff Dryden's appendix (*Hermeneutic of Wisdom*, 243–64), on which I am largely dependent in this footnote. See also Kynes, *Obituary for "Wisdom Literature."* Wisdom 7:24–28 says,

> For wisdom is more mobile than any motion; because of her pureness she pervades and penetrates all things. For she is a breath of the power of God, and a pure emanation of the glory of the Almighty; therefore nothing defiled gains entrance into her. For she is a reflection of eternal light, a spotless mirror of the working of God, and an image of his goodness. Although she is but one, she can do all things, and while remaining in herself, she renews all things; in every generation she passes into holy souls and makes them friends of God, and prophets; for God loves nothing so much as the person who lives with wisdom.

31. Van Leeuwen, "Wisdom Literature." Dunn ("Jesus: Teacher of Wisdom or Wisdom Incarnate?," 80) claims that wisdom is "simply a way of speaking about God's presence among his people and about God's activity on their behalf."

32. Barton, "Gospel Wisdom," 94.

Scriptures' promise of a sapiential messiah, (2) the titles given to Jesus and his opponents in the First Gospel, (3) the specific content of the teaching of Jesus in Matthew, and (4) the immediate context of chapter 13.

First, Jewish literature looked forward to a sage-messiah. Job asks where wisdom and understanding are to be found (Job 28:12). Enoch claims that wisdom found no dwelling place on the earth (1 En. 42.2). The prophets therefore foretold the arrival of wisdom. Isaiah predicted that the sage-messiah would have "the Spirit of wisdom and understanding, . . . knowledge and fear of the LORD" (Isa. 11:2; 2 Chron. 1:10–12).[33] The terms "wisdom," "knowledge," "understanding," and "fear of the LORD" parallel the concepts in Prov. 2:1–8, indicating the hope for a king like Solomon. Isaiah also refers to the servant as one who will "act wisely" (52:13). Later, Isaiah connects this with teaching, claiming, "All your children shall be taught [διδακτούς] by the LORD, and great shall be the peace of your children" (54:13). Jeremiah 23:5–6 speaks of a Davidic "Branch" being raised up, "a King who will reign wisely and do what is just and right" (NIV). Enoch said that the elect one will sit on the throne and out of his mouth will come all the secrets of wisdom, for the Lord of the Spirits has given them to him (1 En. 51.3; 63.2). The desire from times past was to have a wise ruler like Solomon. There is also a long tradition of wisdom being personified (Job 21; Prov. 1; 3; 8; 9; Sir. 1, 24; 11QPs^a 18; Bar. 3–4; 1 En. 42; 4 Ezra 5; 2 Bar. 48; Wis. 1–9).[34]

The second argument for seeing Jesus as the teacher of wisdom is in the specific titles given to Jesus.[35] Matthew prominently presents Jesus as a teacher (διδάσκαλος) and instructor (καθηγητής).[36] The later term is unique to Matthew and portrays Jesus in the role of a tutor (23:10).[37] Jesus therefore has a unique instructor-student relationship with his disciples in Matthew. Matthew

33. Early Jewish and Samaritan literature indicates that Jews expect the messiah to be a teacher of godly wisdom. CD 6.11; 7.18; 4QFlor. 1.11; 11QMelch. 18–20; T. Jud. (A) 21.1–4; T. Levi 18.2–6; Pss. Sol. 17.42–3; 18.4–9; 1 En. 46.3; 49.3–4; 51.3. See this note in Witherington, *Christology of Jesus*, 180.

34. For a discussion of wisdom Christology, see Dunn, *Christology in the Making*, 163–209.

35. In Gospel of Thomas 13, Jesus is compared to "a wise man of understanding." For a wisdom perspective on Matthew, see Deutsch, *Hidden Wisdom*; Deutsch, *Lady Wisdom*; Suggs, *Wisdom, Christology, and Law*.

36. On ancient literacy, see Keith, *Jesus' Literacy*, who provides a more nuanced and helpful view of different levels of literacy and writing. He argues that "Mark and Matthew . . . place Jesus outside the scribal-literate culture" (141). Though I don't have time to respond to his argument in full, this does not work against my thesis. The "scribes of the law" would be particularly incensed by Jesus if he was not educated like them.

37. Winter, "Messiah as the Tutor." Derrett ("Matt 23:8–10") argues that the text is a midrash on Isa. 54:13 and Jer. 31:33–34. In Isa. 54:13 the result of the servant's work is that "all your children shall be taught by the Lord."

refers to Jesus as a "teacher" implicitly or explicitly twelve times (8:19; 9:11; 10:24, 25; 12:38; 17:24; 19:16; 22:16, 24; 22:36; 23:8; 26:18). In Matt. 26 Jesus calls himself "the Teacher," and many times in Matthew's Gospel people come up to him, calling him "Teacher." Witherington argues that Wisdom is regarded as *the* teacher in numerous sapiential texts.[38] Matthew also stresses that Jesus is the son of David (Solomon). Eleven times he speaks of Jesus as the "son of David" compared to four in Mark and Luke and none in John. He and Luke are the only Gospels to have the following words on Jesus's lips: "Behold, something greater than Solomon is here" (Matt. 12:42).

On the opposite end, Matthew contrasts Jesus with the "scribes/teachers [γραμματεῖς] of the law" twenty-one times—negatively describing those who are associated with the Pharisees (2:4; 5:20; 7:29; 8:19; 9:3; 12:38; 15:1; 16:21; 17:10; 20:18; 21:15; 23:2, 13, 15, 23, 25, 27, 29, 34; 26:57; 27:41). The Greek term for "teachers [γραμματεῖς] of the law" is the plural form of the same word as *scribe* in 13:52 (γραμματεύς). Therefore, those coming against Jesus could be rightly translated as the "scribes of the law." Jesus, as the teacher, clashes with the "scribes of the law" but trains his own scribes in the true interpretation of the Scriptures. Jesus trains his scribes in Matt. 5–7 (first discourse); he chastises the scribes of the people in 23–25 (last discourse).[39] Matthew explicitly connects scribes/disciples to the title of teacher throughout his Gospel (8:19; 9:11; 10:24–25; 12:38; 17:24; 22:16). Thus, both the titles for Jesus and the opposition to Jesus in Matthew point toward Jesus as a teacher of wisdom.

The third argument for seeing Jesus as the teacher of wisdom is not only the titles but also the specific *content* of Matthew's Gospel. As Byrskog writes, "Matthew characterizes Jesus not only by means of designations and titles, but also by informing the readers/hearers about what Jesus does."[40] Matthew enhances the portrayal of Jesus as a teacher in a number of ways. He structures his book along five discrete discourses, many of which can be understood along the lines of the wisdom tradition.[41] In fact, the process of gathering teachings together into blocks reflects the process of producing Proverbs.[42] The first summary of Jesus's ministry tells about Jesus and his teaching activity. "And he went throughout Galilee, *teaching* and healing in their synagogues"

---

38. Witherington, *Jesus the Sage*, 351.

39. Eight of the twenty-two references to scribes occur in Matt. 23.

40. Byrskog, *Jesus the Only Teacher*, 201.

41. I agree with Sneed ("Is the 'Wisdom Tradition' a Tradition?"), who pushes back against the concept that Hebrew Wisdom literature represents a worldview, tradition, and movement distinct from those of the priests and prophets. Part of my argument is that Jesus as the prophet-king is also the sage. The titles don't conflict but coalesce.

42. Murphy, *Wisdom Literature*, 49.

(cf. 4:23).[43] The Sermon on the Mount portrays Jesus as one who teaches with authority, not as "their scribes" (7:29). Matthew specifically closes out Jesus's teaching with the remark, "When Jesus had finished saying all these things . . ." (26:1). "All these things" refers not only to the final discourse but also to all the earlier discourses and sayings in Matthew, since the other Synoptic Gospels lack this statement.[44] The Sermon on the Mount specifically portrays Jesus as an authoritative teacher who goes up on the mountain to instruct. Within the Sermon, Jesus asserts his authority over the Mosaic law. Additionally, as already mentioned, Matthew includes a prolonged attack on the scribal authorities of the day in chapter 23. In a section unique to Matthew, Jesus criticizes the Pharisees and scribes as teachers, providing the antithesis and parallel to the Sermon in many ways.

Matthew not only blocks the teaching material of Jesus and gives the antithesis to his teaching, but the teaching itself also mirrors explicit wisdom sayings. As Witherington points out, there are many echoes of Sirach in Jesus's teaching that require explanation (compare Sir. 24:9 and 6:19–31 to Matt. 11:29–30; Sir. 23:9 to Matt. 5:34; Sir. 28:3–4 to Matt. 5:22; Sir. 29:11 to Matt. 6:19). The Sermon on the Mount uses terms and concepts that would have put Jesus in the tradition of a Greco-Roman philosopher as he speaks about what it means to flourish and be whole as a human being.[45] Jesus speaks as a sage when he says that the values of the world will be turned upside down and wrongs will be righted. "The concern for the righting of wrongs in the long run is one of the driving engines of all Wisdom literature, beginning even with Proverbs."[46] Jesus also adheres to the act-consequence theory: good deeds will be rewarded and bad ones will be punished. This is another form that pervades the wisdom tradition. Jesus speaks of himself as having nowhere to lay his head (8:20), and a number of texts speak of wisdom searching for a dwelling place and sometimes finding one and other times not. Sirach 24:8–9 asserts wisdom seeks a resting place, while 1 En. 42.1–2 says, "Wisdom could not find a place in which she could dwell, but a place was found for her in the heavens. Then Wisdom went out to dwell with the children of the people, but she found no dwelling place."

---

43. Byrskog (*Jesus the Only Teacher*, 270–75) argues that the healing is teaching.

44. Carter (*Matthew: Storyteller, Interpreter, Evangelist*, 243), Patte (*Gospel according to Matthew*, 136), and J. Brown (*Disciples in Narrative Perspective*, 139) have all argued that the portrayal of discipleship in Matthew must include an analysis not only of the disciples as they are but also a consideration of discipleship reflected in Jesus's teaching—the disciples as they should be. In other words, one must pay attention to the "actual disciples" and the "ideal disciples."

45. For support of this statement, see Pennington, *Sermon on the Mount*.

46. Witherington, *Jesus Quest*, 191.

Jesus is also first worshiped by "wise men," who bring Jesus gifts as the queen of Sheba brought gifts to Solomon (Matt. 2:1–12). Matthew claims that in Jesus's life "wisdom is justified by her deeds" (11:19).[47] This is Jesus's response to the people's rejection of both John the Baptist and Jesus for their different lifestyles (11:6–9). Jesus comes eating and drinking, and the wisdom tradition itself has quite a bit about banqueting (see Sir. 31:12–32:6). Jesus claims that all things have been revealed to him by the Father (Matt. 11:25–27).[48] In the wisdom tradition, it was Wisdom herself who was entrusted with the secrets or revelation of God (Prov. 8:14–36; Wis. 6:22; 7:7; 9:17). Jesus speaks of creation theology similar to what we find in Proverbs and compares the beauty to the great sage Solomon (Matt. 6:25–30).[49] Sages perceived the cosmic order to have originated at creation and attempted to maintain it by the justice of divine rules. As James Dunn concludes, Matthew "stands alone within the Synoptic tradition in maintaining a full Wisdom Christology."[50]

Finally, and most important for our purposes, are the arguments from Matt. 13 for Jesus being a teacher of wisdom. Three points enhance the portrait of Jesus as a sage in chapter 13. First, the placement of Matt. 13 in the *structure* of Matthew. Chapter 13 sits structurally at the center of the Gospel and is a lens through which to view the entire book.[51] At the center of the chapter Matthew indicates that Jesus's kingdom parables are in fulfillment of Ps. 78:2, "I will open my mouth in parables; I will utter what has been *hidden* [κεκρυμμένα] since the foundation of the world" (AT).[52] The connection between wisdom and what is secret or hidden is a common theme (Prov. 10:14; Job 3:21; 15:18; 28:21; Sir. 20:30; 41:14; Isa 29:14; 45:3).[53] Proverbs speaks of wisdom as something to be sought after like silver, searched for as *hidden* treasures (Prov. 2:4). Throughout the wisdom tradition, wisdom is spoken

---

47. Suggs (*Wisdom, Christology, and Law*) has a long discussion of 11:19's relation to wisdom.

48. Deutsch (*Hidden Wisdom*) argues Matt. 11:25–30 has prominent wisdom themes related to Jewish texts.

49. In 8:19–22 a scribe comes to Jesus, asking if he can follow Jesus, and Jesus replies with a word about his homelessness. Homelessness is a well-known characteristic of wisdom (1 En. 42.1–3; Job 28:20; Prov. 1:28).

50. Dunn, *Christology in the Making*, 206. For other studies on wisdom Christology, see Suggs, *Wisdom, Christology, and Law in Matthew's Gospel*; Deutsch, *Hidden Wisdom and the Easy Yoke*; Witherington, *Jesus the Sage*; Gench, *Wisdom in the Christology of Matthew*; Singsa, "Matthew's Wisdom Christology"; Wainwright, *Shall We Look for Another?*; Gathercole, *Preexistent Son*; Macaskill, *Revealed Wisdom*.

51. Add to this that if Matthew is viewed through the narrative of Israel (as will be argued in the last chapter), then chap. 13 is instructing readers to read this section through the lens of the wisdom tradition.

52. David Wenham ("Structure of Matthew 13") argues for a chiastic structure in Matt. 13.

53. Though the word *hidden* is not always used in these contexts, the concept is regularly connected to treasures, since treasures would be hidden in ancient times.

of as hidden and secret but still able to be found.[54] If we expand our view of the structure as well, Celia Deutsch has argued, the clearest wisdom text is Matt. 11:25–30, which also speaks of the "things . . . *hidden*" by the Father (emphasis added). These five verses sit contextually in a "conflict section," and Matt. 13 is the response and conclusion to this conflict narrative.[55] All sections of 11:2–13:58 have themes of revelation and concealment. Matthew 13 gives the reason for the dynamic of opposition and conflict: Jesus speaks to his disciples in parables about the *secrets* of the kingdom because they have become blind, but he will now enlighten them (13:13–15). What has been hidden (wisdom) is now revealed in Jesus. Notably, the word "understanding" (συνίημι) occurs only in and after chapter 13 in Matthew's narrative.

Second, Matt. 13 should be viewed under the lens of wisdom because of the specific *form* of the chapter. Looking at the form matters because, as Sneed argues, the wisdom tradition was a mode of literature (though diverse) used to train young scribes through short pithy sayings.[56] These instilled the values, beliefs, and norms of ancient Israelite culture into those being trained.[57] According to Justin Martyr, "Jesus' sayings were short and concise" (*1 Apol.* 4.5), possibly with the same aims. Jesus regularly taught using rhetorical forms designated by the Greek terms χρεία and παραβολή, which are connected to the Hebrew word *mashal*. Likewise, NT scholars give the larger label of *aphorisms* to Jesus's teachings (i.e., pithy instructional sayings).[58] Throughout the OT it is the kings who are to be the patterns of wisdom. Matthew 13 specifically contains a collection of parables about the kingdom.[59] Unlike the parallels in the other Gospels, Matthew has nearly every parable in this chapter begin with the phrase "the kingdom of heaven is like." The kingdom is the central theme in Jesus's ministry, and therefore understanding Jesus as a teacher of wisdom pulls the entire Gospel together as Matthew focuses on Jesus's revealing "the secrets" or "the mysteries" of the kingdom in chapter 13.[60] Matthew, as a wisdom teacher himself, cleverly reveals at the center of his Gospel the secrets of his teacher (13:11).

54. Macaskill, *Revealed Wisdom*.
55. Deutsch, *Hidden Wisdom*, 22–23.
56. From an oral perspective, wisdom is not only a form of literature but a mode of speaking as well.
57. Sneed, "Is the 'Wisdom Tradition' a Tradition?," 71.
58. Aune, "Oral Tradition and the Aphorisms."
59. In ancient Mesopotamia, kings presented themselves as accomplished scribes and scholars. Assurbanipal (668–627 BCE) says, "I have learned the hidden secrets of the complete scribal art. With my own eyes I have seen the tablets of heaven and earth." See van der Toorn, *Scribal Culture*, 54.
60. In Dan. 2:27–28, Daniel answers Nebuchadnezzar and says, "No wise men [σοφῶν] . . . can show the king the mystery [μυστήριον] that the king has asked, but there is a God in heaven

Third, the *immediate context* surrounding Matt. 13:52 supports viewing Jesus as a teacher of wisdom. Right before Jesus makes the comment about scribes, he asks the disciples if they have "understood" (συνίημι) his parables (13:51). The disciples answer yes. The term "understand" is used twice in Prov. 2 (2:5, 9) and six more times in Proverbs as a whole (8:9; 21:11, 12, 29; 28:5; 29:7); the concept looms large for the wisdom tradition as a whole. But it is not only the words immediately preceding Matt. 13:52 but also the narrative following 13:52 as well. The story that follows concerns Jesus going to his hometown in Nazareth and "teaching" them in their synagogue (13:53–58, esp. v. 54). The people are astonished and ask, "Where did this man get this "wisdom" (σοφία, v. 56), and they are offended by him because he is the carpenter's son. Matthew intentionally brackets 13:52 with wisdom themes. The next section will argue that the term "treasures" in 13:52 also has wisdom connotations.

Therefore, it is not only the Jewish hopes, the titles given to Jesus in Matthew, or the specific content of Jesus's teaching in Matthew that point to Jesus as a teacher of wisdom, but the very *structure, form*, and *immediate context* of Matt. 13. At the axis of his Gospel, Matthew inserts multiple hints for how he himself reads Jesus's life. Just as Jesus reveals the mysteries of the kingdom as the teacher of wisdom, so Matthew discloses the mysteries of his method (13:11). While "a disciple is not above his teacher" (10:24), Jesus gave his twelve disciples authority (10:1) and bequeathed to them revelation of the kingdom that they can pass on to the next generation. They do understand Jesus's teaching (13:51). Matthew now reveals the secrets of the kingdom in his Gospel (13:11). When Matthew devotes a whole chapter to Jesus explicating the kingdom, he also inserts a statement about how he himself learned to illuminate the kingdom from his teacher-sage. Jack Suggs is right to conclude that Jesus as a wisdom teacher has been neglected in Matthew: "For too long, the traces of wisdom speculation present in Matthew have been treated as tangential or eccentric traditions foreign to the purpose and theology of the evangelist. They constitute, in my opinion, certain proof that one aspect of Matthew's thought has been unfortunately neglected."[61]

---

who reveals mysteries." In the LXX, the word μυστήριον occurs over twenty times, but over half of them are found in Dan. 2. The word is used favorably to describe the way of divine wisdom in Wis. 2:22 and 6:22. As *NIDNTTE* says, "In almost every case where μυστήριον occurs in the NT, the term is found with vbs. denoting revelation or proclamation" (354).

61. Suggs, *Wisdom, Christology, and Law*, 18. For a response to Suggs, see M. Johnson, "Reflections on a Wisdom Approach to Matthew's Christology."

Matthew as the Discipled *Scribe*

Matthew is not only a disciple of Jesus the teacher of wisdom but also a discipled *scribe*. Labeling Matthew as a scribe should inform us about his task and how he will accomplish it. Although the word "scribe" (γραμματεύς) in 13:52 might carry a nontechnical meaning, this does not necessarily mean historical scribal background can't help inform Matthew's usage.[62] In fact, as Duling notes, it would be an oversimplification to suppose that scribes occupied only one category. Duling suggests at least six categories: (1) royal scribes, (2) public and private secretaries, (3) village and local scribes, (4) scribes of voluntary associations, (5) scribes who teach elementary education, (6) learned Torah scribes.[63] But in another sense all scribes were "sapiential scribes" who sought out wisdom (Sir. 39:1–3) and became sagacious.[64] William McKane has even argued that "scribes" and "wise men" were essentially synonymous as a class.[65] The above categories don't have to be put at odds, and it is best to understand Matthew's self-description as the combination of a royal, Torah, and sapiential scribe.[66] To put it more precisely, Matthew becomes wise by learning how to interpret the Torah from his sage-king.

In the OT, scribes were described as "scribes of the king" and "royal scribes" (cf. 2 Kings 12:11; 2 Chron. 24:11). Scribes would "chronicle the kings of Israel" (cf. 1 Kings 11:41; 14:19, 29).[67] In the OT we also learn that kings are faithful by following the Torah. Ezra was a "scribe of the Law of the God of Heaven" (Ezra 7:12), who was filled with wisdom concerning God's law (7:25). Kings who were faithful to the Torah also produced wisdom. Matthew's role was modeled on these portraits. He was a learned Torah-royal-sapiential scholar who penetrated prophecies and studied the hidden meanings of the Hebrew Scriptures.[68] He did so through the new Torah, the new king, or the royal law of Christ.

---

62. France (*Gospel of Matthew*, 544) asserts, "All that we are told about the background from which the Twelve have come gives us no ground to believe that any of them was a 'scribe' in the normal NT sense." My analysis in this chapter suggests otherwise. In BDAG (206) γραμματεύς is defined as one who has special functions in connection with documents, but it also includes as a subcategory "an expert in matters relating to divine revelation."

63. Duling, *A Marginal Scribe*, 263–67.

64. Witherington, *Jesus the Sage*, 346.

65. McKane, *Prophets and Wise Men*, 40–47.

66. E. P. Sanders (*Judaism: Practice and Belief*) doubts that the Torah scribe exists. In *HALOT*, the Hebrew *soper* has four meanings: (1) scribe, secretary; (2) royal official, secretary of state; (3) secretary for Jewish affairs; (4) scholar of Scripture.

67. See Rollston, *Writing and Literacy*, 88.

68. Seraiah was the scribe for David (2 Sam. 8:17); his sons Elihoreph and Ahijah were scribes for Solomon (1 Kings 4:3); Shebnah was the scribe for Hezekiah (2 Kings 18:18); Shaphan was the scribe for Josiah (2 Kings 22); Elishama was the scribe for Jehoiakim (Jer. 36); Jonathan was the scribe for Zedekiah (Jer. 37).

Though it can be tempting to think of scribes merely as those who wrote, most scribes in both Matthew's time and before Matthew's time engaged in at least four activities that mirror and illuminate Matthew's composition: (1) learning (2) writing/interpreting, (3) distributing, and (4) teaching.[69]

The first activity of a scribe can be described as learning.[70] All of the rest of these roles and capacities depend on scribes being learned or educated.[71] A scribe is one who knows things. They learned these things from their sages, kings, or public rulers. The OT evidence indicates that scribes were valued for the wisdom and understanding they possessed (1 Chron. 27:32), and they were known as "wise" (Isa. 33:18; 1 Cor. 1:20). Horsley confirms this, saying that the increasing information about scribes in the ancient Near East confirms that the cultivation of wisdom was integrally related to their function.[72] Ezra, one of the most well-known scribes, is introduced as "a scribe skilled in the Law of Moses that the LORD, the God of Israel, had given" (Ezra 7:6), and "learned in matters of the commandments of the LORD and his statutes for Israel" (7:11). Ezra was responsible not only for reading the Torah to the people (Neh. 8:1–8) but also for its study (8:13). Ezra's fundamental commission sounds similar to Matthew's, especially with the emphasis on the "secrets of the kingdom" (Matt. 13:11). Ezra was to "write all these things that you have seen in a book; . . . and you shall teach them to the wise among your people, whose hearts you know are able to comprehend and keep these secrets" (2 Esd. 12:37).

One of the most famous descriptions of the ideal scribe is provided by Ben Sira, who attributes to scribes all areas of knowledge, government, and fame. The scribe "seeks out the wisdom of the ancients, and is concerned with prophecies" (Sir. 38:24–34; 39:1–11, esp. v. 1). The key thing for a scribe was to seek understanding, to become wise. Ben Sira's consistent description of scribes includes the fervent search for understanding. According to Hebrew sages, there were three ways to gain wisdom: "(1) Careful scrutiny of nature

---

69. Orton (*Understanding Scribe*, 161–62) comes to a similar conclusion when he says the ideal scribe includes the following elements: (1) the exercise of wisdom and the gift of special understanding; (2) the notion of authority; (3) the notion of righteous teaching, including the right interpretation of the law and the prophets; (4) a close association with true prophecy; and (5) a sense of inspiration. Later in the Christian tradition, scribes were known mainly for their copying, but this is not the picture presented by the OT or Matthew.

70. Horsley (*Scribes, Visionaries*, 72) says, "Asking for advice about upcoming events or plans, the scribes searched their repertoire for earlier predictions that might bear on the future events. By interpreting ominous things, wise scribes predicted the future for the king."

71. On the education of scribes, see van der Toorn, *Scribal Culture*, 51–108. For Greek education from the time of Alexander the Great to the end of the Roman period, see Cribiore, *Gymnastics of the Mind*. For Roman book publishing, see Winsbury, *Roman Book*.

72. Horsley, *Scribes, Visionaries*, 71.

and human nature; (2) learning from the traditions of one's elders, the accumulated wisdom of previous generations; and (3) through encounter with God or a special revelation (Prov. 8 and Job 40–41)."[73]

These three points nicely typecast Matthew's wisdom and what it means for him to be learned or educated.[74] Matthew himself has a special revelation of God through the man Jesus Christ (point 3 above). "No one knows the Father except the Son and anyone to whom the Son chooses to reveal him" (Matt. 11:27). Wisdom is a divine gift—it comes from above—and Jesus has come to bequeath this gift to his followers as the son of David. Notably Sir. 39:1–11, when describing the ideal scribe, says, "*If the great Lord is willing,* he will be filled with the spirit of understanding" (v. 6, emphasis added). The implication is that the scribe needs to enjoy some kind of inspiration. When he pours out this knowledge, the scribe does so in a prophetic sense in that he conveys information and wisdom granted to him.

Matthew is also well known as the most Jewish of the Gospel writers. He intersects the Jesus story with the traditions of the elders (point 2 above). This mirrors what Ben Sira's grandson says about his grandfather in the Prologue: "So my grandfather Jesus, who had devoted himself especially to the reading of the Law and the Prophets and the other books of our ancestors, and had acquired considerable proficiency in them, was himself also led to write something pertaining to instruction and wisdom, so that . . . those who love learning might make even greater progress in living according to the law."

Matthew is the scribe who remembers Jesus speaking about the Law and the Prophets, about the new and the old. He demonstrates his expertise in the Hebrew Scriptures, showing interpreters how to put their Scriptures together as a unified whole, and also presents an interpreted view of Jesus's life that relies on Israel's past to explicate Jesus's significance.[75] He therefore comes to modern readers as the specialist on both the life of Jesus and the Jewish Scriptures. To understand one, you must understand the other. This

73. Witherington, *Jesus the Sage*, 12. Witherington adapted this from Crenshaw, "Acquisition of Knowledge."

74. Wisdom can be understood both as a learned skill and as the way a person can teach this practical intuition to another person. When I refer to Matthew's wisdom, I include his learned skill in interpreting both the new and the old. Matthew's and Jesus's wisdom intertwine. We get a sense of Jesus's wisdom only through Matthew's account (and that of the other evangelists).

75. In some ways Jesus and Matthew can be compared to Jeremiah and Baruch. Jesus is the prophet like Jeremiah; Matthew is the scribe like Baruch. Baruch's role as a scribe is an extension of the prophetic activity of Jeremiah. When Jeremiah is instructed to write a prophecy on a scroll (Jer. 36:2, 28), it is Baruch who writes at Jeremiah's dictation. Baruch must have played some role in the formation of the book of Jeremiah, and this was compatible with the profession of a scribe. In the same way Matthew shapes and forms Jesus's life as the scribe. Scribes are not merely redactors and compilers of tradition; they also shape tradition.

emphasis on understanding fits perfectly with how Matthew employs the term in 13:51–52. After Jesus has recounted the kingdom parables, he asks them, "'Have you *understood* all these things?' They said to him, 'Yes.'" Then Jesus continues to speak about the scribe. Matthew's Jesus uses the term "scribe" in relation to the disciples precisely because they have understood the parables.[76] A discipled scribe is one who understands the mysteries of the kingdom of heaven.

Finally and more briefly, as Matthew walks with Jesus, he learns how to scrutinize nature and human nature (point 1 above). Jesus commands them, "Look at the birds of the air. . . ." (6:26). He speaks of the outward performance of the scribes and Pharisees but also of their inward disease (23:1–36). Therefore, for Matthew, to be a scribe is first to be a learner. Matthew walks with his teacher, who claims to be from God, and as he does so, he learns to interpret the Torah from the one who claims to be the new Torah. Jesus instructs him about the tradition of the elders and makes observations about nature as the sage. Matthew thereby *learns* the ways of wisdom.

The second activity of a scribe is "writing."[77] Having learned, Matthew also transmits his learning to future generations.[78] In Jub. 4.16–18, Enoch is identified as "the first who learned writing and knowledge and wisdom . . . and who wrote in a book the signs of the heaven." While scribes worked on various forms of literature, both sacred and nonsacred texts, some evidence shows that sacred texts were handled with more care.[79] Baruch wrote down the oracles "from the mouth" of the prophet (Jer. 36:4 KJV). This image portrays Baruch as a faithful recorder, who transmits Jeremiah's words. Tov notes the restriction for scribes recorded in rabbinic texts, stating that writings by a

---

76. In 13:52 διὰ τοῦτο, then, isn't merely a literary device introducing a saying. Rather, Matthew is using it in a position of climax, linking the two verses together.

77. In the OT, the common Hebrew term for a scribe, סֹפֵר, is derived from the Semitic root סֹפֶר, which means a message that is sent. In the NT, the Greek term for scribe, γραμματεύς, comes from γράμμα, meaning something drawn, most commonly with letters. While one needs to be wary of anachronism and recognize the priority of orality in the first century, scribes were the ones who would certainly have produced the more complex written texts. In David Carr's discussion of Wisdom literature in ancient Israel scribal education (*Writing on the Tablet*, 126–28), he sketches an "oral-written" process in which the oral medium is primary, but writing is still central. Michael Bird (*Gospel of the Lord*, 46–47) notes that it was quite common among the literary elites of the Greco-Roman world to take notes, and Gerhardsson (*Memory and Manuscript*, 160–62) asserts the same for the Jewish context. See also Alan Millard, *Reading and Writing in the Time of Jesus*.

78. My argument does not depend on Matthew being the actual copyist. The "literacy" of Matthew is hard to know for sure. Matthew could have used a scribe for his work but still be the "voice" behind the tradition. This coheres with what we see in Paul and Peter's Letters: "By Silvanus . . . *I* have written briefly to you" (1 Pet. 5:12, emphasis added).

79. See S. Charlesworth, *Early Christian Gospels*.

heretic, pagan, informer, Samaritan, or converted Jew are not acceptable.[80] Other internal evidence exists that scribes corrected their mistakes when they deviated from their base text.

But scribes in this period were more than just recorders; they were also interpreters.[81] Matthew did not just copy Mark's material, nor did he merely sit down and tell a step-by-step story of Jesus. He adapted his narrative for his own purposes and therefore was a unique type of scribe. There is evidence that Ben Sira adapted wisdom traditions for his own purposes. Some of the texts found in the Judean Desert were original compositions rather than copies of earlier sources. As Emmanuel Tov has pointed out, "The majority of persons involved in the transmission of the biblical and other texts took more liberties than copyists of later periods. . . . Many scribes took an active role in the shaping of the final form of the text, and therefore the general term 'scribe' is more appropriate for them than 'copyist,' since it covers additional aspects of scribal activity and could easily include creative elements."[82]

This is important to recognize for Matthew's narrative, because he is not just copying down the life of Jesus but also crafting it. As Orton says, Matthew is a "charismatic, creative interpretation of the scriptures in light of . . . the eschatological events going on around him."[83] More specifically, he crafts it under the shadow of Jewish history. Thus we must recognize both faithfulness and flexibility in the role of a scribe. Matthew is the discipled, careful, and creative scribe, bringing out treasures new and old *through his writing*.[84]

80. Tov, *Scribal Practices and Approaches*, 9.

81. Van der Toorn (*Scribal Culture*, 115) asserts, "We may say that scribes, even in their most instrumental roles, impose their style, language, and ideas on the text. Acting as secretaries and transcribers, they are not phonographs in writing; they mold the material that reaches them orally." Matthew 2:4–6 gives some evidence of interpretation. According to Matt. 7:29, scribes also seemed to teach and therefore interpret. In Matt. 17:10, the saying that Elijah must come first is attributed to the scribes. Matthew 23:2 says that the scribes sit on Moses's seat, implying some sort of interpretation and teaching.

82. Tov, *Scribal Practices and Approaches*, 7.

83. Orton, *Understanding Scribe*, 168. Some may be nervous about this language of creativity, assuming that it contradicts the "correct" sense of the OT text. But by using the term "creative," I am simply asserting something similar to Moo and Naselli. "NT authors do not always use OT language as authoritative proof. . . . So when they appear to deduce a meaning from the OT or when they apply it to a new situation, they are not necessarily misusing the text or treating it as errant" ("Use of the Old Testament," 706). Later (709) they say, "It is unfair to apply a rigid concept of meaning to . . . an OT law and then charge him with misinterpreting the OT for going beyond what the OT specifically intends."

84. See Westerholm, *Jesus and Scribal Authority*. In Matt. 2:4 Herod asks "the chief priests and the *scribes* of the people where the Christ was to be born" (emphasis added). "They told him, 'In Bethlehem of Judea, for so it is written by the prophet'" (2:5). They not only copied texts but also answered questions about the texts and therefore interpreted them.

Scribes were not only learners and writers, but their writings were also *distributed*. The evidence for this third task comes directly from Matthew. While we might think of scribes as writing notes in a dark room, Matthew gives evidence that scribes were "sent out." In Matt. 23:34 Jesus says, "Therefore I send you prophets *and wise men and scribes*." While the statement from Jesus should probably be interpreted as a "divine sending," this is not opposed to distributing but coheres with it. Scribes needed their work to be transmitted to have its effect. They wrote, copied, and interpreted so that they could have a public hearing. If they themselves were "sent out," then they would be the natural ones to "read aloud" the copies and interpret them for people. The scribe portrayed by Ben Sira "appears before rulers" and "travels in foreign lands" (Sir. 39:4). Scribes therefore, it seems, interpreted texts for others and distributed them as needed. Readers get some sense of this reality when Jesus castigates the scribes and Pharisees in Matt. 23, implying that they must have been involved in the distribution.

In Aelius Theon's introduction to his *Progymnasmata* (written about the same time as Matthew's Gospel), Theon says a person who wants to read aloud well and speak well should "write every day."[85] It is challenging for a person to read fluently if they are not skilled at writing. Therefore, it makes sense that at times the scribe would be not only the writer but the reader. All writing in this time period needs to be embedded in the reality of oral communication. Most written texts were inscribed partly or mainly as guides in oral recitation. In a similar way, Matthew sends his scroll out into the future by copying down the record of his narrative. He transmits the knowledge he has obtained through parchment and reed pen and also through oral communication.[86] Many times scrolls functioned as aide-mémoire for scribes as they prepared for an oral performance. Matthew's authority comes from being with Jesus, who sanctions him to be a faithful representative of the message that Jesus taught his followers. In many ways Matthew is "sent" by Jesus so that the message of the kingdom can be spread. "The mission of the NT scribe is the same as of the prophets and wise men."[87] The scribe is a commissioned one and has the task of prophetic teaching. Scribes functioned as custodians, transmitters, and interpreters of the Scriptures. Now that Jesus

85. Aelius Theon, *Progym.* 2.61–62 (ed. Leonhard von Spengel); Kennedy, *Progymnasmata*, 6–7.
86. A vast amount of literature exists on the transmission of oral and written material, which I don't have the space to develop here. A good place to start is to look at Gerhardsson, *Memory and Manuscript*.
87. Penner, "New Testament Scribe," 16.

has arrived, a scribe needs to sit down and explain the Jewish Scriptures in the shadow of the messiah.[88]

Finally, scribes are also viewed as *teachers* and therefore wise.[89] As Matthew walks with Jesus, he becomes wise. Proverbs 13:20 says, "Whoever walks with the wise becomes wise." Matthew 7:29 notes how Jesus "was *teaching* them as one who had authority, not as their scribes" (emphasis added). While the point of this passage is that the scribes *do not* have authority like Jesus, the assumption is that they are supposed to have authority. This authority is confirmed in Matt. 17:10, when the disciples ask Jesus, "Then why do the scribes say that first Elijah must come?" Their question to Jesus implies an authority attributed to the scribes. Matthew 23:2 also establishes the authority of the scribes, with Jesus saying, "The scribes and Pharisees sit on Moses' seat." It seems that in their role as scholar-teachers, the scribes had attained enormous prestige among the people and were given seats of honor and enjoyed esteem from the people. In a similar way, Matthew sets himself up as the authoritative teacher in the same tradition as his rabbi. He presents his Gospel as a learned and trustworthy transmission of Jesus's life and teaching. David claims that the testimony of the Lord is sure, making wise the simple (Ps. 19:7). Readers are therefore not only to learn from Jesus but also to learn from Matthew's *presentation* of Jesus. Matthew is the discipled, careful, and creative scribe who learns, interprets, distributes, and teaches readers about the messiah.

Treasures New and Old

We have seen how Matthew was trained by his teacher of wisdom and more broadly examined the work of a scribe. Now it is time to turn to the specific task of the wise scribe detailed in 13:52: "bringing forth treasures both new and old." Matthew passes on the wisdom of his teacher by being a host who brings out goods for his guests based on his understanding and through interpretation. Treasures (θησαυρός) are not only the person's cherished values, but also more general goods or commodities. These supplies are likely demarcated in the domain of knowledge when connected to the idea of disciple. The use

---

88. Byrskog (*Jesus the Only Teacher*, 245.) asserts that we learn more about the transmission of Jesus's teachings in Matt. 16:13–20, where Peter is given authority to bind and loose. For the best explanation of what this means, see Leeman, *Political Church*.

89. This teaching was oral in nature. I don't want to give the false impression that the first-century culture was a reading culture, for it was mainly an oral culture. Thus Isa. 29:18 predicts a time when "the deaf shall hear the words of a book." See the first chapter of van der Toorn, *Scribal Culture*. Phillips ("Casting Out the Treasure," 12–13) even argues that the verb ἐκβάλλω in Matt. 13:52 could have the sense of "speaking" or "expelling" words.

of treasures probably reflects the OT wisdom tradition.[90] Proverbs 2:1–8 parallels treasures with wisdom, understanding, commands, and knowledge, while having other conceptual parallels to Matthew's language as emphasized below.

> My son, if you accept my words and store up *my commands* within you, turning your ear to *wisdom* and applying your heart to *understanding*—indeed, if you call out for *insight* and cry aloud for *understanding,* and if you look for it as for silver and search for it as for *hidden treasure*, then you will understand the fear of the LORD and find *knowledge* of God. For the LORD gives *wisdom*; from his mouth comes *knowledge* and *understanding*. He holds success in store for the upright, he is the shield to those whose walk is blameless, for he guards the course of the just and protects the way of his faithful ones. (Prov. 2:1–8 NIV, emphasis added)

Proverbs 7:1 also brings the idea of treasures (though in the verbal form) in close connection to commandments. "My son, keep my words and *treasure* up my *commandments* with you" (emphasis added; see also Prov. 21:20).

Colossians 2:3 develops our understanding of these Proverbs by arguing that in Christ are hidden "all the treasures of wisdom and knowledge." Here in Matthew's context, he correlates wisdom with the kingdom, for "the kingdom of heaven is like *treasure* hidden in a field" (13:44, emphasis added). As already noted, the connection between wisdom and what is secret or hidden is a common refrain. The treasure that the discipled scribe is to bring forth is therefore the secrets of the kingdom (Ps. 51:6). On at least three occasions Matthew claims that the disciples "understand" Jesus's teaching (13:51; 16:12; 17:13). The parallel passages in Mark indicate that the disciples do not understand (Mark 6:52; 8:21; 9:10, 32). True disciples of Jesus will understand his teaching in the sense of gaining wisdom.[91] Therefore, it seems likely that Matthew pulls from the wisdom tradition in his use of "treasures" to speak of the secrets of the kingdom he absorbed from his teacher.[92]

90. Sirach parallels wisdom and treasure in Sir. 1:25; 20:30; 41:14 (see also Isa. 33:6). Baruch does as well (2 Bar. 44.14; 54.13).

91. In Exod. 35:31, 35 and 36:1 Bezalel and Oholiab are filled with wisdom (σοφίας) and understanding (συνέσεως) to perform a task of understanding (συνίημι). See also Ps. 107:43; Prov. 21:11; Hosea 14:9; Dan. 1:4, 17; 2:21; 2 Chron. 1:10–12; 2:12–13, where wisdom and understanding are linked.

92. Yieh (*One Teacher*, 248–52) notes that Jesus's teaching tasks can be categorized under four banners: (1) interpreting the Law and the Prophets, (2) speaking the words of God, (3) preaching the kingdom of heaven, (4) calling disciples and building his church. My analysis is complementary and not contradictory to Yieh.

Matthew further defines the content of this treasure, labeling it as both "new and old" (καινὰ καὶ παλαιά; see also 9:17). Many church fathers understood the new and old with reference to the NT and the OT.[93] However, this view, while not entirely wrong, is anachronistic, since the NT as a canonical collection did not exist when Matthew wrote. It is better simply to assert that Jesus himself and his teaching is the new, while the old is the Jewish tradition more generally.

The First Gospel often draws on and quotes from the Jewish Scriptures, but Jesus also interacts a good deal with the oral tradition of the elders and the shaping of the Jewish tradition. Jesus is negative toward the law only when it has been misinterpreted. Jesus himself brings out the old, as confirmed in his teaching in Matt. 5:17–19, where he says that he has come to fulfill the Law and Prophets.[94] Like Jesus, Matthew clarifies the balance between the new and the old because he has been trained in the ways of the kingdom of heaven. He confirms the continuation of the old, when rightly understood, while also uncovering how the new clarifies the old. He does not discard the past and simply cling to the new, but he employs the new to interpret the old. The relevant point for Matthew's Gospel is that the new and the old come in tandem. These elements are defined by each other. The old can be perceived because of the presence of the new, and the new reinterprets the old. Discontinuity and continuity ultimately belong together.[95] As Barton observes "the new has priority over the old. . . . But the conjunction [and] is significant: the old retains its fundamental worth."[96] And as Morris says, "If the word order is significant, the new matters more than the old and Jesus is saying that the new teachings his followers are embracing do not do away with the old teachings (those in the Old Testament), but are the key to understanding them. The new age has dawned, and it is only in recognition of that fact that the old can be understood in its essential function of preparing the way for the new."[97]

93. Irenaeus, *Haer.* 4.9.1. Blomberg (*Matthew*, 225) says it refers to the teaching and meaning of the Hebrew Scriptures while showing how they are fulfilled in the kingdom age.

94. Sirach parallels the Law and Prophets with instruction and wisdom (Sir. prologue 1, 5, 10).

95. Hagner, *How New Is the New Testament?*, 12. Hagner continues by asserting, "While there is plenty of continuity here, at the same time the extent of newness in the Gospels—and indeed the whole of the NT—is such that an unavoidable *discontinuity* with Judaism is created. Fulfillment includes forward movement and thus inevitably involves discontinuity" (20, emphasis original).

96. Barton, "Gospel of Matthew," 122.

97. Morris, *Gospel according to Matthew*, 363. Phillips ("Casting Out the Treasure," 19) notes that the old does precede the new, and apart from ecclesiastical commentary, the new before the old appears only three times in the whole of Greek literature.

Matthew is now this discipled scribe who was so familiar with the OT and Jewish traditions and Jesus's life that he interweaves the two and uses the new-old paradigm as the key for organizing, interpreting, and describing the life of Jesus. The wisdom Matthew learns concerns the mysteries of the kingdom revealed in Jesus himself (the new) and predicted in Jewish tradition (the old). Jesus causes the old era of expectation to burst forth to the new era of realization.

Certainly other NT writers have similar convictions. However, in Matthew's Gospel the relationship and alternation between the new and the old assumes a dominant role.[98] This alternation in Matthew is unique for at least three reasons. First, unlike the rest of the NT outside the Gospels and Acts, Matthew's literature is narrative.[99] His story can parallel and echo the Jewish story in a way that other NT genres are unable to do. The OT and the whole of the Scriptures are primarily carried along by narrative. Even other genres, such as poetry, Wisdom literature, prophecy, and law, find themselves embedded within a narrative framework.

So by using this genre, Matthew can carry on and complete the Jewish hopes in a unique way. He can also insert subgenres into his narrative as the OT did. In the Gospels, we get a more direct sense of the Bible's great story line.[100] The whole of God's revelation is a great story, and the Gospel narratives recapitulate, evoke, and satisfy the old story. This is not to assert that narrative is a superior form of communication, or that the Epistles are secondary, but simply to recognize that the Gospels more than other genres mirror the mainstay of the Hebrew Scriptures. Therefore, the particular *form* of the Gospel of Matthew lends itself to a unique alternation between the new and the old.

Second, this framework of the new and the old is distinctive to Matthew because of his explicit employment of the Hebrew Scriptures. Matthew is not the only Gospel: three other canonical Gospels exist, and all of them depend on the tradition that came before them. So the natural question is "Why couldn't we use this 'new-old' framework for them as well?" Moreover, it is true that anyone reading the Gospels should have their ears attuned to the sounds of the Hebrew Scriptures. However, Matthew's explicit use of the OT sets him apart. As a Jewish writer, he uses forms of the word *fulfill* far more than the others. Richard Hays has asserted that Matthew is the most explicit Gospel in his OT interpretative strategies.[101]

---

98. The other books that could rival Matthew on this alternation between the new and the old are John, Hebrews, and Revelation.

99. For more reflection on this, see Pennington, *Reading the Gospels Wisely*.

100. Pennington, *Reading the Gospels Wisely*, 43.

101. Hays, *Reading Backwards*.

On some countings, Matthew uses some sixty-one quotes from the Hebrew Scriptures. According to the NA[28], forty of these are explicit citations, and twenty-one are quotations without explicit mention of the source. When allusions (which are harder to quantify) are taken into account, the number soars to about three hundred.[102] Therefore, the biblical tradition is the lifeblood of Matthew's presentation. Matthew also divides his narrative into units that naturally compare to the different parts of Israel's story (more on this in the last chapter). Hence, while there is quite a bit of overlap with the other Synoptic Gospels, Matthew assembles his Gospel to indicate his purposes. Donald Hagner says that Matthew provides "exceptionally fruitful ground" for exploring how this Gospel relates to the Scriptures of the Old Covenant.[103] Thus, while this alternation between the new and the old can be found in the other Gospels and could be used in an examination of them, it appears most prominently in Matthew.

The final reason the alternation between the new and the old is pertinent to Matthew's Gospel is because of its canonical placement. Although each writer of the NT recognizes Jesus's fulfillment of OT hopes, a canonical reading recognizes that the First Gospel sends the NT off with this theme. The First Gospel eventually set the table for the rest of the NT meal. Matthew becomes the lens through which to read Mark, Luke, John, Paul, and Peter's literature. If Jesus is the messiah, then the rest of the writers tie up loose ends and explore the implications of this historical reality. So while it is true on one level that the alternation between the new and the old could be applied to all NT books, it is also accurate to say that this theme is particular to and characteristic of Matthew. As R. T. France says, "Where others [NT writers] might be content to quote a few rather obvious texts as 'fulfilled' in Jesus, Matthew explores the nature of fulfillment with remarkable ingenuity, and with systematic attention to the place of Jesus's ministry with the unfolding purpose of God which *affects* and *controls* his presentation of all aspects of the story and the teaching of Jesus."[104] The First Gospel presents Jesus as the continuation and climactic completion of the story of Israel. He shapes his stories to sound like OT narratives to show that his narrative joins seamlessly to God's unfinished work.

What is evident, as Orton notes, is that Matthew is producing new things as well as old from his treasure store of special understanding.[105] The new content of the treasure is Jesus and the gospel of the kingdom. Matthew

---

102. Hays, *Echoes of Scripture in the Gospels*, 109.

103. Hagner, "Balancing the Old and the New," 21. France (*Gospel of Matthew*, 11) states, "But among the gospels Matthew stands out for his sustained and creative presentation of this theme of fulfillment in Jesus."

104. France, *Matthew: Evangelist and Teacher*, 167, emphasis added.

105. Orton, *Understanding Scribe*, 168.

produces material based on the old, but it is still altogether new because "it rests on a living experience of revelation."[106] Stanton argues that Matthew should be thought of as an exegete, or a "creative interpreter," who forms "new" sayings of Jesus.[107] These should not be thought of as creations de novo. Matthew is not some sort of innovator but retells the stories of Jesus as a creative redactor. Stanton rightly says, "Matthew is creative but not innovative: he is committed to the traditions at his disposal, but he endeavors to elucidate them for his own community."[108]

Ben Sira himself saw the Torah as the locus of wisdom, where the wisdom of heaven meets earth. Jesus as the sage teaches Matthew about the telos of the Torah to show that he is Wisdom personified. This is not in opposition to the Torah but in fulfillment of it. The discipled scribe is the one who sees Jesus as fulfilling all wisdom. He sees that in Jesus all spiritual things are discerned by looking to his sage. As the Wisdom of Solomon puts it: "Who has learned your counsel, unless you have given wisdom and sent your holy spirit from on high? And thus the paths of those on earth were set right, and people were taught what pleases you, and were saved by wisdom. . . . Wisdom . . . showed him the kingdom of God and gave him knowledge of holy things . . . so that he might learn that godliness is more powerful than anything else" (Wis. 9:17–18; 10:9–10, 12).

The Gospel of Matthew therefore sits at the climax of the wisdom tradition. It tells readers that wisdom has come—as the Hebrew Scriptures attest—through experience, observation, tradition, and correction.[109] However, it ultimately comes by revelation—the revelation of the Son. Experience can be misunderstood, observation can be faulty, tradition can be corrupted, and correction is not always present. The son of David has brought the kingdom—the revelation of wisdom—in his person and fulfilled all righteousness.

The Alternate Scribal School

Matthew can thus be understood as the discipled scribe who learned from his teacher of wisdom how the new and the old come together. However, careful readers of the First Gospel will immediately think of the negative things Matthew has Jesus hurling at the scribes. Most notably is Matt. 23, where Jesus goes on a tirade against the scribes and Pharisees.

106. Orton, *Understanding Scribe*, 168.
107. Stanton, "Matthew as a Creative Interpreter."
108. Stanton, "Matthew as a Creative Interpreter," 287.
109. These categories come from Longman's book on "sources of wisdom." Longman, *Fear of the Lord Is Wisdom*, 111–26.

Woe to you, scribes and Pharisees, hypocrites! For you lock people out of the kingdom of heaven! (23:13 NRSV)

Woe to you, scribes and Pharisees, hypocrites! For you cross sea and land to make a single convert, and you make the new convert twice as much a child of hell as yourselves. (23:15 NRSV)

Woe to you, scribes and Pharisees, hypocrites! For you are like whitewashed tombs, which on the outside look beautiful, but inside they are full of the bones of the dead and of all kinds of filth. (23:27 NRSV)

It is true that most of the references to scribes in the First Gospel are pejorative. Chris Keith has rightly argued that Jesus as a teacher clashes with the scribal authorities.[110] The scribes disagree with what Jesus teaches and how he teaches, and they say that he does not have the authority to be teaching in the first place. In Matt. 21:23 Jesus enters the temple, and the chief priests and the elders of the people ask him by what authority he does these things and who has given Jesus this authority? As Keener notes, "If Jesus taught some ideas that differed from those of some other teachers of the law, we would expect some disagreements."[111]

But rather than pushing against my thesis, the conflict between Jesus and the scribal authorities actually strengthens it. Part of the way Jesus the sage-rabbi combats the scribal elite is through constructing his own scribal school.[112] The clash of the schools, after all, is centered on Scripture and authority.[113] In most of the controversy narratives, the debate revolves around the interpretation of the Jewish Scriptures. The scribal authorities challenge Jesus's disciples for not washing their hands before eating (Matt. 15:2). The Pharisees ask about the Mosaic exceptions to divorce (19:7). The Sadducees attempt to trap Jesus concerning the resurrection (22:23–33). When Jesus goes into

110. Keith, *Jesus against the Scribal Elite*, 6. Keith more specifically argues that Jesus's reputation as an authoritative teacher of the law was itself debated because Jesus was part of the manual-labor populace, a carpenter. The elite class did not like that Jesus claimed authority as an interpreter of the Torah.

111. Keener, *Historical Jesus of the Gospels*, 38.

112. The new scribal school does not need to be understood in the technical sense, but Jesus's disciples are the ones who will transmit the teachings of Jesus to future generations. Most scholars would say that the first clear evidence of scribal schools comes from Ben Sira (Sir. 51:23), but it is likely that by around 700 BCE there was an informal class of sages. Proverbs 25:1 speaks of a group of people who produced a body of oral and written wisdom material. Witherington, *Jesus the Sage*, 4. Later Israelite kings had sage counselors (2 Sam. 16:23; 1 Kings 4:1–19; 10:1). This data is supported by the fact of early scribal schools in Egypt.

113. Keith, *Jesus against the Scribal Elite*, 112.

the temple (21:12–13), the religious leaders ask him, "By what authority are you doing these things?" (21:23). In sum, they differ on how the new relates to the old—or maybe more precisely, if there is such a thing as "the new."

As Yieh notes, not only does Jesus combat Jewish hostility, but he also defines group identity and forms a new community.[114] From the start of his ministry, Jesus gathers a group of disciples to follow him. He calls Simon, Andrew, James, and John, who are fishermen (Matt. 4:18–22), an anonymous person (8:21), and Matthew, who works at the tax booth (9:9). Jesus begins to teach them the ethics of the kingdom of heaven (5:1–7:29) and explains to them the secrets of the kingdom (13:11, 52). He gives authority to his disciples (10:1) yet also teaches them how to use the authority to serve, not to lord it over the people (20:25). His wish to recruit and train more disciples is clear when he commissions his disciples to "make disciples of all nations" (28:19). Matthew is one of those scribes who transmits his teaching to later generations.

Jesus may thus be using this term "scribe" in 13:52 to describe his disciples as authorized teachers *for* the kingdom of heaven in contrast with the Pharisaic scribes, who have failed to grasp the message.[115] Jesus urges his disciples, through his example in Matt. 13, to be discipled in the ways of the kingdom so they too can bring out riches new and old and teach and instruct with the authority that has been given to Jesus. This view is supported by other texts in Matthew, where he subtly associates scribes and disciples. In Matt. 8:19 it says, "And *a scribe* came up and said to him, 'Teacher, I will follow you wherever you go'" (emphasis added). Notice this scribe comes to his "teacher" (διδάσκαλος) and says, "I will follow [ἀκολουθέω] you." The Greek word for "follow" is the dominant term Matthew uses for the disciples. This is confirmed when the text says in 8:21, "Another of *his disciples* said, 'Lord, . . .'" According to Gundry's analysis, the sequence implies that the two scribes are both labeled as disciples.[116] Matthew elsewhere explicitly connects scribes/disciples to the title of teacher throughout his Gospel (in each case, emphasis added):

- The Pharisees ask the *disciples*, "Why does your *teacher* eat with tax collectors and sinners?" (9:11)
- Jesus says, "A *disciple* is not above his *teacher*," explicitly linking disciples with their teachers. (10:24–25)
- The *scribes* and the Pharisees ask Jesus as the "*teacher*" for a sign. (12:38)

---

114. Yieh, *One Teacher*. Matthew also emphasizes the small size of the group of disciples and contrasts the disciples with two other groups in his Gospel: the crowd and the religious leaders.
115. I am thus taking the dative as indicating advantage or interest: "for." See note 8.
116. Gundry, "True and False Disciples."

- The tax collectors ask Peter (the disciple) if his *teacher* pays the tax. (17:24)
- The *disciples* come to him and call him *teacher*. (22:16)

One final example correlates scribes and disciples. After Jesus castigates the scribes and Pharisees, he speaks in the present tense about sending "prophets and wise men and scribes" to the religious leaders (23:34). Interestingly, Jesus does not say that he sends them evangelists, apostles, or disciples; he uses this alternative triad now in a positive sense. He probably does so to contrast the "scribes" with whom he has just been speaking, those who sit on Moses's seat. But the religious leaders only kill, crucify, flog, and persecute these new messengers. In the narrative, readers have already heard about Jesus sending out his disciples, but nothing more has been made of their mission since then. Here that mission picks up again, and Jesus describes his "sent ones" positively as wise men and scribes. These scribes will find themselves in opposition to the "scribes" of the day, and therefore they represent an alternative school that Jesus is forming.

Thus, in at least three places (8:19; 13:52; 23:34) Matthew correlates scribes and disciples. Although scribes are regularly perceived as the group of characters who oppose Jesus, Matthew speaks of the scribe in a positive sense and probably in contrast to those who oppose him, the trained scribe of the kingdom of heaven who wisely brings out treasures new and old.[117] As Esther Juce contends, Matthew has two objectives in using wisdom imagery. First, to reveal Christ as the fulfillment of the Jewish tradition. Second, to contrast Christ with his opponents.[118] In summary, three points substantiate that Matthew portrays Jesus as a teacher-sage-rabbi forming a new scribal school: (1) Jesus is presented as a teacher-sage, (2) Matthew has three unique and positive uses of scribes where he correlates them to disciples, and (3) he offers negative portraits of the Jerusalem scribal school.

The Purpose of the Scribe

The purpose of this scribal training and profession was the formation of a certain type of person "understood as a higher 'humanity.'"[119] In other words, they were to help form a new community under the rule of the king. In many

---

117. The Gospel of Matthew contains twenty-two references to "scribe(s)." This is compared to ten from Mark, thus showing Matthew's special interest in scribes. Overman (*Matthew's Gospel*, 115) is right to note that in Matthew's perspective there are good and bad scribes. The three positive references are in 8:19; 13:52; and 23:34.

118. Juce, "Wisdom in Matthew," 126.

119. Horsley, *Scribes, Visionaries*, 74.

Sumerian, Akkadian, and Egyptian texts, the scribes learned to copy the works and words of the king, who was viewed as the paradigmatic scribal scholar and embodied the ideal of humanity. On one Egyptian monument, a scribe wrote the following: "I was appointed to be the royal scribe at the palace, and moreover was introduced to the god's book(s), saw the powers of Thoth and was equipped with their secrets. I opened up all their mysteries and my advice was sought concerning all their matters."[120]

As we see in the Hebrew Scriptures, kings maintained order for the society and even the universe by following the Torah. The scribes would copy the king's text to form a group with specialized knowledge and pass on this knowledge to the king's subjects. The scribe thus functioned as an intermediary between the king and the people. The OT specifically names scribes at David's court (Seraiah, 2 Sam. 8:17; Sheva, 2 Sam. 20:25; Shisha, 1 Kings 4:3; Shavsha, 1 Chron. 18:16). They were the royal scribes, or scribes of the king, spreading the king's wisdom.

When one lays this picture over the First Gospel, Matthew's purpose as a scribe begins to come together. Matthew is not only the *discipled scribe* but also *the sapiential scribe*. He too has copied the works and words of the son of David to form a community. Possibly this is why Matthew is the only Gospel writer to refer to the ἐκκλησία (16:18; 18:17).[121] By calling his disciples together and sending them into all nations, Jesus's intention is to build a "church." Matthew, as the royal and discipled scribe, stands as the intermediary who transmits the words of the king to shape and form the king's subjects. Following and assisting his king, Matthew creates a new humanity, one in which justice, love, and mercy prevail.

Matthew thus serves as King Jesus's envoy or representative as he transmits and carries the king's message; he brings good news to the poor. The purpose of scribal training was not only literacy and learning but also the shaping of a kind of person. "The law of the wise is a fountain of life" (Prov. 13:14). Scribes were to follow the established order of the world and transmit the knowledge of past generations to future generations so that they too could live in harmony with divine order. In this way, scribes helped maintain the order established by the king and ultimately by the gods.

---

120. Cited in Horsley, *Scribes, Visionaries*, 74.
121. The Hebrew word *Qohelet* in Ecclesiastes is the feminine active participle of the Hebrew verb *qhl*, which means "to assemble, to gather together."

2

The Scribe's Convictions and Methods

Different maps serve different purposes. Online maps allow people to choose whether they want to see a street view, a satellite view, or a road-map view. Other websites provide elevation cartography, climate statistics, county boundaries, political precincts, or school-district borders. None of these maps is better than the others; they merely serve different purposes. In the same way, while the rest of the book may be compared to a road map with all the same items (such as restaurants) in one area selected, then this chapter can be related to an altitude perspective, where the basic shape of nations or states can be viewed. Before we zoom in on Matthew's wisdom through his narrative, it is helpful to back up and get a wide and expansive view of Matthew's convictions and methods.[1] If Matthew is the discipled scribe who learned wisdom from his sage, then his convictions and method are a part of the wisdom he seeks to transmit to the nations.

While my larger argument is that Matthew brings forth treasures new and old, this is just the tip of the iceberg. Below the water are assumptions and methods that need to be explored. My proposal for what subtly rests beneath the surface for Matthew is the following: Matthew learned from his

---

1. While there are some excellent resources on Matthew's use of the OT (including Beale and Carson, *New Testament Use of the Old*), few attempt to integrate the interpretative stance of each author. Beale himself notes this weakness. The work "did not attempt to synthesize the results of each contributor's interpretative work on the use of the OT in the NT. Consequently, the unifying threads of the NT arising out of the use of the OT are not analyzed and discussed." Beale, *New Testament Biblical Theology*, 13. A notable exception is Richard Hays (*Echoes of Scripture in the Gospels*) in his work on the Gospels.

teacher that the arrival of the apocalyptic sage-messiah fulfills the hopes of Israel; this results in the unification of Jewish history. The method Matthew employs to communicate this conviction is "gospel-narration" through the use of shadow stories. Matthew as the scribe brings out treasures new and old because his teacher-sage has revealed to him the mysteries of the kingdom of heaven (11:25–30; 13:51–52). The rest of this chapter expands on each of these assertions.

Conviction	Israel's hopes fulfilled
Basis/grounds	The arrival of the apocalyptic sage-messiah
Result	Jewish history is unified
Method	Shadow stories

Fulfillment

Matthew's main conviction concerning the relationship between the old and the new can be summed up in the word "fulfillment" (πλήρωμα).[2] Jesus himself taught Matthew this in his statement about the messiah's relationship to the Law and Prophets. "Do not think that I have come to abolish the Law or the Prophets; I have not come to abolish them but to fulfill them" (Matt. 5:17). He fulfills the Law and Prophets as the wise messiah. Law and wisdom are fashioned together, as evidenced by Deut. 4:5–8: "I have taught you decrees and laws . . . so that you may follow them. . . . Observe them carefully, for this will show your *wisdom* and understanding to the nations" (NIV).[3] Matthew uses πληρόω or a form of it sixteen times in his Gospel compared to twice in Mark and nine times in Luke.[4] This section will assert two things. First, I will argue that "fulfillment" means to bring something to fruition in the eschatological

2. Esther Juce ("Wisdom in Matthew," 135) says, "Jesus is seen as the consummate law-giver, the consummate prophet, and the consummate sage, thus completely fulfilling the Hebrew scriptural tradition in all of its three aspects."

3. Some might object that I am losing the wisdom trail here with the statement about the Law and the Prophets. However, as noted earlier, many are now seeing wisdom less as a genre and more as a characteristic like righteousness or holiness. In addition, Longman notes how many of the teachings of the Proverbs, Wisdom of Solomon, and Ben Sira connect wisdom and law. For example, the command to honor your father and mother is echoed in Prov. 1:8; 4:1, 10; 10:1; 13:1, while the command not to bear false witness is echoed in 3:30; 6:18, 19; 10:18; 12:17, 19. Longman (*Fear of the Lord Is Wisdom*, 11, 163–75) argues that wisdom, law, and covenant are more closely associated than many realize (cf. Sib. Or. 5.357; Sir. 23:27; Wis. 9:9; Bar 3:37–4:1; 2 Bar. 5.3–7; 38.2; 77.16).

4. Matthew employs a fulfillment quotation twelve times, compared to Mark's one use and Luke's double use.

sense and is not always tied to predictive prophecy. Second, I will examine the location of the fulfillment formulas, displaying that the theme of fulfillment covers not only sections of the First Gospel but Matthew as a whole.

Declaring fulfillment to be a central theme might seem like a simple statement, one many have made, but the proposals for what πληρόω means are legion.[5] Lexically, BDAG (827) gives at least three options for the gloss of the term: (1) to make full; (2) to complete a period of time, or that which was already begun; (3) to finish, complete, or bring to a designated end. Three depictions are contained in these descriptions. "To make full" is a *spatial* metaphor, like filling a cup. "To complete a period of time" is a *temporal* comparison, such as when a person reaches a certain age. "To bring to a designated end" is a *logical* association. These assorted descriptions are not contradictory but complementary. Words are not like hardwoods, which are difficult to twist and cut through. Words are more like softwoods, with flexibility and pliability but also strength determined by their respective contexts. "Fulfill" has a variety of meanings, and in different contexts certain aspects might be highlighted. Yet largely, we can say that it means that Jesus fills up Jewish history, he completes the time of Israel, and he brings Israel to its logical telos. Another way to put it is that Matthew learned from his teacher that all things are *brought to fruition* in and through Jesus.

The term πληρόω should thus be understood in an eschatological sense: Jesus becomes all that the Law and Prophets have pointed to. He is the terminus, the telos of the Hebrew Scriptures. A new epoch has come with Jesus. The nature of πληρόω assumes a before, center, and after. What came before was not the peak of fulfillment; only at the pinnacle of time is fulfillment found (Gal. 4:4). Fulfillment uncovers its substance at the crosshairs of time. Matthew uses this term because he sees it as bridging the gap between the new and the old. All of the promises made in the OT, all of the predictions spoken, are now "filled up" in Jesus Christ. He fulfills the Law and the Prophets by becoming the one to whom the Law and Prophets point. Jesus is the end of the law, the satisfaction of all of Israel's history. As Moule says, "Jesus is . . . the goal, the convergence-point of God's plan for Israel, his covenant-promise."[6] Jesus, through his coming, begins a new era.

---

5. France (*Gospel of Matthew*, 10) argues that the central theme of Matthew's Gospel is fulfillment. Brandon Crowe ("Fulfillment in Matthew") argues for eschatological reversal; James Hamilton ("'The Virgin Will Conceive'") argues for typological fulfillment; Daniel Kirk ("Conceptualising Fulfilment in Matthew") goes the lexical route and defines it as "to fill up, to complete, to perfect." Carson ("Christological Ambiguities," 99) speaks of fulfillment in that "laws, institutions, and past redemptive events have a major *prophetic* function in pointing the way to their . . . culmination in Jesus." Turner (*Matthew*, 25) argues that fulfillment in Matthew "includes ethical, historical, and prophetic connections. . . . By recapitulating these biblical events, Jesus demonstrates the providence of God in fulfilling his promises to Israel."

6. Moule, "Fulfilment-Words in the New Testament," 301.

"Fulfillment" also means more than *prediction*. According to Matthew, the OT gives us *types* and predictions.[7] As Hays affirms, contrary to first impressions, it is inaccurate to characterize Matthew's method as prooftexting or on a prediction/fulfillment model.[8] This is because Matthew's use of "fulfillment" does not simply mean the completion of a previous prediction, although that is what English readers normally assume. For example, the following formula quotations arguably do not introduce a messianic prophecy in their strict historical context: 1:22 (virgin birth); 2:15 (son called out of Egypt); 2:17 (Rachel weeping); 13:35 (opening mouth in parables); and 27:9 (thirty pieces of silver). They are messianic after Jesus has come but only because he fills up their meaning. For Matthew, the word "fulfillment" "stands as an invitation to view Israel's Scriptures as the symbolic world in which his characters and his readers live and move."[9]

Pennington therefore speaks of a *fulfillment spectrum*. "Fulfillment . . . does not depend on prediction per se, while it still leans forward to a time when God will bring to full consummation all his good redemptive plans."[10] Prediction is a subset of the bigger ideas of fulfillment or figurations.[11] According to the fulfillment spectrum that Pennington proposes, "The way the Jewish Scriptures are re-contextualized and re-read and re-understood in light of Jesus is varied—sometimes predictions are fulfilled, while sometimes texts are taken up and re-applied in a new way, and everything in between."[12] He represents it visually like this.

Fulfillment Spectrum

Predictions	Types	Figurations	Allusions	Re-contextualizations

Matthew seems to represent all of these ways of reading, and we must have a model that accommodates all of Matthew's strategies and does not sideline some

7. Bruner, *Christbook*, 33; Turner, *Matthew*, 25. France (*Gospel of Matthew*, 12) agrees: "Fulfillment for Matthew seems to operate at many levels, embracing much more of the pattern of OT history and language than merely its prophetic predictions."

8. Hays, *Echoes of Scripture in the Gospels*, 186.

9. Hays, *Echoes of Scripture in the Gospels*, 186.

10. Pennington, review of *Hidden but Now Revealed*.

11. Hays (*Echoes of Scripture in the Gospels*, 186) rightly asserts, "For Matthew, Israel's Scripture constitutes the symbolic world in which both his characters and his readers live and move. The story of God's dealings with Israel is a comprehensive matrix out of which Matthew's Gospel narrative emerges. The fulfillment quotations, therefore, invite the reader to enter an ongoing exploration of the way in which the law and the prophets *in their entirety* find fulfillment (Matt. 5:17) in Jesus and in the kingdom of heaven."

12. Pennington, review of *Hidden but Now Revealed*.

of them or overemphasize one of them.[13] The overall point is that "fulfillment" is the word Matthew employs to teach future disciples about the relationship between the new and the old, and it expresses the eschatological, spatial, temporal, and logical dimensions of Jesus's relationship to Jewish history. It includes predictions, but also much more because it is an eschatological concept.

The Location of the Fulfillment Formulas

While it would be a mistake to focus only on the times the word πληρόω is used, now is a good time to look at the fulfillment quotations as a whole since they will be divided up and parsed throughout the rest of the work.[14] As is well known, Matthew's Gospel contains ten fulfillment quotations that follow a certain formula: "to fulfill what was spoken through the prophet, saying . . ."[15] The existence of the fulfillment quotations helps readers ascertain the fulfillment theme. Of all the Gospels, Matthew is the most explicit in letting his readers know that Jesus fulfills the hopes of Israel. Yet the placement of these quotations has caused much consternation. At first glance, the distribution seems haphazard.

The two chapters of the infancy narrative contain four fulfillment quotations. The next thirteen chapters of Matthew's Gospel concerning Jesus's Galilean ministry also include four, and then the rest of the Gospel (almost thirteen chapters long) contains only two fulfillment quotations. The fulfillment quotations drop off at a stunning rate.

Location	Number of fulfillment quotations	Percentage per chapter
Infancy narrative (1–2)	4	20%
Galilean ministry (3:1–16:12)	4	3%
Jerusalem and beyond (16:13–28:20)	2	1.5%

13. Fulfillment is both a method and a conviction, but it can be helpful to put different terms on what Matthew is doing so that categories can be more clearly divided. As Aquinas says, Jesus fulfilled the law in five ways: (1) by fulfilling the things prefigured in the law (Luke 22:37); (2) by fulfilling its legal prescriptions to the letter (Gal. 4:4); (3) by doing works through grace, through the Holy Spirit, which the law was unable to do in us (Rom. 8:3–4); (4) by providing satisfaction for the sins by which we were transgressors of the law, and when the transgressions were taken away, he fulfilled the law (Rom. 3:25); (5) by applying certain perfections to the law, which were either about the understanding of the law or for a greater perfection of righteousness/justice (Heb. 7:19; confirmed by Matt. 5:48). See Aquinas, *Commentary on Matthew*.

14. Huizenga (*New Isaac*, 19) notes that the lure of the formula quotations in Matthew has left the more covert allusions less examined.

15. As in 21:4. While the quotations in 2:5–6 and 13:14–15 have also been considered under this category, at this stage it is important simply to look at the ones introduced by a formula.

This distribution is odd because Matthew is a rather systematic author. Is Matthew indicating that the beginning of Jesus's life fulfills Israel's Scriptures more than the end? M. J. J. Menken has provided a convincing explanation for the uneven distribution of the fulfillment quotations:[16] "The distribution seems at first sight rather arbitrary but on closer consideration it appears to be well-thought out."[17] Matthew sets up his story in the infancy narrative, making sure his readers don't miss the fulfillment theme. Then the rest of the fulfillment quotations in the Gospel are placed in summary sections that do not cover only one little detail of Jesus's life but rather large swaths of Matthew's narrative. In other words, as the fulfillment quotations continue, they function like hedges blocking in large gardens of Matthew's material. For example, during Jesus's ministry in Galilee, the four fulfillment quotations (4:14–16; 8:17; 12:17–21; 13:35) have been added not to individual narratives but to summaries that describe the general traits of Jesus's ministry.

In Matt. 4:14–16 the fulfillment quotation is a summary of Jesus's ministry in Capernaum: "The people dwelling in darkness have seen a great light, and for those dwelling in the region and shadow of death, on them a light has dawned" (4:16). In. 8:17 the quotation speaks of Jesus taking illness and bearing diseases: "He took our illnesses and bore our diseases." This comes in the middle of two chapters (8–9) and covers all of Matthew's first presentation of Jesus's deeds. In chapter 12 the antagonism against Jesus grows while Jesus heals outsiders, and a significant shift toward a gentile audience occurs. So, in 12:17–21 Matthew quotes from Isaiah, speaking of Jesus as proclaiming justice to the gentiles (12:18). Finally, 13:35 comes partway through the kingdom parables chapter, and there Matthew quotes from Ps. 78:2, saying that Jesus will speak to them in parables. Matthew therefore, as the narrative continues, inserts the fulfillment quotations at key junctures of his narrative to summarize Jesus's words and actions for multiple chapters.

The same pattern occurs in the Jerusalem narrative (16:13–28:20). Although here Matthew uses only two explicit fulfillment quotations, his strategy has not changed. The first fulfillment quotation occurs in 21:4–5 and tells of Jesus coming to Zion on a donkey. "Behold, your king is coming to you, humble, and mounted on a donkey, on a colt, the foal of a beast of burden" (21:5). This quote again does not merely summarize the chapter in front of it, but reaches all the way back to Peter's confession, when Jesus says he must go to Jerusalem (16:21). A few times Matthew draws attention to Jesus's journey to Jerusalem (19:1; 20:17–18; 21:1), and Jerusalem is finally reached in 21:10.

---

16. Menken, "Messianic Interpretations."
17. Menken, "Messianic Interpretations," 486.

Therefore the journey to Jerusalem, started back in chapter 16, comes to fulfillment when Matthew (21:5) quotes Zechariah (9:9).

In a similar way, the function of the fulfillment quotation in 27:9–10 is the final point of rejection by the Jewish authorities. "They took the thirty pieces of silver, the price of him on whom a price had been set by some of the sons of Israel" (27:9). Though this is a specific quotation, the antagonism toward Jesus in the narrative thread actually begins in chapter 12, when the Pharisees decide that they will destroy Jesus (12:14). In chapter 27 this antagonism and betrayal comes to a climax. So both fulfillment quotations in Matt. 16:13–28:20 are part of pericopes in which important narrative threads come to an end: Jesus's journey to Jerusalem and his rejection by the Jewish authorities.[18]

The Fulfillment Quotations and Large Narrative Blocks

Topic	Fulfillment quotation	Narrative block
Ministry in Galilee	4:14–16	4:12–16:20
Suffering servant who heals	8:17	8:1–9:38
Servant's ministry to Gentiles	12:17–21	4:12–16:20
Speaks in parables	13:35	13:1–58
King comes humbly to Jerusalem	21:4–5	16:21–21:10
Rejection of Jesus	27:9–10	12:14–28:20

Although Matthew's use of fulfillment quotations sharply declines throughout his narrative, Matthew is not haphazard with his placement of them, and they color the way readers engage the entire Gospel. Matthew begins with more fulfillment quotations to let his readers in on his strategy. It is as if he shouts his themes at the beginning to wake his readers up, and then he quiets down when he knows they have caught on.[19] Therefore he diminishes his explicit use of OT quotations, allowing his interpreters to go searching for more clues in his narrative. It is not merely the infancy narrative where Jesus's life is mimicking OT events, institutions, and persons but his entire life. At key junctures in the narrative, Matthew places fulfillment quotations to show that all of Jesus's life is in fulfillment of Jewish hopes.

We have seen how Matthew spreads out his fulfillment quotations, thereby showing us that all of Jesus's life fulfills the OT. Many studies on Matthew have too much of a love affair with the fulfillment quotations, neglecting and abandoning the other Matthean allusions. There is much more to explore in

18. Menken, "Messianic Interpretations," 485.
19. See a similar point in Hays, *Echoes of Scripture in the Gospels*, 106.

Matthew, and therefore the rest of the book will also look to the less explicit references. We have also looked at how fulfillment should be understood in the eschatological sense and how it functions as a summary of Matthew's conviction for his scribal work: Jesus fills up, completes, perfects the history of Israel. This is Matthew's major conviction, which caused him to write about Jesus in the form he did. Now we need to turn to the reason Matthew wrote a fulfillment document.

Appearance of the Apocalyptic Sage-Messiah

The conviction that the fulfillment of all things has come is based on the arrival of the apocalyptic sage-messiah. Each of these terms will be taken in turn. First, *the arrival, the coming, the appearance* of Jesus is the key that unlocks the fulfillment door. While many works on Matthew focus on fulfillment, few explicitly tie this to the coming of Jesus—not because commentators disagree with this, but because it is assumed. Yet when we assume something, it gets sidelined. While the coming of Jesus centers on his incarnation, it is not limited to it. For the biblical authors, the incarnation and atonement of Jesus are two sides of the same coin.[20] To put this another way, the incarnation paves the way for atonement.[21] Though the purposes for Jesus coming to earth are numerous, one of the key reasons is to teach his people wisdom as the messiah and thereby reestablish the relationship between God and human beings and bring forth the kingdom. This happens through the incarnation, instruction, and ultimately the death of the God-man on the cross. Matthew writes because Jesus has appeared on earth, taught him about the kingdom of God, and died for the sins of his people. Wisdom personified suddenly has appeared in history, and things must change after his coming. The appearance of Jesus is the most basic cause for Matthew seeing things in terms of fulfillment. To put this negatively, without the emergence of Jesus, there is no fulfillment.

Second, Jesus's coming is *apocalyptic*. Though this term runs the risk of overuse, it still retains the sense I am attempting to get across. What I mean here is not that Matthew's writing is an apocalypse; rather, in Matthew Jesus reveals mysteries. He reveals the secrets of wisdom.[22] Matthew as the scribe of

20. Although these are theologically loaded terms that many in biblical studies might attribute to the early church, this is a propensity that stems from Kantian and Enlightenment thinking. As Matthew clarifies earlier Jewish hopes, so too early church developments clarify and define Christology.

21. See Crisp, *The Word Enfleshed*; Allison, *Constructing Jesus*, 31–43.

22. Macaskill (*Revealed Wisdom*) argues for the mutual presence of sapiential and apocalyptic elements in Judaism and early Christianity.

Jesus's life may employ an apocalyptic worldview without writing an apocalypse per se. Hagner goes so far as to say, "From beginning to end, and throughout, the Gospel makes such frequent use of apocalyptic motifs and the apocalyptic viewpoint that it deserves to be called *the apocalyptic Gospel*."[23]

Orton emphasizes the apocalyptic nature of scribal activity. He found in Sirach, apocalyptic literature, and the Qumran documents "that the principle underlying *true* scribalism . . . is that the teaching offered by the true scribe derives from divine revelation; it is a matter of inspiration. This is reflected constantly in the emphasis on God-given insight, the claim to special access to divine mysteries, and on the ideal scribe's commission to instruct his posterity in understanding and true righteousness."[24] In light of scribal backgrounds, Orton asserts, the apocalyptic understanding works far better than some notion of Matthew as a rabbinic author.[25]

Jesus's coming is apocalyptic not only in that it is revelatory but in that it is an upheaval, a liberating invasion of the cosmos. The turning of the ages occurs; the introduction of a new epoch begins. Jesus enters not merely the history of the first century but the history of the cosmos. His crucifixion is the crucifixion of the cosmos; sin and death are now defeated. New creation invades the present evil age. The first words of Matthew are evidence of this: βίβλος γενέσεως. This phrase harks back to the creation of all things in Gen. 2:4 and 5:1. Jesus is inaugurating the *new* heavens and the *new* social order in the midst of a world of darkness.

Apocalyptic thus maps onto the term "new" in Matthew's new-old paradigm. While continuity exists with what came before, there is also discontinuity.[26] Modern "biblical theology" may be too focused on stability and continuity, not recognizing that the arrival of Jesus upsets the political, social, and religious orders (even Jewish orders!). Mystery and newness surround Jesus. Matthew is the scribe who brings out the "new" and the "old" (καινὰ καὶ παλαιά, 13:52). The instigation for Jesus's death is evidence of the newness of Jesus's message. If he merely came and did all that the first-century

23. Hagner, "Apocalyptic Motifs," 60. He also states that an apocalyptic perspective "holds a much more prominent place than in any of the other Gospels" (53).

24. Orton, *Understanding Scribe*, 167–68.

25. Orton (*Understanding Scribe*, 175) asserts, "We hope to have demonstrated that Matthew in some essential respects—in his sense of vested authority and mission, in his apocalyptic understanding of scripture and in his insight into the essence of Jesus' instruction in understanding the mysteries of the kingdom and the will of God for the righteous—sees Jesus, the church and himself standing squarely in the tradition of the prophets and in the quasi-prophetic tradition of the apocalyptic scribes."

26. While I don't follow "apocalyptic theology" or its adherents in their proposal for radical disjointedness, a view that trims the sharp edges from their thought is on target.

Jewish leaders expected, then he would not have been crucified. There is new revelation—the secrets of the kingdom of heaven are exposed.

Third, Jesus comes as the apocalyptic *teacher-sage*. Jesus comes in Matthew as the personification of wisdom. As Witherington argues, it may be that the personification of wisdom arose partly because although it was understood that wisdom was hidden, Jews also believed that their God was one who revealed himself. Their God reveals wisdom to his people. A particularly key passage for this comes from Matt. 11:25–27.[27] The context begins with John the Baptist asking Jesus who he is, for he has heard of "the deeds of Christ" (τὰ ἔργα τοῦ Χριστοῦ, 11:2). Jesus answers with a quote from Isaiah, who also prophesied that the Spirit of wisdom would rest on the messiah. The short episode ends with a reference to the deeds of wisdom (ἡ σοφία ἀπὸ τῶν ἔργων αὐτῆς, 11:19) paralleling the "deeds of Christ" in 11:2.[28] Yet in 11:20–24 Jesus denounces the towns he has traveled in because they have rejected him. This leads Jesus to thank his Father in heaven for having "*hidden* these things from the *wise* and *understanding* and *revealed* them to little children" (11:25, emphasis added). Many key wisdom terms and concepts occur here: revelation, hidden, wise, understanding. Jesus goes on to say, "No one knows the Father except the Son and anyone to whom the Son chooses to reveal him" (11:27).[29] As the messiah, Jesus was the apocalyptic inbreaking of Wisdom into this world. He was the very embodiment of wisdom, the incarnation of the kingdom of heaven.

This is further supported by the nature of Jesus's sayings in the Gospels. Though we usually think of Wisdom literature as a fixed form, such as parables or short sayings, we should remember that since there is considerable influence of the wisdom tradition on the prophetic tradition, the whole of Scripture could be described as a wisdom text.[30] Therefore it might be that our view of the wisdom tradition is narrower than the ancients' view. For example, the Wisdom of Solomon (composed around the first century AD) offers extended exhortation in discourse form and chooses to offer something of a historical review. The prophets seemed to take this wisdom tradition and modify it into narrative form to serve their concerns. Jesus as the teacher-sage drew on a variety of Israelite traditions so that he could intermix aphorisms and narrative *meshalim*. In fact, most of his material takes one of these two

27. I deal more with this text in the chapter on Moses, where I discuss the parallels of "yoke" with the wisdom tradition.

28. For a more detailed analysis, see Walter Wilson, "Works of Wisdom."

29. Wisdom 8:21 says, "But I perceived that I would not possess wisdom unless God gave her to me" (NRSV).

30. Dryden argues this in *Hermeneutic of Wisdom*.

forms. Scribes were responsible for the preservation and production of all sorts of genres. However, the narrative nature of Matthew's Gospel should also not blind readers to the particularity of Jesus's teaching. Witherington even says that by a conservative estimate, at least 70 percent of the Jesus tradition is in the form of some sort of wisdom utterance, such as an aphorism, riddle, or parable.[31]

> I submit that the vast majority of the Gospel sayings tradition can be explained on the hypothesis that Jesus presented himself as a Jewish prophetic sage, one who drew on all the riches of earlier Jewish sacred traditions, especially the prophetic, apocalyptic, and sapiential material though occasionally even the legal traditions. His teaching, like Ben Sira's and Pseudo-Solomon's before him, bears witness to the cross-fertilization of several streams of sacred Jewish traditions. However, what makes sage the most appropriate and comprehensive term for describing Jesus is that he either casts his teaching in a recognizably sapiential form, or uses the prophetic adaptation of sapiential speech—the narrative *mashal*.[32]

Though I disagree with Witherington that "sage" is the most comprehensive term, it is one term among many that throws light onto Jesus's life and Matthew's recounting of it. The implication of Jesus's various wisdom sayings indicates the presence of Wisdom on the earth in the arrival of Jesus.

Fourth, the substance of this conviction revolves around the term *messiah*. Although early Jewish literature cannot produce a checklist of what the messiah will do, and there were diverse opinions about the messiah, we can read backward from Matthew's presentation to get a better understanding of what was expected.[33] Many biblical scholars are wary of appealing to later writings, thinking that they confuse and distort our picture of early Jewish hopes. In other words, they assert that it is anachronistic to force later views on earlier texts. But could it be that the passing of time clarifies anticipations rather than concealing them? The coming of Jesus actually defines the hope rather than obscuring it. As Wright says, although we can't re-create a single unified picture of Jewish messianic expectation, such expectation, though

31. Witherington, *Jesus the Sage*, 155–56.
32. Witherington, *Jesus the Sage*, 158–59.
33. I acknowledge that this method is not popular in biblical studies, but either we approach the Gospels with suspicion, or we approach them with trust. As J. Charlesworth ("From Messianology to Christology," 35) claims, "The gospel and Paul must not be read as if they are reliable sources for pre-70 Jewish beliefs in the Messiah." It is fine for historians to examine sources and compare them and respect their historical placement, but this is also a view of history that fails to see how later writings can shed light and new meaning on earlier writings.

not unified, certainly existed. "The early Christians . . . took a vague general idea of the Messiah, and redrew it around a new fixed point, this case Jesus, thereby giving it precision and direction."[34]

W. D. Davies argues that Matthew redraws and defines messianism around David, Abraham, Moses, and the Son of Man.[35] The genealogy begins by asserting nothing less than that Jesus of Nazareth is Israel's long-awaited messianic king. While the Davidic connotations govern Matthew's presentation, they are also balanced by Matthew's description of Jesus as the son of Abraham. Messianism is defined by both a particular and a universal focus. Jesus is a Jewish messiah whose goal is to bless the nations. But he is also the new messianic Moses who fulfills the law by both accomplishing all and teaching others to do the same. By being the Danielic Son of Man, Jesus also balances out these portraits because he comes as judge. As Davies notes, messianism also has a dark side: it can lead to unrealistic, visionary enthusiasms that prove destructive. Matthew tempers and defines those messianic hopes by fashioning the messianic hope according to these four figures.[36]

Wright argues that messianic hopes were transformed by the NT writers in at least four ways: (1) they lost their ethnic specificity and became relevant to all nations; (2) the messianic battle was not against the worldly powers but against evil itself; (3) the rebuilt temple would be the followers of Jesus; and (4) the justice, peace, and salvation that the messiah would bring to the world would not be a geopolitical program but the cosmic renewal of all creation.[37] Messianic hopes were primarily transformed by the reality of a suffering messiah (as Isaiah predicted). The Gospel writers' central conviction revolves around the cross. It is important to recognize here that the thread of messianic hope runs through diverse terrains, and readers can't siphon them off and lock them in their respective rooms. Yet Matthew also employs the suffering messiah as the gravitational axis through which all the other terms travel. So while I won't devote an entire chapter to Jesus as the suffering messiah, each chapter should be read as defining what Matthew means by asserting that Jesus is the Christ.

---

34. Wright, *New Testament and the People of God*, 310.

35. Throughout this work, I will argue that while Davies's proposal is right, Matthew's portrayal of the messiah is also more expansive than this. He defines Jesus the Messiah around Moses and around Israel as well.

36. W. Davies, "Jewish Sources of Matthew's Messianism," 511: "His messianism, in short, is a corrective messianism, corrective of excesses and illusions, even as it recognizes ethnic privacy (or particularity) and at the same time affirms universalism." While I disagree with Davies that we can precisely identify the nature of the dark side of the Matthean communities' hope, I argue that Matthew is providing some sort of corrective, and this corrective is best found in *how* Matthew defines and redefines messianic hope.

37. Wright, *Resurrection of the Son of God*, 554–55.

In sum, Matthew brings out the new because of the arrival of the apocalyptic sage-messiah who inaugurates the kingdom. Old Testament texts are *consummated in the person and work of Jesus the Messiah*. He is not taking out his "messianic searchlight" and finding texts that adhere to his program. The opposite is the case. Neither Matthew nor the NT has this searchlight, but the OT is the "messianic searchlight."[38] The messiah fulfills these hopes in that they were "shadows" before he came, but now these texts are "filled" with reality. What earlier was dark now comes to light in Jesus. Alternatively, to change the metaphor, the Prophets and the Law give a blurry or foggy view of the messiah. The bits and pieces are there, but when Jesus comes, the substance is now present. As Paul says, "All the promises of God are Yes and Amen in Christ Jesus" (2 Cor. 1:20 AT). Jesus satisfies the hunger for eschatological consummation throughout the OT story. Matthew's theology inspires, determines, and controls his hermeneutical approach to the OT Scriptures. As Matthew writes, in every Scripture "something greater is here" (Matt. 12:6, 41–42). Every shadow dancing across the pages of Matthew's narrative is cast by some greater eschatological substance. Matthew recalibrates these texts to have them refer to God's apocalyptic agent.

History Unified

Because Jesus has come and fulfilled all things, the result is that Jewish history (and all history) is now unified. While the apocalyptic nature of the messiah maps onto the "new," the newness paradoxically also brings forth the "old." The Hebrew Scriptures are fulfilled in that their history is now viewed through the window of Jesus. History, at the most basic level, is about people, time, and place. In Matthew's Gospel, all three of these meet in the messiah. The people (Moses, Abraham, David, et al.), the places (mountains, rivers, temple, desert, etc.), and time (new and old) all incorporate together under the banner of Jesus.

Time is presented in duality for Matthew as he constructs both a linear chronology and presses in on the reality of "higher time." Linear chronology views time in sequence; "higher time" views events as not detached but joined together. For example, the exodus from Egypt happened in the past (chronological), yet it is also recapitulated (higher time) in Jesus's departure from Egypt (Matt. 2:15).[39] Robert Jenson put this another way: a biblical

---

38. I first heard this metaphor from Sailhamer, "Messiah and the Hebrew Bible," 14.
39. For more on this distinction, see Levering, *Participatory Biblical Exegesis*.

understanding recognizes time as neither linear nor cyclical but perhaps more like a helix, "and what it spirals around is the risen Christ."[40]

This distinction is important to comprehend in Matthew. Chronologically speaking, Jesus comes on the scene at a certain time, after many events have been completed. But Matthew contends time can be compared to a casting net. When the center line is drawn up, the points on the edges are drawn together. For Matthew, the moments in the OT suddenly draw together at a higher time in the person of Christ. Higher time does not overrun linear time but recognizes the simultaneity of distinct, previously unconnected moments in time. Matthew does not impose alien meanings onto the biblical text and avoid historical meaning. Rather, he is persuaded that the OT events are contiguous with their christological fulfillment in the NT—a fulfillment often incomprehensible until the arrival of Jesus.

These assertions are similarly true about space and place in Matthew's narrative. Many biblical theologies form time-based readings of the text, but a neglected area of reflection lies in the spatial perspective.[41] For Matthew, places can be both separate and unified: Matthew conceptualizes separate mountains as coinciding, the water crossings as holding together in simultaneity, heaven as bending down to touch earth, and Jesus as looking out over the land in Matt. 28 as Moses did at the end of Deuteronomy. Earthbound events suddenly participate in heavenly realities because the God-man has come to be with his people.

The same casting net employed for time and space is also used for people. As the center line is drawn up, the people through the corridors of time begin to point toward their destination. Matthew draws the line, and suddenly Moses's life is not black and white but filled with color; the promises to Abraham begin to fill out, the covenant with David is fulfilled, and all Israel as a nation mirrors the actions of Jesus. Because of Matthew's conviction about history, his shadow stories can have multiple references. These manifold references are not contradictory but complementary. Is Jesus's going through the water in his baptism a picture of Moses, Israel, Joshua, the new creation, or the kingdom? The answer is yes. These can all coalesce because Jesus is the gravitational force that pulls all things together.

Northrop Frye writes that the immediate context of a sentence is as likely to be three hundred pages off as to be the next or preceding sentence.[42] This is because not only the characters participate in the drama of God; history

---

40. Jenson, "Scripture's Authority in the Church," 35.
41. Schreiner, *Body of Jesus.*
42. Frye, *The Great Code,* 208.

itself, including time and space, does as well. "Jesus Christ constitutes the center of linear and participatory history as the Incarnate Word."[43] Another way of putting this is that Matthew's theory of history is not one in which random fluidity is the core idea, but history progresses to a determined end. History has a telos. It is an arena of promise and fulfillment; it is the stage upon which the creator God speaks and acts.

The Scribe's Methods

Convictions produce methods and techniques. For example, photographers will normally shoot at sunset because they are persuaded that the lighting is best at dusk. Their convictions drive their methods and systems. In the same way, the scribe's method flows from his persuasions about his teacher. Matthew therefore tells the story of Jesus in (1) the form of an ancient biography, indicating how his subject is worthy of emulation. Another influence on Matthew's writing is (2) the historical narrative of the Hebrew Bible. The early church and the evangelists understood the four narratives about Jesus as "gospels" and therefore as continuing the great story of God. The First Evangelist particularly shapes, embeds, and builds his narrative in the apparel of other Jewish texts. Shadow stories govern his presentation of the story of Jesus. For Matthew, the best way to show how Jesus disrupts and completes the story of Israel is to employ Israel's texts in the repainting of Jesus's life. The form of Matthew's work (biography and OT narrative) conveys his conviction and the wisdom received from his sage: the new completes the old.

Genre and Purpose

Though some still argue that the Gospels are sui generis, the work of Richard Burridge has turned the tide toward viewing the Gospels as ancient biographies (βίοι), though with some differences.[44] In the ancient world biographies presented their subjects as exemplars. Plutarch, for example, draws a distinction between comprehensive histories and the writing of his βίοι.[45] "I do not tell all the famous actions of these men, nor even speak exhaustively at all in each particular case, but in epitome for the most part. . . . For it is not Histories that I am writing, but Lives; and in the most illustrious deeds there is not always a manifestation of virtue or vice."[46] Plutarch specifically says

---

43. Boersma and Levering, "Spiritual Interpretation and Realigned Temporality," 590.
44. Burridge, *What Are the Gospels?*
45. I was made aware of this reference by Dryden, *Hermeneutic of Wisdom*, 100.
46. Plutarch, *Alexander* 1.1–2, in *Lives*, trans. B. Perrin, LCL 99, 7:225.

he does not include everything in a person's life because he is concerned with the virtuous character of his subjects. This use of stories to promote moral exemplars is commonly used in Greco-Roman and biblical discourse. Matthew therefore puts his writing of Jesus's life into this genre because he wants to encourage wisdom by highlighting the actions and teachings of his sage.

But readers must progress past the Greco-Roman tradition for influence upon Matthew. Major inspiration comes from the historical narratives of the Hebrew Bible.[47] Early on, the term "gospel" began to be employed as a sort of genre description of Matthew, Mark, Luke, and John. The term "gospel" (εὐαγγέλιον) and its verbal cognate "gospelize" (εὐαγγελίζω) point to the oral proclamation or message of good news. Why did the early church begin referring to these written documents as "Gospels"? The answer comes from looking at the first words of Mark, the first written Gospel. It has been widely argued that the opening words of Mark's Gospel are not simply an introduction to his work but most likely serve as a title or heading: "the beginning of the gospel of Jesus Christ, the Son of God" (Ἀρχὴ τοῦ εὐαγγελίου Ἰησοῦ Χριστοῦ υἱοῦ θεοῦ).

Not only do we have some hints in the evangelists' works themselves that these should be labeled as "Gospels," but the early church witness also supports this. As early as the first half of the second century (ca. AD 150–55), the noun εὐαγγέλιον was used in Justin's *Apology* to refer to the Gospel books.[48] In addition, the superscriptions added to the four evangelists in the second century were consistently "the Gospel according to X." So the followers of Jesus early on seemed to follow Mark in labeling these works as "Gospels." However, the more important question for this study is the implication of these being labeled as "Gospels."

In the OT, and more specifically Isa. 40–66, the term "gospel" refers to the hope of the future restoration of God's reign through his chosen servant. For example, in Isa. 52:7 εὐαγγελίζω is put in parallel to the reign of God (βασιλεύσει σου ὁ θεός).

> How beautiful upon the mountains
>   are the feet of him who brings *good news*,
> who *publishes peace*, who brings *good news* of happiness,
>   who *publishes salvation*,
>   who says to Zion, "*Your God reigns*." (Isa. 52:7, emphasis added)

47. Alexander, "What Is a Gospel?"
48. For more on the development of the use of this term from oral to written, see Pennington, *Reading the Gospels Wisely*, 13–16, and esp. 6–10: "From 'Oral Gospel' to 'Written Gospel,'" in chap. 1.

The good news is described here as the reign of God, or peace, happiness, and salvation. The larger context is that Israel sits in exile, and the people await the return of their God to bring them out of exile and back into their home. The context of Isa. 40–66 also speaks of them in exile and suffering because of their sin. Jesus clarifies for Israel that the main problem with Israel is not what others are doing to them but what they have done to themselves. The good news can only be understood after they have realized the bad news. The good news they are waiting for is a Savior, a representative to enact the reign of God. Thus the gospel of the evangelists means the reinstatement of the reign of God.

Therefore, when Jesus comes proclaiming "the gospel of the kingdom" of God (Matt. 4:23; 9:35), the disciples must have understood that Jesus's ministry fulfills the hopes of which Isaiah spoke. It was thus appropriate for the disciples and the early church to label their stories as "The Gospel according to X" because in these stories we learn how Jesus satisfies the gospel expectations.[49] The Gospels are stories about Jesus, and Jesus's message is that the kingdom of God, the reign of God, is here in his person.

Matthew chooses to tell this "Gospel" because it *completes the great story line of the Scripture.* The trained scribe understood himself as continuing the ancient story of God's dealings with his people, beginning with Adam and Eve and going through Abraham, Moses, and David. At its core the whole Bible is a narrative of God's work in the world, and Matthew completes this portrayal with the story of Jesus. The hopes and dreams of Israel centered on the announcement of good news and more specifically the good news that their God reigns over the whole earth. Matthew, as the scribe, illustrates for his readers that his rabbi is the representative of God who will bring God's kingdom. These are not just any stories, but stories of the Jewish messiah, the king from David's line, the son of Abraham.

The combination of these two genres (ancient biographies and OT narratives) instructs readers both that Matthew presents Jesus as a figure to emulate and that this story is the climax of the great narrative of Israel. Matthew, and the other Gospel writers, take the wisdom sayings of Jesus and connect them with the narrative mode of the Hebrew Bible. According to Dryden this

---

49. About the larger context of Isa. 40–66, Pennington says: "Isaiah describes it [the gospel] with a full artist's palette of vibrant colors. It is comfort and tenderness from God (40:1, 2, 11; 51:5; 52:9; 54:7–8; 55:7; 61:2–3), the presence of God himself (41:10; 43:5; 45:14; 52:12), help for the poor and needy (40:29–31; 41:17; 55:1–2), the renewing of all things (42:9–10; 43:18–19; 48:6; 65:17; 66:22), the judgment of God's enemies (42:13–17; 47:1–15; 49:22–26; 66:15–17, 24), the healing of blindness and deafness (42:18; 43:8–10), the forgiving of sins (44:22; 53:4–6, 10–12), and the making of a covenant (41:6; 49:8; 55:3; 59:21)." Pennington, *Reading the Gospels Wisely*, 15–16.

means that the Gospels function as wisdom: they "teach practical wisdom by instilling in readers a personal allegiance to a particular value-laden picture of the world."[50] Matthew writes of Jesus's life in these particular forms so that we might see the values of Wisdom embodied as the new and the old intermix in his discourses and actions.

Shadow Stories

Matthew provides an ancient biography peppered with the Hebrew Bible. But we need to press more into the *manner* of how he tells this story of Jesus, for this instructs us about the wisdom learned from his sage. The First Gospel can be understood on a basic narrative-development level: Jesus is born, baptized, begins his ministry, is challenged, dies, and rises from the dead. Yet the shadows of the Torah nearly always shape Matthew's historical rendering. The OT Scriptures constitute the "generative milieu" of Matthew's story. It is somewhat like the baby boomers experiencing the first generation of Star Wars movies and then watching the 2015 installment *The Force Awakens*. The director J. J. Abrams explicitly made the film in a way that both new and old fans could appreciate. There was the basic plot line, which carried the movie forward, yet when Star Wars fans saw certain scenes, they couldn't help but be reminded of earlier movies. The point is that there is the text (*The Force Awakens*), and then there is the subtext (earlier Star Wars films). They cohere with one another in some ways and differ in others, but those with ears to hear and eyes to see end up seeing more than the uninformed viewer does.

Yet exactly how Matthew (and the other NT authors) employ the OT is debated. The dispute pertains to both the terms used to describe the method and the actual practice behind these terms. Some prefer the name typology, others intertextuality, or inner-biblical exegeis, or figural representation, or midrash, or allegory.[51] The division between these camps creates deep divides among interpreters (though there is probably more commonality than they realize). I don't attempt to solve the debate here, but I do want to point out one oversight and attempt to correct it in my presentation. The problem with some of the aforementioned terms is that they unintentionally produce tunnel vision rather than viewing parallels together. If Matthew's gospel-narration

---

50. Dryden, *Hermeneutic of Wisdom*, 123.

51. Hays (*Echoes of Scripture in the Letters of Paul*, 14) popularized the term "intertextuality." Some debate whether biblical scholars should be using this term at all unless they adhere to the reader-oriented approaches. See Kristeva, *Desire in Language*; Kristeva and Roudiez, *Revolution in Poetic Language*; Bakhtin, *Dialogic Imagination*. Fishbane prefers the term "inner-biblical exegesis." See Fishbane, "Revelation and Tradition"; Fishbane, *Biblical Interpretation in Ancient Israel*.

of Jesus's life reflects and completes the *persons, places, things, offices, events, actions, and institutions* of the OT, then these should be viewed together.[52] The combination of all these things produces a story.

I will therefore use the term *shadow stories* as the comprehensive term partially because shadow stories are unique to the Gospels' narration.[53] They connect large swaths of narrative rather than just points or dots in the story. The point here is to push people past simply looking for similar terms and to look for a combination of these factors and the development of a narrative through quotes, allusions, and echoes. The main importance of this is that as we study Matthew, we should be looking for more than "word" connections; we should watch for "narrative" echoes as well. Associations are made to Jesus's life that demonstrate how all the types in the Hebrew Scriptures are fulfilled in the antitype. This makes sense, for a story consists not only of persons but also of events, institutions, things, offices, and actions.

So, for example, Jesus is presented as the new Moses (person). In portraying Jesus as the new Moses, Jesus is set on mountains (places) mirroring Sinai and other such imagery. At times, he is even portrayed in shining clothes (things), showing that he is near to God, like Moses. As the new Moses, Jesus is thus the new prophet (office), who speaks for God and leads his people on a new exodus (event). He does this by the sprinkling of his blood (action), which establishes the new covenant (institution). Readers should not take these out and only assess them individually, as if they stand on their own. Rather, they should examine how Matthew's narrative develops the portrait of Jesus as the new Moses. The narrative as a whole is shaped in a way that imitates, duplicates, and replicates a previous story, not only individual pieces of it.

Explicit or Subtle?

Many scholars notice how explicit Matthew's use of the OT is, and the abundance of fulfillment quotations support this contention, but Matthew

52. Another way to categorize the relationship between the new and the old is summarized by Moo and Naselli ("Use of the Old Testament," 736–37), whose argument is not far from what I have proposed. They are looking at the entire canon and assert the following: (1) A canonical approach provides the interpretive framework by answering the "why" question. (2) Typology describes one critical way in which the two Testaments within one canon can be seen to relate to each other—the "how." And (3) *sensus plenior* is the "what": the fuller or deeper sense that NT writers find in OT texts as they read canonically. The NT authors discern a "fuller" meaning in OT passages by placing those texts in a wider context than the original authors could have known.

53. I picked up this term from Senior, "Lure of the Formula Quotations," 115. When I say I will use the term, this does not mean I won't use *typology* or *figural interpretation* as well for the sake of variety.

can also be subtle.[54] Sometimes his overt fulfillment statements distract readers from seeing other shadows dancing across his pages.[55] Dale Allison says that while Matthew made much clear, he did not trumpet all his intentions; a careful reader will note this even in the first few verses.[56] Matthew's style is not only overt but also full of allusions and implications. It is not a contradiction to assert that Matthew is both explicit and subtle. He is explicit on the surface level but subtle on a deeper level. Sometimes the overt words of Matthew are plain so that a modest reader can get his point, but his *form* is subtle. Other times the individual words seem plain, but then when comparing them with an OT text, one realizes much more is going on.

For example, Matthew cloaks his introductory narrative about who Jesus is (chap. 1) and where he is from (chap. 2) with distinctly torahaic robes. Using a string of fulfillment quotations in chapter 2, Matthew shows his readers how to interact with his unfolding story. Jesus's birth in Bethlehem is to fulfill the prophecy that a ruler will come from Bethlehem (Mic. 5:2). His life in Nazareth fulfills the expectation that he will be called a Nazarene (Isa. 11:1). On one level the meaning is plain, but when one examines the OT, no quote exists that says, "One is coming who shall be called a Nazarene." Matthew surely knew this, so he must want his readers to see something more than what was on the surface. Many therefore conclude that Matthew executes a wordplay with Isa. 11:1, which says, "Then a shoot will spring from the stem of Jesse, and a branch from his roots will bear fruit" (NASB). In Hebrew, the word for "branch" is *netzer*, which in the Hebrew consonantal text would appear as *NZR*, the letters occurring also in NaZaReth. Matthew is thus explicit on one level but subtle on another.[57]

Matthew can be subtle, ambiguous, and "untidy" at times because, like a good artist, he knows words on a slant are sometimes more effective. In the words of R. T. France, there is a surface meaning but also a "bonus meaning" that conveys the increasingly rich understanding of the person and role of Jesus.[58] The point is not that Matthew is "a verbal juggler, but [an]

54. Hays (*Echoes of Scripture in the Gospels*, 106) overstates it when he says Matthew leaves nothing to chance in his OT references.

55. The nature of the people seeing only the explicit references may be tied to the tunnel vision I spoke of earlier.

56. Allison, *New Moses*, 284.

57. Leithart (*Jesus as Israel*, 77–78) claims from this use of Nazareth that Matthew "also indicates that we need to read poetically, even punningly, if we are going to understand how Jesus fulfills the prophets. He does not always fulfill prophecy in a straightforward, literal manner."

58. This language of "surface meaning" and "bonus meaning" is adopted from France, "Formula-Quotations of Matthew 2." Consider the example of formula quotations: only one of the formula quotations exactly repeats the text of the LXX. In most cases Matthew's quotation

innovative theologian whose fertile imagination is controlled by an overriding conviction of the climactic place of Jesus in the working out of the total purpose of God."[59] The First Gospel is a mnemonic device, a trigger for intertextual interchanges that depend on an imaginative and careful reading.[60] So Matthew provides stories about Jesus, but these stories have shadows lurking both in the foreground and the background. Some of these shadows have clear outlines, while others require more work on the part of the reader.

Reception and Production

As I have argued, Matthew is convinced that the coming of the apocalyptic sage-messiah has fulfilled Israel's expectations. Shadow stories look more to the larger narrative patterns and note that events, persons, institutions, places, things, and offices can't ultimately be separated. But *how* does Matthew find these figures and shadow stories? Does he read backward from Jesus's life, or forward from the OT? David Orton is right to state that Matthew's method was probably more natural than parsed out.

> Matthew may not himself have been fully aware of the *mechanics* of his own method, since it plainly operates on an intuitive level, involving a high degree of lateral thinking and unconscious allusion. For Matthew the exercise is certainly not an academic one, some kind of word-game, or even a rabbinic-type exegesis; it is a product born of extended reflection and meditation on the written words of scripture and of his Jesus-sources.[61]

While Matthew may have not been aware of his mechanics, it is useful to step back with hindsight and categorize what he is doing. Matthew seems to employ a reading of both reception and production.[62] Reception focuses on how Matthew received meanings generated by the OT text. Production refers to the way in which Matthew exposed or inserted meanings in earlier texts. In simpler terms, Matthew reads both forward and backward. He sees things latent in the OT text before Christ's advent and also sees things that can be recognized only retrospectively, after the coming of Jesus.

---

seems to be a creative yet faithful rendering of the passage, adapting the text to more clearly point out how Jesus's life completes the OT story (see Matt. 27:9–10 and Zech. 11:12–13). A study of only the explicit OT predictions merely scratches the surface. Matthew's concept is far broader and more complex.

59. France, *Matthew: Evangelist and Teacher*, 183.
60. This language comes from Allison, *New Moses*, 285.
61. Orton, *Understanding Scribe*, 174.
62. See Alkier, "Intertextuality and the Semiotics" and "Categorical Semiotics."

While the prospective reading is not provocative, some are uncomfortable with a retrospective reading. Kaiser states, "If it is not in the OT text, who cares how ingenious later writers are in their ability to reload the OT text with truths that it never claimed to reveal in the first place?"[63] I care, especially if Matthew the scribe is the one reloading the text. The crux of the argument comes down to what "in the OT text" means. Matthew is not taking the text for a spin that the original authors would not have recognized. Rather, their view was hazy because the fullness of time had not yet arrived. This does not mean that Matthew is finding things in the OT text not already there. Instead, the nature of their *thereness* transforms with the coming of Jesus.[64] As Moo and Naselli state, "Does the OT intend the NT's typological correspondence? We would answer 'no' if 'intend' means that the participants in the OT situation or the OT authors were always aware of the typological significance. On the other hand, we would answer 'yes' if 'intend' means that the OT has a 'prophetic' function."[65] These readings are not contradictory to the OT texts but truly retrospective readings. To put it another way, it is divinely intended but recognized retrospectively.

An example outside the Scriptures of how retrospective readings work may help here. Daniel James Brown's best-selling book, *The Boys in the Boat*, tells the story of the Washington University crew team who won the gold under Hitler's glaring eye. At the end of the book Brown reflects on what Hitler saw that day in 1936, connecting two events that could only be done so retrospectively. Brown says:

> It occurred to me that when Hitler watched Joe and the boys fight their way back from the rear of the field to sweep ahead of Italy and Germany seventy-five years ago, he saw, but did not recognize, heralds of his doom. He could not have known that one day hundreds of thousands of boys just like them, boys who shared their essential nature—decent and unassuming, not privileged or favored by anything in particular, just loyal, committed, and perseverant—would return to Germany dressed in olive drab, hunting him down.[66]

Brown, as the narrator, brings two events into association: the day the Washington crew won the gold and the day when American soldiers invaded Germany. He acknowledges that Hitler could not have known, but he, as the

63. Kaiser, "Lord's Anointed."
64. As Sequeira ("Eschatological Fulfillment in Christ," 5) says, "Although the author's use of a text may *transcend* its original meaning, it is always a *legitimate outgrowth* of this original meaning."
65. Moo and Naselli, "Use of the Old Testament," 727–28.
66. D. Brown, *Boys in the Boat*, 368.

author who stands on the other side of the war, sees the prefigurement of the American heart in the boys in the boat.

This is similar to Matthew's method. Many of the Hebrew Scriptures are certainly prophetic, and Matthew sees them straining forward toward the messiah. However, other texts only shine after the messiah has come. Brown admits that Hitler could not have known what lay before his eyes, but now that the war is over, the two events can be held in simultaneity. This is true of all history. The whole truth concerning an event can only be known afterward, and sometimes only long after the event itself has taken place. The OT authors are not at fault for not knowing the future or how it will shape the events they are experiencing. If we believe that new events in history bring light and meaning to previous events, then how can we not also believe this for the coming of the Son of God? The apocalyptic coming of the messiah casts new light on old stories: the lamp of Jesus reveals corners that were dark and musty. Only after the fact of Jesus is Matthew able to see certain connections. So, like Brown, Matthew reads backward.

The process of reading and interpretation is a complex interplay between a retrospective and prospective reading. For example, if you read a detective novel and the key is revealed at the end, then all the hints in the first part come together. Suddenly the reader sees that the clues were present the whole time, but the key needed to be revealed. The early church described Jesus as the "key" of the Scriptures. Once the key is revealed, readers see the clues contained all along in Scripture. Retrospectively they seem patent; prospectively they seem more latent. The process of reading and interpreting Scripture is usually even more complex than a simple detective novel: once you reach a conclusion, it is hard to tell whether "the new" was discovered prospectively or retrospectively.

Other NT authors and indeed Jesus's words on the road to Emmaus in Luke (where he interprets for them from "Moses and all the Prophets" all "the things concerning himself"; Luke 24:27) confirm this method. The new law stands over the old law and determines how we are to interpret the old law. This is because all of the NT authors read the Scriptures under the banner of Christ. Hugh of St. Victor says, "All of Divine Scripture is one book, and that one book is Christ."[67] Therefore, their exegesis of the OT is paradoxical, for though the authors viewed the Torah as authoritative, they also extended the text by pointing to its fundamental telos. The word spoken in the Torah was never meant to be self-referential but now dwells in Christ.[68]

---

67. As quoted in Billings, *Word of God for the People*, 166.

68. Yet the Torah also points forward to Jesus. In Jesus's ministry, he constantly asks, "Have you not read?" "Do you not see?" "Have you not understood?" Perhaps the best way to put it is in Matthew's explicit language: "Do not think I have come to abolish the Law or the Prophets; I

Matthew's language in chapter 13 supports this idea of reception and production. In one sense, according to the context of Matt. 13—and indeed the entire Gospel—this newness is not really "new." These things have "been hidden since the foundation of the world" (13:35). Jesus is not changing God's plan, for God has been slowly painting his canvas all along. At the same time, the revelation of these things through the Son is new. These are new/old truths, and the discipled scribe brings out a plate of goods for the benefit of others. According to Matthew, the message of the kingdom of heaven does not do away with the old but builds on top of it. Matthew shows his readers that in their enthusiasm for finding the new, they must not disregard the old. The old is not thrown away but brought out in fresh clothing. As Frederick Bruner says, "The new does not displace the old but accompanies it."[69]

Yet at the same time, the order of the "new" and then the "old" in Matt. 13:52 is unexpected. It indicates that the old order is now to be interpreted in light of the new order.[70] Augustine famously said, "The New Testament is latent in the Old, the Old patent in the New."[71] The difficulty comes in trying not to err on either side of this balance beam. Some of the richest reflections on the Scriptures come from exploring the connection between promise and fulfillment. Matthew demonstrates that to understand the Scriptures well, one must steady these two weights and see Jesus as the balance of it all. Therefore, Matthew gives his readers their first hermeneutical lesson in the form of a story about Jesus, not in a list of directives that can become a new law. Narrative resists tabulation and requires wrestling. An expansion of Augustine's words puts it this way:

> The New is in the Old contained,
> The Old is in the New retained;
> The New is in the Old concealed,
> The Old is in the New revealed;
> The New is in the Old enfolded,
> The Old is in the New unfolded.[72]

---

have not come to abolish them but to fulfill them" (5:17). Matthew's strategy of reading shows us how he sees the new and the old interacting in complex ways, but the new seizes priority and reinterprets (or clarifies) the old while, at the same time, the old informs the new. Both of these statements must be held in tension, something Matthew does throughout his Gospel.

69. Bruner, *Churchbook*, 56.

70. See Matt. 9:16–17; 2 Cor. 5:17; Heb. 8:13; and 1 John 2:7 for other references where the new is mentioned before the old.

71. Augustine, *Quaestiones in Heptateuchum* 2.73. The Latin is "*quamquam et in Vetere Novum lateat, et in Novo Vetus pateat,*" which could also be translated "The New Testament in the Old lies concealed, the Old in the New is revealed."

72. Augustine, *Quaestiones in Heptateuchum* 2.73.

Conclusion to the Scribe

Matthew is the discipled and trained scribe from Matt. 13:52 who learned wisdom from his teacher. More than maybe any other NT author, Matthew centers on the relationship between the new and the old. He summarizes the association through the word "fulfillment."[73] The First Evangelist teaches his readers his method in the writing of his Gospel, where readers find a complex yet consistent interchange between the new and the old.

This is not unlike the relationship of Jesus to the Hebrew Bible. Jesus is the singular candlelight that is best understood and seen through the reflection of thousands of surfaces in the Hebrew Bible. But in a similar way, without the candlelight, those surfaces are dark.[74] Matthew unearths connections between the new and the old by reading both backward and forward. Sometimes he sees predictions about Jesus in the OT that are blatant, and other times he reconsiders nascent old texts in light of Jesus's coming. He also is quite generous with his language. He does not simply look for word-for-word correspondences, but he uses his encyclopedic knowledge of Jewish beliefs and practices to construct his image of Jesus. At times he is explicit with these shadows; other times he is subtle. As a skillful scribe, Matthew goes in and out of these techniques, not always telling his reader which tactic he will use next. By so doing, he encourages his reader to engage and open their minds to the wonder of Jesus as the key not only to the OT but also to all of heaven and earth.

Where did Matthew get this method? Where is wisdom to be found? Who is responsible for this original, concrete, and even flexible exegesis? Although the typical answer hails and salutes either the early church, postmodern or modern theories, or early Jewish interpretation, it was C. H. Dodd who pushed further into this question. He said, "Creative thinking is rarely done by committees," but individual minds usually originate creativity.[75] Who was this originating mind? His answer: "The New Testament itself avers that it was Jesus Christ himself who first directed the minds of his followers to certain parts of the scriptures as those in which they might find illumination upon the mission and destiny."[76] God's wisdom is found in Jesus the Son of God.

The early disciples rethought their OT because the origin of this rethinking came from Jesus, their teacher and sage. Matthew is *discipled* by the messiah.

---

73. This chapter has focused more on theory, while the following chapters will examine how this theory is put to use in the different pictures of the messiah.

74. Like all analogies, this one breaks down at certain points. In one sense the Hebrew Bible produced its own light, which pointed to the greater light.

75. Dodd, *According to the Scriptures*, 109–10.

76. Dodd, *According to the Scriptures*, 110.

"Messianic exegesis—the interpretation of Scripture with reference *to* the messiah—is ultimately based on interpretation of Scripture *by* the messiah. Jesus, it appears, is his own best exegete."[77] My argument is that the best exegete, the most skilled rabbi, passed down these skills to his disciple: Matthew the scribe. Fulfillment, at its base level, is not so much a methodology as a presupposition,[78] or even better, it is a presupposition, a conviction, which produces a methodology. I agree with France when he says, "I am not so sure that a neat distinction can be drawn between the hermeneutical technique and the theology of fulfillment which inspires it."[79]

My plan is to trace the scribe's writings through the contours of Matthew's narrative, focusing on how he has the new interact with the old. Studies like this have tended to focus on the titles and the identity of Jesus and forget that much of what we learn about Jesus is from his role and function within the larger narrative. Therefore, for each subject I deal with, I will not simply be doing a word study but attempting to keep my ear close to the ground of Matthew's narrative. I will allude back to the section on Matthew's method simply to point out more specific examples of shadow stories, history unified, reception and production, and apocalyptic-messianic fulfillment. The best methods are supported with evidence, not simply asserted.

77. Knowles, "Scripture, History, Messiah," 69–70.

78. Saying that fulfillment is more of a presupposition than a method does not mean principles can't be garnered from what Matthew and other NT authors do. But that it is a presupposition also explains why so many people argue about which "methodology" and description is actually the correct one. This probably proves that we try too hard to fit these ideas into neat modern boxes rather than being comfortable with some fluidity.

79. France, *Matthew: Evangelist and Teacher*, 182.

PART 2

The Scribe
AT WORK

A disciple is not above his teacher, but everyone
when he is fully trained will be like his teacher.

Jesus (Luke 6:40)

3

Jesus and the Journey
of the Davidic King

In the ancient world people used seals to make deep impressions on surfaces. The purpose, whether it was on a document or stone, was for authentication, communicating a message, or giving representation. We get this sense from Heb. 1:3, where the author says Jesus is "the exact imprint" (χαρακτήρ) of God's "nature." Jesus is the seal, representation, and distinctive mark of God's nature. Even though we don't use signet rings anymore in America—though some official documents may receive an authenticating stamp or seal—we know that the seal of a signet ring attests to the authority and veracity of its bearer. In the same way Matthew molds his impression of Jesus through seals, stamps, and images. This method authenticated Jesus's ministry, communicated a message, and gave a representation so that people could read the life of Jesus through a familiar image.

Though Matthew is most famously known for his portrayal of Jesus as the new Moses, Matthew also shapes and impresses Jesus's life in the mold of a Davidic king.[1] I intentionally begin with David because Matthew's first descriptions of Jesus are that he is the messiah, the son of David (1:1). The inaugural images function as the threshold through which readers are required to pass before entering the house of Matthew's Gospel. They set the tone and tenor for the rest of the narrative; to neglect them, or not let

---

1. Interestingly, the Qumran scrolls qualify King David as a "scholar" and a "scribe" because he wrote the book of Psalms. See 11QPs^a (= 11Q5) XXVII, 2.

them direct the rest of Matthew's picture, is to distort the image. Matthew is the scribe trained by his teacher and is convinced that Jesus fulfills the life of David. The wisdom that the scribe learned from his sage is that while Jesus's coming was new, it also reached far back into Jewish history. For Matthew, presenting Jesus as the Davidic messiah was a high priority, maybe the highest.[2]

However, if you read some modern scholars, you might suppose that they have not ventured far into Matthew. James Charlesworth says, "The NT writings do not elevate Jesus as a type of David. Jesus was not celebrated by his earliest followers as 'a' or 'the' new David."[3] Alan Richardson claims that paltry evidence exists for the new-David theme in the NT: "It is truly astonishing, in view of the weight of OT prophecy concerning the Davidic messiah, how little the NT makes of the matter. The evangelists represent Jesus as the new Moses, the new Joshua, the new Elijah, and so on; but there is perhaps only one pericope in the tradition which sets forth Jesus as the new David, viz. the Walking through the Cornfields on the Sabbath (Mark 2:23–28)."[4]

Other scholars do affirm the importance of Davidic traditions.[5] For example, W. D. Davies says, "Of all the New Testament writers it is Matthew who most emphasizes that Jesus is of Davidic ancestry. . . . It was apparently Matthew's most characteristic designation for the earthly Jesus, the Messiah."[6] Donald Verseput similarly says, "Matthew has placed the Davidic Messiah at the heart of his presentation. This for him is of central importance. It determines the dynamic of the gospel's plot, it explains the mission of Jesus, and it remains of confessional validity."[7] I line up with

2. Though in another sense, no one title is adequate to contain Jesus, and Matthew's narrative does not require a preeminent title. On this point, see Allison, "Son of God as Israel." This prioritization of "son of David" in some ways goes against J. D. Kingsbury's thesis in *Matthew: Structure, Christology, Kingdom* that "son of God" is the most prominent title. The titles are not mutually exclusive, as the "son of David" is the "son of God" (cf. 2 Sam 7:11, 14; Pss. 2:7; 89:27–28).

3. J. Charlesworth, "From Messianology to Christology," 9.

4. Richardson, *Theology of the New Testament*, 126.

5. Willitts (*Matthew's Messianic Shepherd-King*, 30) even says, "I attempt to read it [Matthew] narratively and in sequence, allowing the beginning of the Gospel, with its Davidic Messianism, to be the interpretive key for the whole." See also Gibbs, "Purpose and Pattern"; Kingsbury, "Title 'Son of David'"; Duling, "Solomon, Exorcism, and the Son of David"; Quarles, *Theology of Matthew*; Hays, *Echoes of Scripture in the Gospels*; Konradt, *Israel, Church, and the Gentiles*; Novakovic, "Jesus as the Davidic Messiah"; Chae, *Jesus as the Eschatological Davidic Shepherd*; Piotrowski, *Matthew's New David*; Zacharias, *Matthew's Presentation of the Son of David*.

6. W. Davies, "Jewish Sources of Matthew's Messianism," 500.

7. Verseput, "Davidic Messiah," 102.

the latter scholars, who think David is at the heart of the scribe's presentation.[8]

In the following two chapters my aim is to trace Matthew's management of Jesus as the Davidic messiah and demonstrate that he operates from a monarchal worldview. The traditions of David, his life and his writings, form the ballast by which the animation of Jesus is stabilized. Matthew employs the life, writings, and traditions of David to a great extent to define and delineate Jesus's life, thus exploring Jesus as the Davidic messiah who brings the kingdom, wisdom, and righteousness. This chapter more specifically concerns the *geographic journey* of the Davidic king. Without seeing Jesus's journey to the cross, readers will miss *how* the wise king installs and reunites the kingdom. Matthew presents Jesus as the enthroned, faithful, and suffering son of David (both like David and Solomon). However, there is an order to these descriptors: Jesus is the revered-contested-exiled-faithful-sorrowful one and then enthroned as the Davidic king.[9] This pattern should not be surprising, because David's life follows a similar arrangement.

David is also appointed, contested, exiled, and then enthroned. Samuel anoints David as king (1 Sam. 16:1–13), and Saul accepts David at the beginning when he defeats Goliath (17:1–54). However, Saul becomes jealous of David and banishes him from his court (18:6–30). Although David and Jonathan covenant together at Ramah (1 Sam. 20), David must flee to Nob to escape Saul (1 Sam. 21). David then flees to Gath, a Philistine city; he hides at the cave of Adullam (22:1–5), and Saul pursues David at Engedi (Ps. 54). David flees to Gath a second time (1 Sam. 27:4) and then moves to Ziklag with his men (1 Sam. 27:6). David serves the Philistines for over a year (1 Sam. 29:3). Notice that even after David has been anointed as the king, he is constantly on the run (or exiled). Even after being appointed as king, David must leave his city because of his son Absalom's revolt (2 Sam. 15–19).

If the Jews were expecting a red carpet to be rolled out for the new Davidic king, then they have not been paying close attention to the story of David's kingship. David's journey to his kingship is anything but smooth. This chapter will therefore examine the *progression* of Jesus's Davidic kingship—looking first to the king's lineage, then to his birth and infancy, where he is worshiped

8. Supporting this notion is the fact that kingship and kingdom are Matthew's main descriptors for the life and death of Jesus. Jesus came proclaiming the kingdom of heaven (Matt. 4:23; 9:35), and he sent his disciples out with the same message (10:7). Yet it is not just any kingship or kingdom that they declare; rather, this kingdom is filled in with the hues of the Davidic monarchy.

9. The use of both terms—*exile* and *reuniting*—is intentional. Exile is already a major theme in Matt. 1–2, with the explicit mention of exile in the genealogy and of Egypt and Ramah in Matt. 2. In addition, Zebulun and Naphtali refer to the Northern Kingdom (Matt. 4:15).

and rejected as king. This leads to the exile of the king, where he reunites what Solomon's son split; yet on his return to the city, he is not installed on the throne but suspended on the cross for the sins of the people and to unify the nation. The journey of the king is one of deportation and distress. He suffers righteously as the king and is enthroned on the cross. This specific movement, this journey that Matthew traces, is *the way* the kingdom is inaugurated. To miss the journey of the Davidic king is to neglect how kingdom hope is fulfilled and thereby bypass the insight the scribe learned from his teacher of wisdom.

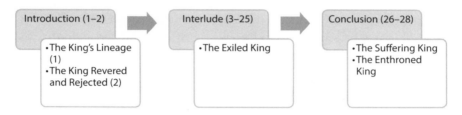

The King's Lineage

Both Matthew and Mark begin in an odd way. Maybe you have read the opening lines of Matthew and Mark so many times that it does not strike you anymore. Yet they both begin by fronting their conviction about Jesus. Mark begins with declaring that Jesus is the messiah, "Christ, the Son of God" (Mark 1:1). Matthew also starts with his beliefs, but they are stated differently from those of Mark. He launches his Gospel with Jesus's family line and three titles meant to help readers understand who this Jesus figure is. The titles he uses for Jesus are arranged as a triad: "An account of the genealogy of Jesus, [1] the messiah, [2] the son of David, [3] the son of Abraham" (Matt. 1:1 AT). All three interpret one another. The messiah is the son of David, and the son of Abraham is the messiah. While Mark begins his Gospel by declaring that Jesus is the messiah and Son of God, Matthew interprets Jesus's life through the window of *specific* Jewish figures.

Though three titles are employed in Matthew, there may be a special emphasis on the center of the triad, the "son of David." Three indicators point in this direction. First, while the genealogy follows a chronological order, the title at the beginning reverses that trend. Matthew lists David before the patriarch Abraham. This unexpected order places special prominence on the person of David. According to the description that Matthew employs right after honoring Jesus as messiah, Jesus is of the lineage of David. He is not only the messiah, but the Davidic messiah.[10] Second, David's importance is evident by the way Matthew arranges the three sets of fourteen generations. The forty-two generations are divided into three periods of Israel's history:

1. Abraham to David: growth of Israel into a kingdom
2. David to Josiah: the decline of the kingdom
3. Jechoniah to Jesus: destruction of the kingdom until Jesus's arrival

Matthew has evidently omitted many generations, and therefore this is a theological retelling. Many are convinced that Matthew's emphasis on the number fourteen is purposeful and an example of gematria. Gematria is a form of biblical interpretation using the numerical value of the letters to make a theological point. In Hebrew, *David* consists of three letters and has the numeric value of fourteen (*dalet* [4] + *waw* [6] + *dalet* [4]). The periods are divided to emphasize both the kings and the success or failure of the kingdom of Israel. This fits Matthew's theological retelling of the OT story in the triadic structure of three.

Third, the name David is placed at the fourteenth and fifteenth spot in the genealogy, putting David right at the pivot of the list (1:6). David is also named at the beginning and the end of the genealogy (1:1, 17). Jesus is the fivefold son of David.[11] Thus, the genealogy is in some sense the Davidic genealogy. Right at the outset of his Gospel, therefore, Matthew wants readers to see Jesus through the person of David and see David through the person of Jesus. The genealogy—and the entire Gospel, for that matter—is about how Jesus is David's son. This point is reinforced in the immediate narrative aftermath when the angel of the Lord appears to Joseph in a dream and addresses Joseph as the "son of David" (Matt. 1:20), fortifying Joseph's Davidic lineage and thus the identity of Jesus as a legal descendant of David.

Matthew begins his Gospel this way because he is the scribe who is well read in the Hebrew Scriptures. Matthew hears the sounds of the OT and

10. *Messiah* and *David* interpret one another. As Willits (*Matthew's Messianic Shepherd-King*, 1) affirms, "*Davidic* Messianism must be treated as *a kind* of Messianic expectation." Matthew redraws messianism around the person of David and Solomon. While Bultmann (*Theology of the New Testament*, 4) is right to say, "No saying of Jesus mentions the Messiah-king who is to crush the enemies of the People," it is also true that Matthew takes great pains to present Jesus as the Davidic messiah. Either we can conclude that Matthew's testimony is flawed and that we moderns have a better understanding of messianic hopes than first-century writers or we can interpret with trust and openness.

11. Stephen Carlson ("Davidic Key") argues that Matthew's double-counting of David in 1:5–6 is intentional (42 rather than 41) and thus is the key to the genealogy. Though readers should also note that Jechoniah is also counted twice (1:11–12).

assaults and arrests his narrative with these hopes. Numerous passages in the OT speak of another king who is coming in the line of David.[12] When Matthew thinks of Jesus, he thinks of the promises in the Hebrew Scriptures. More specifically, he contemplates the promise given to David that one of his sons would sit on the throne forever. The forever-Davidic messianic king has arrived, claims Matthew. Therefore he begins his narrative with numerous indications that to understand Jesus's life, readers need to see it through the lens of the hopes for the Davidic kingdom. While all this is interesting, fewer go on to ask the harder question, the *why* question. Why does Matthew begin this way? Is it just to let us know that Jesus is like David? A deeper answer exists and must be plumbed.

Implications of the First Words

At least two interrelated reasons for Matthew beginning this way rise to the surface. First, most obviously, it teaches us that when the scribe draws Jesus, the most noticeable feature is the crown on his head. Through the genealogy Matthew is indicating that readers should view Jesus as the king, more specifically as a king in the line of David. Just as Samuel comes to the house of Jesse to anoint David as king "in the midst of his brothers" (1 Sam. 16:13), so too Matthew anoints Jesus as king in the midst of his brothers in the genealogy.

Kingship is thus the "root metaphor" for Matthew, the one image he wants all other images to revolve around. This suspicion is confirmed by Matthew's continual emphasis on the kingdom of heaven / gospel of the kingdom (ἡ βασιλεία τῶν οὐρανῶν / ὁ εὐαγγέλιον τῆς βασιλείας) as the driving summary for Jesus's ministry (4:23; 9:35). Since Jesus's message is encapsulated in the term "kingdom," the natural corollary is that there must be a king. Every aspect of Jesus's life in Matthew should be interpreted through the lens of monarchy and kingdom.

Second, by linking Jesus to David's line in the genealogy, Matthew indicates that Jesus is the wise messiah, who will bring the people out of exile, unite their kingdom, and sit on the throne promised to a son of David (2 Sam. 7). The forever kingdom and wisdom are paired in Wis. 6:20–21: "So the desire for wisdom leads to a kingdom. Therefore if you delight in thrones and scepters, O monarchs over the peoples, honor wisdom, so that you may reign

---

12. Isaiah 9:6–7; 22:21–23; Jer. 23:5–6; Ezek. 37:24–25; Amos 9:11; Hosea 3:5. Witherington (*Jesus the Sage*, 353) notes that the precise Greek phrase translated "the son of David" is not attested before Pss. Sol. 17.21. However, though the precise phrase might not be used, the concept is quite prevalent.

forever" (NRSV). Through the genealogy, Matthew announces to his readers that Jesus fulfills God's covenant with David. Matthew's portrait is the royal book of origin. The advent of the son of David ends the exile and brings the people to their long-awaited kingdom. But while the Davidic title at the beginning informs readers about Matthew's portrait, it also raises the question of *how* Jesus will restore the kingdom.[13] At the narrative level, it tells us that the Davidic king is on the scene, but it does not explicitly clue readers in on how the king will usher in his kingdom. The veiled hint might be that he is like David's son Solomon, who has wisdom and builds the temple but does not embody Solomon's flaws. Rather than splitting the kingdom, he will unite it through his wise teaching and deeds. Overall though, while Matthew reveals in his first words, he also conceals and makes readers wade through the Gospel to see the kingdom enacted. In some ways, the first words reveal enough to make the reader curious to see the journey of the Davidic king.

Matthew opens by establishing Jesus as the appointed king, but he is not the enthroned king yet. He *will* inaugurate the new covenant and establish his people forever. God *did* not lie to David (Ps. 89:35), and "his offspring shall endure forever, his throne as long as the sun before [Yahweh]" (89:36). Yahweh *is* no longer hiding; he *is* fulfilling his promises to David in the birth of Jesus. Yet we still don't know exactly in what way this will happen. Matthew, as the scribe, makes his confessional stance on Jesus plain through beginning his scroll by naming Jesus as the son of David. Jesus wears the Davidic crown, and he will restore the kingdom, but we must journey with Matthew to see *how* this will be accomplished.

The Wise King Revered and Rejected

The lineage crystallizes the thought that Jesus comes as a king like David, but the genealogy tells readers little about the realization of the kingdom. Therefore, Matthew continues the parallels to David to fill out the picture. Though Matt. 2 is usually noted for its Mosaic parallels, David and Solomon also make convincing appearances. Matthew not only begins his parchment by defining Jesus as the Davidic messiah; he also carries these similarities into Jesus's infancy. Not just the lineage points to Jesus as the Davidic messiah

---

13. At another level, many readers would already know Jesus's future, and thus this work could be viewed as an apologetic or something to calm their fears. Early readers may have been questioning whether the man crucified on a Roman cross could really be the Davidic messiah. In his first words Matthew answers their question. It is only through the cross that the kingdom will come.

but even the circumstances of his birth. The scribe continues to relate the life of Jesus to David, and at least four indicators in Matt. 2:1–23 point toward Jesus as the *revered* but also the *rejected* wise son of David. First, Jesus is born in Bethlehem, the city of David. Second, Matthew quotes the prophet who says a ruler shall come from Judah. Third, the wise men see a star in the east and bring gifts to the new sage-king. Fourth, Jesus is called a Nazarene (the branch) who will be filled with wisdom.[14] Jesus is therefore born in the city of the king, but largely rejected and therefore exiled into Galilee. As David was accepted by some and rejected by others, so too Jesus must first be challenged before he sits on the throne. Most of the texts Matthew alludes to (or quotes) have strong messianic interpretations in the Dead Sea Scrolls and other early Jewish and Christian writings. Each reaches back to the life of David, confirming Jesus as the Davidic messiah for whom the people of Israel have been waiting. The king is not just born as the king; Yahweh continues to enact his kingship, yet in a surprising way.

Born in Bethlehem

Matthew begins chapter 2 unassumingly: "Now after Jesus was born in Bethlehem of Judea." Readers are prone to speed past this statement and get to the aftermath of Jesus's birth, but Matthew has chosen his words carefully. That Jesus was born in Bethlehem was a sign that a king like David was appearing on the scene. "David was the son of an Ephrathite of Bethlehem in Judea, named Jesse, who had eight sons," says 1 Sam. 17:12. Anticipation lingered in the hearts of the prophets that a new David would come and hail from the same town in which David was born.[15] Matthew releases the Davidic king into the world with place-names, saluting Jesus as the promised king.

Although Matthew does not stop and give us a theology of Bethlehem in 2:1, he assumes that his readers' ears will perk up when they hear Bethlehem. And in case their ears are stopped up, he makes the link explicit in 2:6. By saying that Jesus was born in Bethlehem, the city of David, Matthew indicates that the new king is entering the scene. Yet Matthew's point is not only that. Jesus is born in the city of the king, but the narrative makes clear that there

---

14. Readers may wonder why I do not engage with Matt. 2:15 and the quote from Hosea 11:1. There are three reasons for my omitting it at this point. First, the text will be examined briefly in the chapter on Jesus as the new Israel. Second, this quote has received the bulk of scholarly attention in Matt. 2, and I don't want to repeat all the research on the topic. Third, the chapter was already long enough. Having said this, Jesus's deportation to Egypt foreshadows his deportation to Galilee and therefore nicely aligns with my argument in this chapter.

15. Micah 5:2, which is quoted later in this passage, speaks of a ruler coming from Bethlehem.

is another king, the king of Jerusalem, who opposes him. Jesus comes as a second king, and second kings are never welcome. Tension will inevitably come. Two kingdoms cannot coexist. Matthew launches the outworking of the Davidic kingship of Jesus by thrusting him immediately into conflict. The echoes of the Davidic nature of Jesus's infancy set up the struggle and describe how the king becomes not only the *anointed* king but also the *exiled* and *deported* king. The king is here, but he is not going to stroll into his kingdom; he will have to toil to crawl back to his city and throne.

A Ruler Shall Come from Judah

The conflict becomes explicit with the second Davidic resonance. In 2:6 Matthew quotes Mic. 5:2. However, notice who speaks these words in Matthew's context. It is the "scribes of the people" (γραμματεῖς τοῦ λαοῦ) who report where the Christ is to be born. Herod, the rival king, seeks to destroy Jesus and therefore asks the scribes where he might find this king. Matthew provides another early clue of his scribal theme. The scribes of the people have been corrupted and lured in by political power. Although one might be tempted to read this more innocently, the rest of Matthew's narrative confirms the depravity of the Jerusalem scribes. Jesus says he will be delivered and suffer at the hands of the chief priests and scribes (16:21; 20:18). He pronounces woes on them in chapter 23, and it is the scribes and elders who gather together against Jesus (26:57)[16] and mock him (27:41).[17] Jesus will therefore need to form an alternative wise scribal school.

The corrupted scribes provide the following quote from Mic. 5:2: "In Bethlehem of Judea, for so it is written by the prophet: 'And you, O Bethlehem, in the land of Judah, are by no means least among the rulers of Judah; for from you shall come a ruler who will shepherd my people Israel'" (Matt. 2:5–6). Ironically, through the words of these shameful scribes, Matthew indicates that the messiah is the ruler from Bethlehem who shepherds his people. Messiahship, kingship, and shepherding are all brought together to define and enlighten messianic hopes. Yet despite the thematic clarity, the citation differs from the LXX and the MT. A number of changes have been introduced to the LXX text, as seen below.

16. The language of "gathering together" should remind readers of Ps. 2:2, in which the rulers take counsel together against the Lord and his Anointed.

17. Compare this to the story of Joseph, where Pharaoh is also *troubled* (ταράσσω) and summons the magicians and wise men—thus paralleling the scribes of the people with wise men (Matt. 2:3; Gen. 41:8). Similarly, in the days of Moses Pharaoh summons the wise men (Exod. 7:11).

Micah 5:1 LXX	Matthew 2:6
Καὶ σύ, Βηθλεεμ	καὶ σὺ Βηθλέεμ,
οἶκος τοῦ Εφραθα,	γῆ Ἰούδα,
ὀλιγοστὸς εἶ τοῦ εἶναι ἐν χιλιάσιν Ιουδα·	οὐδαμῶς ἐλαχίστη εἶ ἐν τοῖς ἡγεμόσιν Ἰούδα·
ἐκ σοῦ μοι ἐξελεύσεται	ἐκ σοῦ γὰρ ἐξελεύσεται
τοῦ εἶναι εἰς ἄρχοντα	ἡγούμενος,
ἐν τῷ Ισραηλ,	
καὶ αἱ ἔξοδοι αὐτοῦ ἀπ᾽ ἀρχῆς	
ἐξ ἡμερῶν αἰῶνος.	
	ὅστις ποιμανεῖ τὸν λαόν μου τὸν Ἰσραήλ.
And you, O Bethleem,	And you, O Bethlehem,
house of Ephratha,	in the land of Judah,
are very few in number to be among the thousands of Ioudas;	are by no means least among the rulers of Judah;
one from you shall come forth for me to become a ruler	for from you shall come a ruler
in Israel,	
and his goings forth are from of old, from days of yore. (NETS)	
	who will shepherd my people Israel. (ESV)

Note: Targum Mic. 5:1 attaches messianic import to the quotation.

Each substitution Matthew introduces further clarifies the kingly nature of Jesus. In other words, Matthew adjusts this text to make the kingly notes resound.

France suggests that the substitution of Judah for Ephrathah may reinforce the christological point already stressed in the genealogy, that Jesus really did derive from the royal tribe from which the Davidic messiah would come.[18] Genesis 49:10 says, "The scepter shall not depart from Judah, nor the ruler's staff from between his feet." A second change occurs when Matthew adjusts the phrase "who are too little to be among the clans of Judah" (ESV) to "who are by no means least among the rulers of Judah." Here Matthew promotes a small role for Bethlehem into a significant position as the birthplace of the king.

I find this a fascinating move. Matthew felt free to adapt the text with a simple adverb οὐδαμῶς.[19] The passing of time and the fullness of revelation caused him to be comfortable with altering the significance of Bethlehem: from insignificant to significant.[20] Interpreters need to be careful not to

18. France, "Formula-Quotations of Matthew 2."
19. Hagner (*Matthew 1–13*, 29) proposes another solution: "If in the MT the initial ל were read as the negative particle (לֹא, lōʾ), i.e., with the slight change of לִהְיוֹת, lihyôt, to לֹאהְיוֹת, lōʾhĕyôt, a reading is produced that coincides with Matthew's Greek rendering of the passage." But this seems to be reaching for an explanation.
20. Some argue that Micah sees Bethlehem as small but still significant.

pose false dichotomies here. Matthew is not playing fast and loose with the text, but he is also not performing the typical grammatical-historical exegesis. To try to argue either one does not respect Matthew's careful but intentional playfulness with the text. He looks at a former text in light of current circumstances and adapts it based on the birth of Jesus. Bethlehem was insignificant, and now it is significant because of the coming of the apocalyptic messiah.

The third change in this text comes at the end, where Matthew substitutes the description of the ruler "whose coming forth is from of old" (ESV) with words from 2 Sam. 5:2, "who will shepherd my people Israel." Many times Matthew uses combined double quotations. This specific change further imports an echo of King David. "The words from 2 Samuel 5:2 would only convey a special meaning if recognized as an intrusion. But to those who had the necessary detailed knowledge of Scripture, these variations of wording would powerfully reinforce the message of the Davidic character of the Messiah which has already been so strongly stressed in chapter 1."[21]

Matthew is already pointing to what type of king this new David will be. The surface meaning of the text is plain, but for those who have eyes to see, extra gems reveal that this child born in Bethlehem is the ruler in the line of King David. As France says in conclusion, "All these three alterations, . . . while not at all necessary for the surface meaning of the text, combine to convey a deliberate Christological message to those who can recognize them."[22] So the scribe shapes the text of the scribes in a Davidic way.[23] If he does this molding with a quotation from the OT, then he surely constructs the narrative of Jesus in a similar way. In his explicit quotation from Micah, Matthew, the true scribe, portrays Jesus as the ruler who comes from Judah, thus linking promises of the OT to Jesus's life.

While these changes by Matthew are interesting and certainly highlight the Davidic nature of Jesus's kingship, the point is one of contrast in two ways. First, Matthew places this quote in the mouths of those who inform Jesus's nemesis. Matthew himself stands as the fulfillment of Jesus's new discipleship group, who knows to whom these texts point. Second, the thrust of the passage (and the Davidic nature of the quote) centers on the competing nature of the earthly kingdom with the heavenly sourced kingdom. Herod massacres the children of Israel, while Jesus comes to shepherd and protect the children of Israel. Herod is the king of Jerusalem, while Jesus is the king

21. France, "Formula-Quotations of Matthew 2," 243. See also Hays's analysis of 2 Sam. 5:2: *Echoes of Scripture in the Gospels*, 146–47.

22. France, "Formula-Quotations of Matthew 2," 242.

23. In this sense, Matthew becomes the true scribal editor.

from Bethlehem. Bethlehem previously was of small significance, but now it is of great significance.

The Davidic resonances prove to heighten the conflict, not subdue it. Jesus is from the tribe of Judah, so he holds the scepter. However, he will not wield the scepter in the expected way. Instead, his family flees from the danger threatening this king. The king and his family must run for their lives and wait for the scepter to be revealed. The true Davidic king is on the scene, but he must go on a journey to be enthroned. He must show the people what it means to be the wise shepherd (Ps. 1). The text leaves readers with a question: Which scribe will you listen to, and which king will you follow?

Magi and Star in the East

Matthew not only alters the way one is to think about how Jesus wields the scepter; he also reverses the expected reverence paid to Jesus. It is not Jerusalem who bows before Jesus but the wise men from the east. Jerusalem is "troubled" by Jesus's birth, and the scribes tell Herod where the king is to be born; the wise men bring gifts. Only Matthew includes the magi as the first worshipers of the son of David: "Behold wise men [μάγοι] from the East came to Jerusalem, saying, 'Where is he who has been born king of the Jews? For we saw his star [τὸν ἀστέρα] when it rose and have come to worship him'" (Matt. 2:1b–2).[24] Readers should note that the "wise" are the first to worship the newly arrived sage-king.[25] Tertullian said that while the magi were astrologers by profession, they were also considered kings.[26] The medieval church preferred this designation, but the Reformers were dismayed with this conclusion.[27]

Two OT texts give some support for associating the magi with kings and therefore sages as well. First, in the book of Daniel the "wise men" and Daniel battle for an interpretation of the king's dreams. Then after Daniel rightly interprets the dreams and visions, he is promoted to a kingly status. Second, an older story tells of Joseph, who also interpreted the dreams of a king and proved himself to be better than the wise men of Pharaoh, and he

24. In 2 Sam. 22:44–45 David says, "You delivered me from strife with my people; you kept me as the head of the nations; people whom I had not known served me. Foreigners came cringing to me; as soon as they heard of me, they obeyed me." This passage has some remarkable parallels to the wise men coming to David as the "head of the nations" and obeying him.

25. Powell ("Magi as Wise Men") goes against the majority interpretation when he argues that Matthew presents the magi's learning not as wisdom but as foolishness. Their foolishness qualifies them for divine revelation.

26. Tertullian, *Answer to the Jews* 11 (ANF 3:162).

27. Calvin, *Harmony of the Evangelists*, vol. 1, sect. 1, Matt. 2:1–6.

too was raised up to the right hand of the throne.[28] Although these two texts don't conflate kings and wise men, it does bring them into close association.[29] Tertullian saw the text concerning the magi bringing gifts to Jesus as fulfilling Ps. 72, as in verse 10 (NIV): "May the kings of Sheba and Seba present him gifts."[30] But he also saw an allusion to Isa. 60:3, 6 (NIV): "Nations will come to your light, and kings to the brightness of your dawn; . . . and all from Sheba will come, bearing gold and incense and proclaiming the praise of the LORD." Jesus is the new wise Solomon to whom the wise men come (1 Kings 4:34; 2 Chron. 9:23). Therefore, both early patristic literature and OT witnesses support viewing the magi as associated with kings. While we may never know if they were literal kings, Matthew seems to be presenting these magi through the OT witness as both wise men and kings of the earth.[31] The sage-kings from the east are coming to worship the son of David.

The magi come not only to worship but also to offer their gifts. These gifts are an important part of the narrative and complete at least two open-ended stories from the Hebrew Scriptures. The first comes from the story of the queen of Sheba, who visits Solomon.

> When the queen of Sheba heard about the fame of Solomon and his relationship to the LORD, she came to test Solomon with hard questions. Arriving at Jerusalem with a very great caravan—with camels carrying spices, large quantities of gold, and precious stones—she came to Solomon and talked with him about all that she had on her mind. (1 Kings 10:1–2 NIV)

During her visit, the depth of Solomon's wisdom took her breath away: "In *wisdom* and *wealth* you have far exceeded the report I heard" (1 Kings 10:7 NIV, emphasis added). Laying her gifts of gold, spice, and precious stones

---

28. Arguments exist for Daniel being a type of Joseph: both king Pharaoh and Nebuchadnezzar have a dream, both are troubled (Gen. 41:8; Dan. 2:1), both call for their magicians, both recount their dreams, both have a captain of the guard who is aware of a captive who can interpret dreams (Gen. 41:10–12; Dan. 2:14). Then both Joseph and Daniel are honored for their dream reporting (Gen. 41:40; Dan. 2:46), they are given gifts (Gen. 41:42; Dan. 2:48), and both are promoted to rulership in a foreign land (Gen. 41:40–41; Dan. 2:48). In addition, Longman (*Fear of the Lord Is Wisdom*, 78–93) argues that Joseph and Daniel are paradigmatic "wise men" in the Hebrew Scriptures. It could be that the "wise men" in Matthew come as a fulfillment of the pattern of Joseph and Daniel, and the scribes of the people are now those who oppose the king.

29. In ancient literature outside the Scriptures, we also find magi receiving royal honors. In *Histories* 3.62–97, Herodotus tells of two magi brothers who staged a coup for the Persian Empire. After the king died, one of the magi, Smerdis, sat on the throne as king.

30. Tertullian, *Answer to the Jews* 11 (ANF 3:162).

31. In the following chapter I will argue that the king embodies and lives the law, and therefore he is the "wise king."

before him, she blessed the Lord for making Solomon king. Martin Luther read the story of the magi in light of David's son Solomon and the story of the queen of Sheba. Just as the queen of Sheba bowed before Solomon the king, so too the sage-kings from the East bow before Jesus. The wisdom of God is found in the city of David, to whose son those from the east come with reverence. Matthew's first story after the birth of Jesus declares that wise men came to worship the new sage-king just as the queen of Sheba came bearing gifts to Solomon.

The second story comes from the days of Hezekiah, long after Kings David and Solomon lived.[32] In the days of Isaiah, King Hezekiah let an envoy from Babylon come and view Jerusalem's "silver, the gold, the spices, the fine olive oil" (Isa. 39:2 NIV). Isaiah warns Hezekiah that because he has done this the Babylonians will come and take it all away. "Nothing shall be left" (Isa. 39:6). In 587 BCE the Babylonians came and plundered Judah and took all of its silver and gold. Daniel himself recounts that the Babylonian king used the golden cups from the Lord's temple (Dan. 5:1–4). Matthew may be indicating that the gifts the magi bring are the true homecoming of Jerusalem's treasures from exile.[33] Thus, with the coming of the magi, the treasures of the temple are returning. The three kings travel from the East and bring with them the gold, frankincense, and myrrh that was stolen from David's and Solomon's house. This child is restoring David's house, which Isaiah promised would happen (Isa. 60).

The appearance of the star and its connection with Num. 24 also confirms the point about Jesus as the son of David being revered by those outside Israel.[34] Stars were frequently associated with kings, and the star the magi see is commonly linked to Balaam's prophecy in Num. 24:17: "I see him, but not now; I behold him, but not near. A star will come out of Jacob; a scepter will rise out of Israel" (NIV).[35] In Balaam's (the *magus*) prophecy, he sees someone, but his sight is foggy. He is coming, but not now; he is not near. Because of this forward-looking statement, all four Pentateuch Targums paraphrase the passage in messianic terms. The word for "star" is replaced in Aramaic by "king."

32. This connection was pointed out to me first by my friend Chad Ashby.

33. Some of the articles of the temple were brought back in the 500s and 400s BCE. See Ashby, "Magi, Wise Men, or Kings?"

34. A. T. Robertson (*General Epistles and the Revelation*, on Rev. 22:16) gives us a picture of how the Scriptures present the star: "The Davidic King is called a star in Numb. 24:17; Luke 1:78. This 'day-star' (φωσφόρος) is interpreted as Christ (2 Pet. 1:19). In Revelation 2:28 the phrase 'the morning star' occurs in Christ's words, which is here interpreted. Christ is the Light that was coming into the world (John 1:9; 8:12)."

35. Hebrews 1:8, quoting Ps. 45:6, calls it a scepter of "uprightness" (εὐθύτητος), which means "straightness" or "righteousness." Righteousness and wisdom are often paralleled in Proverbs, indicating that this is a scepter of wisdom.

In the Dead Sea Scrolls the long-awaited messiah is sometimes referred to as the "scepter."[36] Messianic interpretation of Num. 24:17 is widely attested in traditions dating to the first century and earlier. In Numbers, Balaam speaks of a star coming out of Jacob, a scepter rising out of Israel that will "crush the foreheads of Moab."

Matthew includes a few striking parallels with the passage in Num. 24. First, in both texts we have outsiders who bless God's people. Matthew 2:2 is the only utterance of the magi that Matthew records, and the magi search for a way to worship Jesus and pay him honor. Second, Balaam is also a *magus* in Num. 22–24, like the wise men.[37] Matthew not only has the scribes of the people read a text, but a sorcerer's prophecy about the wise king fulfilled. Finally, both Balaam and the magi are kept from acting in a manner that would be destructive to God's purposes. Balaam can't curse Israel, and the magi are told in a dream not to return to tell Herod about the child.[38] Already Matthew shows his readers that the truly wise are those who follow the son of David. The star both signals the ruler in Matthew and is the ruler in Numbers.[39]

Therefore, Matthew presents Jesus as the star to whom the sage-kings from the east bring their treasures and to whom all kings of the earth pay tribute, while the scribes of Jerusalem look for prestige in another kingdom. In the genealogy, Matthew indicates that Jesus will fulfill the kingdom promises to David, but he does not say *how*. Here readers begin to get more specificity. Jesus activates reversal of the exile and the curse by being the prophesied wise king. Just as in David's day the Moabites and the surrounding regions are defeated and bring tribute/offering to David (2 Sam. 8), so too the magi come from the east, bringing tribute. As Isaiah foretold, there will be a redeemer to whom the nations will stream, and he will reestablish the house of the Lord. The magi bring the treasures back to Jerusalem because the Davidic messiah rebuilds the walls of the city and the temple of Jerusalem.[40] This is precisely what the Jews hoped for from their messiah.

36. "For God has established you as a scepter over rulers" (1QSb V, 27–28); "The scepter is the prince of the congregation" (4Q161 frags. 2–6 II, 27). See Collins, *Scepter and the Star*.

37. Jewish historian Philo (*Mos.* 1.276) refers to Balaam (Num. 22) as a *magus*. This anachronism indicates that by the first century AD, the word may have been adopted for more general use.

38. The flurry of revelation by dreams in the first two chapters of Matthew may indicate one of Matthew's themes: wisdom comes by revelation.

39. Nolland (*Gospel of Matthew*, 111) gets too literal when he says that specific links are not to be found because the star in Numbers does not *signal* the ruler but *is* the ruler. In other words, in Numbers the star is identified with the ruler, but in Matthew it shows the way to the ruler. But this is probably more a modern disposition than a biblical one.

40. Wisdom and temple are correlated in 8:21–9:8, where Solomon asks for wisdom to build the temple.

Jesus also establishes the city and brings back the treasures from exile, but as the scepter rises, only those outside the city perceive this. As Keener says, "Whatever these Magi's religious commitments, Matthew's audience would probably recall the Magi of their Greek translation of the OT: they were Daniel's enemies, whom Daniel's narratives portray in a negative light as selfish, incompetent, and brutal pagans (cf. Dan. 2:2, 10). This is even clearer in some later Greek versions of the Old Testament."[41]

The magi have come to worship Jesus, but Jerusalem, the scribes, and Herod the king are *troubled* when they hear that a new king has appeared on the scene. The narrative reverses the symbolism of the place of exile. The place that was far from God is now the place of true obeisance. Matthew confirms that the king is on the scene, but his own people don't recognize him. As in the Wisdom literature, wisdom demands a choice between two ways. As Matthew indicated in the genealogy, Jesus is not only the king of the Jews but now also the king of the whole world. Jesus both fulfills the old covenant and inaugurates the new. The star is in the east because the king has come to welcome those "east of Eden" (cf. Gen. 3:24; 4:16) who were cast out so long ago.

Nazarene

The story so far has indicated that Jesus is the son of David (like Solomon), who is born in the city of the king (but there is another king), will act like David (unlike Herod), and to whom the magi bring their gifts (but Jerusalem and the scribes work against him). Now Matthew indicates that, like David, Jesus must be deported and exiled to be spared. At this point in the narrative, the king is not to square off with the kings of the earth but to flee. We have become so comfortable with the story that we forget what a shock this would be to those who first heard it.

The final adumbration, and a key passage for this chapter, is that Jesus is a Nazarene. In 2:23 the scribe says Joseph and his family "went and lived in a city called Nazareth, so that what was spoken by the prophets might be fulfilled, that he would be called a Nazarene." However, no specific OT passage contains the words "He will be called a Nazarene," and thus interpreters must try to figure out what Matthew alludes to. One important clue is given: Matthew uses the plural form of "prophet" to describe the source. Through the use of the plural, he might be indicating more than one source. Many see him alluding to the messiah as "the branch," which is found in Isa. 4:2; 11:1;

---

41. Keener, *Gospel of Matthew*, 99.

Jer. 23:5; 33:15. In early readings of Isa. 11, there seems to be some coherency of identifying this branch as the messiah.[42] Here the branch is the righteous descendant of David and empowered by the Spirit. In Hebrew, the word for "branch" is *netzer*, which in an unpointed text (i.e., without written vowels) would appear as *NZR*, the key consonants in NaZaReth.

Matthew skates across an etymological pond to label Jesus's new home as the "branch place" and Jesus is the "branch person" who possesses wisdom. While this might seem far-fetched, when combined with the evidence we have seen above, it coheres nicely with the theme throughout. Jesus is the wise king from the line of David to whom wise men come and give their gifts. Now he is also the "branch place" and the "branch person" because the branch is the descendant of David. In the OT, this branch is especially associated with wisdom. The branch shall "deal wisely, and shall execute justice and righteousness in the land" (Jer. 23:5). The branch "shall build the temple of the LORD" (Zech. 6:12), like the action of wise Solomon. The branch shall have "the Spirit of wisdom and understanding" resting on him (Isa. 11:2).

Many note these correspondences but miss the most important point: *Jesus is in Nazareth of Galilee*, not in Jerusalem or Bethlehem! Because of the rejection of Jesus's kingship, the wise king must flee first to Egypt and then to Nazareth (northern part of Israel). The Gospel of John indicates that being from Nazareth was a stumbling block for Jews (John 1:46), and therefore Matthew provides this fulfillment quotation and this unique material as an apologetic for Jesus's Nazarene origins (Matt. 21:11; 26:71). Nazareth in Galilee, therefore, is Jesus's exile from his city. Two realities indicate this, one historical and the other textual. First, while Galilee was in the region of the former Northern Kingdom of Israel, it still was largely separated from the southern region by a number of factors. *Racially*, it had a more mixed population (ever since the Assyrian conquest in the eighth century BCE). It is even known as the district of the gentiles (Isa. 9:1). Not only was it racially removed, but it was also *geographically* removed because it was detached from Judea by the non-Jewish territory of Samaria. *Politically*, Galilee had been under an administration separate from Judea for almost all of its history, since the tenth century BC. *Culturally*, Judeans despised their northern neighbors because of their lack of Jewish sophistication and their openness to Hellenistic influence. *Linguistically*, Galileans spoke a distinct form of Aramaic that was immediately noticeable (cf. Matt. 26:73). *Religiously*, the Judean opinion was that the Galileans were lax in the observance of proper

42. In the Dead Sea Scrolls, Isa. 11 is taken to be messianic in 4QpIsa[a] frags. 7–10 III, 22–29 and echoed in 1QSb V, 21–26.

ritual, and this was primarily based on the distance of Galilee from Jerusalem, the city of the king.[43] As France says,   .

> Even an impeccably Jewish Galilean in first-century Jerusalem was not among his own people; he was as much a foreigner as an Irishman in London or a Texan in New York. His accent would immediately mark him out as "not one of us," and all the communal prejudice of the supposedly superior culture of the capital city would stand against his claim to be heard even as a prophet, let alone as the "Messiah," a title which, as everyone knew, belonged to Judea.[44]

To miss this geographic distance is to miss one of Matthew's major points. France again says, "To read Matthew in blissful ignorance of first-century Palestinian sociopolitics is to miss his point. This is the story of Jesus *of Nazareth*."[45]

Second, it is not only the history but the narrative that supports that this is Jesus's exile. Between the geographic references to Bethlehem and Nazareth is the overlooked town of Ramah (2:18). Ramah is the place from which Israel was taken by Babylon into exile (Jer. 40:1). The wise king must be exiled from his birthplace like his people. Matthew the scribe informs readers that wise kings embody the actions of the nation. The genealogy lets readers know that Matthew views Jesus as the son of David who will restore the kingdom and build the temple, but now readers are seeing that Jesus must first be exiled. Ironically, he is exiled to the branch place because he is the descendant of David. His exile does not dull his Davidic kingship. Rather, it confirms that he is worthy and full of wisdom.

Summarizing the Son of David in Matthew 1–2

From the moment Matthew puts his pen to his scroll, he thinks of Jesus as the wise son of David.[46] In both Matt. 1 and 2 he fills his text with Davidic allusions and echoes so that readers can recognize Jesus as the son of David. But if Matt. 1 asserts that Jesus is the king who fulfills the Davidic covenant, then Matt. 2 tells readers that Jesus is the wise king and rival kingdoms are not going down quietly. The Davidic resonances escalate and

---

43. This summary was helpfully condensed by Justin Taylor in his blog. He was summarizing R. T. France.

44. France, *Gospel of Matthew*, 6.

45. France, *Gospel of Matthew*, 7.

46. Jeremiah speaks of the "scribal pen" (σχοῖνος, 8:8 AT). The Septuagint writers render the Hebrew *et* with the Greek word κάλαμος (reed, Ps. 45:1). The scribe, using a reed pen, also wore around the waist a "scribal palette" or "scribal pen case" ("writing case," Ezek. 9:2, 3, 11). In the case may have been a scribal knife (Jer. 36:23) used to cut parchment and papyrus.

accelerate the conflict rather than smoothing and facilitating the path to the throne.

Notably, all the allusions to Jesus's Davidic descent in Matt. 2 center on geography. If Matt. 1 is about the *people* of the king, then Matt. 2 is about the *place* of the king. He is born in the city of David but exiled to Nazareth, where he will minister as the wise king reuniting the split kingdom. Though we didn't explore Egypt and Ramah in depth, both are places associated with exile, thus confirming the exile theme in miniature in Matt. 2 and setting up the larger exile in Matthew's entire narrative.[47]

Bethlehem →	Egypt →	Ramah →	Nazareth
southern Israel →	exile →	exile →	northern Israel

As David had to flee from Saul (1 Sam. 21:10) and Absalom (2 Sam. 15:14) and leave the city of his home, so too Jesus flees from King Herod and the scribes and inhabitants of Jerusalem. The journey of the Davidic king has begun. Matthew is a creative scribe, filling out Jesus's life with echoes from the OT and asserting that something new is here, but the new is like the old.

The Return of the Exiled King

Some scholars, following Kingsbury, stop finding parallels to the life of David after Matt. 22:45, since the name "David" never occurs after that. Kingsbury even asserted that the title "son of God" becomes the most prominent title in light of this lexical fact.[48] At least three arguments work against dropping a focus on David at the end of Matthew's narrative. First, as we have already seen, Matthew has a tendency to dilute more explicit fulfillment references as his narrative proceeds. Second, readers should be looking not only to the titles but to narrative parallels. Third, the title "son of David" and "son of God" are not antithetical or mutually exclusive but work together (cf. 2 Sam. 7:11, 14; Pss. 2:7; 89:27–28).[49] The rest of this chapter will display that David traditions play an important role in the arrest, trial, and crucifixion.

The "interlude" begins with Jesus's exile to Nazareth at the end of Matt. 2. For most of the narrative, Jesus ministers in Galilee, embodies the way of

---

47. Ramah is the place from which the Judean captives left for Babylon (Jer. 40:1). Jeremiah's image of Rachel weeping is a sign that a new exile is taking place, and the larger context of Jer. 31 points to the hope for the end of exile.

48. Kingsbury ("Title 'Son of David,'" 596–97) influentially maintained that Matt. 22:41–46 shows Matthew moving away from Jesus as the "son of David" and toward the "Son of God."

49. N. Johnson, "Passion according to David," 249.

wisdom, and forms a new scribal school (Matt. 3–20). Then in chapter 16 he turns his face toward Jerusalem to return to the city that had already rejected him once. Upon entering the city, he experiences a mixture of celebration and confrontation. The geographical overlay of Matthew, with the journey of the king, can appropriately be described as *the return of the exiled wise king to confront the city of his forefather's throne.* He comes conquering through humility; he does not let pride destroy him as it did Solomon and his sons. Matthew has Jesus walking the dusty Galilean path because, as David was sent away from his home and chased by Saul before he became king, so too Jesus must walk these paths before he is enthroned. As the sitting king seeks Jesus's life, so too David fled for his life from King Saul and from David's own son, who sought David's life so that he might become king. Jesus spends most of his time in Galilee, north of Jerusalem,[50] but Jesus's goal is to return to the city of the king, and on his way through Galilee he teaches his people wisdom concerning the content and character of the kingdom. Now that Jesus has entered his city, will he go to his throne, or will Jerusalem reject their king again? If readers have been following the pattern and the predictions, they know that the high priests and scribes, who are supposed to welcome Jesus, will not be favorable to this new son of David. As the wise king, Jesus will (1) allow himself to suffer as the wise servant. He will then (2) be enthroned on the cross as the exalted one who leads by sacrifice rather than by power and might.

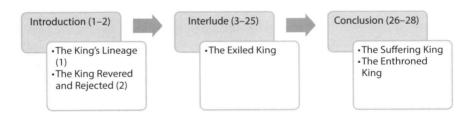

The Wise Suffering Servant

The Davidic parallels don't cease once Jesus returns to Jerusalem; rather, they pick up in new and unique ways. Upon entering the city, Jesus mimics

---

50. Willitts (*Matthew's Messianic Shepherd-King*, 31) argues Jesus is in Galilee because his ministry is to the "lost sheep" of Israel, which refers to the remnants of the former Northern Kingdom of Israel who continued to reside in that land. The mission of Jesus centers on the restoration of Israel.

David as the wise suffering servant who is (1) betrayed, (2) innocent, and (3) forsaken as David was in his life.[51] A number of arguments tie the servant in Isa. 53–55 to a Davidic figure in Isa. 1–39.[52] First, outside of Isaiah, the title "servant" is applied to David more than any other figure, especially when one considers "servant" with its possessive pronouns.[53] Isaiah himself references King David as "my servant" in Isa. 37:35, suggesting that these two figures are one and the same. Second, both the king and the servant are tasked with establishing justice (9:7; 42:1–4), bringing light to the nations (9:2; 42:6–7), and opening the eyes of the blind (32:3; 42:7). Third, in many ways, the titles "son of David," "son of God," and "servant" collide in the textual tradition. This is most evident in Jesus's baptism when God declares Jesus to be his beloved Son, with whom he is well pleased (Matt. 3:17). This statement likely reflects influences from both Ps. 2:7 (son of David and son of God) and Isa. 42:1 (the servant).[54] Fourth, Isaiah describes the king and the servant with botanical imagery (11:10). He grows up like a young plant, like a root out of dry ground (53:2). This last point coheres with the branch bearing the Spirit of wisdom and understanding, the Spirit of knowledge and fear of the Lord (11:1–3). In other words, if one looks at the narrative of Isaiah as a whole, rather than dividing it into sections, the servant and the Davidic king are equated or at least related.[55] But not only that. The suffering servant is also the emblem of a wise king par excellence. Every picture of his suffering can and should be put under the banner of wisdom.

Heinz Held notes that Matthew does not simply hand on the traditions he receives but rather retells them.[56] This is certainly the case where Matthew presents Jesus as the wise suffering servant. Like David, Jesus's friends betray him, false witnesses rise up against him, Jesus declares his innocence, he is silent before his accusers, and finally he is mocked as the king. Matthew's presentation is even more explicit than Mark's in portraying Jesus as undergoing righteous suffering. In one instance, Matthew even indicates awareness of the tradition

51. Leroy Huizenga ("Incarnation of the Servant") argues that this is not the case on the level of the historical production of the text, but that we can now read the text this way only because of the modern Christian encyclopedia such as the OT as the dictionary. As this section shows, I disagree with Huizenga and assert that we can read it this way on the historical level. See also Rikki Watts, "Messianic Servant."

52. See Treat's argument for this in *Crucified King*.

53. "Servant" = David (23×), Jacob (13×), and Moses (8×); "servant" with possessive pronoun = David (66×) and Moses (19×).

54. Beaton (*Isaiah's Christ in Matthew's Gospel*) argues that the image of the servant is central to Matthew's overall portrayal of Jesus.

55. N. Johnson ("Rendering David a Servant") also argues David is presented as the servant in Pss. Sol. 17.21.

56. Held, "Matthew as Interpreter," 165.

in the Hebrew Scriptures by adding a quotation where Mark has only an indirect reference (Matt. 27:43//Ps. 22:8). On other occasions Matthew reproduces Mark's material to maintain the parallels already there (Matt. 27:34//Ps. 69:21; Matt. 27:35//Ps. 22:18; Matt. 27:39//Ps. 22:7; Matt. 27:46//Ps. 22:1). Both Pss. 22 and 69 play prominent roles in the development of the theme of the righteous sufferer and the Psalms are like floating wisdom hymns sung by the sage-king.

Both of these psalms also have first-century Davidic associations within the Psalter; their use thus indicates Matthew's continued interest in Jesus as the Davidic messiah. "Three of Matthew's longer expansions to Mark in his account of the trial are carefully positioned to highlight Jesus' innocence."[57] But rather than merely focusing on a horizontal reading and how Matthew adapts Mark's literature, it is more important to see Matthew develop his own narrative of the righteous suffering Davidic messiah. Matthew suggests Jesus is the wise suffering servant through (1) betrayal before the cross, (2) his silence and innocence at the trial, and (3) his forsakenness at the cross. The kingdom comes, but it arrives not through violence but by the Davidic servant submitting himself to death.

Betrayal before the Cross

Suffering and betrayal were always predestined for this wise king. Several predictions of Jesus's suffering are made before the actual events. These pick up with fervency after Peter confesses that Jesus is the messiah (16:21; 17:12, 22–23; 20:18–19). Once the suffering begins, the parallels with David's life blossom, especially with regard to Judas's betrayal and its similarity to the revolt of Absalom and Ahithophel. First, as Van Egmond and N. Johnson note, Jesus's movement from Jerusalem across the Kidron Valley to the Mount of Olives parallels an episode in the life of David.[58] Second, as Jesus goes up to pray on the Mount of Olives, Matthew employs the same verb that describes David's journey from Jerusalem during the revolt of Absalom and Ahithophel (2 Sam. 15:12–18:18). Therefore, Matthew sets up Jesus's time of prayer and betrayal with the same geographical movement and even some of the same words as a Davidic episode. Third, as Absalom and Ahithophel conspire against David, so Judas conspires against Jesus.[59] Fourth, David prays

---

57. Van Egmond, "Messianic 'Son of David,'" 60.

58. Van Egmond, "Messianic 'Son of David,'" 62; N. Johnson, "Passion according to David."

59. N. Johnson ("Passion according to David," 249–52) rightly asserts that while Matthew reproduces around 80 percent of Mark's material, the arrest scene and Judas's death are redacted to a great extent. He notes the following parallels. First, once on the Mount of Olives, Jesus falls down and prays, as David did. Second, the weariness of Jesus's and David's followers is emphasized. Third, both leaders tell their followers, "Arise, let us go (flee)."

that the counsel of Ahithophel will be turned to foolishness (2 Sam. 15:31), and in a similar manner the counsel of Judas to the religious leaders turns to foolishness because it leads to Jesus's enthronement and Judas's death. Fifth, when Judas hangs himself (Matt. 27:5), readers should also be thinking of Ahithophel's suicide (2 Sam. 17:23).[60] They are the only two characters in the entire Bible to hang themselves.[61]

The allusions to a Davidic figure continue as Matthew then transitions to Jesus in the garden and puts words in his mouth that suggest an echo with the suffering king from the psalms, especially a close mirroring of Ps. 42:5–6. Jesus prays, "My soul is very sorrowful, even to death; remain here, and watch with me" (περίλυπός ἐστιν ἡ ψυχή μου ἕως θανάτου· μείνατε ὧδε καὶ γρηγορεῖτε μετ' ἐμοῦ, Matt. 26:38). The parallels in the first part of the psalm are notable:[62]

> Why are you cast down, O my soul,
>   and why are you in turmoil within me?
> Hope in God; for I shall again praise him,
>   my salvation and my God.
> My soul is cast down within me;
>   therefore I remember you. (Ps. 42:5–6)

> ἵνα τί περίλυπος εἶ, ψυχή,
>   καὶ ἵνα τί συνταράσσεις με;
> . . . .
> πρὸς ἐμαυτὸν ἡ ψυχή μου ἐταράχθη·
>   διὰ τοῦτο μνησθήσομαί σου. (Ps. 41:6–7 LXX)

David also arrived on the Mount of Olives in emotional distress; he wept as he walked (2 Sam. 15:23, 30). After Jesus has finished praying that this cup would pass from him, Judas arrives with a crowd of armed soldiers (Matt. 26:47). Although no verbal parallels with the Psalms occur here, there are thematic parallels. David speaks of deadly enemies surrounding him (Ps. 17:9). He tells of the Lord preparing a table before him in the presence of his enemies, which suggests a fulfillment in the Last Supper (Ps. 23:5). David pleads to be rescued from the hands of his enemies and his persecutors (31:5); he complains that his enemies trample him all day long (56:2) and that they consult together, watching for his life (71:10).

60. See N. Johnson, "Passion according to David," 252–56.
61. Origen (*Sel. Ps.* 3.1.29, 36 [PG 12:1120c]) also drew parallels between Ahithophel and Judas, as did Chrysostom (*Exp. Ps.* [PG 55:103]).
62. Although Ps. 42 is a psalm of Korah, the entire Psalms collection is generally regarded as from David.

When Judas approaches, Jesus says, "Friend, do what you are here to do" (Matt. 26:50 NRSV). This use of "friend," both ironic and excruciating, refers to the pain of a companion's betrayal.[63] A psalm also speaks of the pain of a friend's betrayal:

> For it is not an enemy who taunts me—
>   then I could bear it;
> it is not an adversary who deals insolently with me—
>   then I could hide from him.
> But it is you, a man, my equal,
>   my companion, *my familiar friend.*
> We used to take sweet counsel together;
>   within God's house we walked in the throng.
> . . . .
> My companion stretched out his hand *against his friends*;
>   he violated his covenant.
> His speech was smooth as butter,
>   yet war was in his heart;
> his words were softer than oil,
>   yet they were drawn swords. (Ps. 55:12–14, 20–21, emphasis added)

After Judas has arrived with his band of soldiers, the opportunity for violence arises. Jesus, however, denounces violence, though it is clear that he has authority to wield such power (26:51–53; cf. 5:38–42). This action both aligns with and contradicts the David narrative. Sometimes he too resisted violence (as with Saul and Shimei; 1 Sam. 24:4; 2 Sam. 19:21–23). However, David also benefited from violent help and was known for killing tens of thousands, but "Jesus refuses identification with . . . a militant Davidic messiah."[64] He acts as the servant. The story is new and old.

Matthew thus presents the betrayal of Jesus in the matrix of Davidic passiocentric wisdom-like texts. The First Gospel employs unique material to show Jesus acting as a type of David as his friend betrays him at his most emotional moment.[65] Rather than responding with violence, he submits himself to sword and corruption. "He was despised and rejected by men; a man of sorrows" (Isa. 53:3). As both the Psalms and Isaiah predict, the messiah

63. Matthew adds this use of "friend" to Mark's narrative, and the term is unique to Matthew in the NT. Of the seventeen uses in the LXX, eight of these are employed in the Davidic succession narrative. N. Johnson ("Passion according to David," 254–55) also notes that in rabbinic literature Ahithophel is known as the "friend" of David in the Psalms.

64. N. Johnson, "Passion according to David," 272.

65. See Senior ("Matthew's Special Material") on the material unique to Matthew in the passion. He notes the Judas episode.

has returned to Jerusalem to be betrayed by his enemies and now even his friends.

Silence and Innocence at the Trial

Matthew continues to depict Jesus as the Davidic wise suffering servant when the scene shifts to the trials. Here readers see the false testimonies against the Lord's anointed and Jesus's silence and innocence as the servant (Isa. 53:7, 9). Both of these themes have resonances with David's life and that of the servant. In the trial before the Sanhedrin (Matt. 26:57–68), the chief priests and the whole council are seeking "false testimony" (ψευδομαρτυρίαν) against Jesus. In the Psalms, David similarly cries out, "Give me not up to the will of my adversaries; for false witnesses have risen against me" (Ps. 27:12). "For wicked and deceitful mouths are opened against me, speaking against me with lying tongues" (109:2). "Deliver me, O LORD, from lying lips, from a deceitful tongue" (120:2). As in the Psalms, Jesus is surrounded by lying tongues and false testimony. They ask him about the temple, and then they adjure him to tell them if he is the Christ, the Son of God (Matt. 26:63). Jesus answers in the affirmative. The whole scene fulfills Ps. 2, where the kings of the earth set themselves against the Lord's "Anointed."

In the trial under the authority of Pontius Pilate (Matt. 27:1–26), Matthew again focuses on Jesus's innocence and silence. The echoes of Ps. 2 continue as the chief priests and the scribes take council (συμβούλιον ἔλαβον, Matt. 27:1) against Jesus to kill him.[66] The chief priests and the scribes also gathered against Jesus in Matt. 2:5. Jesus stands before the governor, who asks Jesus whether he is the King of the Jews (27:11). Jesus gives no answer (27:12). Pilate is confused and asks him why he does not answer. David likewise speaks of waiting for God alone in silence (Ps. 62:1, 5). However, Matthew's emphasis on silence also harks back to Isaiah and the suffering servant, who "was oppressed, and he was afflicted, yet he opened not his mouth; like a lamb that is led to the slaughter, and like a sheep that before its shearers is silent, so he opened not his mouth" (Isa. 53:7). Later, Isaiah pairs the servant's silence with his innocence as Matthew does: "They made his grave with the wicked and with a rich man in his death, although he had *done no violence*, and there was no deceit in his mouth" (Isa. 53:9, emphasis added).

---

66. Judas himself says he has betrayed "innocent blood" and departs to hang himself (Matt. 27:4–5). This act by Judas relates to the emphasis in the Psalms on God's defeating all of David's enemies: "For you strike all my enemies on the cheek" (Ps. 3:7); "All my enemies shall be ashamed and greatly troubled" (6:10); "Now my head shall be lifted up above my enemies all around me" (27:6).

Pilate marvels at Jesus's silence, so he tries to get out of the situation by offering the criminal Barabbas to the crowd rather than Jesus "for he knew that it was out of envy that they had delivered him up" (Matt. 27:18). The juxtaposition of Barabbas and Jesus is intentional. Barabbas is probably a member of the *sicarii*, a militant Jewish movement seeking to overthrow Rome by violence (contra Isa. 53:9). The crowd has a choice between the innocent and silent sufferer or a revolutionary. While the crowd deliberates, Matthew notes how a word comes to Pilate's wife in a dream, telling Pilate to have nothing to do with the innocent man (Matt. 27:19). This is the third recognition of Jesus's innocence.

However, the crowd answers that they want the revolutionary set free and the wise one to be crucified (27:21–22). Pilate ironically washes his hands, trying to assert his innocence before the innocent one after he has condemned Jesus to die (27:24). The psalmist says, "All in vain have I kept my heart clean and washed my hands in innocence" (Ps. 73:13). Although Pilate thinks he is cleansing himself, Matthew makes clear that only one innocent person is in their midst.[67] They release Barabbas and have Jesus scourged and delivered over for crucifixion (Matt. 27:26). The revolutionary is free. The exiled sage-king rejects violence and marches toward death.

Forsaken at the Cross

The third scene that displays Jesus as the wise suffering servant is the crucifixion. Plenty of seemingly insignificant details surface in the crucifixion scene: Matthew speaks of what he drank, his clothes, the actions of those who pass by Jesus, and Jesus's last words. In between all these details, Matthew slips in the small phrase "when they had crucified him" (σταυρώσαντες δὲ αὐτόν, 27:35). He surrounds this momentous event with scriptural allusions. Without the scriptural background, the focus on these particulars might seem peculiar. The crucifixion is a new event, but it is bookended with scriptural allusions to David and the servant.

First, Jesus is offered wine mixed with gall, alluding to Ps. 69:21.[68] Initially, the wine mixed with gall seems like an odd element to include (Matt. 27:34). Of all the things that explain the circumstances of the crucifixion to us, Mat-

---

67. Hays (*Echoes of Scripture in the Gospels*, 133) notes that when the people ask for Jesus's blood be upon them and their children (Matt. 27:25), it resonates with David's wrathful response to the Amalekite messenger who brings the report of Saul's death. David declares to him, "Your blood be on your own head, because you have killed the Lord's anointed" (2 Sam. 1:16 AT).

68. Maybe there is also a narrative allusion to 2 Sam. 23:15–17, where David said with longing, "'Oh, that someone would give me water to drink from the well of Bethlehem that is by the gate!' Then the three mighty men broke through the camp of the Philistines and drew

thew includes this eccentric aspect about what was offered to Jesus to drink. Yet this surely alludes to Ps. 69:21, which says, "They gave me poison for food, and for my thirst they gave me sour wine to drink." Psalm 69 as a whole is a cry from David for Yahweh to save him:

> Save me, O God!
>> For the waters have come up to my neck.
> I sink in deep mire,
>> where there is no foothold;
> I have come into deep waters,
>> and the flood sweeps over me.
> I am weary with my crying out;
>> my throat is parched.
> My eyes grow dim
>> with waiting for my God. (Ps. 69:1–3)

The psalmist continues, with David saying that he has become a stranger to his brothers (69:8), and calling out for the Lord to save him and to redeem his soul (69:18). If Matthew alludes to the entire psalm then again on the cross, he portrays Jesus as the wise suffering servant like David, who also had sour wine given to him to drink by his enemies while he was suffering.[69]

Second, a number of allusions to Ps. 22 occur: the dividing of Jesus's clothing, the wagging of heads, and Jesus's last words. Psalm 22 begins with David asking why God has forsaken him and his crying to God day and night. David says, "All who see me mock me, they make mouths at me; they wag their heads; 'He trusts in the LORD; let him deliver him; let him rescue him, for he delights in him!'" (Ps. 22:7–8). In a similar way, Matthew describes people passing by, deriding Jesus, wagging their heads, and saying, "You who would destroy the temple and rebuild it in three days, save yourself! If you are the Son of God, come down from the cross" (Matt. 27:39–40). A few verses later the text says, "The robbers who were crucified with him also reviled

---

water out of the well of Bethlehem that was by the gate and carried and brought it to David. But he would not drink of it."

69. Nolland (*Gospel of Matthew*, 1191) says, "Various features of the psalm could illuminate Jesus' situation, and certainly the broad theme of the psalm, the suffering of the righteous, is an important one." Although some suppose this detail is included because it was a custom in crucifixions (as mentioned in the Talmud), Matthew's pattern is to include these details as a fulfillment of Scripture. He more likely includes this because he wishes to confirm the continual mocking of Jesus. "He was despised and rejected by men" (Isa. 53:3). As Gundry (*Use of the Old Testament*, 202) says, "The offer of the bitter drink is not an act of mercy, but an act of mockery." The sour wine is like poison, a mockery of the pure wine that a true king would drink.

him in the same way" (27:44). In a similar way, the enemies of the righteous man in Wis. 2:12–20 use comparable language: "Let us see if his words are true, and let us test what will happen at the end of his life; for if the righteous man is God's child, he will help him, and deliver him from the hands of his adversaries" (2:17–18).

The account of the guards dividing his garments by casting lots for them (27:35) also comes from Ps 22. Psalm 22:18 says, "They divide my garments among them, and for my clothing they cast lots." This is in a psalm of lament from David. Through using this quote, Matthew laments the treatment of the Davidic king. Just as David was mistreated by his enemies, so now even Jesus has been stripped of his clothes. Rather than being clothed with royalty, he is strung up naked on the cross. The point of both the division of the clothing and the mockery is that the king fulfills the suffering of David. Not only is the king exiled like David, but he also suffers a thousand deaths like David.

Finally, Jesus cries out the same words from Ps. 22:1: "My God, my God, why have you forsaken me?" (Matt. 27:46). Isaiah says that he was "smitten by God, and afflicted" and that "it was the will of the LORD to crush him; he has put him to grief" (Isa. 53:4, 10). This is the final cry of anguish from the one of David's lineage. The first lines of Matthew declare Jesus to be the Davidic king. Yet the journey Matthew portrays is not a pretty picture. The first breath that Jesus breathes garners hatred from the pseudo-king Herod. Now the last breath that Jesus cries is one of forsakenness and anguish. How could this be the king? How could this be the one? Matthew skillfully positions Jesus on the cross as the new David, who suffers at the hands of his enemies. Not only the words of Jesus carry the melodies of the Psalms, but even the actions of those who crucify Jesus point back to David.

The Wise Suffering King in Perspective

For Matthew, no contradiction exists between declaring Jesus to be the son of David and portraying him as the wise suffering servant who rejects violence. In fact, he is both *more* like and unlike David because of these realities. He is betrayed by his friends, innocent of the charges against him, and forsaken at the cross. Jesus already said to his disciples, "Whoever would be great among you must be your servant" (20:26). By highlighting parallels from the Psalms and Isa. 53, Matthew demonstrates the divine plan was for Jesus's messianic identity to be revealed in precisely this way.[70]

---

70. It is hard to avoid the idea that Matthew may have been writing to fellow Jews at this point. He looks at his scroll and tells them that this suffering figure is meant not to be a stumbling stone or rock of offense but the fulfillment of all their hopes.

The trajectory of Matthew's Gospel is one in which he fills in the portrait of Jesus with more depth as he goes along. It is as if at the beginning we discern only the outline, but life comes into the picture as we see that Jesus is exiled like David and is the righteous sufferer like David. Matthew has Jesus standing in continuity with the writers of the OT, but there is also a sense of escalation and newness. When people read about David's innocence, they would also think about his sins. When people read about David's enemies, they will also remember that David was not able to build the temple because he was a man of war. Jesus is like David in many regards, but he is also dissimilar. He fulfills the role of David and therefore is not just "like" David, but "better than" David. Jesus was truly innocent and truly wise; he forgave his enemies. The suffering on the cross was more than anything David ever had to endure. Therefore, when David cried out, "My God, my God, why have you forsaken me?" it meant something different from when Jesus cried these same words. It is still congruent with David's words, but the mystery is now revealed. We have covered how Jesus is "like" David in many respects, but we have not detailed how Jesus is enthroned as king. To have a king without his exaltation is to have no king at all. The ceremony of anointing and the ritual of his ascending to his throne are the confirmation of kingship. To this ceremony we finally turn.

The Enthroned King

Ultimately Matthew is able to declare that Jesus is the son of David in 1:1 because he observes Jesus's enthronement. Jesus is born as the king, exiled, and then suffers as the wise suffering servant. The destiny and journey of the king was always meant to lead to kingship. This is his journey. Yet Matthew shows that Jesus's enthronement occurs on the cross.[71] Jesus's enthronement is wrapped in irony as his opponents install him in jest. But between the lines, it is evident that what is done in derision vindicates his authority. Just as the scribes and the chief priests have been blind to Jesus's Davidic descent throughout the entire narrative, they are now blind to his enthronement on the cross; they are consecrating the one they have endeavored to eliminate. The cross is the only way to kingship for Jesus; it is his glorious and inglorious ceremony.

71. George Nickelsburg (*Resurrection, Immortality, and Eternal Life*) has proposed the existence of a traditional genre of suffering and vindication stories that can be seen in Jewish stories such as Joseph in Gen. 37–42; Esther; Dan. 3–6; Susanna; and 2 Macc. 7. The parallels between Joseph's life and Jesus's are striking. Joseph's death is plotted by his kin, his clothes are stripped, he is betrayed, sold for silver, and taken by others.

Seated at the Right Hand of God (26:62–64)

When Jesus suffers like David, he is also enthroned and exalted as the Davidic king in Matthew's narrative. This theme begins when Jesus faces the Sanhedrin (26:57–68). If Matt. 1–2 is the window through which we are to view the entire Gospel of Matthew, then the trial with the Sanhedrin is the window through which we can view the passion of Jesus. I have already commented on how Jesus is falsely accused and remains silent. However, Jesus *does* open his mouth at an important point.

When the high priest asks him, "Tell us if you are the Messiah, the Son of God," Jesus answers, "You have said so" (Matt. 26:63–64 NIV). Matthew employs the label *messiah* only a few times in direct quotations in his narrative, and therefore this is an important text. Jesus clarifies what type of messiah he is in the following words, with a combined quote from Dan. 7 and Ps. 110: "You will see the Son of Man seated at the right hand of Power and coming in the clouds of heaven" (Matt. 26:64). While it was clear that the messiah would be from the line of David (see Matt. 22:42b), in Ps. 110 David (or Israel's king) refers to two individuals above him, both called Lord. "The LORD says to my Lord: 'Sit at my right hand, until I make your enemies your footstool'" (Ps. 110:1).[72] The first "LORD" (with small caps) is clearly Yahweh. Yet as Jesus has shown back in Matt. 22, he himself is the second Lord. He is both David's son and David's Lord. Therefore, when Jesus is on trial and they ask him whether he is the messiah, he cites a Davidic psalm that speaks of him as Lord and seated at the right hand of God. By combining this psalm with Dan. 7, Jesus asserts that he will be exalted to the highest position, as the son of David, as the cloud rider.[73] When the Pharisees ask him if he is the messiah and he answers with this composite quotation, he declares that he *is* the about-to-be-enthroned *Davidic* messiah.

By placing these words in Jesus's mouth at this point, Matthew indicates for his readers that it is precisely through this suffering, through death on the cross, that the Son of Man is glorified and enthroned. The cross is Jesus's throne. The discipled scribe takes the Jewish Scriptures and explains them

72. Solomon is also opposed as king but promised the throne (1 Kings 1:13, 17, 30, 37, 47; 2:12).

73. A number of articles exist on the title "son of man" in Matthew. Luz ("Son of Man in Matthew") argues that Matthew uses "son of man" to reinforce Jewish misunderstanding of Jesus but also teaches his disciples through the employment of the title. After 16:13 Jesus speaks only to the disciples about himself as the son of man (20×). The only exception is 26:64 before the Sanhedrin. Kingsbury ("Title 'Son of Man'") argues that "son of man" is a public label, while "son of God" is a confessional label and that the two complement each other. Pamment ("Son of Man") asserts that Jesus uses the term "son of man" to define his destiny and to call his disciples to participate in it.

in light of Jesus, but the Scriptures also explain Jesus. Aspects of how this Son of Man would be enthroned were locked in the shadows, and now Jesus reveals them. Jesus's mission is also foggy to everyone around him, but when he quotes from Ps. 110 and Dan. 7, then readers and listeners should understand that he fulfills the Torah. Although he is in the midst of being judged, through judgment he is given authority to judge.

The King before Pilate (27:11–14)

After Jesus finishes with the chief priests and the elders of the people, they plot against Jesus to put him to death. They bring him before Pilate (the governor) because the Jewish leaders do not have authority to put him to death; so they call on Pilate, a Gentile ruler, to sentence him. As Jesus stands before the governor, he asks Jesus, "Are you the King of the Jews?" (Matt. 27:11).[74] Matthew has already answered this by identifying Jesus as the son of David, but now he is in the throes of answering *how* Jesus becomes king. The point is multivalent for Matthew.

First, it ironically culminates the ploy of Israel's leaders to get Jesus into trouble. The chief priests and scribes are not thoughtless; they "plot" to put Jesus to death (26:4), so they must come up with a charge that will stick, and they know that a claim to kingship will ruffle political feathers. Second, it shows that Jesus is pitted against not only the Jewish leadership and kings but also the kings of the earth. Jesus is not really the one on trial; earth is on trial, and it has been found wanting. Third, the title is an interpretative key for understanding what has come before. Jesus is on trial for kingship. Matthew is basically pleading with his readers to again go back through the narrative and read Jesus's life through the lens of royalty. Jesus is on trial for being king because he lived his life as *the* king. Finally, it brings to a close the story of what the Gentile kings and the Jewish leaders will do with this king. They will rage and conspire against him (Ps. 2:1–3), just as they did the last time he was in Jerusalem (Matt. 2). While the *wise* worship the king of the Jews, the *foolish* either plot Jesus's death or step aside for political protection.

Mocked as King (27:27–31)

Matthew continues to carry the monarchal theme forward when Jesus is mocked by the soldiers as king. The scribe includes many sardonic details of the treatment Jesus receives. All of them revolve around mocking Jesus as

74. Readers can compare this question from a Gentile king with Matt. 2, where Gentile wise men worship the king of the Jews, bringing him gifts as the new Solomon (1 Kings 4:34).

king (cf. Pss. 22:7; 74:10; 119:51). First, they strip him and put a scarlet robe around him (27:28). Scarlet robes were associated with royalty, and this is their attempt to mock him as king. This is confirmed by their putting a crown of thorns on his head and a reed in his right hand as they mock him and say "Hail, King of the Jews!" (27:29; see Ps. 89:39). A reed is a fake scepter, which they later use to strike him (27:30; Ps. 2:9). The soldiers mock Jesus according to his condemnation. They spit on him and take his own reed and strike him on the head. Isaiah predicted that the servant would give his back to those who strike him, his cheeks to those who pull out his beard, and he would not hide his face from disgrace and spitting (Isa. 50:6). Then they strip him of his robe and lead him away to be crucified. The soldiers crown him as king and then strip him of his kingship.

Matthew records the treatment of Jesus not only to make us feel sorry for him, but also to communicate reversal. When Jesus is stripped of his clothes, he is crowned. When he is struck with a reed, he is handed a scepter. When the scarlet robe is torn from his bloody back, he is covered in robes of royalty. The spit parodies the kiss of homage with which eastern subjects greeted their rulers. Through this narrative Matthew illustrates for his readers that their anticipated kingdom and king have come; he just traveled down the stream of suffering and disdain. On a larger biblical-theological level, Jesus is taking the curse on himself. The crown of thorns echoes the sin of Adam, where thorns would grow up and be a nuisance to flourishing. The reed by which Jesus is struck is a metaphor of humanity taking good gifts of God and turning them into weapons. The king takes the sins of the people, lays them on his shoulders, and heaves them up on the cross. King David has come!

The Titulus (27:32–44)

The final scene has Jesus ascending Golgotha with Simon of Cyrene. Simon carries Jesus's cross like those who would carry the king's throne and goods as he enters the city in the parousia as the conqueror.[75] Jesus arrives not at his city but at the "Place of a Skull" (27:33). The parousia of the king is the procession to his death. After the soldiers cast lots for the king's possessions, Matthew notes that they put over Jesus's head a sign that reads, "This is Jesus, the King of the Jews" (27:37). Origen, Augustine, and Aquinas viewed this scene through the lens of Ps. 2:6: "I have set my king on Zion, my holy hill."[76] The titulus becomes an ironic proclamation of Jesus's kingship. Interestingly,

75. Simon's carrying the cross also points to Simon becoming a disciple of the new king.
76. Ferda, "Matthew's Titulus." Already Matthew has noted that the people "gather together" against Jesus (2:4; 12:30; 22:34, 41; 26:3; 26:57; 27:17, 27, 62; 28:12).

none of the Gospels agree on the wording of the title. Unique to Matthew and John is the inclusion of the name "Jesus," which Ferda ties back to Matt. 1:21, where the angel says to Joseph, "You shall call his name Jesus, for he will save his people from their sins."[77] The Romans thus declare to the world why this man is being crucified, but in a satirical twist Matthew pronounces to his readers that the king has been enthroned. The sign declares to the whole world that Jesus is "the King of the Jews." Readers who have been following Matthew's narrative carefully will remember that this was the one whom Matthew said is the son of David, born in Bethlehem like David, exiled like David, and suffering like David. The sign completes the dye on the narrative with the scarlet hue of royalty and brings the kingship theme to its climax. Now readers can return to Matt. 1:1 and read it with a fuller understanding.

The mocking continues as the chief priests, scribes, and elders—along with the two thieves crucified with Jesus—ask why, if Jesus is the king of Israel, he can't deliver himself (27:42–44). They mock him for not being able to "save" himself. This helps readers understand that kingship and salvation are linked. The king should save his people and also protect himself, but *this* king is strapped to a wooden beam and can't even save himself. At the beginning of his Gospel, Matthew declares that Jesus is given his name because "he will save his people from their sins" (1:21). The Davidic king is here not simply to assert his authority and demonstrate his righteousness, justice, or compassion, but to save his people.

Although some accuse the Gospel writers of not developing a theology of the cross in their passion narratives, this theology surfaces upon closer inspection of the details and circumstances surrounding Golgotha. Through mocking, Matthew communicates that salvation comes through the king's enthronement on the cross. He saves the people through sacrifice and letting himself fall under the weight of sin. Although this is not explicit in Matthew's narrative, it is underneath the words of the lampooners. The conquering of the king comes in overpowering his enemies through love and sacrifice, not by the sword and war horses. The fulfillment of the Davidic king is upon them, but it is also redefined.

Why does Matthew employ an abundance of irony here? Why not be more explicit in declaring that this is the enthronement of Jesus? The answer comes in reflecting on the nature of irony. Irony allows Matthew to wisely assert two things at once, rather than just one. First, it allows readers to see that Jesus is opposed and crucified not because of something he has done, but on account of false accusations. They want him dead. They deny their king,

---

77. Ferda, "Soldiers' Inscription."

thus fulfilling Ps. 2. They deny the ruler of the universe. But *by* denying him, they set him up as king. Second, it allows Matthew to connect the cross and the throne and his suffering with his wisdom. Without this strategy, one of these points is lost. Matthew affirms that *through* mockery and defeat, Jesus is enthroned.[78]

Conclusion

This chapter has focused on the wisdom of Matthew in presenting the journey of the king to his throne from a geographic perspective. Jesus's life begins in Jerusalem and ends in Jerusalem, but his ministry takes place mostly in Galilee. While Matthew announces that Jesus is the Davidic king in 1:1, he makes readers go through his narrative to see how Jesus becomes king of the kingdom:

- Jesus is declared to be the son of David (Matt. 1:1).
- He is exiled by the king of Jerusalem to Nazareth of Galilee (Matt. 2).
- Ministry in Galilee ensues (Matt. 3–20).
- He suffers as the wise servant (Matt. 26–28).
- Jesus is enthroned on the cross (Matt. 27–28).

The exile of Jesus to Galilee is key because through this movement he mimics David's exile from his throne and unites the north and the south as the wise king.[79] Upon his return to the city, he is crowned as the king on the cross.

The bookend chapters of the Gospel (1–2; 26–28) can be viewed as *passive* instances where Jesus is portrayed in Davidic hues. All of the examples in chapters 1–2 depict Jesus as being acted upon or sovereignly placed. For example, Matthew's genealogy paints Jesus as the son of David. Even before

---

78. The scene of mockery is similar to what happens as David leaves the city and Absalom sets himself up as king. In 2 Sam. 16:5–14 Shimei (one of Saul's relatives) follows along and curses David: "And he threw stones at David and at all the servants of King David, and all the people and all the mighty men were on his right hand and on his left. And Shimei said as he cursed, 'Get out, get out, you man of blood, you worthless man!'" (2 Sam. 16:6–7). Abishai offers to kill the man for David, but David tells Abishai and his servants to leave Shimei alone, for maybe the Lord will look upon David and bless him for the wrong done to him this day. The narrative functions on a number of levels. As David flees for his life, and readers might be questioning if this will be David's downfall, Shimei is inserted to prove that David is still a righteous man. When he is cursed, he does not curse back. The foil characters reveal David's true identity, just as Jesus's identity is revealed at the cross through those who mock him.

79. In the next chapter I speak more about fulfilling the covenant requirements during the exile.

Jesus could act intentionally, God has sovereignly placed him in David's family. So while Jesus is "passive" in one sense, Matthew's "active" imagination makes the connection. The same activity from the scribe and passivity from Jesus are found in Jesus's infancy narrative in chapter 2. Jesus is *placed* in Bethlehem, *visited* by the magi, *challenged* by a rival king, and then *brought* to Egypt and Nazareth. These are all passive activities. Matthew deftly puts a Davidic quote in the mouths of the chief priests and the scribes, allowing readers to see a deeper meaning. He also calls him a Nazarene, letting readers know that this Jesus is the branch of David.

The "passive" example of Jesus continues at the end of the Gospel (chaps. 26–28). Like David, Jesus suffers as the wise servant. He is acted upon, mocked, ridiculed, and treated shamefully. He is passive because he allows himself to suffer although he has all authority.[80] He also allows himself to be hoisted on the cross, permitting others to enthrone him. Jesus's life begins and ends under the control of others. He suffers under the hands of those who oppose him, but they unwittingly exalt him when they lift him up on the cross. Even in all these instances of others acting on him, Jesus still fulfills the life of David.

Usually when studies are done on Jesus as the new David (or the Davidic messiah), scholars focus on the specific mentions of David. While these references have an important role to play, narratives are meant to be read for their development. It is quite unsatisfactory to dissect the narrative, cut it to pieces, and then try to reassemble it and say, "See, here is David." Such an approach is more typical of the hard sciences than of the soft sciences. What I have attempted to do is trace a narrative view of Jesus as the Davidic messiah in Matthew, looking more at his broad brushstrokes and the development in the story than merely at the occurrences of David's name.

My argument here is that the writer of the First Gospel takes his readers on the geographic journey of the Davidic king. The king is born into the family of David, grows up in the city of David, is exiled from his home, and then returns to the city of the king, conquering through humility, suffering righteously, and finally being enthroned on the cross. The story is old, but it is also new. The discipled scribe has brought forth treasures—his wisdom—and described how the king is crowned. The next chapter will look more specifically at what this king accomplishes during his exile.

---

80. In another sense this is an active passivity from Jesus. In the trial, those who put Jesus on trial think that they are in charge, but Jesus is directing these episodes as the victim.

4

Jesus as the Ideal and Wise King

Monarchy is the chief metaphor Matthew employs to illuminate Jesus.[1] The First Gospel presents Jesus as the Davidic king who leads Israel in faithfulness to the wisdom found in the Torah. He shepherds the people toward flourishing and righteous living, thus securing the nation's territory. The king is the conduit through which God will bless and prosper his nation, thereby blessing the world. Yahweh rules through the obedience of his appointed monarch. This idea is not unique to Israel, for in the ANE numerous cultures viewed their king as the intermediary between the divine and the mundane worlds (sometimes labeled "sacral kingship"). While the discipled scribe presents Jesus as the Davidic messiah whose purpose is to restore his nation, the way in which he does so is unique and clarifies the promises that came before. Matthew wisely brings out treasures both new and old through the employment of shadow stories.

If the last chapter provided a bookend to the journey of Jesus, showing the geographic journey of the king, then this chapter takes a plunge into Jesus's Davidic actions while in exile—the actions of the ideal and wise king.[2]

---

1. By chief metaphor, I am not arguing that Matthew sidesteps Moses, for Moses is also compared to Israel's kings (see Deut. 18). However, Matthew begins by relating Jesus to Abraham and David, not to Moses.

2. Support for labeling Jesus's ministry in Galilee as an "exile" comes from Matt. 2. Jesus is born in the city of Bethlehem but must leave because of the rival king. He flees to Egypt (2:13–15). Then after Herod dies, Joseph brings his family back up to Judea but passes through and on up to Nazareth because of Archelaus (Matt. 2:22). Between these two movements, Matthew inserts a fulfillment quotation from Jer. 31:15, which speaks of Rachel weeping for her children

Matthew does not begin his Gospel with a theme and then leave it to shiver in anonymity. He extends it through his account, indicating the introduction and conclusion are the windows to the rest of his world. He invites readers to look more closely at the life of Jesus and to see him through the life of David. The previous analysis concerned Jesus's birth and infancy and finally his reentry into Jerusalem and his death. In these we saw how Jesus was crowned as the king. He undergoes rejection, exile, suffering, and mockery, which is his path to the throne, as was David's. Jewish readers should have been expecting an unsteady trip to the throne since this was David's experience too.

In this chapter, we examine a different angle of Jesus's Davidic kingship: the *activities* of this king while he is in exile (Galilee).[3] In Galilee Jesus personifies what it means to be the true and wise king by embodying the Torah, thereby showing both Israel and the world the shape and character of his kingdom. In exile Jesus seeks the good of the city. Although this chapter can't be exhaustive, three specific Davidic actions will be explored.

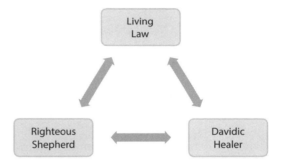

Jesus not only gives the new law as the prophet in the Sermon on the Mount; he *embodies* the law as the wise king. Kings were meant not only to be lawgivers but also to live the law and demonstrate to their subjects what it means to be a citizen of their kingdom. The next two points then intertwine and function subordinately to the manner in which Jesus lives the law. First, Jesus personifies the law by acting as the righteous Davidic shepherd who watches over his flock—being the merciful, arbitrating, and sacrificial shepherd in contrast to the religious leaders of the day. Second, Jesus enacts *justice* as the Davidic merciful healer (which also has shepherding impressions). While

---

at Ramah. Ramah is the place from which the people were taken into exile (Jer. 40:1). Matthew thus indicates that Jesus's not being able to return to his birthplace is a type of exile, but he also points to the hope of a return from exile. Hays, *Echoes of Scripture in the Gospels*, 115.

3. I will step outside this so-called exile to note some framing passages that instruct readers on how to view his exile.

in Galilee, Jesus restores those around him as they call out to the "Son of David." Jesus does not neglect the weightier matters of the law: "justice and mercy and faithfulness" (23:23). In all of these actions, Jesus actively fulfills the role of the ideal and wise Davidic king, and the discipled scribe illustrates how the new interprets the old, and the old reveals the new.

The Living Law

Jesus has been introduced as the Davidic king in the genealogy; he is revered and rejected, and then exiled to Galilee. As Jesus begins his ministry, he is officially anointed as king in his baptism (3:16). Jesus claims that this is "to fulfill all righteousness" (3:15), which means to fulfill the total will of God for the earth by being its king. Not surprisingly, the word "righteousness" is regularly connected to wisdom in the wisdom tradition (Deut. 16:19; Ps. 37:30; Prov. 1:3; 9:9; 10:31; Eccles. 7:16; 9:1; 10:2; Jer. 23:5; 1 Cor. 1:30). John the Baptist, the last prophet of the old age, anoints him, and the Baptist later ends up being killed by King Herod.[4] As David proves himself as fit to be the people's deliverer by demonstrating his power over Goliath (1 Sam. 17), so too Jesus also proves himself as fit to be the people's king by resisting Satan (Matt. 4:1–11). Both are loyal to God (1 Sam. 17:26; Matt. 4:10) and are dependent on God (1 Sam. 17:37; Matt. 4:4). David does not put on the normal armor of the king but clothes himself in humility (1 Sam. 17:38–40); Jesus defeats Satan by clothing himself not with the power of a normal king but with the armor of dependence on God's word (Matt. 4:4).

This leads Jesus to declare that the kingdom is here through his *teaching* and *healing*. "He went throughout all Galilee, teaching in their synagogues and proclaiming the gospel of the kingdom and healing every disease and every affliction among the people" (Matt. 4:23).[5] The actions of the king in the exile are a combination of both authority and mercy. He "teaches" and "proclaims" the kingdom, but he also "heals" every disease and affliction. Jesus is the ideal and wise king. Camelot, so to speak, has arrived in King Jesus. These two tasks define and delineate the kingdom, and therefore Matthew devotes the rest of his narrative to an alternation between the teaching and the healing of Jesus.

4. Samuel also fears the wrath of the king when he is told to anoint a son of Jesse (see 1 Sam. 16:1–2). Samuel has the children of Jesse parade before him, but David is brought to him and described as a man who knows psalms (εἰδότα ψαλμόν, usually translated as "skillful in playing"), a man of intelligence, a man of war, a wise and good man, and "the LORD is with him" (1 Sam. 16:18). David is described as being with the sheep and watching them.

5. Sirach says, "Wisdom becomes known through speech, and education through the words of the tongue" (Sir. 4:24).

Matthew's first major discourse (teaching section) of Jesus comes in the famous Sermon on the Mount (Matt. 5–7). But when it comes to Jesus's teaching, most commentators run to Jesus as a prophet. Nevertheless, much of the confusion concerning Jesus and his attitude toward the law stems from a narrow prophetic lens, forgetting that Matthew has begun the Gospel by announcing that Jesus is king. While I will be interacting with Jesus as the prophet in the next chapter, significant clarity comes to Jesus's attitude toward the law if we begin by viewing Jesus as the Davidic king. Looking at the Sermon through the lens of royalty smooths out the rough hills, and separating kingship themes from the νόμος (law) wreaks havoc on our understanding of Jesus's relationship to the law. Law and wisdom come in tandem in the Scriptures and in a king's reign.

Although the title David never appears in the Sermon, and only once does the noun "king" occur (5:35), it would be a severe mistake to overlook Jesus as king here. At least three reasons present themselves for viewing the Sermon through the lens of royalty. First, the very occurrence of βασιλεία (kingdom), both throughout the Sermon and in the narrative leading up to the Sermon, give warrant for viewing each discourse as a kingship discourse. As just noted, Matthew speaks of Jesus "proclaiming the gospel of the kingdom" in two summary statements (4:23; 9:35), which are meant to act like an abbreviated canopy thrown over the entire narrative. The Beatitudes are framed with "kingdom of heaven" statements (5:3, 10), and the term kingdom (βασιλεία) occurs eight times in the discourse. The Sermon on the Mount is the king's speech.

Second, it would be odd for Matthew to begin with the Davidic theme so clearly and then drop it once Jesus enters his ministry. In Matthew's case, he must have come to understand Jesus as the Davidic messiah *through* the ministry of Jesus's teaching, healing, (and) dying. Jesus's ministry is a vibrant example of Jesus being in the line of David, which caused Matthew to write his introduction as he did. It isn't legitimate to view one part of Matthew's Gospel through the lens of this theme and exclude other parts. The Sermon isn't hermetically sealed off from the rest of the narrative but integral to it.

Third, and most important for my purpose, kings in ancient times were not only to instruct in the law but also to "embody the law internally and produce good legislation that transforms the people and leads them in obedience to the law."[6] Evidence exists both in the ANE and the biblical text that kings were to be living embodiments of the law who instruct through both teaching and example what it means to follow the law. As the king goes, the nation goes. Jesus is the Davidic king who becomes the living law (à la wisdom). The true

---

6. Jipp, *Christ Is King*, 45. What follows applies to Jipp's observations on messiah in Paul and to Matthew's presentation of Jesus.

and wise king will live the Torah (Deut. 17:19; Ps. 1:2). Sirach even identifies wisdom with the Torah of Moses (Sir. 24:23). Jesus's approach toward the law cannot be sufficiently explored by looking only at the places where νόμος occurs, but that is a place to start. Jesus's best-known statement about the law comes in the Sermon on the Mount.

> Do not think that I have come to abolish the Law or the Prophets; I have not come to abolish them but to fulfill them. For truly, I say to you, until heaven and earth pass away, not an iota, not a dot, will pass from the Law until all is accomplished. (Matt. 5:17–18)

In Matt. 5, Jesus's statement about fulfilling the law has been the subject of much debate. In what way does he fulfill the law? By extending it? By showing its true intention? By bringing it to its end? Clarity emerges by seeing Jesus as fulfilling the law by "living it" as the ideal and wise king. To put this another way, as the king, he embodies the law: he meets its demands and thereby fulfills it. Some scholars reject this meaning for "fulfill."[7] Leon Morris claims, "We must bear in mind that 'fulfil' does not mean the same as 'keep'; Jesus is speaking of more than obedience to regulations"; yet it is also true that "fulfill" does not mean less.[8] To understand what "fufill the law" means from a monarchal perspective, one must put oneself into the first-century context and the common notion about kings.

As Joshua Jipp has shown, both Hellenistic and OT kingship discourses assert that virtuous kings submit to the law and thereby internalize it. "It is only through this royal 'living law,' whereby the king's subjects imitate the king who provides the perfect pattern for their own character, that they are able to fulfill the demands of the law. The results of the people's imitation of the royal living law are harmony, friendship, and the eradication of dissension among the king's subjects."[9] Although Jipp is not referring here to the Sermon, this quote brings remarkable clarity to Jesus's first speech. Jesus is not only the new Moses going up on the mountain to give the law; he is also the new king, fulfilling the demands of the law by instructing the people how to imitate him and live in harmony with the law.

The theme of the king as embodying the law is strewn throughout Hellenistic and kingship discourse. A few examples should suffice. In the Neo-Pythagorean essays "On Kingship," Archytas of Tarentum presents the good

---

7. Nolland (*Gospel of Matthew*, 218) dismisses the idea that "fulfill" means Jesus lives out the requirements of the law.
8. Morris, *Gospel according to Matthew*, 108.
9. Jipp, *Christ Is King*, 45.

king as the animate law: "Laws are of two kinds, the animate law, which is the king, and the inanimate, the written law. So law is primary; for with reference to it the king is lawful, the rulership is fitting, the ruled are free, the whole community happy. . . . So it is proper for the better to rule, for the worse to be ruled. . . . The best ruler would be the one who is closest to the law."[10]

According to this text, the wise king is the one who embodies the law, who rules in accordance with the law. He is the animate law to be imitated by his subjects. Plutarch in a similar way says that kings shape their own character by the laws so that their subjects fit their pattern.[11] The just king obeys the law and becomes a wise copy of the things the law commands. While the OT does not use the language of "living law" to describe Israel's ideal king, it does speak of the task of Israel's ruler; he is to write out, read, and obey the Torah.

> When he sits on the throne of his kingdom, he shall write for himself in a book a copy of this law, approved by the Levitical priests. And it shall be with him, and he shall read in it all the days of his life, that he may learn to fear the LORD his God by keeping all the words of this law and these statutes, and doing them, that his heart may not be lifted up above his brothers, and that he may not turn aside from the commandment, either to the right hand or to the left, so that he may continue long in his kingdom, he and his children, in Israel. (Deut. 17:18–20)

The king was to be a scribe who wrote the law so that he might *fear the Lord* and keep his statutes.[12] A wise king would be centered on the law, learning himself how to internalize the law, thereby becoming an embodiment of the law. As Philo says, "Other kings indeed have staves for their scepters, but my scepter is the book of Deuteronomy, . . . a symbol of the irreproachable rulership which is copied after the archetype, the kingly rule of God."[13] As the OT continues, each of Israel's kings and rulers is evaluated on whether he has internalized the Torah.

This internalizing of the law is exactly what Israel was called to do in Deut. 4:6 to become wise: "Keep them and do them, for that will be your *wisdom* and your *understanding* in the sight of the peoples, who, when they hear all these statutes, will say, 'Surely this great nation is a *wise* and *understanding*

10. Thesleff, *Pythagorean Texts*, 33.8–13; Goodenough, "Political Philosophy of Hellenistic Kingship," 59–60. See Jipp, *Christ Is King*, 49.

11. Plutarch, *Moralia* 780B.

12. The word "fear" and the phrase "fear of the Lord" are employed consistently in the wisdom tradition: Pss. 2:11; 5:7; 9:20; 15:4; 19:9; 22:23, 25; 25:14; 31:19; 33:8, 18; 34:7, 9, 11; 36:1; 40:3; 55:19; 60:4; 61:5; 66:16; 67:7; 72:5; 85:9; 86:11; 90:11; 102:15; 103:11, 13, 17; 111:5, 10; 115:11, 13; 118:4, 6; 119:63, 74, 79, 120; 135:20; 145:19; 147:11; Prov. 1:7, 29; 2:5; 3:7; 8:13; 9:10; 10:27; 14:26–27; 15:16, 33; 16:6; 19:23; 22:4; 23:17; 24:21; Eccles. 3:14; 5:7.

13. Philo, *Spec. Laws* 4.160–64, quote from 164.

people'" (emphasis added). Matthew, as the discipled scribe, goes to great lengths to show that Jesus not only teaches on the law but also internalizes it and thereby fulfills it.[14] In fact, when Jesus teaches on a topic, Matthew makes sure to emphasize that Jesus performs it as well.

- Jesus teaches his disciples to be meek (5:5), and Matthew describes him as meek and lowly of heart (11:29; 21:5).
- Jesus calls them to not neglect justice, mercy, and faithfulness (9:13; 12:7), and he goes about as king and willingly touches a leper, a hemorrhaging woman, and a girl believed to be dead in the house of a gentile (chaps. 8–9).
- Jesus tells his scribes to prioritize loving God and others (22:36–40), and his entire ministry is in service to God his Father and his people.
- Jesus requires mercy and humility (5:7; 9:13; 12:7; 18:4; 23:12), and the scribe portrays him as merciful and humble. People who need help even cry out to him, "Have mercy" (9:27; 11:29; 15:22; 18:4; 20:30).
- Jesus blesses those who are persecuted for the sake of the kingdom (5:10), and he himself suffers while Pilate declares, "What evil has he done?" (27:23).
- Jesus teaches and demands faithfulness to the Torah (5:17–20; 23:1–2), and Matthew shows the sage faithfully keeping and interpreting the law throughout his life (8:4; 12:1–8; 15:1–20).
- Jesus tells his disciples to turn the other cheek when someone strikes them (5:39), and in the trials Jesus allows others to spit in his face and strike him (26:67; 27:30).
- Jesus teaches his disciples not to give pearls to pigs (7:6), and Jesus at first refuses to speak to the Canaanite woman (15:23), and also when he is at his trial he remains silent at key points (26:63; 27:12–14).
- Jesus calls his disciples to be truthful in their speech (5:37), and while Jesus is on trial, he does affirm that he is the messiah while he is under oath (26:64).
- Jesus teaches his disciples to pray that God's will be done (6:10). In the garden, when Jesus faces the prospect of death, he uses the same words three times (26:37–44).
- Jesus, as the sage, warns his disciples about mammon and keeping wealth for themselves (6:19). Jesus also does not store up treasure, has

14. See the lists in the following two books, from which my list is borrowed: Davies and Allison, *Matthew*, 3:715–16; Hood, *Imitating God in Christ*, 77–79.

nowhere to lay his head (8:20), and denies the opportunity the devil gives to him to seize sovereignty over the whole world (4:8).

- Jesus instructs his disciples to take up their crosses and follow him (16:24), and he also carries his cross (27:31–32).
- Jesus blesses his people who mourn (5:4), so too he mourns and grieves (23:37).
- Jesus calls his disciples to hunger and thirst for righteousness (5:6), and he hungers and thirsts for God's kingdom to be manifested (9:38).
- Jesus commands his disciples to be pure in heart (5:8), so too he is pure (4:10).
- Jesus teaches his disciples that self-sacrifice will lead to honor and glory (16:24–27; 19:27–30), and he denies himself (4:8) and lays down his life, thereby receiving all authority (25:31–32; 28:18).
- Jesus lives the law as the king showing the people the way of righteousness (3:15), a righteousness that even exceeds that of the scribes and Pharisees (5:20).

Jesus did not come to set aside or nullify the law. Rather, he affirmed it, accomplished it, and brought it to reality. Jesus embodies and lives the law that he delivers in the Sermon and in the rest of the Gospel. The standard responsibility of ancient kings was the task of enacting justice for his people. Moreover, related to his procuring justice for the king's subjects is the task of executing judgment upon the wicked.[15] Matthew's dramatization of the law throughout his Gospel cannot be separated from Jesus's kingship because Matthew's programmatic statement about Jesus's ministry is that he "went throughout all Galilee, teaching in their synagogues and proclaiming the gospel of the kingdom and healing every disease and every affliction among the people" (4:23). The Sermon on the Mount is part of the wise king's message about the kingdom of heaven. He teaches on the kingdom (Matt. 5–7), and then he heals every disease in anticipation of the kingdom (Matt. 8–9) and enacts the double love command.

Royalty and the Law of Christ

That the king is the living law is an old message, one that appears quite frequently in Hellenistic and OT literature. However, this message is also new because it is filtered through a new king. Unlike David, Solomon, and

---

15. Jipp, *Christ Is King*, 216.

all the other kings, this king never breaks any of the laws. He embodies the law and teaches the people how to flourish under the law. For Jesus to fulfill the law at least partially means he comes and performs all it commands. In this way, Jesus does not abrogate the law but fulfills it. Not a jot or tittle goes away, because the law is wrapped up in him as the Davidic messiah. As Nolland says, "The fulfilment language represents a claim that Jesus' programmatic commitment, far from undercutting the role of the Law and the Prophets, is to enable God's people to live out the Law more effectively."[16] In one sense Jesus transcends the law, not by extending it or going beyond it, but by being a more perfect embodiment of the divine will than has ever happened before.[17]

The framework that Matthew has set up so far suggests that it is not until the arrival of Jesus, the divinely appointed heir of David's throne, that the Deuteronomic curses (Deut. 27–28) begin to be reversed. Deuteronomy pronounces curses on those who lead the blind astray (27:18), who withhold justice from the foreigner (27:19), who do not uphold the words of this law (27:26). Jesus reverses the curses while in exile by fulfilling the law as the king: he heals the blind (Matt. 9:28–29; 11:5), shows mercy to a Canaanite woman (15:22), and keeps the law instead of abolishing it (5:17–20). The messiah's apocalyptic appearance marks the end of the age of wrath and the renewal of God's presence with Israel. The forgiveness of Israel's sins provides the basis for the reestablishment of the kingdom of Israel. Jesus as the wise king reinforces the identity of the community of his kingdom. This community is in line with the Israel of old, but they also have their new king who embodies the law perfectly. The king as the living law continues in exile with Jesus acting as (1) their righteous shepherd and (2) enacting justice (healing them). It is to these themes that we turn.

The Righteous-Shepherd Motif

Jesus is not merely like David in his geographical movement but also in the *way* he carries out his kingship during his exile. One way he enacts his kingship is by being the Davidic righteous shepherd. In a defining and pivotal text, David's kingship is linked with the idea of shepherding (2 Sam. 5:2).

16. Nolland, *Gospel of Matthew*, 219.
17. If that is all people mean by saying that Jesus transcends the law, then I agree, but I fear that most are not careful with their language and are asserting something different. Some seem to imply that Jesus transcends the law in that he contradicts the law and gives a new law that negates the Torah in certain ways.

The context of 2 Sam. 5:2 concerns the transition from Saul to David. All the elders of Israel come to the king at Hebron. David makes a covenant with the people, and they anoint David as king over Israel (2 Sam. 5:3). The Lord defines for David what his kingship is to be. He says, "You shall be shepherd of my people Israel, and you shall be prince over Israel."

2 Samuel 5:2 LXX	2 Samuel 5:2 MT
Σὺ ποιμανεῖς τὸν λαόν μου τὸν Ισραηλ, καὶ σὺ ἔσει εἰς ἡγούμενον ἐπὶ τὸν Ισραηλ.	אַתָּה תִרְעֶה אֶת־עַמִּי אֶת־יִשְׂרָאֵל וְאַתָּה תִּהְיֶה לְנָגִיד עַל־יִשְׂרָאֵל:

The word sometimes translated "prince" (ἡγούμενον) can also mean simply leader or ruler. Therefore, at the beginning of David's rule, his kingship is defined by the metaphor of being a shepherd.

R. Hunziker-Rodewald correctly notes that, from the perspective of the narrative, the function of shepherding is the starting point for conceptions of David's career and the presentation of his kingship is a "shepherdship" (*Hirtenschaft*).[18] The Bible's characterization of David's story can be aptly summarized as a transformation from shepherding his father's flock to shepherding Yahweh's flock (2 Sam. 7:8; Ps. 78:70–71). Thus it is little surprise that Matthew, the Jewish scribe who knows his OT so well, picks up this motif and applies it consistently to Jesus. Though it is not sufficient to examine the occurrences of "shepherd" in Matthew, because all of Jesus's ministry should be viewed under the lens of a shepherd, it is a good place to start. Matthew uses "shepherd" (ποιμήν) three times in his Gospel (9:36; 25:32; 26:31) and the verb ποιμαίνω once (2:6). The shepherd image is also implied in 15:24 and 18:12. The Gospel of Matthew employs the shepherd motif more than either Mark or Luke and explicitly links it to christological phrases like "Son of David" and "Son of Man" and typological themes like the "new Moses" and the "new David."

As Willitts argues, the "Shepherd-King tradition and the phrase should be investigated within the sphere of a concrete-political Davidic Messianism."[19] As David was the shepherd of Israel, so too Jesus will shepherd his people. I will divide this section into two parts. First, I will step back and examine the relationship between kings/shepherds in the ANE and the Scriptures. Second, I will walk through five Matthean texts in which Jesus's kingship is developed with the shepherd motif. My argument is that Matthew takes up the tradition of the historical and prophetic books to portray Jesus as the Davidic shepherd

18. Hunziker-Rodewald, *Hirt und Herde*, 46. See Willitts, *Matthew's Messianic Shepherd-King*, 53.
19. Willitts, *Matthew's Messianic Shepherd-King*, 3–4.

in his exile. This is set in contrast to the Jewish leaders, who are characterized as evil/false shepherds both explicitly and implicitly.[20]

Background to the Shepherd Motif

The shepherd metaphor is widespread in the ANE and Greco-Roman traditions and regularly connected to kingship and leadership. Many different deities of Mesopotamia are referred to as shepherds. The Greco-Roman world also linked a number of gods to the shepherd image: Hermes carries the lamb over his shoulders, and Pan is the god of herds and shepherds. The *Iliad* employs the image of a goat herder who separates and orders the flock as a hero-king.[21] In the later Greco-Roman period, the philosopher (king/ruler) is the one who becomes the shepherd. Xenophon says the duties of a good shepherd and king are alike.[22] The shepherd metaphor was evidently widespread in both the ANE and Greco-Roman literature and regularly linked to the gods and kings.

In the Hebrew Scriptures this pattern continues. Two primary traditions inform the shepherd/sheep metaphor. First, Yahweh is described as the shepherd of Israel. Jacob speaks of God as his shepherd (Gen. 48:15) and later uses the imagery again when he prays to the "Mighty One, . . . the Shepherd, the Rock of Israel" (49:24 NIV). The description of Yahweh as shepherd is also found in Ps. 80:1, "Give ear, O Shepherd of Israel, you who lead Joseph like a flock. You who are enthroned upon the cherubim, shine forth." The metaphor of Yahweh as shepherd is also extended by David in Ps. 23: "The LORD is my shepherd." At other times Yahweh is depicted as feeding, gathering, and carrying his flock. In the Moses/exodus tradition, Yahweh leads his people like sheep and guides them through the wilderness like a flock (Ps. 78:52).

Not only is Yahweh portrayed as a shepherd, but also the leaders who guide Israel are considered undershepherds of God's people. According to Gen. 4:2, "Abel was a keeper of sheep." Early in Genesis, the patriarchs are described as shepherds. When Pharaoh asks the brothers of Joseph, "What is your occupation?" they say to Pharaoh, "Your servants are shepherds, as our ancestors were" (47:3 NRSV). In Num. 27:17 Moses prays that God will provide a shepherd for them. Later the psalmist describes the role of Moses: "You led your people like a flock by the hand of Moses and Aaron" (Ps. 77:20). But the most prominent undershepherd in the Hebrew Scriptures is King David.

20. This thesis is similar to Hedrick's work. See Hedrick, "Jesus as Shepherd," 7. The following section is in large part dependent on his work, since to my knowledge it is the most comprehensive treatment of this theme.
21. Homer, *Iliad* 2.474–77.
22. Xenophon, *Memorabilia* 2.1–4.

Since rulers were shepherds in the ANE and the Greco-Roman literature, this stamp on David's past is natural. The first time a reader meets David is as the shepherd of his father's flock, when Samuel comes to Jesse to anoint one of his sons as the future king. After Samuel has gone through Jesse's children, and the Lord has rejected them all, he asks, "Are all your sons here?" And Jesse says, "There remains yet the youngest, but behold, he is keeping the sheep" (1 Sam. 16:11). David is first described as a shepherd. This characterization continues when David is appointed to the service of Saul as a musician in 1 Sam. 16. Saul summons David by sending messengers to Jesse with the request: "Send me David your son, who is with the sheep" (16:19). David's identity as a shepherd also arises a few times in the Goliath narrative (17:15, 34, 40).

This task transforms when David becomes the shepherd of Yahweh's people. The tribal leaders of Israel join together to make David king over their united kingdom. They say, "In times past, when Saul was king over us, it was you who led out and brought in Israel. And the LORD said to you, 'You shall be shepherd of my people Israel'" (2 Sam. 5:1–2). David's activity as a literal shepherd turns into a figurative, military, and national shepherding of Israel. The point is further emphasized when Nathan the prophet gives a promise to David from Yahweh in 2 Sam. 7:5–17.

> Now, therefore, thus you shall say to my servant David, "Thus says the LORD of hosts, I took you from the pasture, from following the sheep, that you should be prince over my people Israel. And I have been with you wherever you went and have cut off all your enemies from before you. And I will make for you a great name, like the name of the great ones of the earth." (2 Sam. 7:8–9)

The terms *rulership* and *shepherding* again cohere, as they do in 2 Sam. 5:2. The legacy of David as a shepherd continues to abide in the memory of Israel. In Ps. 78, amid a long recital of Israel's story, this is what is said of David: the Lord "chose David his servant and took him from the sheepfolds; from following the nursing ewes he brought him to shepherd Jacob his people, Israel his inheritance. With upright heart he shepherded them and guided them with his skillful hand" (Ps. 78:70–72).

In the LXX, Ps. 151 also resumes the tradition of David as the shepherd of his people. David is described as the shepherd in verse 1, and it emphasizes his humility and faithfulness to his father's sheep. Whenever the text slows down to give a summary of David's kingship, it regularly employs the metaphor of a shepherd. According to the Hebrew Scriptures, David is the shepherd-king. In the Prophets, the use of the shepherd/sheep motif continues but is expended mainly in contrast to David and Yahweh (the good shepherds); the prophets castigate those leading the people as false shepherds (see Mic. 5:1–4; Jer. 23:1–6). Ezekiel explores the meaning of the exile, which also includes the hope of a Davidic messiah (Ezek. 34:23–24), and this whole section is notably framed with the most extended use of the shepherd/sheep metaphor.[23]

Jesus as the Davidic Shepherd in Matthew

With this background in mind, it is no surprise that Matthew employs the shepherd motif to further portray the nature of the Davidic messiah. While in exile, Jesus shepherds his people back to Yahweh by embodying the Torah as the wise king. The shepherd imagery is a fundamental vehicle for Matthean Christology. Five Matthean texts (2:1–6; 9:32–38; 15:21–28; 25:31–46; 26:30–35) employ the shepherd/sheep metaphor relative to Jesus's ministry. The first text is found in Matthew's introduction (2:6), while the last one is found in the conclusion (26:31); the theme stretches across the entire narrative. Though these two texts do not describe this ministry during Jesus's exile, they set up and conclude how we are to view Jesus's actions during his deportation.[24] The distinctive themes found in the introduction and conclusion are developed and expanded upon through the rest of Matthew's narrative.

For the sake of space, I will limit this discussion to the explicit references to Jesus as a shepherd, but readers should note that the theme encompasses the Gospel just as the fulfillment quotations bracket large sections of the narrative.[25] The explicit occurrences simply give readers categories for them to interpret the rest of the story.

The Development of the Davidic
Shepherd Motif in Matthew

Matthew	Motif
2:6	The royal shepherd
9:36	The ministering shepherd
15:24	The merciful shepherd
25:31–46	The shepherd-judge
26:31	The sacrificial shepherd

23. Zechariah 9–12 also contains many shepherd/sheep motifs where the good shepherd is contrasted to the existing shepherds who exploit the people.

24. In some ways, we should not divide the actions of Jesus during his ministry in Jerusalem and his ministry in Galilee. In other ways, it enlightens and clarifies what sort of king this Jesus is going to be.

25. Luz (Matthew, 1:162) even says, "The formula quotations are notably frequent in the prologue, because here the evangelist introduces those viewpoints and accents which are important for the whole Gospel and which the reader must keep in mind while perusing the entire Gospel. The formula quotations which are scattered in the rest of the Gospel are then reminders."

THE ROYAL SHEPHERD IN MATTHEW 2:6

The first explicit shepherd reference occurs in Matt. 2:6 and sets up how readers are to engage with the rest of the narrative. It comes in the birth and infancy narrative of chapters 1 and 2. In this larger context Matthew has the chief priests and the scribes answering Herod's question about where the Christ is to be born but also curiously includes what type of messiah he will be (a shepherd). Herod asks where. Matthew gives an answer that includes both *where* and *what kind*. Matthew usually breaks his narrative flow to let his reader know that what just took place fulfills some prophecy. However, this is different. Matthew artfully places the fulfillment quote in the mouths of the actors in his narrative. Even more surprisingly, he puts the fulfillment quote on the lips of those opposed to Jesus. The chief priests and the scribes of the people read the Scriptures and even correctly know "where" the messiah is to be born, but they cannot see the deeper meaning relating to *what kind of king*. They have an understanding of the literal sense of the text but not the *sensus plenior*.

They can point to where the Davidic messiah is to be born, but they can't recognize the messiah. In fact, as the narrative develops, this group will bring the messiah to his death (16:21; 20:18; 26:57; 27:41). The text the chief priests and scribes quote is a double citation, combining Mic. 5:2 (5:1 LXX) and 2 Sam. 5:2. Why does Matthew include the shepherd motif here? At the narrative level, it seems that Matthew desires to further define what type of king Jesus is going to be. He is not only born in the city of David, but he will also be a shepherd and ruler like David.[26] The motif defines, characterizes, and typifies the type of kingship. This is in direct contrast to the current "ruler" (King Herod) they lived under. The combined metaphor of a ruler who shepherds his people would summon messianic and eschatological expectations. As W. D. Davies and Dale Allison note, "To a first-century Jew, a reference to a ruler coming forth to 'shepherd my people Israel' would have conjured up the eschatological expectation of the ingathering of the twelve tribes of Israel (cf. Ezek. 34:4–16; Mic. 5:1–9; Pss. Sol. 17; 4 Ezra 13.34–50; 2 Bar. 77–86), an expectation apparently shared by Matthew (19:28)."[27] The kingdom Solomon's sons split, this wise shepherd will unite.

THE MINISTERING SHEPHERD IN MATTHEW 9:36

Matthew 9:36 is the second text that mentions the shepherd motif. The text reads as follows: "When he saw the crowds, he had compassion for them,

---

26. Heil, "Ezekiel 34," 699–700.
27. Davies and Allison, *Matthew*, 1:243.

because they were harassed and helpless, *like sheep without a shepherd*. Then he said to his disciples, 'The harvest is plentiful, but the laborers are few; therefore pray earnestly to the Lord of the harvest to send out laborers into his harvest'" (Matt. 9:36–38, emphasis added). The verses occur at a transition point, and scholars debate whether they more naturally relate to the previous two chapters (8–9) on the deeds of Jesus or whether they fit better with what follows, the sending out of the twelve disciples in chapter 10. In other words, is 9:36–38 primarily a conclusion to the healing narrative or an introduction to the Mission Discourse? The best solution is that the verses are transitional, both looking back to what precedes and forward to what follows. As Davies and Allison argue, "9:35–10:4 is a door that closes off one room and opens another. Structurally the pericope belongs equally to what comes before and to what comes after (as one door belongs to two rooms)."[28] While this might seem like a pedantic debate, it helps readers understand the role of the shepherd motif in Matthew.

If this section is like a door, it helps us understand the shepherd motif in two ways. First, it points *back* to Jesus's ministry of healing and teaching in chapters 5–9. Chapters 5–9 can be described as the shepherd-king watching his flock.[29] Second, it points *forward* and claims that in the sending out of the disciples, Jesus is still being the shepherd. "The harvest is plentiful, but the laborers are few" (9:37). In many ways, this text covers everything in Matthew from chapter 5 through chapter 10 and probably up through chapter 13. The exiled king is thus reaffirmed as the ministering shepherd.

This expansive reading of shepherd also puts a little more flesh on the bones of what it means for Jesus to be the Davidic shepherd. He heals and teaches the people as the shepherd. His activity indicates both how Jesus will save them from their sins (1:21) and how he will be Immanuel to them (1:23).[30] But not only that. He also authorizes his disciples to be Davidic shepherds in power. As *the* shepherd, he trains and empowers undershepherds. As Willitts notes, connecting this to the sending out of the Twelve points to restoration themes.[31] This text points to the need of the nation and implicitly contrasts Jesus with the current shepherds, who are not doing their job.

---

28. Davies and Allison, *Matthew*, 2:143. Matthew 9:35 closes off the narrative of chaps. 8–9, and the reader is introduced to the second block of instruction, the Mission Discourse in chap. 10. So together, 9:35–38 and 10:1–4 function as a hinge between the passages, introducing readers to the second major discourse.

29. Hence, this is another argument for the Sermon on the Mount to be viewed under the banner of kingship.

30. Heil, "Ezekiel 34," 701.

31. Willitts, *Matthew's Messianic Shepherd-King*, 119.

In Num. 27 Moses passes the leadership baton so that a new generation can take the mantle. Moses asks Yahweh to appoint a man over the congregation "who shall go out before them and come in before them, who shall lead them out and bring them in, that the congregation of the LORD may not be *as sheep that have no shepherd*" (Num. 27:17, emphasis added; see also 1 Kings 22:17; 2 Chron. 18:16). This text is likely in the background for Matthew not only because of the linguistic parallels but also because a new phase is about to be introduced into Jesus's ministry, as in Moses's; the disciples are now to share in the management of the kingdom mission. Moses is concerned that the people will be left leaderless, and Jesus views the situation of the crowd with their current leaders and concludes that they are leaderless. The vacuum needs to be filled by the righteous Davidic shepherd *and* his followers.

THE MERCIFUL SHEPHERD IN MATTHEW 15:24

The third text employing the term "shepherd" is Matt. 15:24. Jesus withdraws to the district of Tyre and Sidon, where a Canaanite woman comes out, crying, "Have mercy on me, O Lord, Son of David; my daughter is severely oppressed by a demon" (15:22). Jesus pretty much ignores her and says, "I was sent only to the lost sheep of the house of Israel" (15:24). She pleads with him again, and Jesus recognizes her faith and heals her daughter (15:28).

Three interesting details occur in this text. First, Jesus describes himself as a shepherd of "the lost sheep of the house of Israel," but it comes in a context where someone calls him the "Son of David." Matthew develops the theme of Jesus as the righteous Davidic shepherd by linking the woman's statement about Jesus being the son of David and Jesus's role as shepherd to Israel and all the nations.[32] Second, the shepherd son of David claims that his mission is to the "lost sheep of the house Israel" (τὰ πρόβατα τὰ ἀπολωλότα οἴκου Ἰσραήλ). Willitts argues that this phrase refers to the northern tribes of Israel.[33] Already Jesus had sent his disciples to the "lost sheep of the house of

32. Identifying Jesus as the "Son of David" in this text opens up the possibility that Matthew could also be alluding to Ezek. 34:23–24, which prophesies that the Lord will set up over them one shepherd, "my servant David." Ezekiel is also famous for the new-covenant passages that say Yahweh will pour out his Spirit on all people. No matter what interpreters decide to do with the allusion, the lost sheep of Israel implies the existence of a leadership crisis. With this shepherd metaphor, Jesus redefines his leadership style and defines his Davidic kingship.

33. Several texts form the background to Jesus's reference to the "lost sheep of . . . Israel" (Num. 27:17; 1 Kings 22:17; 2 Chron. 18:16; Ps. 119:176; Isa. 53:6; Jer. 50:6; Ezek. 24:23–25; 34:5; Zech. 13:7). Jeremiah 50:6 alludes to the theme of people as "lost sheep," and in the context it is the shepherds who have led the people astray and caused them to be lost. Willitts (*Matthew's Messianic Shepherd-King*, 219) argues that "the lost sheep of the house of Israel" refers to the northern tribes of Israel and that the Davidic messiah is going to them. He distinguishes going

Israel" (10:6) and told them to go nowhere among the gentiles or Samaritans. The implication is that when Matthew has Jesus describe both his mission and the disciples, it centers on the reunification of the north and south. This son of David restores and mends the split kingdom by his staff.[34]

Third, Matthew indicates that while Jesus has a priority in his shepherding ministry, it is not exclusive. When the Canaanite woman appeals for mercy, Jesus initially is reluctant, which heightens the tension of the story, but then the son of David shows himself to be the merciful shepherd who has compassion even on gentiles. The shepherd who was sent to the lost sheep of Israel also has compassion on the gentiles who have faith. Although the mission of the son of David is first to the house of Israel, he is also merciful to those who display great faith in Israel's king. Jesus's activity in his exile is not only to restore the unity of Israel; he also welcomes all who are loyal to his kingship. The compassion of the shepherd will eventually lead to trouble.

The Shepherd-Judge in Matthew 25:31–46

The fourth text develops the Matthean motif of Jesus as the shepherd judge (Matt. 25:31–46). The section functions as a conclusion to the eschatological discourse of 24:1–25:46. In the larger context of Matthew, it concludes the formal teaching of Jesus that Matthew has gathered into five large blocks throughout his Gospel. The scene is one of judgment: the Son of Man sits on his throne, gathers all the nations before him, and separates the people into two groups. He places the "sheep" on his right and the "goats" on his left, just as David protected Israel and destroyed its enemies.

The focus of the text is on separation by the king, which is how the passage both begins and ends. In the middle, Matthew details why people have been divided into their respective groups. He combines three metaphors/titles here. Jesus is the Son of Man, the shepherd, and the king. The Son of Man is enthroned to exercise judgment, and he is seated on this glorious throne (25:31) and described as "the king" (25:34), but the king is also the shepherd who both gathers his people and separates/judges those who are against him. The metaphors inform each other. The shepherd is the judge, and the Son of Man is the shepherd.

---

to them from gathering them (8:11–12; 24:30–31). This would be taking the genitive phrase "of the house of Israel" as a partitive genitive (the lost sheep are a subset of Israel), whereas taking it as an epexegetical genitive would indicate that the "lost sheep" refers to the whole nation.

34. Hays (*Echoes of Scripture in the Gospels*, 128–29) notes that the language of "lost sheep" echoes Jer. 50:6–7. Jeremiah 50 is a judgment oracle against Babylon and predicts the return of Israel from exile.

The background to this text may come from Ezekiel's extended meditation on good and evil shepherds in Ezek. 34. The chapter starts with the word of the Lord coming to Ezekiel and telling him to prophesy against the shepherds of Israel because the shepherds have been feeding themselves (34:2). They have not helped the weak, and so the sheep are scattered because they have no shepherd. The Lord pronounces judgment against the shepherds and says he is against them (34:10). Yahweh will rectify the situation by himself searching for his sheep and seeking them out (34:11). He will rescue them from the places in which they have been scattered and gather them together again. "I myself will be the shepherd of my sheep, and I myself will make them lie down, declares the Lord GOD" (34:15). Then in verses 17–19 he turns to his flock and speaks words from which Matthew may be drawing.

> As for you, my flock, thus says the Lord GOD: *Behold, I judge between sheep and sheep, between rams and male goats.* Is it not enough for you to feed on the good pasture, that you must tread down with your feet the rest of your pasture; and to drink of clear water, that you must muddy the rest of the water with your feet? And must my sheep eat what you have trodden with your feet, and drink what you have muddied with your feet? (Ezek. 34:17–19, emphasis added)

The sound of the text is appropriately similar because Jesus is the shepherd who now judges between sheep and goats. However, now the sheep are not limited to the people of Israel but include all the righteous and wise.[35] The text begins by castigating the current shepherds (the leaders of Israel), and then Yahweh pronounces that he will be the shepherd to regather them and feed them. Jesus has come as Yahweh's representative to feed his people (Matt. 2:6), to send out others to teach them and guide them (9:36), and to welcome those not of Israel (15:24–28). But if they reject him, he comes with wrath. He is not only the merciful and ministering shepherd but the shepherd-judge.

THE SACRIFICIAL SHEPHERD IN MATTHEW 26:31

The final shepherd text, Matt. 26:31, is a marked quotation from Zech. 13:7.[36] Contextually, it sits within the passion narrative begun in Matt. 26 and colors the rest of the narrative in shepherd imagery. The opening verses of the chapter set the stage for the arrest and crucifixion of Jesus at the hands of the Jewish leaders, thus becoming an implicit critique of their leadership. The leitmotif of Jerusalem leaders being false shepherds, which starts in chap-

---

35. Heil, "Ezekiel 34," 705.
36. Willitts (*Matthew's Messianic Shepherd-King*, 146) argues that it is a composite quotation from Zech. 13:7 and Ezek. 34:31.

ter 2 with King Herod, comes to a climax here with the sacrificial shepherd enduring all for the sake of his sheep. This last reference to the shepherd is fitting, for the wise shepherd will ultimately gather his sheep through sacrifice (Isa. 53). The text appears as Jesus and the disciples go to the Mount of Olives and wait for Judas to betray Jesus. As they come to the Mount of Olives, Jesus reveals his foreknowledge of the situation. "You will all fall away because of me this night. For it is written, 'I will strike the shepherd, and the sheep of the flock will be scattered.'"

The text functions on several levels. First, it reveals the shepherd protects by his own sacrifice. He guards his flock by giving himself over to the predators.[37] Second, the passage speaks not only of the sacrifice of the shepherd but also of the departure of the sheep. They abandon him when he is struck. At the end of the section, Jesus says, "All this has taken place so that the Scriptures of the prophets might be fulfilled." At that critical point "all the disciples left him and fled" (Matt. 26:56). Third, as Carson notes, the fulfillment quotation shows "that the disciples' rejection, though tragic and irresponsible, does not fall outside of God's sovereign plan."[38] Although the faithful shepherd is rejected, this is the path laid out for the Davidic messiah. Fourth, on the eschatological horizon, Willitts is right to hold that this quote points toward the restoration of Israel. "Zechariah 13:7 is taken from a discrete passage whose limits are 13:7–9. The unit has a poetic design that sets it apart from the previous section and consists of three statements. The first concerns the death of the Shepherd-King (13:7a), the second the scattering of the flock (13:7b) and the third: purification and restoration of the remnant of insignificant ones who remained in the Land (13:7c–9)."[39] Through the sacrifice of the shepherd, Jesus reunites the kingdom. Though he is betrayed and left alone, he still purifies, atones for, and redeems his people.

In this story, Judas and the chief priests and scribes act as a foil to the righteous sacrificial shepherd. In Matt. 27 Judas admits that he has betrayed innocent blood, but the chief priests and the elders don't care because they have captured the shepherd who was disturbing their flock. This story reminds readers of Jonathan, who defends David to Saul and asks his father. "Why then will you sin against innocent blood by killing David without cause?" (1 Sam. 19:5); but Saul continues to pursue David, to end his life. So too Judas

---

37. One might think of David, who offers to sacrifice himself for his sheep. In 2 Sam. 24:17 when he sees the angel of the Lord who is striking the people, David speaks to the Lord and admits that he, not his sheep, has sinned and acted wickedly. So David pleads with the Lord for the angel's hand to be against himself and against his father's house rather than against his sheep.

38. Carson, "Matthew" (1984), 540.

39. Willitts, *Matthew's Messianic Shepherd-King*, 150.

throws the pieces of silver down in the temple, and the chief priests take the money and do not put it in the treasury but buy a field with the money (Matt. 27:6–8).

The text aligns Judas with the elders of the people as worthless shepherds. The quote from Zech. 13:7 provides scriptural warrant for Jesus's announcement that he is both coming to his death and that his disciples will abandon him. In Zechariah, the shepherd whose sheep are scattered "is one of the Judaic kings in the line of David whose rule comes to a violent end in the sixth century BC."[40] But interpreters should also connect Zech. 12:10 to chapter 13. The shepherd who is struck down is also the one "they have pierced."

This sacrificial and struck shepherd is the messianic Davidic king who stays true to his mission while his followers all fall away. His enemies betray innocent blood, and the disciples fall away because of fear: only one shepherd turns the other cheek when he is struck and gathers his sheep. At the end of Matthew's Gospel, Jesus is the only true shepherd left standing. All other people have paid to get rid of him or flee when he is arrested. The shepherd must go to Jerusalem, where he will suffer. The text from Zechariah clarifies that this is the wise righteous shepherd who will be left alone to face the wolves of Jerusalem. David sometimes protected himself, and at other times put his life on the line for his sheep. Jesus is both like and unlike David.

The Davidic Healer

This chapter has argued that Jesus is the "living law," the wise king who embodies the Torah during his exile, as Deuteronomy instructs the later monarchy to do. One of the ways in which the king embodies the law is by being the righteous shepherd. The second way he lives the law is by performing justice and mercy through healing. While this theme only furthers the Davidic shepherding motif, it can also be looked at separately for the sake of clarity. While Mark is more interested in presenting Jesus as an exorcist, Matthew centers on Jesus's healing ministry, while not excluding exorcisms. As Paffenroth notes, "there are nearly three times as many occurrences of the verbs θεραπεύω [to serve, take care of, heal] and ἰάομαι [to heal] in Matthew than in Mark."[41] Additionally, Matthew summarizes Jesus's ministry as one of "teaching" and "healing" (4:23; 9:35).

Matthew also stands apart from the other Gospels in that he links Jesus's healing activity to the title "Son of David." Quite a few texts exist in Matthew

---

40. Blomberg, "Matthew," 91.
41. Paffenroth, "Jesus as Anointed and Healing Son of David," 548.

that tie the Davidic Son to the healing ministry of Jesus. Nine times Matthew refers to Jesus as the "son of David," as against the three Markan times and four Lukan times.[42] Five of the Matthean occurrences associate Jesus and his Davidic ancestry with healings. However, David was not explicitly known as a healer, which leaves interpreters with a question. Why would Matthew connect David with healing? Three reasons arise, two in continuity with the Davidic line, and one in discontinuity.[43]

First, it could be that this puts readers' eyes on the son of David: Solomon. Solomon, the patron of wisdom (1 Kings 4:29–34) and the last great king of a united kingdom, was known as a powerful exorcist and magician.[44] In the Testament of Solomon, David's son is consistently presented as one who subdued demons. This act is regularly connected to Solomon's wisdom (T. Sol. 3.5; 4.11; 22.1, 3). But as already noted, Matthew emphasizes healing, not exorcisms. However, it is also true that Matthew lumps exorcisms under the banner of healings in Matt. 4:23–24 when he summarizes Jesus's ministry as "proclaiming" and "healing" in verse 23. Verse 24 expands on the healing ministry of Jesus and includes "those oppressed by demons." When John the Baptist asks who Jesus is, Jesus claims that he is the one who fulfills Isa. 35:5–6, who heals the blind, deaf, lame, and mute (Matt. 11:2–6). In Isaiah this healer is a Davidic king. Already we have seen how the suffering servant is tied to a Davidic king. Matthew 8:16–17 makes explicit the connection between Jesus's healing ministry and his suffering.[45] In addition, the verses from Isa. 35 exist in a larger section of Isaiah where Yahweh promises Israel that he will turn their desert (exile) into a garden (kingdom). He will bring them back to Zion on a highway, and they shall come in singing (Isa. 35:8–10). Already Isaiah has said this will be accomplished by the Davidic branch who will have the spirit of wisdom on him (Isa. 11:1–2). Therefore, Matthew could stress the healing ministry of Jesus to show that he is the new son of David (Solomon) who has come to unite the kingdom and bring them back from exile.

Second, Wayne Baxter and Young Chae have argued that Matthew's leading warrant for the use of David as a healer stems from Ezek. 34 (a further

---

42. Matthew 1:1; 9:27; 12:23; 15:22; 20:30, 31; 21:9, 15; 22:42; Mark 10:47, 48; 12:25; Luke 1:32; 3:31; 18:38, 39.

43. Novakovic (*Messiah, the Healer of the Sick*) also ties the healing Christ to Matt. 1:21, where she argues that their sins encompass both his atoning death and his healing ministry.

44. See Duling, "Solomon, Exorcism, and the Son of David"; Davies and Allison, *Matthew*, 1:157.

45. "That evening they brought to him many who were oppressed by demons, and he cast out the spirits with a word and healed all who were sick. This was to fulfill what was spoken by the prophet Isaiah: 'He took our illnesses and bore our diseases'" (Matt. 8:16–17).

connection between shepherding and healing).[46] In Ezek. 34 the son of man (Ezekiel) prophesies against the shepherds of Israel because they have not fed the sheep (Ezek. 34:2) and have neglected the flock: "The weak you have not strengthened, the sick you have not healed, the injured you have not bound up, the strayed you have not brought back, the lost you have not sought, and with force and harshness you have ruled them" (34:4).

Overlaying this verse onto Jesus's ministry in Matthew seems to fit as a puzzle piece. The religious leaders of Jesus's day are also guilty of neglecting the sick and marginalized (Matt. 9:10–13), failing to exercise compassion (12:7, 10), and exploiting the flock (23:4, 14). Ezekiel says that the people are "scattered because there was no shepherd" (34:5), and in Matt. 9:36 Jesus observes that the people are "like sheep without a shepherd." Later in Ezek. 34 Yahweh promises that he himself will search for his sheep and seek them out (34:11). This promise is specified as the narrative continues when he says, "I will set over them one shepherd, my servant David, and he shall feed them: he shall feed them and be their shepherd. . . . My servant David shall be prince among them" (34:23–24).

Third, a point of discontinuity also appears in relation to David as a healer. Paffenroth suggests that Jesus is contrasted and not compared with his father David in the healing episodes.[47] Jesus is acclaimed the son of David both when he enters Jerusalem and when he heals the lame and the blind in the temple (21:9, 14–15). In contrast, when David conquers Jerusalem he shuns the lame and the blind. The relevant text is as follows:

> Nevertheless, David took the stronghold of Zion, that is, the city of David. And David said on that day, "Whoever would strike the Jebusites, let him get up the water shaft to attack '*the lame and the blind*,' who are hated by David's soul." Therefore it is said, "*The blind and the lame shall not come into the house*." (2 Sam. 5:7–8, emphasis added)

David therefore excluded the lame and the blind from his house, while Jesus welcomes the lame and the blind.[48] Jesus also calls the scribes and Pharisees blind (15:14; 23:16–19) and excludes them from the temple people. As Hays says, "the textual echoes [to 2 Sam. 5:7–8] both establish the link and, at the same time, hint at Jesus's peaceful reshaping of Israel's messianic

---

46. Baxter, "Healing and the 'Son of David,'" 37. Chae, *Jesus as the Eschatological Davidic Shepherd*.

47. At the beginning of this book I noted how continuity and discontinuity exist together. Paffenroth, "Jesus as Anointed and Healing Son of David," 553.

48. The lame and the blind whom David attacks and does not welcome are Jebusites, who are Canaanites (Gen. 10:15; Josh. 18:16).

hope."[49] Jesus is the greater Davidic healer of whom Ezekiel prophesied. While David showed himself fit to deliver God's people by demonstrating his power over Goliath, Jesus shows himself fit to deliver God's people by demonstrating his power over sickness, the demonic realm, and ceremonial impurity. David shunned those with needs; Jesus welcomes them. The wise king creates order out of chaos, peace in the midst of combat. Now it is time to examine some of the specific Davidic healing texts to further the argument that Jesus acts as the ideal and wise king while in exile.

Blind Men and a Canaanite Woman See

The first text that pairs the healing ministry of Jesus with the title "Son of David" comes near the conclusion of Matthew's first block of Jesus's deeds (9:27–31). Two blind men follow Jesus and cry out, "Have mercy on us, *Son of David*" (9:27, emphasis added). Jesus asks them if they believe he is able to heal them, and they say that they do (9:28). Therefore Jesus touches their eyes and says, "According to your faith be it done to you" (9:30). Then he warns them not to tell anyone about this, but they go "and spread his fame through all that district" (9:31). As noted in the previous section, Matthew frames both the Sermon on the Mount and the healing chapters 8–9 under the banner of the kingdom. Jesus is acting as the king, enacting justice for those whom he meets on his travel ministry.

Most commentators see the miracles in Matt. 8–9 as occurring in three groups of three. In the third group, Jesus heals a ruler's daughter and a woman with a blood discharge (viewed as one story), two blind men, and a demon-possessed man. All of them are social outcasts. The ruler is in some position of power, colluding with the enemy; the woman with the discharge of blood is unclean; the blind men are deemed of little use to society; and the demon-possessed man is a sinner and shunned. Jesus has mercy on all of them. Yet in this block of miracles, only the two blind men explicitly recognize Jesus's royal Davidic status.

Two blind men in 20:29–34 also acknowledge Jesus's kingship. Jesus goes out of Jericho, and two blind men cry out, "Lord, have mercy on us, *Son of David!*" (emphasis added). The crowds rebuke them, but the men keep calling out to Jesus. Jesus takes pity on them and opens their eyes. In both stories Matthew has the blind men acclaiming Jesus's Davidic status. Despite their condition, they recognize and identify Jesus with this specific reference. By placing this phrase on the mouths of blind men, Matthew indicates it takes a

---

49. Hays, *Echoes of Scripture in the Gospels*, 149.

certain kind of sight to see who Jesus is; not like the sight of the chief priest and scribes. It is not physical sight but spiritual sight.[50] They can see past the miracles and recognize that since Jesus is portraying the new David, he is fit to be their king. As David defeated the forces of darkness for Israel, so too Jesus now defeats the powers of darkness that also indwell the people of Israel.

"Outsiders" also recognize Jesus's authority, as in 15:21–28, when a Canaanite woman approaches Jesus and cries out, "Have mercy on me, O Lord, *Son of David*; my daughter is severely oppressed by a demon" (Matt. 15:22, emphasis added). Jesus initially turns a cold shoulder to her, saying that he "was sent only to the lost sheep of the house of Israel" (15:24). But she keeps pleading, and Jesus recognizes her great faith and heals her daughter (15:28). Like the blind men, she has insight into the nature of Jesus. Matthew communicates that while in exile in Galilee, this "son of David" is revealing himself to those who normally would be considered "outside" the kingdom.

These texts are scattered throughout Jesus's exile, and therefore taken together they confirm that the Davidic king redefines the kingdom during his deportation. The kingdom of Israel is for the meek, the blind, the rejected. But Jesus also tells each one he heals that they are not to spread his fame around the region because if they do, people will misconstrue what type of messiah figure he is. The blind men can see, but his fame should not be extolled because Israel would misunderstand Jesus's mission. Blind men and the Canaanite woman are given special intuition that Jesus is a messiah figure in the form of David. If the Jewish leaders hear that this is a Davidic figure, they will become jealous and have certain expectations for this new leader. The time for the inglorious enthronement of Jesus is not yet. That will have to wait until he comes to Jerusalem.[51]

The Children Cry "Hosanna"

In Matt. 21:14–15 the blind and the lame come to Jesus in the temple, and he heals them. While the chief priests and scribes are jealous, the children in the temple cry out, "Hosanna to *the Son of David!*" (emphasis added). "Hosanna" occurs in Ps. 118:25 and is translated as "help" or "save." The term is also used as a shout of praise in Jeremiah 31:7, and although most might conclude that the children are using it in this latter sense, a case could

---

50. Loader ("Son of David") argues that this sight and blindness parallels the blindness of Israel and the sight of gentiles.

51. A second text concerns a similar healing, but the focus is on the crowd. A demon-oppressed man who is blind and mute is brought to Jesus in Matt. 12:22, and Jesus heals the man so that he can speak and see. However, unlike the text in Matt. 9, here the crowd is amazed and asks, "Can this be *the Son of David?*" (12:23, emphasis added).

be made that they are observing his action in the temple and requesting Jesus to save/help them from their current oppressors.[52] In fact, Ps. 118 serves as a liturgy for the Feast of Tabernacles, and verse 26 says, "Blessed is he who comes in the name of the LORD." This image is particularly suited for the Davidic king leading in procession to Yahweh's house. Thus the children may be employing it as a shout of praise and as a request. These two uses of language do not have to be at odds.

The chief priests and scribes are indignant at the children and their employment of language. Clearly, the children's speech is evocative. The juxtaposition between the two groups is evident. "Hosanna," the term the children address to Jesus, annoys the Jewish leaders. *The Jewish nation rejects Jesus as their king, and the children have the eyes to see Jesus as David's heir.* Jesus replies to the chief priests and scribes by affirming what the children have attributed to him. He quotes from Ps. 8:2, saying, "Yes; have you never read, 'Out of the mouth of infants and nursing babies you have prepared praise'?" Readers should be thinking back to the Sermon, where Jesus proclaims, "Blessed are the meek" (Matt. 5:5). Psalm 8 is a hymn of praise to God, who created the universe. Despite their lack of knowledge, even infants praise God; therefore how much more should those who understand the things of God? Jesus picks up this text and uses it in the same way. Even the children can see that Jesus is the son of David; how much more should the chief priests and scribes be praising Jesus as the messiah? As God's acts in creation elicit praise, so should the acts of Jesus in healing people in the temple. As God is the creator of all, Jesus is the royal son of David who through healing re-creates all things. The blind and the lame are made well, and only the children recognize that this is David's heir. During his deportation, the king redefines the kingdom.

As David returned from battle with the Philistines and was met with tambourines, songs of joy, and musical instruments (1 Sam. 18:6), so too Jesus enters his city with the songs of praise on the lips of the people. Yet Saul was jealous that the people were praising David: "Saul was very angry, and this saying displeased him. He said, 'They have ascribed to David ten thousands, and to me they have ascribed thousands, and what more can he have but the kingdom?' And Saul eyed David from that day on" (1 Sam. 18:8–9). The chief priests and the scribes respond in a similar way to what the children shout. "But when the chief priests and the scribes saw the wonderful things that he did, and the children crying out in the temple, 'Hosanna to the Son of David!' they were indignant" (Matt. 21:15).

52. Yet Silva (*NIDNTTE* 5:746) notes that by the time of the NT, "Hosanna" had become a full "cultic cry," like the LXX use of the loanword ἀλληλουϊά, from the Hebrew.

In the flow of Matthew's narrative, what comes to the surface here is the heightened opposition to the son of David. While in chapter 2 Jerusalem is only troubled at the birth of this king, now in chapter 21 the chief priests and the scribes are *indignant*. This is similar to the life of David. After David defeated Goliath, opposition grew toward David in 1 Sam. 18–20. The chief priests and the scribes know their Scriptures and think that the children should not be applying messianic language to this man from Nazareth. But Jesus knows the Scriptures better, and so does Matthew. Matthew flips this scenario on its head and has Jesus quoting another psalm, where the children ascribe praise to their messianic redeemer. The scribes think they know the Scriptures and the nature of the one who is coming. Through his narrative Matthew teaches them that they "know neither the Scriptures nor the power of God" (Matt. 22:29). He is the scribe, teaching them to mine their Scriptures and see that Jesus fulfills all their hopes.

Summary of the Davidic Healer

Though David is not formally known as a healer in his life, there were prophetic hopes expressed by both Isaiah and Ezekiel that a Davidic king would come and heal the nation. This is exactly what this new son of David does while exiled to Galilee. Matthew indicates this by having key people cry out to the "Son of David." They see the relationship between this Jesus and David, even if it is muddy to the current regime. Generally, kingship is evaluated based on the prosperity of its citizens. Evil kings are condemned because their people suffer, and good kings are celebrated because they lead the people into wholeness and security in their land. As David demonstrates compassion to Mephibosheth (2 Sam. 9:6–7), so too Jesus shows kindness to all his covenant people. Now his covenant people are redefined as those who have a new heart. Like Mephibosheth, they will always eat at the king's table. But unlike David, Jesus will also welcome *all* the lame and blind to his new city (2 Sam. 5:7–8). He is like David but also better than David. Matthew is persuaded that Jesus is both like and unlike David, and he reveals this not in the mouths of the religious leaders but in those who would most naturally be outside the kingdom. This is because Matthew exposes what the Davidic king is to do and what sort of kingdom this is to be. His actions do not contradict what kings are to perform, but Jesus performs these actions *for those* whom the religious leaders are neglecting.

Matthew brings the new out of the old. If the religious leaders go back to the prophets and learn not only where this figure is to be born but also what he is to accomplish, then they will see that the Davidic Son will lead the nation not merely in military victory but in personal and communal healing. Jesus expands the kingdom for those outside of Israel. He turns their world upside down, but this does not contradict what the Scriptures say. Rather, it fulfills what the prophets whisper. The righteous branch who is full of wisdom and knowledge rises up; the question for Israel is whether they will recognize this branch or reject it out of fear and jealousy. Matthew uses his scribal techniques on the other side of Jesus's resurrection to show his readers that they need to look harder at their OT texts and also take a hard look at their own hearts. The kingdom is not for those in power but for the humble, the meek, the thirsty.

The Ideal and Wise King

My argument has been that Jesus embodies the law during his exile as the wise king, thus uniting and saving the nation. He fulfills the law not only by being the one to whom the law points but by living it. He internalizes the law, giving the people a true picture of a Torah follower. Jesus therefore comes not only as a teacher but as one who exemplifies his own instruction. Both Hellenistic and OT discourses presented ideal kings as those who epitomized the law. This internalizing of the law would make both the king and the nation wise (Deut. 4:6). The true and wise king lived the Torah (Deut. 17:19; Ps. 1:2).

This "living of the law" can be seen in his *healing* and *shepherding* motifs. As David was known as the shepherd of Israel, so too Jesus holds forth both his staff and a rod. He welcomes, gathers, and draws his sheep to his side, but he also castigates those who will not listen to him. He is the royal shepherd who leads his nation to flourishing rather than attacking them like King Herod (Matt. 2:6); he is the shepherd who teaches and heals, instructing Israel on the law of Christ, and also gives his disciples authority to go out and perform the same tasks (9:36); he is the merciful shepherd, whose mission is first to the lost sheep of the house of Israel (northern Israel) but also the one who will welcome gentiles (15:24); he is the shepherd-judge, who separates the sheep from the goats; finally he is the sacrificial and struck shepherd who lays down his life for his sheep, even as they all turn their backs on him (26:31).

Jesus is also the Davidic healer whom both Isaiah and Ezekiel prophesied would come. The son of David describes his own ministry in the following words: "The blind receive their sight and the lame walk, lepers are cleansed and the deaf hear, and the dead are raised up, and the poor have good news preached to them. And blessed is the one who is not offended by me" (Matt. 11:5–6). Blind men, a Canaanite woman, and children cry out to this son of

David. They have true spiritual sight, while the leaders of Israel stumble over the stumbling stone. Jesus's healing ministry is also put in the vortex of the suffering servant, for as Jesus heals, Matthew claims it fulfills Isa. 53:4: "He took our illness and bore our diseases." Jesus's sacrificial ministry extends beyond the cross, even while culminating on the cross.

This shepherding, healing, and sacrificial ministry of Jesus departs from the labels given to the chief priests and the scribes, who "clothe [them]selves with wool, . . . slaughter the fat ones, but . . . do not feed the sheep" (Ezek. 34:3). They do not strengthen the sick or bind up the injured, but they rule with force and harshness. They even pay to get rid of those who would oppose them. The imagery in Ezek. 34 is similar to Matt. 9:36, where the people are described as "harassed and helpless." The fact that the people in Matthew are described as "harassed and helpless" implies that this condition has been inflicted upon them by a lack of leadership. Jesus must lead and create a new scribal school. Ezekiel castigates the shepherds for their harshness but also tells of a time when God will gather his people through a Davidic messiah who will embody the law by being their shepherd and healer.

Conclusion

While some deny or at least question that the Gospel writers portray Jesus as the Davidic messiah, I find this conclusion quite unconvincing. David's life is woven into the garments of Jesus's life. Matthew does this not just through fulfillment quotations but also through plot, characterization, geographical movement, cities, and even numbers. The previous chapter looked at the journey of the Davidic king, while this chapter examined his actions while in Galilee. David's life looms large for Matthew. Although the Davidic allusions are diverse, they can all be gathered under the banner of the messianic Davidic king who unites the kingdom, brings the people back from exile, establishes the temple, installs the new covenant, and instructs his people in wisdom. The king is to embody the Torah, heal the nation, rebuild the temple, shepherd the flock, and be enthroned in the city of Jerusalem. "The desire for wisdom leads to a kingdom" (Wis. 6:20).[53] Matthew grasps each of these themes and fastens them to the life of Jesus. He tells a shadow story.

But Matthew, as the wise scribe, also subverts these themes in Jesus's life. Rather than rebuilding the temple, he pronounces its destruction. Rather than affirming the Jewish leader's interpretation of the law, he clarifies that they

---

53. The text continues by saying, "Therefore if you delight in thrones and scepters, O monarchs over the peoples, honor wisdom, so that you may reign forever" (Wis. 6:21).

are neglecting justice and mercy. Rather than entering the city as a warrior, he arrives humbly. Rather than being enthroned and worshiped, he is mocked and crucified. In one way, these things are old; in another they are new. Brandon Crowe rightly says that fulfillment reverses "the sinful trajectories of Israel's history by the obedience of the messianic king, which was necessary for the eschatological blessings to accrue to the messianic community."[54] Fulfillment does not mean absolute continuity but also includes reversal. Just as an acorn stands in continuity and discontinuity with an oak tree, so too Jesus is the new and old fulfillment of David. Jesus is the apocalyptic Davidic messiah who is both the new king and the king of old.

In 2 Sam. 7 David is given a promise that one of his children will sit on the throne forever. Jesus is that heir who will sit on the throne forever. He acts like David in his life, and he dies as a type of David. The journey to his throne runs through the cross because he needs to die for his people. The king is to save his people from their enemies, and their enemies are both the spiritual forces waging war against them and the darkness arising from within their own hearts. The Jewish leaders are a symbol of this rejection for Matthew. Through David's life we understand Jesus's life, and through Jesus's life we see David's life fulfilled. Matthew is telling his readers to look harder and more closely at Jesus. There is a way to read Jesus's life and miss many of the echoes reverberating back into Israel's past. Matthew's narrative embosses some of these allusions with clarity, but he also is sometimes subtle in his approach. He does this because he shows his cards at the beginning and expects readers to perk up as he moves along.

Matthew's method reminds me of the scene in the movie *The Lion King* when Rafiki tracks down Simba.[55] Simba tells Rafiki to go away because he doesn't even know who he is. But Rafiki replies, "I sure do, you're Mufasa's boy." Simba replies, "Well, my father is dead." But Rafiki says, "No, he is alive!" He takes him on this wild reckless chase through the woods, brings him to a small pond, and instructs Simba to look into the water. Simba slowly does and says, "That's not my father; that's just my reflection." Rafiki says, "Look harder. . . . You see, he lives in you."

In a similar way, Matthew takes his readers on a journey through Jesus's life, yet all the while we are looking at this figure who looks like David. He tells the Jews to "look harder." See Jesus's life. They too have forgotten who he is, who his father is. Matthew tells his readers, "This is David's boy!" They have forgotten who David was, and they need to return to the Scriptures. They

---

54. Crowe, "Fulfillment in Matthew," 48.
55. *The Lion King* (Burbank, CA: Walt Disney Pictures, 1994).

need to remember who David was, that this Jesus is David's son, the one true wise king. David lives through Jesus. Like Simba, they need to "see," and so Matthew has us peer into the pool so that we all can see the reflection with a crown on his head. He does not provide a simple, unadorned historical portrait of Jesus. No, he interprets each detail of Jesus's life and looks to the past to show his readers that Jesus is the Davidic messiah.

5

Jesus and the Mosaic Exodus

No NT author develops the portrait of Jesus as the new Moses quite like Matthew.[1] My argument throughout this book is that Matthew is the *discipled scribe* who has learned from his teacher of wisdom to bring out treasures new and old. Part of the way he does this is through shadow stories: weaving the Hebrew Scriptures into his narrative as a seamstress would carefully and skillfully sew up a dress. While other NT writers have similar methods, Matthew stands above the rest in this respect.[2] He clothes Jesus in the apparel of the old and presents his life in a way that invites comparison with those who came before him. As Matthew opens his treasure chest of wisdom, he continues the comparison of Jesus to OT events by linking Jesus figures associated with specific events.

As in the previous two chapters, rather than merely focusing on the occurrences of the name "Moses" in the text, my approach will be to look at the *narrative* of Matthew and the *narrative* of Moses. But for some, questions about Jesus as a new Moses still remain.[3] Questions such as "Does this

---

1. See the excellent argument by Allison as well as the other studies that contain reflections on Moses: Allison, *New Moses*; Baxter, "Mosaic Imagery"; R. Brown, *Birth of the Messiah*; Teeple, *Mosaic Eschatological Prophet*; Pitre, *Jesus and the Last Supper*, 53–443; Hays, *Echoes of Scripture in the Gospels*, 143–45.

2. By "stands above" I do not mean that his presentation is superior. See chap. 1 for the three reasons I give for Matthew uniquely embodying this technique. John, Hebrews, and Revelation are the other books of the NT filled with OT quotes or allusions.

3. Witherington (*Jesus the Sage*, 350) says that the Jesus-as-Moses-figure motif is minor at best in Matthew because Jesus is portrayed more as a messianic king, Wisdom, and Son

Mosaic typology even exist, or have scholars begun to insert into the text what they are searching for?"[4] To the surprise of some, Jesus in Matthew is never directly given a title such as "the prophet like Moses" or even "the new Moses." Although Moses is explicitly mentioned only seven times in five passages in Matthew (8:4; 17:3–4; 19:7–8; 22:24; 23:2), I will argue that the Mosaic imagery is thickly laced throughout the Gospel and that it would be a mistake to observe only the explicit occurrences of Moses's name.

Take Matt. 19:7, for example. In this account the Pharisees come to Jesus, questioning him about divorce. Moses enters the dialogue when the Pharisees ask, "Why then did Moses command . . . ?" While we can learn a great deal about the Pharisees, their intentions, and what they thought of Moses through this text, the passage provides very little for reconstructing Jesus as the new Moses. It gives us some information, but to build a case on the explicit references to Moses doesn't respect the more narratival and sometimes elusive nature of Matthew's narrative. In the words of Gowler, there is a difference between "direct definition" and "indirect presentation" within a narrative. Matthew more commonly uses "indirect presentation" through the lens of speech, action, external appearance, environment, and comparison/contrast.[5] It is not only the *facts* but also the *form* of the Gospel that contains Matthew's witness to the messiah.

Matthew can give a more indirect presentation because careful readers of the Jewish Scriptures would have already been waiting for the new Moses. Two foundations support this. First, in Deuteronomy God promises the coming of a prophet like Moses.[6]

> The LORD your God will raise up for you a prophet like me from among you, from your brothers—it is to him you shall listen—just as you desired of the LORD your God at Horeb on the day of the assembly, when you said, "Let me not hear again the voice of the LORD my God or see this great fire any more, lest I die." And the LORD said to me, "They are right in what they have spoken. I will raise up for them a prophet like you from among their brothers. And I will put my words in his mouth, and he shall speak to them all that I command him." (Deut. 18:15–18)

---

of God. But why put these things at odds? Witherington seems to avoid subtle connections to Moses in Matthew but highlights subtle connections to Jesus as a wisdom teacher and sage.

4. Hay ("Moses through New Testament Spectacles," 245) says, "Thus we find many claims that Moses bears witness to Jesus' glory but very few that Jesus is like Moses. The latter idea may have appealed to some early Christians, and certain New Testament passages may have been shaped to oppose it."

5. See Gowler, *Host, Guest, Enemy, and Friend,* 72.

6. Wisdom 10:16 says that wisdom "entered the soul of a servant of the Lord, and withstood dread kings with wonders and signs." In context, "servant" refers to Moses.

The second foundation for the biblical hope of a new Moses is that the future age of salvation is molded in terms of the deliverance of Israel from Egypt. Redemption and exodus are the main terms to identify Jesus as the new Moses. Isaiah speaks of a future salvation in the imagery of a new exodus.

> "I am the LORD, your Holy One, the Creator of Israel, your King." Thus says the LORD, who makes a way in the sea, a path in the mighty waters, who brings forth chariot and horse, army and warrior; they lie down, they cannot rise, they are extinguished, quenched like a wick: "Remember not the former things, nor consider the things of old. Behold, I am doing a new thing; now it springs forth, do you not perceive it? I will make a way in the wilderness and rivers in the desert." (Isa. 43:15–19)

Other prophetic writings continue this theme. In Hosea, Yahweh promises to bring Israel out "into the wilderness" so that the people will return to him as when they "came out of the land of Egypt" (Hosea 2:14–15). Jeremiah says the future deliverer will come who will bring them out of the land of Egypt. "Therefore, behold, the days are coming, declares the LORD, when they shall no longer say, 'As the LORD lives who brought up the people of Israel out of the land of Egypt'" (Jer. 23:7). Micah says restoration will be modeled after the exodus (7:14–15).

These two foundations interconnect. The identity of Jesus as the new Moses and the shape of salvation as a new exodus cannot be estranged. Putting these two foundations together, we can say in advance: *Matthew portrays Jesus as the new Moses who leads his people on the new exodus.* While many focus only on Jesus's relationship to Moses as the new prophet, Matthew gives a more expansive narrative view. Jesus has authority like Moses as a prophet, mediator, teacher, redeemer, and miracle worker.[7] These roles don't need to be put at odds but are brought into coherence by exodus themes and the establishment of a new covenant.[8] Matthew renders Jesus as like Moses in that he is

1. a redeemer who is preserved (Matt. 1–2),

2. a prophet who delivers the new Torah (all of the Matthean discourses),

7. Kirk (*Man Attested by God*, 452) notes the following, which aligns with my view of not focusing on Moses as just a prophet: "Although scripturally Moses is remembered as the great prophet and David as the great king, the lines between prophet and king were blurred at times in the history of interpretation, Moses being depicted as a king (cf. Philo, *Mos.* 1.155–58; Ezek. Trag. 68–89) and David being referred to as a prophet (e.g., Acts 2:30). Both figures were also said to be taken from shepherding sheep in order to fill their roles as leaders of God's people (Exod. 3:1; 1 Sam. 16:11–12; 17:15)."

8. Another foundation not mentioned here is the expectation of a new Moses in terms of a "servant." Pitre, *Jesus and the Last Supper*, 60.

3. a miracle worker who redeems his people (all of the Matthean narratives),
4. a mediator who meets with God and shows the goal of the law (the transfiguration),
5. a paterfamilias who explains the terms of the new covenant (the Last Supper), and
6. a leader who instructs his people what to do when they enter the land (the Great Commission).

Jesus is like Moses in many respects, but the discipled scribe's goal in comparing Jesus to Moses is to show how Jesus escorts his people through new waters and liberates them through his death. According to one text in the Dead Sea Scrolls, the coming of the eschatological prophet will coincide with the coming of a new priest and a new king.[9] In this way the Davidic messiah, the new Moses, the coming kingdom, and the eschatological exodus cannot be disjointed, but they can be distinguished.

A Redeemer Who Is Preserved

Matthew wastes little time before he brings Moses into the picture.[10] The story of Jesus's birth echoes Moses's birth and paints Jesus as the redeemer-king. Yet the comparison comes not in the form of a great act of Moses or of Jesus rescuing his people but a preserving act of God. Yahweh controls every detail in the life of both these figures; he sustains their lives and prepares the way for them to lead the people through the water. Even before Jesus is able to act on his own, the events surrounding his life have a strong sense of déjà vu. In Matt. 2, Jesus is born in a land where a jealous and anxious king resides. "Now after Jesus was born in Bethlehem of Judea in the days of Herod the king" (2:1). When Herod hears from the wise men about this Jewish king, he and all of Jerusalem are troubled (ἐταράχθη, 2:3). Herod proceeds to kill the children in Bethlehem to stamp out this upstart king.

Like many of Matthew's stories, this narrative echoes a previous story, Moses's infancy. As Jesus is born under the power of a foreign king, so too

9. 1QS IX, 9–11: "They should not depart from any counsel of the law in order to walk in complete stubbornness of their heart, but instead shall be ruled by the first directives which the men of the Community began to be taught, until the prophet arrives, and the Messiahs of Aaron and Israel" (*DSSSE* 1:91, 93).

10. Crowe ("Song of Moses") even argues that Matt. 1:20 draws from Deut. 32:18 and the Song of Moses to show that Israel fails to be the faithful son of God, while Jesus is the obedient Son.

was Moses: "Now there arose a new king over Egypt, who did not know Joseph" (Exod. 1:8). When the Egyptians saw Israel increasing, they decided to act shrewdly with them: they made them work harder. When that failed, they told the Hebrew midwives to kill any son born to the Hebrew women (Exod. 1:16). However, the midwives feared God (like the wise men from the east) and did not do as the king of Egypt commanded them. The king of Egypt discovered their treachery and told them to cast every male newborn into the Nile. Into these circumstances, Moses was born.

The parallels between Moses's birth and Jesus's birth are unmistakable and not coincidental. Both are born as helpless children in a doomed home and under a foreign power. Both kings (Pharaoh is labeled as "king" in Exod. 1:15, 17, 18) seek to kill male Hebrew children who threaten to upset the balance of power in the nation.[11] Both stories show the persecution and preservation of God's people. Both Moses's and Jesus's family are told by God to return to the land, and both stories display how God sovereignly preserves his chosen one in the most unlikely of circumstances. Matthew portrays Herod the Great as an evil and paranoid ruler, much like Pharaoh.

God preserves his redeemers in the midst of the persecution because he has greater plans for them. They both travel through water to enter into the land where they will do their ministry. Both stories also conclude with the Lord telling them to return to their land. In Exod. 4:19 the Lord says to Moses in Midian, "Go back to Egypt, for all the men who were seeking your life are dead [τεθνήκασιν γὰρ πάντες οἱ ζητοῦντές σου τὴν ψυχήν]." In Matt. 2:20 the Lord appears to Joseph in a dream and says, "Rise, take the child and his mother and go to the land of Israel, for those who sought the child's life are dead [τεθνήκασιν γὰρ οἱ ζητοῦντες τὴν ψυχὴν τοῦ παιδίου]." The language here is the same. As Moses is commanded to return, so also Jesus's family, after fleeing to Egypt, is told to return. Matthew's description of Jesus's birth is wrapped in the robes of Moses's birth.

Implications for Our Reading

Moses's birth narrative informs Matthew's narrative, and Matthew's birth narrative informs Exod. 1–2. Matthew exemplifies how to read both forward and backward, prospectively and retrospectively. Both stories are theological portraits of the war between the kings of the earth and the king of heaven. The battle between Moses and Pharaoh is a battle of kingship. When Exod.

---

11. Philo himself repeatedly emphasizes the kingly nature of Pharaoh (*Mos.* 1.8, 10, 13, 15, etc.).

1–2 is read in the silhouette of Matt. 1–2, then the kingly nature of both Pharaoh and Moses comes to the forefront.

Although Moses is not explicitly called a king (and in one sense the king of heaven is warring with the king of the earth), there are indications in Moses's early life that he is to be read in the line of his forefathers. His forefathers Adam, Abraham, Isaac, Jacob, and Judah are all presented as kings. As the narrative continues, we read of Moses taking Zipporah as his wife, whom he meets at the well (Exod. 2:17). This is similar to how Jacob meets Rachel (Gen. 29:2–14) and how Isaac's wife, Rebekah, is found (24:10–28). As Sailhamer notes, these repeated patterns should cause us to link these texts and tie Moses to his kingly forefathers.[12] Thus, when the early life of Moses is read in light of Matt. 2, the battle of the kings comes to full force.[13]

While one king seeks destruction, the preserved king redeems his people (Matt. 1:21). The vocation of the king is the salvation of his people. Pharaoh's murder of Hebrew children is meant not merely to provide fodder for storybook Bibles but to show the difference between a redeemer who comes to serve and a redeemer who comes to be served. Pharaoh is a typological picture of all those who war against the offspring of the woman. Jesus's birth is presented in the form of Moses's infancy story to enable readers to see him as their new redeemer, their new Moses, who will bring them on the new exodus. As Moses is born under a foreign king and with little hope of redemption, so too Jesus is born under a foreign king and has little hope for a prosperous life. But Moses ends up leading the people out of Egypt in the most unexpected way, and Jesus will also lead the people out of slavery.[14]

If readers fail to see the Moses insinuations, they might read this story at a mere historical level: Jesus is born, and then he must leave his land to be spared. But when the Moses traditions come to life, then the readers' viewpoint expands. This is not simply about Jesus being rescued but about *the*

---

12. Sailhamer, *Pentateuch as Narrative*, 244.

13. Philo himself reads the Moses story in such a way. After Moses has killed the Egyptian for persecuting his people, Philo notes, the Egyptian authorities plant suspicion in the mind of the king, saying that Moses is plotting to deprive him of the kingdom: "He will strip you of your crown. He has no humble designs or notions. . . . He is eager for the kingdom before his time" (Philo, *Mos.* 1.46). Philo reads the story of Moses as an attack on the kingship of Pharaoh. This could be in part because Matthew's narrative has filled in the holes of Moses's story to make it sound as if Philo has read Matthew here! The connection between Pharaoh and Herod the Great reveals more about Pharaoh than the first reading. Although this reading is seminal to the OT text itself, it is not brought into prominence until Matthew's infancy story is laid on top of Moses's infancy story.

14. The location of Egypt as a place of refuge is both new and old. Jesus must flee to Egypt as Israel did, but Herod has also come like Egypt, which persecuted Israel. Leithart, *Jesus as Israel*, 69.

rescuer. The redeemer-king is spared so that he may lead God's people out of slavery. The Mosaic imagery is employed in service of a larger purpose; that purpose is freedom. God places a sanctuary around both of these figures because he cares for his people and has promised to rescue them. Their miniature safeguarding stories seal a larger coming redemption. God has sworn to liberate his people, and he plans to do this through a leader. The Mosaic imagery and the new exodus coincide.

Once the Mosaic imagery is lit, the burning bush of Moses shines brightly. Matthew's method here casts the narrative structure as an echo rather than using explicit fulfillment quotations. Thus, in Jesus's birth Matthew is simultaneously obvious and deft with his comparisons. He echoes multiple stories at once.[15] The story of Jesus's birth takes up a mere twenty-three verses but is in fulfillment of four prophets, and also of the Moses narrative (and probably more). Matthew does not limit Jesus's story to only one OT referent or prophecy: he weaves them all together into a beautiful whole. This is because he perceives the entire OT as one unified story that can be stitched together. The cornerstone on which this unity is built is the messiah. If it is not a unified story about Jesus, then his method would be madness. As it stands, it is art.

The Prophet Who Fulfills the Torah

In the infancy narrative, Matthew depicts Jesus as the redeemer-king, whose life is spared like Moses so that he can lead them on the new exodus. While Matthew presents Jesus like Moses in many respects, this does not mean the typical image of Jesus as the prophet-teacher like Moses takes a back seat. Matthew insists that Jesus be viewed as the teacher-prophet like Moses. For Matthew, in fact, the descriptions of Jesus as redeemer and prophet don't have to be at odds. They interpret each other, and to artificially separate them does damage to our understanding of how they interlace. The redeemer can only redeem because he instructs people in how they are to live. The teacher-prophet teaches so that he can redeem them. The goal or purpose of bringing

---

15. While Matthew is known for his explicit fulfillment formulas, in this example he is more subtle in his presentation of Jesus as a Moses figure. Some readers might miss this echo and focus mainly on the overt reference to the OT in this section. For the story is also said to be in fulfillment of Micah (Matt. 2:6), Hosea (Matt. 2:15), Jeremiah (Matt. 2:18), and Isaiah (Matt. 2:23). It is surprising to some, however, that Matthew says nothing about this being a fulfillment of the Moses infancy narrative. That is why some scholars still cast cold water on the fire of Mosaic imagery in this narrative. However, this seems to be a hermeneutical presupposition more than a close reading of the text. It falls under the assumption that Matthew can only allude to intertexts in an explicit way. Few throughout history have read the Bible in such a way.

the people out of Egypt is so that they can live in wisdom and worship under the ruling hand of Yahweh: to do this they need the law (Ezra 7:25–26). At the beginning of Proverbs, Lady Wisdom stands in the streets speaking both as a prophet and teacher (Prov. 1:20–33).[16] Law, exodus, and wisdom are therefore allied. Moses stands as the mediator of the Torah, delivering and applying the law to the people. Jesus, in the same way, teaches the Torah so that the people will no longer live under slavery to sin, flesh, and death.

If there is any Gospel that emphasizes the prophetic or teaching function of Jesus, it is Matthew. Matthew shortens the busy activity of Mark's Jesus to fill about half of his Gospel. Another quarter of his Gospel, on the teaching of Jesus, he shares with Luke. The remaining quarter of the material is distinct to Matthew and focuses on the teaching of Jesus. Matthew divides his Gospel into narrative and discourse sections, each of the five having a distinct theme.

Matthew's Discourses

Chapters	Theme
5–7	Blessings, entering the kingdom
10	Mission Discourse
13	Parables of the kingdom
18	Community discourse
23–25	Woes, coming kingdom

The point here is clear: Moses is dubbed the teacher of Israel; similarly, Matthew gathers Jesus's teaching into a large block, paralleling him with the teacher of Israel. While much could be said about Jesus as the teacher like Moses, I will concentrate on (1) the Sermon on the Mount's introduction, (2) the key paragraph in Matt. 5:17–20, (3) the true intention of the law in Matt. 5:21–48, and finally (4) Matt. 11:28–30, where Jesus tells his hearers to take his yoke. These verses succinctly explain Jesus's relationship to the Torah as the new prophet like Moses.

While it is easy to become distracted amid the details of Jesus's relationship to the law, readers must remember to connect it with the new exodus. Confirming this connection is the plot that comes before the Sermon, which gives the same sequence as Exodus.

Exodus	Slaughter of infants	Return of hero	Passage through water	Temptation	Mountain of lawgiving
Matthew	Slaughter of infants	Return of hero	Passage through water	Temptation	Mountain of lawgiving

16. See Deutsch, *Lady Wisdom*, 18–20.

The upshot of this is that the Mosaic parallels should be considered together, not in isolation from each other. By virtue of their order and relatedness, the presentation develops a figural sequence that should inform how one reads the Sermon. Not only do the allusions and citations echo the Tanak, but the plot of Jesus recapitulates the plot of Moses.

Setting Up the Sermon

Matthew does two interesting things to set up the Sermon on the Mount to portray Jesus as the new Moses. First, just prior to the Sermon, in Matt. 4:12–17, there is an important transition from John the Baptist to Jesus. Jesus hears that John the Baptist has been thrown into prison. The significance of John's imprisonment can hardly be overestimated. Matthew 3 portrays John as an OT prophet, yet John himself prophesies that one greater than he is about to come (3:11–12). Matthew immediately identifies Jesus, through the account of his baptism, as the one who is greater than John (3:13–17). Readers should thus be attuned to the sequence of Matt. 4 into Matt. 5: John, the OT prophet, is arrested and his ministry ends; only at that point does Jesus begin his own ministry. Something important has ended, and something even more important has begun.[17] John is the *last* of the OT prophets (11:13–14), and when he passes from the scene, an eschatologically new era commences. Now *the Prophet* has come, and he is about to give his first teaching.

The second part of the introduction to the Sermon deserving attention is the first verse of chapter 5. Matthew, in merely one verse, gives three hints that Jesus is the new Moses. To set up the Sermon, he makes sure the reader is thinking about Sinai and the prophet Moses. First, the words "he went up on the mountain" (ἀνέβη εἰς τὸ ὄρος) are a verbatim quotation of Exod. 19:3 (ἀνέβη εἰς τὸ ὄρος), which describes Moses as ascending Mount Sinai to receive the law. As others have noted, this particular phrase occurs only three times in the Greek OT. Each of the three times it is in reference to Moses's ascent of Sinai (Exod. 19:3; 24:18; 34:4).

Second, Matthew describes Sinai as "the" mountain (τὸ ὄρος). Matthew usually does not use a definite article when referring to a mountain unless a mountain is mentioned in the preceding context (Matt. 8:1; 17:9). This would be called the anaphoric use of the article. But in 5:1 no immediately preceding mountain is mentioned. This indicates it is a par excellence use of the article (identifying someone or something in a class of their own). Matthew invites a comparison with the most prominent mount in the OT.

---

17. These observations come from Jonathan Pennington's teaching notes if I recall correctly.

Finally, Matthew describes Jesus as sitting down to teach. This recalls Moses's stance when he receives God's law on Mount Sinai. Although the verb in the Hebrew is debated, references in the Talmud show that Jewish interpreters regarded Deut. 9:9 as meaning that Moses sat down on the mountain. All three of these details place the Sermon under the lens of Sinai. Unfortunately, many note these opening Mosaic parallels and then stop, but the parallels continue throughout the Sermon. Matthew's point seems to be to connect the law of the Torah with the law of the new covenant. Jesus delivers the new-covenant teaching as the new Moses.

Fulfilling the Law

I agree with many who argue that the central verses of the Sermon come in 5:17–20. In the previous chapter, we examined these verses under the rubric of royalty; here we will peruse them with a prophetic lens. These verses certainly provide rich reflection on how Matthew intermingles the new and the old and how the new eschatological prophet stands at the center of the turn of the ages. If these are the central verses, then the Sermon is all about how the prophet interacts with the Torah. In other words, the Sermon presents Jesus as the new Moses. However, that does not make the interpretation any easier. The compactness of 5:17–20 is at once its power and its difficulty:[18]

> Do not think that I have come to abolish the Law or the Prophets; I have not come to abolish them but to fulfill them. For truly, I say to you, until heaven and earth pass away, not an iota, not a dot, will pass from the Law until all is accomplished. Therefore whoever relaxes one of the least of these commandments and teaches others to do the same will be called least in the kingdom of heaven, but whoever does them and teaches them will be called great in the kingdom of heaven. For I tell you, unless your righteousness exceeds that of the scribes and Pharisees, you will never enter the kingdom of heaven.

The central point is that Jesus has come to fulfill the law.[19] The tension between the new and the old is illustrated and encapsulated in this word "fulfill." France, for instance, calls fulfillment "the essential key to all Matthew's theology."[20] Jesus as a teacher of wisdom affirms the message of Ecclesiastes: "All has been heard. Fear God and keep his commandments" (12:13). As Davies and Allison say, this paragraph anticipates two misunderstandings:

18. Pennington, *Sermon on the Mount*, 171.
19. Moo ("Jesus and the Authority of the Mosaic Law") argues that this perspective can be found in all three Synoptic Gospels.
20. France, *Gospel of Matthew*, 38.

(1) that Jesus came to set aside the law, and (2) that Jesus simply came to say that the law continues in the same way. Jesus did not come to abrogate the law nor to simply affirm it; he came to fulfill it. One can view this as a spectrum of misunderstandings, with the middle as the message:

Abrogated	Fulfilled	Affirmed

The Law and the Prophets are not set aside but completed. Another way to put this is that the Law and the Prophets have found their telos (end, goal, purpose) in Jesus. As Banks says, "It is not so much Jesus' stance towards the Law that he [Matthew] is concerned to depict: it is how the Law stands with regard to him, as the one who brings it to fulfillment and to whom all attention must now be directed."[21] The major point here is that in the Sermon Jesus affirms the validity of the law through the word "fulfillment" as the new prophet brings his people on the new exodus. Clarity concerning 5:17–20 comes from examining 5:21–48, where Jesus explains in more detail the implications of his fulfilling the law.

The True Intention of the Law

The Sermon continues by fleshing out Jesus's statement in Matt. 5:17–20 with more specific comments on the law. As the teacher, Jesus gives not merely proverbial esoteric statements but examples illustrating and clarifying what he means. Yet many interpreters have still been confused by what follows in 5:21–48. Ridderbos regards these antitheses as more detailed expositions of the law.[22] Meier holds that Jesus clearly abrogates the commandments of the OT in some instances.[23] Strecker says that the antitheses largely replace the demands of the OT by way of new regulations.[24] W. Davies claims, "We cannot speak of the Law being annulled in the antitheses, but only of its being intensified in its demand, or reinterpreted in a higher key."[25] Allison even asserts, "It does not surprise when 5:21–48 goes beyond the letter of the law to demand more."[26]

These views initially seem right, considering that six times Jesus says, "You have heard it was said. . . . But I say to you."[27] Even the innocent title

21. Banks, *Jesus and the Law*, 226.

22. Ridderbos, *The Coming Kingdom*, 299.

23. Meier, *Law and History in Matthew's Gospel*, 135.

24. Strecker, *Der Weg der Gerechtigkeit*, 146.

25. W. Davies, *Sermon on the Mount*, 29.

26. Allison, *New Moses*, 183.

27. But as Loader (*Jesus' Attitude towards the Law*, 173) says, "Thus Jesus' words in the antithesis, 'but I tell you,' do not set Jesus in competition with God (or Moses), but express

of "antithesis" tilts toward understanding Jesus as going beyond the law. Glancing at what was said before and seeing what Jesus said seem to point to an intensification of the law.

- Moses forbids murder (Matt. 5:21), but Jesus forbids anger (5:22).
- Moses condemns the adulterous act (5:27), but Jesus condemns the adulterous thought (5:28).
- Moses permits divorce (5:31), but Jesus restricts this permission (5:32).
- Moses gives rules for taking oaths (5:33), but Jesus rules that oaths should not be taken at all (5:34).
- Moses declares the precept "eye for eye, tooth for tooth" (5:38), but Jesus denies the precept's application to personal disputes (5:39).
- Moses requires love of neighbor (5:43), but Jesus also requires love of the enemy (5:44).

While the proposal that Jesus extends or intensifies the law is attractive, if this section (5:21–48) is read in light of its preamble (5:17–20), then the indication is that these statements are not overturning the Torah but fulfilling it—or showing the law's true intention.

The clue lies in the preamble. Jesus does not add laws, or even deepen them, but recovers what God has always required in the law from of old. However, this does not mean nothing new is to be found. There is a sense of newness, but newness understood rightly. Jesus is now the prophet who is the arbiter of the truth of God (e.g., 7:24, 29) because no other prophet could say "But I say to you" in response to Torah without eyebrows being raised. Jesus rebuts a wrong interpretation of the Torah and supplies the reader with wisdom.[28] A newness exists, but it also has continuity with the past. Each statement that Jesus delivers in this section can be appreciated in this way.

When Jesus compares murder to anger in 5:21–26, he shows that the intention of the law is not merely to prevent murder but also to prohibit selfish anger and serve as a stimulus for reconciliation. "You have heard that it was said to those of old, 'You shall not murder; and whoever murders will be liable to judgment.' But I say to you that everyone who is angry with his brother will be liable to judgment; whoever insults his brother will be liable to the

---

the authority which belongs to the divinely created Son of God, Israel's Messiah, the one who will come as the world's judge. He comes not to abolish, but to uphold and expound Torah on the basis of the authority which is his."

28. Longman (*Fear of the Lord Is Wisdom*, 123) points out how wisdom comes through tradition, but tradition can also be corrupted.

council; and whoever says, 'You fool!' will be liable to the hell of fire" (Matt. 5:21–22). The intent of this law, even in the Torah, is not merely to prevent murder but also to warn the people against anger, insults, and disunity. It is to be a stimulus for love, so Jesus points them back to the law and says, "This is what it always meant, but I as the messiah needed to show you how." Verse 23 confirms this interpretation, for it makes little sense for Jesus to go beyond the law and then immediately follow it up by an example where one is observing the law. "If you are offering your gift at the altar . . ." Like any law presented to humans, there is a tendency for us to twist it to fit our likings until the purpose of the law is entirely lost. Jesus stands up as the new Moses and does not intensify the law but returns to the original intention of the law.

In a similar way, the prohibition against adultery is still in force (Matt. 5:27–30), but Jesus gets to the heart of the matter. "But I say to you that everyone who looks at a woman with lustful intent has already committed adultery with her in his heart" (5:28). He condemns not only adultery but also what leads to adultery—adulterous thoughts. This was the intention of the law the entire time, but the heart of the matter needed to be spelled out. Matthew's words on divorce are more difficult: "It was also said, 'Whoever divorces his wife, let him give her a certificate of divorce.' But I say to you that everyone who divorces his wife, except on the ground of sexual immorality, makes her commit adultery, and whoever marries a divorced woman commits adultery" (Matt. 5:31–32). The difficulty is that the law does allow a divorce with a certificate. Moreover, it seems Jesus intensifies this command and says that there is only one instance where a divorce is legitimate. Should we conclude that Jesus is abrogating the law? Jesus could also be correcting a misinterpretation of Deut. 24:1–4. It is better to say Jesus fulfills the ultimate purpose of the OT law. God's original intention is grasped in Genesis. This law should not have been used to justify divorce; rather, it is a concession due to the hardness of human hearts (Matt. 19:8). The intention of God's command is clear in Genesis. The certificate has become a license for liberty rather than a concession for a sinful, broken world.

The prohibition of all oaths again might seem like Jesus sets aside the OT law that permits oaths: "Again you have heard that it was said to those of old, 'You shall not swear falsely, but shall perform to the Lord what you have sworn.' But I say to you, Do not take an oath at all, either by heaven, for it is the throne of God, or . . ." (Matt. 5:33–34). But if this command is viewed through the lens of the preamble, then the OT laws enshrine the importance of truthfulness. The language of Jesus is, therefore, hyperbolic. Jesus reminds people of the original intention of the law. His words create a community of truthfulness, where oath taking is unnecessary since men and women speak the truth.

Many have seen an abrogation of the law in verses 38–42, since Jesus seems to reject the OT law of "an eye for an eye and a tooth for a tooth." Instead, he calls on his hearers to not take revenge for evil: "But I say to you, Do not resist the one who is evil. But if anyone slaps you on the right cheek, turn to him the other also" (Matt. 5:39). John Meier claims that Jesus's teaching regarding the lex talionis is perhaps the clearest and least disputable case of annulment in the antitheses. This view, though popular, is probably mistaken. What Jesus counters is a misinterpretation of the command to exact an eye for an eye and a tooth for a tooth. The lex talionis was designed to limit violence (Lev. 24:19–21). The command simply affirms that the punishment should fit the crime. However, the lex talionis had come to perpetuate rather than arrest violence. The heart of the disciple is to be one of forgiveness and nonretaliation. Therefore, Jesus again corrects a misuse of the law. He brings out treasures both new and old. They are new because Jesus teaches a way to overcome the flesh and enact the justice of God, but old in that these are still the same commands given in the Torah.

The last section concerning loving your neighbor should be interpreted similarly, where Jesus says, "You have heard that it was said, 'You shall love your neighbor and hate your enemy'" (Matt. 5:43). There is no OT command saying that one should love one's neighbor and hate one's enemy. Thus this last example confirms that throughout Jesus responds to some distortion of what the people thought the Torah taught. The true meaning of Lev. 19:18 is that believers should love all people—friends and enemies alike. "You shall not take vengeance or bear a grudge against the sons of your own people, but you shall love your neighbor as yourself: I am the LORD."

The law has always called on Israel to love, and Jesus returns to this idea of both loving your enemies and praying for those who persecute you. Jesus turns their eyes toward the true intent of the law. "But I say to you, Love your enemies and pray for those who persecute you" (Matt. 5:44). Matthew has Jesus, as a teacher like Moses, presenting the old-fashioned law. This is the old message that Moses has already given, but now it is wrapped in the robes of the messiah. He fulfills the law by both performing the law (see the previous chapter) and giving its true interpretation (see this chapter).

Taking His Yoke

A fitting way to conclude a reflection on how Jesus is a prophet like Moses, who fulfills the Torah, is by looking at how Jesus instructs his disciples to take his yoke upon them. The relationship between wisdom, law, and the new exodus are evident in Matt. 11:28–30:

> Come to me, all who labor and are heavy laden, and I will give you rest. Take
> my yoke upon you, and learn from me, for I am gentle and lowly in heart, and
> you will find rest for your souls. For my yoke is easy, and my burden is light.

As David, the kingdom, and wisdom were joined, so too in this text Moses, the
new exodus, and wisdom meet. Wisdom 10:18–11:16 speaks of Lady Wisdom
as the one who rescued Israel from Egypt with miracles, brought them across
the Red Sea, led them through deep waters, drowned their enemies, opened
their mouths to sing praises, prospered the works of Moses, gave water from
the rock, and tested the generation as a parent.

Three indications in the text support viewing this statement by Jesus
under the banner of the Torah and the next exodus, with wisdom at the
center. First, Jesus calls his disciples to come to him, and he will give them
rest (ἀναπαύω, 11:28–29). This Greek word, ἀναπαύω, is the same word
employed for Sabbath rest (Exod. 23:12; 31:15), but even more importantly
for the promised land. In Deut. 12:9–10 the word "rest" parallels their inheritance and relief from their enemies.[29] This is repeated in Josh. 1:13 when
Joshua reiterates the words of Moses: "The LORD your God is providing you
a place of rest [καταπαύω] and will give you this land." The phrase "rest for
your souls" also alludes to Jer. 6:16, which is a scathing judgment oracle.
The offer stands, but refusal of wisdom leads to disaster (Prov. 1:20–33;
8:35–36). Intertextual allusions therefore confirm that when Jesus calls for
people to come to him and find *rest*, he holds out to them the promise of
a new exodus. However, to obtain this rest, they need a solution to the law
they fail to keep.

Therefore, second, Jesus tells them to take his yoke upon them. Yoke
is an image for both Torah and wisdom. Jesus teaches them that to find
rest they need to become his disciples, who receive Jesus's yoke: "Take my
yoke [ζυγός] upon you, to learn [μάθετε] from me. . . . For my yoke is easy
and my burden is light" (Matt. 11:29–30).[30] Deutsch notes that the sage in
Sir. 6:18–37 and 51:23–26 speaks of a yoke that is wisdom, which is also
equated with the Torah.[31] Then 2 En. 34.1 says, "They have rejected my
commandments and my yoke." And 2 Bar. 41.3–4 says, "I see many of your
people have withdrawn from your covenant, and cast from them the yoke

29. See also Deut. 25:19; Josh. 21:44; 22:4; 23:1; 2 Sam. 7:11; 1 Kings 5:4; 8:56; Ps. 95:11;
Isa. 11:2; 28:12; 66:1.
30. In Sir. 24:19–22 and Prov. 8:1–6 and 9:5–6, Lady Wisdom calls her hearers to heed her
instruction. Isaiah 9:4 also speaks about the light whose yoke of burden has been broken.
This is the same text used for Jesus going into Galilee and being a light to the northern region
(Matt. 4:15–16).
31. Deutsch, *Hidden Wisdom*, 115.

of your law."[32] In the table, the text from Sirach is compared with the text from Matthew.[33]

Matthew 11:25–30 ESV	Sirach 51:1, 23–28 NRSV
At that time Jesus declared, "I thank you, Father, Lord of heaven and earth. . . .	I will give you thanks, O Lord and King. . . .
Come to me, all who labor and are heavy laden, and I will give you rest.	Draw near to me, you who are uneducated, and lodge in the house of instruction. Why do you say you are lacking in these things? . . .
Take my yoke upon you, and learn from me, for I am gentle and lowly in heart, and you will find rest for your souls. For my yoke is easy, and my burden is light.	Put your neck under her yoke, and let your souls receive instruction; it is to be found close by. See with your own eyes that I have labored but little and found for myself much serenity (rest).

Therefore, in Matt. 11:28–30 Jesus invites Israel to rest by calling them to learn his wisdom—specifically to be his disciples in both his embodiment and interpretation of the Torah. They are to embrace Jesus's teachings and to imitate him as he goes to the cross. They can enter the land only if they follow Jesus as he fulfills the Torah and empowers them to do likewise.[34]

Third, Matt. 12, which immediately follows this passage, also supports the yoke and Torah interrelation, with Jesus reinterpreting the Sabbath commandment. The Pharisees and scribes impose heavy yokes on the people, but Jesus's way of the Torah is freeing, not burdensome; it leads to rest. "The disciple therefore, learns the yoke of Jesus, i.e., the Torah, as it is interpreted by Jesus himself, as illustrated in 12:1–8, 9–14."[35] These three points combine to form a picture of Jesus as the new Moses, who leads the people to the promised land of rest by discipling them in wisdom cocerning the Torah. He takes the law upon himself as their wise leader. In this way he surpasses Moses, who could only mediate the law but never fully accomplish it.

The New and Wise Lawgiver

If Jesus is the new Moses, then would it not be natural to expect Jesus to deliver a new revelation? This assumption has tilted people into saying that

32. See also 2 En. 48.9.

33. Strauss was the first one to draw attention to the relationship between Matt. 11:25–30 and Sir. 51. See Betz ("Logion of the Easy Yoke," 11), who does some work on the history of interpretation. See also Sharbaugh, "Light Burden of Discipleship."

34. See Hays (*Echoes of Scripture in the Gospels*, 154–59) for a longer analysis of the relationship between Sir. 51 and Matt. 11.

35. Deutsch, *Hidden Wisdom*, 43.

Jesus "extends" the law in the Sermon. Yet the first premise is questionable. If Jesus is the new Moses, he might also simply be the one to whom the law always pointed. The new fulfills the old, and the old informs the new. He is still another lawgiver because he embodies the new law and clarifies the true intention of the law. So is there anything new to what Jesus is saying?

While continuity exists with the instructions of the Torah, there is also discontinuity relative to the old covenant that comes from the apocalyptic new-covenant era that Jesus has inaugurated. A transformation occurs through the coming of the new covenant. The eschatological transformation means not that he contradicts the law but that the law now resides in a new era. The law is still the law, but it now is in the mouth of the true lawgiver, law abider, and law liver. He takes the entire Torah (the yoke) upon himself. The *authority* of the OT law continues, but it does not *function* in the same way, because it inhabits a different epoch.

By bringing his people into a new epoch and taking their yoke upon himself as the Moses-sage, Jesus leads them on the new exodus.[36] While Moses led Israel into the promised land, the people found that sin still resided in their hearts. Jesus provides a redemption that transfers not only their location but also their allegiance. The Sermon and the rest of Jesus's teaching on the law displays that while the law was always destined to lead them toward a right relationship with God, a wide-angle lens displays that obedience can come only through death. The law is good, but sin has corrupted the law. As Israel needed to die for their sins, now a representative of Israel is going to die for the sins of the people. The only way to live a kingdom life in accord with the Sermon is to follow the teacher-prophet to the cross. Too often the Sermon is read in isolation from the rest of the Gospel. The Sermon and the new exodus overlap like the Torah and the exodus intersect for Moses. Jesus is the eschatological prophet to whom the Law and the Prophets pointed. He can lead them on the new exodus because he has accomplished all that the law requires.

Jesus interprets the law as a musician performs Mozart's *Violin Concerto No. 1*. Good performances add nothing to the score, not a jot or tittle. Yet at the same time, the performance is not wooden but is an act releasing what is inherent in the text itself. The music is realized through the performance and interpretation. It comes to life in the performance, and although the performer exercises self-restraint in not adding to the piece, there is a newness

---

36. Hays (*Echoes of Scripture in the Gospels*, 123–24) notes that Jesus's admonitions to renounce anger (5:21–26) and practice forgiveness (6:12, 14–15) closely parallel the wise counsel of Sir. 27:30–28:7, thus labeling Jesus as the wise teacher.

to each performance. In the same way, Jesus does not add to the law, but his performance and presence bring new life to it. The new covenant, in a similar way, is both like and unlike the old covenant. A different νόμος is at work, because Jesus brings forth the new covenant. There are not new commands, but the law is now within—written on the heart—and God will be with his people (Jer. 31:33).

Jesus is the teacher, unlike Moses, who enables Israel to overcome the flesh rather than acquiesce to it. He fulfills the newness like a musician playing Mozart. The new covenant instituted by Christ is the old covenant revealed, and the old covenant is the new concealed beneath dark hearts. Jesus instructs the people on the law as the new Moses and tells them to pray for the new exodus as he leads them into the land he has promised their forefathers. Matthew's strategy here is to string the teaching material together so that readers can trace the pearls all the way back to Sinai. This connection reveals how to interpret the Sermon, how to view Jesus, and how to see the placement of Sinai on the canvas of God's redemptive history.

This examination of Jesus as the teacher-prophet and his stance toward the law was necessary because the law and the exodus cannot be fragmented. The law is given immediately after Yahweh has redeemed his people, because the goal was always for Israel to be free to worship Yahweh as he stipulated. Therefore, the law is not some afterthought to their redemption—it is the very purpose of redemption. Maybe this is why Matthew also presents Jesus as the teacher par excellence in his Gospel. The new exodus and the Torah are hitched in the Pentateuch, and so they must be in Matthew's presentation as well. The Sermon and Jesus's teaching largely is not merely a nice little compilation of Jesus's sayings but a charter for the new people of God. If Jesus's blood and death are the means by which the door of the new exodus will swing open, then the teaching of Jesus is the law for the reconstituted people of God.

The Miracle Worker Who Redeems

As Jesus is the redeemer-king like Moses (Matt. 2) and the teacher-prophet like Moses (Matt. 5–7, 11), he is also a miracle worker like Moses. After the Sermon, one might suppose that the Moses imagery would begin to fade, but in chapters 8–9 Matthew continues to portray Jesus as the new and better Moses. We can view Moses's life as a narrative of God working miracles through him. Moses mediates many of the wonders that Israel sees, and these are all centered on the exodus. A pillar of cloud and fire guards the multitude (Exod. 13:21–22), a strong wind makes a path for them through the sea (14:21–29), bitter waters are made sweet and drinkable (15:22–25), water comes from a rock (17:2–6), the wind brings quail (Num. 11:31), Miriam is cured of leprosy (12:5–15), Aaron's staff buds (17:1–10), and the people are healed by looking at the snake on a bronze pole (21:4–9). Yahweh is the one who performs these miracles, but he performs some of them through the mediator Moses.

Early writers also recognized the connection between Moses the miracle worker and Jesus the miracle performer. In the Acts of Pilate, Nicodemus says the following to Pilate: "What do you intend to do with this man? . . . If the signs are from God, they will stand; if they are from men, they will come to nothing. For Moses also, when he was sent by God into Egypt, did many signs which God commanded him to do" (Acts of Pilate 5.1). Eusebius similarly said that Jesus's miracles paralleled Moses's: "Moses by wonderful work and miracles authenticated the religion he proclaimed; Christ likewise, using his recorded miracles to inspire faith in those who saw them, established the new discipline of the gospel teaching" (*Dem. ev.* 3.2). Philo also speaks of Moses as being greatly grieved and indignant that when the Egyptians oppressed his people, he could not assist them (*Mos.* 1.40). So he gave them assistance "like a good physician" although their taskmasters returned and oppressed them with greater severity (*Mos.* 1.42). In Matt. 21:15 the chief priests and scribes witness the "wonderful things" (θαυμάσια) that Jesus does. This term is widely used in the LXX of the marvelous deeds of God, and especially of the exodus wonders. Matthew likely wants readers to see the connection. Three specific examples will help readers see how Matthew develops his portrait of Jesus as the new Moses in terms of the miracle worker who brings his people on the new exodus.

Three Signs

Moses is given three signs so that people might believe him and listen to his voice (Exod. 4:1). The three signs Moses assumes correspond to Jesus's life. Moses is able to (1) grasp the serpent, (2) bring waters of salvation and judgment, and (3) resurrect dead flesh. The ability to grasp the serpent (Exod. 4:2–5) recalls the promise in Gen. 3:15, where one will come who will conquer the serpent. The authors of the NT and Matthew specifically present Jesus as this promised offspring of the woman. Matthew makes that clear by starting with the genealogy, which displays Jesus as the culmination of the line of promise. His entire life satisfies the seed promise in Genesis as he restores creation to an ordered relationship with its Creator. The ability to grasp the serpent was a sign of dominion and fulfillment of the role that humans are meant to have over creation. Jesus, in a similar way in Matthew, controls and dominates the serpent during his temptations and declares his rightful authority over all heaven and earth.

The waters of judgment and salvation are the second sign given to Moses. Throughout Moses's life, the water motif continually reappears. His name comes from the fact that he is drawn up out of the water (Exod. 2:10). When Moses flees to Midian, he draws water for the priest of Midian (2:16–19). The water Moses takes from the Nile becomes blood (7:19–20). In the climactic scene at the Red Sea, Moses stretches out his hand, and the water crashes upon the Egyptians, destroying them (14:26–27). In the wilderness, water becomes an issue at Marah until Moses casts a log into it to make it sweet (15:23–25). At Horeb, God instructs Moses to strike a rock to make it pour forth water (17:6). Moses's downfall comes when he strikes a rock at Kadesh instead of telling it to yield its water, as God had commanded (Num. 20:7–12).

As Moses's life begins by being drawn up out of the water, Jesus begins his ministry at his baptism. After Jesus comes up out of the water (Matt. 3:16), he goes on to cross water, walk on water, and calm the water in his ministry. Matthew specifically highlights the story of Jesus walking on the water in chapter 14 and Peter stepping out of the boat and walking with Jesus (Matt. 14:29). No longer does the water pose a threat to Jesus, because he is sovereign over the water in a way Moses never was. Matthew ends his narrative with Jesus commanding his followers to make disciples by baptizing them with water, symbolizing that they are taking part in a story begun with Moses and consummated in Jesus.

Finally, Moses is given the sign of resurrecting dead flesh: healing a leprous hand. The first miracle that Matthew records in Jesus's ministry is the cleansing of a man with leprosy (8:1–4). There are a number of indications that Matthew uses this introductory miracle to point to Moses.[37] Two different times in Moses's ministry the leprosy theme arises. The first miracles in Moses's ministry are the transformation of a rod into a snake and the healing of leprosy (Exod. 4:1–9). In Exod. 4:6–7, God commands Moses to place his hand inside his cloak. Leprosy covers his hand when he withdraws it. However, when he withdraws it a second time, his hand is cleansed. The second example of a leprosy healing story takes place in Num. 12:1–16: Miriam is struck with leprosy for speaking against Moses. Moses intercedes for her, and she is healed.

---

37. This is at the least the third introduction to some part of Jesus's life that mirrors Moses. Jesus was born like Moses, he revealed the law to the people like Moses, and now he heals like Moses. In all these, Matthew is using his introductory material in a purposeful way.

Matthew employs a particular phrase to explain how Jesus performs this healing of the leper. Jesus "stretched out his hand" (καὶ ἐκτείνας τὴν χεῖρα, Matt. 8:3). Although this term occurs over a hundred times in the OT, it appears in Exodus by far the most. Moreover, many of those occurrences appear in Exod. 3–14. Interestingly, the story concludes with Jesus telling the leprous man, now healed, "Go, show yourself to the priest and offer the gift *Moses commanded*, as a testimony to them" (8:4 NIV, emphasis added). In his inaugural miracle in Matthew, Jesus imitates the characteristic gesture of Moses and heals leprosy (both uniquely identified with Moses).

These miracles in Exodus are enclosed by the larger narrative of Moses leading his people out of Egypt. They are enacted so that the people might go to worship Yahweh and obtain their own land. In many ways, these miracles are meted out to those who are needy, sick, and in slavery. In Matt. 9:12 Jesus says, "Healthy people don't need a doctor, but those who are sick" (AT). This could be seen as the major motif of chapters 8–9, where Jesus goes around healing those who need his help. The miracles show not only his divinity but also his healing power in delivering his people from their oppressors. As Matthew begins Jesus's life and teaching as mirroring Moses, now as Jesus begins to perform miracles, these are also patterned after Moses.

Manna from Heaven

Another miracle in Jesus's life that matches Moses is the provision of food. Twice in Matthew's narrative, Jesus feeds people (14:13–21; 15:29–39). Both of these stories recall the miraculous provision of manna in the wilderness. When the people grumbled against Moses in the wilderness, Yahweh rained bread from heaven on them (Exod. 16:4). The text in Exodus repeatedly notes that the people were filled with bread (16:12, 15). In the same way, Matthew's first feeding story is in the wilderness (14:15). Jesus feeds them with bread and fish. Manna is identified as a sort of "bread" (Exod. 16:8; Deut. 8:3; Neh. 9:15) or "bread from heaven" (Exod. 16:4). Both feeding stories in Matthew are followed by a water-crossing miracle, certainly reminiscent of Exodus imagery.[38]

In the first miracle there is mention of five thousand men being present, besides women and children. Similarly, in Exod. 12:37, the number of people in the wilderness was six hundred thousand men on foot; as Dale Allison notes, the Hebrew original indicates this count as being "besides women and children."[39] As Matthew has two feeding stories, so the Pentateuch contains

---

38. See Hays, "Canonical Matrix of the Gospels."
39. Allison, *New Moses*, 238–42.

two different accounts of the miracle of manna (Exod. 16; Num. 11). In Matthew's second account of a feeding story, there are clear parallels with the Sermon, where Jesus goes up on the mountain, sits down, and the people come to him. This mirrors Moses's ascent to Sinai after leading Israel through the sea and feeding them.

Modern commentators are divided over why Matthew includes two feeding stories. Some posit that the two feedings are a doublet, two accounts of the same event, but this seems implausible for several reasons. First, there are a number of differences in the stories themselves: (1) only the second story takes place on a mountain; (2) here the initiative lies with Jesus and not the disciples; (3) only here in chapter 15 is the crowd said to be with Jesus for three days; (4) the numbers are not the same; (5) the word for baskets is different.[40] Second, as Carson remarks, "Even if one of Mark's or Matthew's readers knew there was only one miraculous feeding, and that of Jews, the point about the gentiles would be lost and the credibility of the two evangelists impugned. . . . The validity of the theological point depends here on the credibility of the historical record."[41]

Carson's point is that early readers would have been confused by the inclusion of two feeding stories if they knew there was only one. Even so, why would Matthew include two feeding stories when they are so similar? Would not one do to make a connection with Moses? Matthew uses the two feeding narratives as an opportunity to bring out treasures new and old. Jesus surpasses Moses by feeding the whole world and not only Israel.[42] The feeding of the five thousand stands for Israel, while the feeding of the four thousand stands for gentiles. Moses fed his people in the wilderness; Jesus feeds the whole world.

Implications for the New Exodus

Without recognizing that Jesus mimics Moses's miracles, it is hard to realize that Jesus is more than a wonder-worker or a food distributor. As Pitre says, "Jesus' act of feeding the multitude . . . is best explained as a prophetic sign to signal Jesus' identity as the long-awaited 'prophet-like-Moses,'" *who will redeem them.*[43] In Jewish tradition, eschatological hope

---

40. For a list of differences, see Davies and Allison, *Matthew*, 2:562–63. Admittedly, the differences do not directly support a different feeding, but based on other evidence, the differences do make it more likely.

41. Carson, "Matthew" (2010), 407.

42. Jesus's feeding the whole world will be a point developed in greater detail in the next chapter.

43. Pitre, *Jesus and the Last Supper*, 69.

was accompanied with new manna. Second Baruch 29.6 says, "And it will happen at that time that the treasury of manna will come down again from on high." One of the Dead Sea Scrolls known as the Songs of the Sage says, "With the lyre of salvation [may] they [op]en their mouth for God's kindness. May they search for his manna."[44] Each miracle of Jesus connecting with Moses points both *to* Moses and *past* Moses. His feeding in the wilderness points back to Moses and the exodus, but it also points forward to the eschatological exodus.

A second aspect of these feedings deserving mention is the double-natured aspect of them. By including two feeding stories when one could have sufficed, Matthew shows how Jesus constitutes the people of God anew, made up of both Jews and gentiles. As Moses fed the people of God in the wilderness, so Jesus feeds the whole world, which both transcends Moses (new) and fulfills OT prophetic passages (old). In the OT, Yahweh shows his people that he will invite *all peoples* to come to him. Matthew indicates that Jesus is not merely Moses but the better Moses. Moses works wonders for Israel, while Jesus works them for the whole world. Matthew reads the OT as a whole, seeing the forward movement, the advancing progression that begins in the garden and has high points in Moses yet goes beyond Moses. Jesus comes to fulfill this messianic feast, where all nations are gathered before him on the mountain. As Dale Allison says:

> In Matthew's Jewish-Christian world the exodus from Egypt, the last supper, and the messianic banquet were not three isolated events. An intricacy of association rather obtained among them. . . . Matthew therefore did not envisage the exodus, the eucharist, and the messianic banquet as three [discrete] events on the world's time line; instead they were for him superimposed images, and all three reproduced a fundamental pattern of Jewish religious experience, one involving redemption, bread, and covenant.[45]

On the mountain, Jesus provides for Jews and gentiles alike. In the same way, his healing of the leper and his other miracles point both to and beyond Moses. The lepers whom Moses healed still died. The people whom Moses brought out of Egypt were still enslaved to their own sin. However, Jesus's healings bring in the new creation.

Whereas Moses conquered the water at one point through Yahweh's power, the water also ultimately conquered him. Moses grasped snakes, but it is Jesus who crushes the snake. Moses resurrected dead flesh, but Jesus's own

---

44. 4QSongs of the Sage [4Q511], frag 10, 9.
45. Allison, *New Moses*, 242.

dead flesh is resurrected to eternal life. In Jesus, it is not only the hand or the head that is healed but the entire body. Moses's miracles were pointers to the resurrection coming in Jesus. The type foreshadowed the antitype, which is a fuller and more complete revelation of what God is doing in Christ. The imagery of healed flesh in the Exodus narrative was a sign of what was to come in Christ.

Matthew intentionally evokes Moses's miracles as he narrates the miracles of Jesus to indicate that Jesus inaugurates the new exodus. This is a point often missed, but when seen, people regularly run to that pole and remark that the miracles do not merely show Jesus's divinity. Jews are not expecting that. While there is some truth to this claim, it is important to see that while Moses mediated the miracles of Yahweh, Jesus does not need to mediate the miracles. He performs them of his own authority. The miracles show both that Jesus is restoring Israel and that he is divine. These two options don't need to be pitted against one another. Through the miracles of Jesus, Matthew instructs his readers about what is new in Jesus and what was spoken of old. Not only that, but the feedings also anticipate what Jesus will accomplish at the Last Supper. The memories of the exodus will culminate in Jesus's words and actions when he again eats with his disciples.

The Mediator on the Mountain

We have seen how Jesus leads his people on a new exodus as the new Moses in the infancy narrative (redeemer-king), in his teaching (teacher-prophet), and miracles (miracle worker). Another vibrant comparison to Moses arises in the transfiguration (Matt. 17:1–8). Through this scene Matthew indicates to his readers that Jesus is the new mediator on the mountain. For Jews and early Christians, Moses was the mediator between God and his people on Sinai. Particular laws are even introduced with phrases like "Moses said" or "Moses commanded" (Mark 7:10; Matt. 8:4; Luke 20:28). Through the transfiguration scene, Jesus is portrayed as the new mediator of revelation. This revelation is in continuity with what came before it, yet the revelation is also superior to what came earlier.

All three Synoptic Gospels include the account of Jesus and three disciples on the Mount of Transfiguration. In each of them, the event is interpreted by using Sinai motifs (from both Exod. 24 and 34). Matthew, in particular, seeks to associate Moses and Jesus. Unlike Mark, Matthew lists Moses first in the naming of Moses and Elijah (cf. Mark 9:4). He also is the only one with a reference to Jesus's shining face. Like the other Gospels, Matthew also includes the allusion in the divine utterance about the prophet like Moses in Deut. 18:15. Except for the addition of the command "Listen to him" (ἀκούετε αὐτοῦ), the statement spoken of Jesus is identical to the one at Jesus's baptism: "This is my beloved Son, with whom I am well pleased." In Deut. 18:15, Moses commands the people that when the prophet like him comes, "To him you shall listen" (αὐτοῦ ἀκούσεσθε). The forms of these phrases are nearly identical in Greek. These are merely the overt allusions; there are many others. We will discuss the other correspondences below.[46]

Parallels between the Transfiguration and Sinai

Matthew's description of the transfiguration	Mount Sinai in Exodus 24 and 34
On a high mountain (17:1)	On a high mountain (24:12, 15–18; 34:2–3)
After six days (17:1)	The cloud covers the mountain for six days (24:16)
Three individuals are given special privileges: Peter, James, John (17:1)	Three individuals are given special privileges: Aaron, Nadab, Abihu (24:1)
A cloud descends and covers the mountain (17:5)	A cloud descends and covers the mountain (24:15–18; 34:5)
Jesus's face shines like the sun (17:2)	The skin of Moses's face shines (34:29)
The voice speaks from the cloud (17:5)	Yahweh calls out to Moses from the cloud (24:16)
The disciples are terrified (17:6)	Israel is afraid when they see Moses's face (34:30)
The disciples are comforted by Jesus's voice (17:7)	The congregation is comforted by Moses's voice (34:31)

Matthew's transfiguration narrative divides into three sections—introduction, body, and conclusion—each corresponding with Sinai in some way. His introduction contains three statements pointing to Sinai.

First, Jesus and three disciples go up on a high mountain (ὄρος ὑψηλόν).[47] Sinai is the "highest" mountain in the Jewish Scriptures, thematically and theologically speaking, the space where heaven and earth meet and God reveals himself. Second, they go up after six days. Similarly, in Exod. 24:16 the glory of Yahweh dwells on Mount Sinai, and the cloud covers it six days. Third, Matthew notes the exclusivity of the group involved: just Jesus, and with him are Peter, James, and John. Matthew explicitly says they are by themselves (κατ᾽

---

46. I found Quarles's table after I had constructed mine. He had the line about the cloud descending and covering the mountain, which I added after I saw his. He did not include the words of comfort from Jesus and Moses, which I have included. See Quarles, *Theology of Matthew*, 45.

47. The mountain theme will be developed later.

ἰδίαν, 17:1). This corresponds to Exod. 24:1, where Moses, Aaron, Nadab, and Abihu alone draw near while the others worship from afar.

The body of the narrative in Matthew also matches a few of the details on Sinai. The three descriptions Matthew uses for the transfiguration are that (1) Jesus's face shines like the sun, (2) his clothes become white as light, (3) Moses and Elijah appear and talk with Jesus. Only Matthew notes that Jesus's face "shone like the sun" (Matt. 17:2). This is a reference to Exod. 34:29–35. When Moses came down from the mountain, his face shone because he had been talking with God. From then on, Moses put a veil over his face when he came out from speaking with the Lord because of the brightness of his face. Next, as Yahweh called out to Moses from the clouds in Exod. 24:16, so also a voice speaks out of the cloud in Matt. 17:5.

Finally, the conclusion to Matthew's narrative or the resulting action echoes Sinai. Matthew 17:6 says that when the disciples heard this, they fell on their faces and were terrified. In a similar way the people of Israel were afraid when they saw Moses's face (Exod. 34:30). The Israelites returned to Moses once he had comforted them, and likewise the disciples are comforted and return to Jesus at the sound of his voice (Matt. 17:7–8).

The correlations between Matthew's transfiguration account and the text of Moses going up to Mount Sinai are numerous, varied, and occur in each section of the narrative. Matthew undoubtedly wants the Sinai imagery to be the filter through which the transfiguration is read. Because of the prevalence of Sinai themes in this section, some have even proposed that this event was fabricated. Instead, we must realize that Matthew is doing his favorite thing: telling a shadow story. The new narrative is shaped and molded by what has come before it. This is not disingenuous but enlightening. As any good historian does, Matthew not only recounts the past but interprets it. The Gospels were never meant to give the bare facts; they are inspired readings of Jesus's life.

The Transfiguration and the Goal of the Exodus

Careful readers will rightly ask, "How does the transfiguration relate to the new exodus?" This question can be answered only by going back to the original context of the exodus. When Moses received the law and was himself transfigured, this revealed the aim of the law all along: transfiguration *coram deo* (in the presence of God). The goal of the exodus was to place Israel in their land under the rule of Yahweh, beholding his face and thereby becoming like him. Therefore, the giving (or receiving of the law by Moses) was part and parcel of the goal of the exodus. God did not bring them out of Egypt to simply let them go back to their old ways in Egypt. He brought them out to be a new people. When Jesus is transfigured before the disciples and Moses shows up beside him, this all points to an eschatological hope of the people living under the rule of Yahweh. As Moses revealed the will of God in the law, so Jesus reveals the will of God in his person. The transfiguration is the goal of the exodus.

Second, and related, as God revealed himself to Moses on Mount Sinai, so too Jesus reveals himself on this high mountain. Moses went up on the mountain to meet with God and see his glory, and through the eyes of the disciples Matthew invites readers up on the mountain to see the revelation of God. However, what happens on the mountain is unexpected: God is revealed through the face of Jesus Christ. God showed his back to Moses but is revealed in and through Jesus on the Mount of Transfiguration; Jesus himself is the revelation of God. A cloud descends in both narratives, but Matthew's pen clears the fog.

The old covenant was about God revealing himself to Moses through the covenant, and now God reveals himself through Jesus in the new covenant. Moses and Elijah appear, which help the disciples understand that this revelation is the fulfillment of the Law and the Prophets. The old is feeding into and buttressing the new. This emphasis on revelation makes Jesus *the* prophet of whom Moses spoke. Formerly the prophets received the Word of God; Jesus *is* the Word of God. The interplay between these two mountaintop experiences is key to how Matthew understands Jesus's role. As Moses was the mediator of the old covenant, who went in and spoke with God for the people, so now Jesus is the mediator of the new covenant, where all people will know God.

The old covenant is closely associated with Moses and was frequently called "the law of Moses." When Moses appeared on the Mount of Transfiguration, the disciples should have immediately seen Jesus did not abolish the Law and the Prophets; he fulfilled them. This fulfillment comes in the inauguration of the new covenant, where the people will see God face-to-face. So Jesus is a prophet like Moses, revealing God; he is a mediator like Moses, standing between the people and God; and like Moses, he is associated with a particular covenant.

While Moses's face reflects God's glory, Jesus's face is God's glory. A shining face is used in the Scriptures as a metaphor to denote grace and compassion, usually in reference to Yahweh making his face shine upon individuals (Num. 6:24–26; Eccles. 8:1).[48] As Yahweh allows his grace and compassion

---

48. In Jewish tradition, the priestly messiah shines with the light of the sun. Cf. 1 En. 38.4; 4 Ezra 7.97; 2 Bar. 51.3. See Joshua Philpot's work ("Shining Face of Moses," 3) to which I am indebted here.

to shine forth from his being, so too Jesus allows the three disciples to see his shining face. Jesus stands as Yahweh to his people; he bestows grace and compassion on them through the new covenant. He gives them new hearts that can serve him. Unlike Moses, who gave them a ministry of death, Jesus is giving them a covenant of life. However, the Law and Prophets paved the way for this covenant. They are not opposed to one another; rather, Matthew shows Jesus and Moses and Elijah—the Law and Prophets—conversing on the mountain. A significant question remains as the transfiguration light fades: How will the new covenant, new exodus, and transfiguration for Jesus's followers be established? The answer comes through suffering and blood. As Moses came down from the mountain and threw the blood of the covenant on the people of Israel (Exod. 24:8), so too God's servant will sprinkle the people with blood. Moses was a passionate intercessor (32:11–13, 31–32), but the servant "makes intercession for the transgressors" (Isa. 53:12).

Jesus's Death as the New Exodus

When comparing Jesus to OT figures, too many times the cross is viewed as an unintentional minor note. The reasons for this are varied. Some rightly assume that the cross is a unique event in Jesus's life, unrepeatable and distinctive. Others argue that the narration slows during the passion and does not permit the creative storytelling that the early narratives afford. In other words, as the details of the story become more prominent, the connections with the OT fall by the wayside. Yet even though the cross is a unique event, Matthew still portrays the last days of Jesus as a fulfillment of the Scriptures.[49] Indeed, it would seem odd if he painted only Jesus's life in this way and not his death.

But how does Jesus's death integrate with the Mosaic traditions? In Jesus's death he is portrayed as the priestly Moses, leading the people on their new exodus. There is a typological parallel between the historical exodus and the messianic salvation that Christ accomplishes on the cross.[50] The clearest place to see the new-exodus theme in Jesus's death is the Last Supper. Here Jesus synchronizes his coming crucifixion in light of the redemption from Egypt. One might object that the Last Supper is quite a bit before Jesus's

---

49. See Matt. 21:4–5; 26:53–54, 56; 27:9.
50. As Fisher ("New and Greater Exodus," 69) notes, there are four elements to the pattern of exodus deliverance that define it. First, it was a deliverance accomplished by God. Second, it was a deliverance from bondage and oppression to the freedom and dignity of sonship. Third, it was a deliverance that God accomplished through a man. Fourth, it was a deliverance that created a lasting relationship between God and his people.

death, but it is also true that in all of the Gospels, the Last Supper is *where* the death of Jesus is interpreted. Each Gospel writer leaves the description of Jesus's death quite bare. Perhaps this is because they want Jesus's own words about his death at the Supper to provide the interpretation and convey the significance of the event. While the imagery gives hints of the significance of Jesus's death, it is safe to say that the clearest explanation of Jesus's death occurs at the Last Supper.

The Meal, Blood, and Covenant

Three things should be pointed out about the Last Supper that tie closely to the ministry of Moses and point to the cross as a symbol for the new exodus: (1) the Last Supper and its relationship to the Passover meal, (2) the specific use of blood and bread, and (3) the explicit mention of covenant. For Jews, the exodus and the Passover meal are twin siblings. The exodus signifies the key moment of redemption in the OT. Redemption from Egypt was political, spiritual, economic, social, and linked tightly to this meal.

Matthew is explicit in his presentation of the Last Supper as a Passover meal. Matthew 26:17–19 says, "Now on the first day of Unleavened Bread the disciples came to Jesus, saying, 'Where will you have us prepare for you to eat the Passover?' He said, 'Go into the city to a certain man and say to him, "The Teacher says, My time is at hand. I will keep the Passover at your house with my disciples."' And the disciples did as Jesus had directed them, and they prepared the Passover." Jesus sends his disciples to prepare to "eat" the Passover. This is a meal and has history and symbolism woven into every part of it. Ritual meals in the ANE are times of remembrance, celebration, community, and worship.[51] The Passover meal aligns nicely with these points, for this specific dining experience celebrates Israel's deliverance from bondage in Egypt. Thus, in eating the meal they are to remember their dependence on God, Yahweh's provision for them, and participate in joyful worship of Yahweh's goodness. The meal is to be a time when they recall what God did for them in Egypt.

The basic elements of the meal are described in Exod. 12: the Passover lamb (*pesach*), bitter herbs (*maror*), and unleavened bread (*matzah*).[52] The point is

---

51. Adam Day ("Eating before the Lord") has argued that in Deuteronomy, the last book of Moses, food (1) leads to a recognition of dependence on God, (2) points to Yahweh's provision for his people, (3) teaches Israelites to fear and trust Yahweh, (4) shows that true satisfaction is found in Yahweh's word, and (5) is a means of participating in joyful worship of Yahweh's goodness and cultivating thankfulness.

52. The Mishnah (m. Pesahim 10.5) indicates that they eat *pesach* because God skipped over the houses in Egypt. They eat the *merorim* because the Egyptians embittered the lives of Israel in Egypt, and *matzah* because they were redeemed.

that the food symbolizes an event in history. In the Passover, Israel is to remember their exodus from Egypt; in the Last Supper, Jesus calls his people to realize that he is leading them on a new exodus. The relevant elements are not the lamb or the bitter herbs but the bread and the wine. Jesus thus reinterprets the Passover in relation to his own impending death. This was an old meal, but an old meal now transformed. The scribe is bringing out treasures both new and old.

Second, not only the meal but also the blood and bread point to the Mosaic covenant. Jesus acts as the paterfamilias who recounts the story of the exodus and explains to the family why they perform the ritual. As the head of the company, Jesus takes the bread and the wine and explains to them the significance.

> Now as they were eating, Jesus took bread, and after blessing it broke it and gave it to the disciples, and said, "Take, eat; this is my body." And he took a cup, and when he had given thanks he gave it to them, saying, "Drink of it, all of you, for this is my blood of the covenant, which is poured out for many for the forgiveness of sins. I tell you I will not drink again of this fruit of the vine until that day when I drink it new with you in my Father's kingdom." (Matt. 26:26–29)

The words "This is my blood of the covenant" appear to echo Exod. 24:8. In Exod. 24 Moses comes down from the mountain and ratifies the covenant between the Lord and the people by sprinkling blood on them. Moses says about the blood, "Behold the blood of the covenant that the LORD has made with you in accordance with all these words" (Exod. 24:8). That Jesus's blood is poured out for many indicates that his death is a covenant sacrifice for the atonement of sins. As the blood of animals was "poured out" (Lev. 4:7; 18, 25, 30, 34), so the blood of Jesus represents a sacrifice for the atonement of sins. In addition, as Jesus celebrates the Last Supper with his twelve disciples, who represent the twelve tribes of Israel, so too Moses offers the blood of the covenant with the twelve tribes of Israel, symbolically represented by "twelve pillars" around the altar (Exod. 24:4).

In the original Passover, blood was smeared on the two doorposts and the lintel of the houses (Exod. 12:7). The blood was to be a sign for them. When Yahweh saw the blood, he would pass over the house, and no plague would befall them. The significance of the covenant of blood is revealed in its fullest clarity and beauty in these two feasts. The Passover meal is now a covenant meal through Jesus's reenactment.

Brant Pitre also directs our attention to the bread.[53] The bread of the Presence is mentioned in the same section as the blood. In Exod. 25:30 Moses is

---

53. This paragraph is in large part dependent on Pitre, *Jesus and the Last Supper*, 121–47.

instructed to put the bread of the Presence on the table before Yahweh's face always. This bread functioned as a symbol of the heavenly banquet, where Moses and the elders beheld the God of Israel while they ate and drank in Exod. 24 (esp. v. 10). As Pitre notes, this has implications for the connection between the bread and the blood: "The link between the bread and the presence and the blood of the covenant is significant: it is the covenant sacrifice at the foot of the mountain that enables Moses and the elders to ascend into God's presence and celebrate the heavenly banquet with him at the summit of the mountain."[54] The blood paves the way for the bread of Presence, where they see the face of God. In the same way Jesus is telling his disciples to drink of his blood and eat of the bread so that they may enjoy the new-covenant blessing of being in the presence of God.

Third, when Jesus speaks of establishing a new covenant (Matt. 26:28), he echoes prophetic oracles that speak to a future covenant. Zechariah 9 says, "Because of the blood of my covenant with you, I will set your captives free from the waterless pit" (9:11–13). Ezekiel asserts that Yahweh will "establish . . . an everlasting covenant" with Israel (16:59–63). Jeremiah connects the new covenant with the forgiveness of sins (31:31–34). Interestingly, Jeremiah also associates the new covenant with the covenant mediated by Moses at Mount Sinai (31:31–32). In each of these texts the new covenant accompanies the restoration of the twelve tribes of Israel. Zechariah speaks of God's plan to restore both Judah and Ephraim (9:13). Ezekiel speaks of a covenant being established with Jerusalem, Samaria, and even Sodom (16:61). Jeremiah says the new covenant is made with Israel and Judah (31:31). In the same way, when Jesus partakes of the Last Supper, he does so with his disciples (Matt. 26:17).

Exodus and Passover

Matthew follows his rabbi in his interpretation of the exodus, the Passover meal, and Jesus's death. When Jesus celebrates the Passover meal with his disciples, he reinterprets Scripture in light of current events. He does not deny the meaning of the Passover or the exodus; he clarifies their meaning. But now the meaning is mediated through Jesus's actions, and these actions are mediated to us by Matthew. The new context of Jesus's own death enables Jesus to read the tradition of the Passover in a different way. The redemption from Egypt provides the conceptual framework by which to understand Israel's current divine deliverance. In the same respect, the present deliverance reinterprets the significance of the events in the exodus—treasures new and old.

54. Pitre, *Jesus and the Last Supper*, 126.

Matthew was sitting in the room with Jesus when all this took place. As a good Jewish man, he had all the right associations with this meal and grew up celebrating it. He knew what the meal, blood, and bread symbolized, and he knew the meal was a part of their covenant tradition. The combination of these three factors—a meal, the food, and the covenant—provokes Michael Barber to say, "That all four accounts have Jesus linking his *blood* with the motif of *covenant* while celebrating a *meal* mirrors not only Moses' words concerning the 'blood of the covenant' but also the fact that the ceremony in Exod. 24 culminates in a sacred *feast* (cf. Exod. 24:8–11). These points of contact are too strong and numerous to be written off as mere coincidence."[55]

Yet it was probably not till after Jesus's death that Matthew realized the true significance of Jesus's act. Matthew was probably confused when Jesus compared wine to blood. In the old covenant the blood of animals was not to be consumed, but now his rabbi told him the blood was to be ingested. That this blood is now to be ingested—not the blood of animals but the blood of Jesus—indicates that the covenant of blood has reached its fulfillment. God now not only passes over them and spares their firstborn, but he also forgives their sins with the blood of the new lamb. Moses does not lay down his life for his followers, but Jesus is the sacrificial lamb. Moses goes through the wilderness with the people but dies before he enters the promised land, while Jesus conquers in the wilderness. Jesus is like Moses, but superior to him in every respect. Matthew learned the importance of this meal by associating it with the Passover and thinking about how Jesus fulfilled all that Israel was hoping for. Matthew is now the scribe, teaching us how to interpret not only Jesus's life but also his death, because his teacher taught him what it means.[56]

The Last Supper thus points backward to the old covenant and the redemption from Egypt and forward to what is about to be accomplished by Jesus and the wedding feast to come. This scene confirms Moses as a main figure in Matthew's typology. For when Matthew reaches for a symbolic action that explains Jesus's death, he latches onto a meal that speaks of the exodus. The image with which Matthew interprets Jesus's death is the climactic event of Moses's life. Redemption from Egypt is a shadow; the reality is enacted

55. Barber, "Historical Jesus and Cultic Restoration Eschatology," 601, cited in Pitre, *Jesus and the Last Supper*, 95. After I had done my work on this section, I found that Pitre brought these three items together as well.

56. Readers should be expecting that if Jesus is the new Moses, then he leads them on the new exodus as their new Savior. This is because, as Josephus explains, Moses's name means to be saved out of the water: "Hereupon it was that Thermuthis imposed this name *Mouses* upon him from what had happened when he was put into the river; for the Egyptians call water by the name of *Mo*, and such as are saved out of it, by the name of *Uses*; so by putting these two words together, they imposed this name upon him" (*Ant.* 2.228).

through a meal and a death. But Jesus's death is also not like Moses's. Moses dies on a mountain, unable to enter the land. Jesus is raised to life and meets with the disciples on a mountain, looking out over the land.

A Leader Who Commissions His People

The Gospel of Matthew closes with Jesus on a mountain. Otto Michel says Matt. 28:18–20 is the key to understanding the whole book; others have likewise noticed how all the themes of Matthew run through this text.[57] Jesus states that all authority on heaven and earth has been given to him. He commands his followers to go and make disciples of all nations by baptizing them and teaching them and then promises them he will be with them always.

Similar to the last scene of Jesus, the last scene of Moses depicts him on top of a mountain, looking out over the land. Deuteronomy 34:1–4 describes the scene:

> Then Moses went up from the plains of Moab to Mount Nebo, to the top of Pisgah, which is opposite Jericho. And the LORD showed him all the land, Gilead as far as Dan, all Naphtali, the land of Ephraim and Manasseh, all the land of Judah as far as the western sea, the Negeb, and the Plain, that is, the Valley of Jericho the city of palm trees, as far as Zoar. And the LORD said to him, "This is the land of which I swore to Abraham, to Isaac, and to Jacob, 'I will give it to your offspring.' I have let you see it with your eyes, but you shall not go over there."

As Moses looks out over the whole land and thinks of the promises to Abraham, Isaac, and Jacob, so too Jesus looks out over the whole land and knows that the promise of the new covenant is completed in him. He promises his followers that he will be with them—in contrast to Moses, who dies on the mountain. Jesus also commands them to go and make disciples of all nations. This is based on the authority that has been given to him. In both of these phrases, spatial ideas are present. Jesus has authority over all space—heaven and earth—and because of this, he sends his disciples forth into every space, all nations. He wants their bodies to fill the land with blessings as Yahweh promised to Abraham.

The two steps to making disciples in the verse are *baptizing* and *teaching*. As Israel was baptized in the sea and taught by Moses, so the disciples' commission is to reprise the history of Israel. Baptism is a going through the water. Jesus also went through the water, and he wants his followers to follow

57. Michel, "Conclusion of Matthew's Gospel," 35.

him in this sacramental act. He went through the water because Israel also passed through the water in the exodus led by Moses. Matthew the scribe predictably also emphasizes teaching because he sat at the feet of his rabbi, and his rabbi taught him like Moses taught Israel. Jesus wants his followers to go out and imitate their messiah, in this way spreading his law so that people will be transfigured *coram deo*. At the end, on the mountain, Matthew lays out two commands that mirror Moses's ministry.

Not only does Jesus mirror Moses in the spatial outlook, but how Jesus commissions his successors in light of the task before them is also similar. Moses commissions Joshua at the end of his life and promises him that Yahweh will be with him, never to leave him or forsake him: "Then Moses summoned Joshua and said to him in the sight of all Israel, 'Be strong and courageous, for you shall go with this people into the land that the LORD has sworn to their fathers to give them, and you shall put them in possession of it. It is the LORD who goes before you. He will be with you; he will not leave you or forsake you. Do not fear or be dismayed'" (Deut. 31:7–8). At the beginning of Joshua, Yahweh speaks to Joshua and promises that every place the sole of his foot touches will be given to him (Josh. 1:3). As the chosen successor to Moses, his task is to go out and conquer the land. Matthew does not recount Jesus's departure, because the emphasis is on the disciples' task for the whole world and on Jesus's abiding presence among them as they accomplish this task.

As Moses looked out over the land of Israel, so Jesus looks out over the whole world. Moses was given authority over Israel, but Jesus is given authority over all heaven and earth. Moses did not join with the people in entering the land, but Jesus has put his feet on the land to transform it. By closing in this way, Matthew indicates his eschatological outlook toward Jesus: Jesus is not just Moses but also Joshua, and he is not only Joshua but also Israel. As Moses led the people out of the land of Egypt, Jesus leads the people into the new heaven and the new earth. The promised land of Israel foreshadowed the new heavens and the new earth. According to Matthew, Jesus is the one who fulfills the life of Moses. It is not sufficient merely to look at the occurrences of Moses's name in Matthew. No, the parallels occur not only where Matthew mentions Moses explicitly but also where Jesus travels, walks, and sleeps and the place from which he departs.

Conclusion

Shadow stories do not negate history; they enlighten and clarify it. Although some have waved an apprehensive wand, denying Moses typology because it is not as explicit as they would like, the discipled scribe does not stoop to the wishes of modern or premodern interpreters. Dale Allison has shown that Moses typology was used quite frequently in early Jewish literature, and Matthew seems to be stepping into that tradition rather than swerving from it.[58] Although Matthew's Moses typology is not always explicit, this survey has demonstrated "that Matthew embroidered brighter and thicker Mosaic threads into the fabric of history than many have allowed."[59]

At the beginning of this chapter, I asked whether Jesus was simply the new prophet like Moses or if the parallels were more expansive than this. My argument has been that the exodus tradition brings a centralizing force to all that Moses is and was. Jesus is not merely *like* Moses as a teacher, mediator, lawgiver, redeemer, king, prophet, and physician. Rather, Jesus surpasses Moses in every respect. All of these titles and descriptors interact with one another and form a holistic picture of Jesus as the new Moses. He is the redeemer, who is the prophet, their savior, their lawgiver, and their king. All of these images are means to an end—the new exodus. A later rabbinic tradition shows that Matthew's rich storehouse of examples was a pattern in early interpretation.

> R. Berekiah said in the name of R. Isaac: As the first redeemer [Moses] was, so shall the latter Redeemer [Messiah] be. What is stated of the former redeemer? "And Moses took his wife and his sons, and set them upon an ass" (Exod. 4:20). Similarly it will be with the latter Redeemer, as it is stated, "Lowly and riding upon an ass" (Zech. 9:9). As the former redeemer caused manna to descend, as it is stated, "Behold, I will cause to rain bread from heaven for you" (Exod. 16:4), so will the latter Redeemer cause manna to descend, as it is stated, "May he be as rich as a cornfield in the land" (Ps. 72:16). As the former redeemer made a well to rise (Num. 21:17–18), so the latter Redeemer brings up water, as it is stated, "And a fountain shall come forth of the house of the LORD, and shall water the valley of Shittim" (Joel 4:18 [3:18 Eng.]).[60]

58. Allison, *New Moses*.

59. Allison, *New Moses*, 267. Further connections could be exegeted between Jesus leading Israel as a shepherd leads the sheep (Matt. 9:35–38) and Moses the shepherd of God's people (Num. 27:17), between Jesus as the servant (Matt. 12:15–21) and Moses the servant of Yahweh (Exod. 14:31), or between those who challenged Jesus by asking for a sign (Matt. 12:38) and Moses's demonstrating his authority by performing a sign (Exod. 7:8–10). Other possible connections to Moses remain to be found in Jesus's arrival in Jerusalem, his eschatological discourse, and his leading the twelve disciples to their new land. I have dealt with the clearer allusions to Moses. It seems that Matthew's introduction and conclusion ring most clearly with the Moses typology. How an author sets up and concludes the narrative indicates how the rest of the tale is to be read.

60. Qohelet Rabbah 1.9. I found this quote in Quarles, *Theology of Matthew*, 34.

The rabbis understood that the messiah would enact many parts of the Moses story. Philo seems to agree when he says, "Having shown that Moses was a most excellent king, and lawgiver, and high priest, I come in the last place to show that he was also the most illustrious of prophets" (*Mos.* 2.187). Matthew is our teacher and scribe, showing how the new interprets the old and how the old informs the new. In so doing he instructs about both the life of Jesus and the life of Moses. Matthew treats the life of Moses like a richly woven fabric to be trimmed and tailored into a beautiful cloak. He uses scenes, themes, titles, and descriptions to compare Jesus's life to Moses. *Matthew employs this Mosaic shadow story to show how Jesus leads his people on the new exodus.*

In ancient Jewish practice and belief, it was commonly held that the future age of salvation would be heralded by the coming of a new Moses, who would introduce and complete the new exodus. Matthew draws his readers' minds back to the time when Moses stands on the shores of the Red Sea, or when he provides manna for Israel, in order to reimagine the significance of the event. New events reinterpret old events. As Dale Allison puts it,

> For Matthew, Jesus was the hermeneutical key to unlocking the religious meaning of the Jewish Bible, it is also true that the Jewish Bible was for him the hermeneutical key to unlocking the religious meaning of Jesus. . . . The past informs the present, and the present informs the past. . . . The typological lines between Jesus and Moses are bidirectional: informed understanding of Jesus requires true understanding of Moses, and true understanding of Moses requires informed understanding of Jesus.[61]

Parallels between Jesus and Moses

Matthew	Pentateuch	Subject
1–2	Exod. 1:1–2:10	Infancy narrative
3:13–17	Exod. 14:10–13	Crossing the water
4:1–11	Exod. 16:1–17:7	Wilderness temptation
5–7	Exod. 19:1–23:33	Mountain of lawgiving
11:25–30	Exod. 33:1–23	Reciprocal knowledge of God
17:1–9	Exod. 34:29–35	Transfiguration
26:17–30	Exod. 12:31–51 / 24:1–18	The Last Supper/Passover
28:16–20	Deut. 31:7–9 / Josh. 1:1–9	Commissioning of successor

Source: Adapted from Allison, *New Moses*, 268.

Through the discipled scribe's presentation, we learn that Moses existed to teach us about Jesus. By revealing Jesus through the garb of Moses, Matthew

61. Allison, *New Moses*, 289.

uncovers the purpose of Moses. Whereas Moses was sent to deliver the nation out of slavery in Egypt, Jesus was sent to deliver all nations from spiritual slavery to the sins in their hearts (Matt. 1:21). Moses spoke the words he received from God, but Jesus is the very Word of God, who declares, "I say to you" (Matt. 5:21–48). Moses received the law, but Jesus fulfills the law. Moses fed Israel in the wilderness, but Jesus spreads a banquet for Jews and gentiles on the mountain (Matt. 14:13–21; 15:29–39). Whereas Moses's face shone with the reflection of the glory he had seen, Jesus's face shines by his own divine glory (Matt. 17:2). Moses mediated temporarily between the people and God; Jesus mediates eternally for his people by the shedding of his own blood (Matt. 27:51).[62] Moses died looking out over the land that was to be for Israel; Jesus was raised from the dead and tells his disciples to go out to all nations (Matt. 28:18–20). Moses's body cannot be found because no one knows where he was buried (Deut. 34:6), but Jesus's body cannot be found because he is risen (Matt. 28:6).

Jesus is therefore not merely the new prophet; he is also the new mediator, the new servant, the new leader, the new miracle worker, the new teacher, and the new redeemer. He is all the things Moses was and more, and he leads the people on a greater exodus than Moses could have ever imagined. Although the old informs the new, and the discipled scribe fills in Jesus's life with the colors of the old, it is the new that drives Matthew's narrative. He does this because he was instructed in this understanding by his teacher of wisdom.

62. The tearing of the temple curtain signified that the presence of God was now open to all through the blood of Jesus.

6

Jesus and Abraham's New Family

Father Abraham certainly had many sons, but in another sense, he only had one Son. Paul makes this argument in Galatians. When Moses spoke of the "seed" of Abraham, he was not referring to many, but "to one: 'And to your offspring,' who is Christ" (Gal. 3:16). Jesus is the seed of Abraham par excellence, and as the seed he completes the family of Abraham. Paul must have been reflecting on the Jesus traditions when he wrote these words because the first words of Matthew relate Jesus to two figures: David and Abraham (Matt. 1:1). Although David and Moses usually get the lion's share in studies on Matthew, Abraham is actually the second figure whom Matthew names. Jesus is certainly draped in robes of royalty, and he also carries Moses's redeemer staff in his hand, but Matthew also portrays Jesus as the new Abraham, who welcomes all of Abraham's children to his side by his sacrificial death.[1] The last chapters were about Jesus establishing his kingdom (as the new David) and bringing about the new exodus (as the new Moses); this chapter is about *who* is part of the kingdom and *whom* he leads on the path back to their home.[2]

1. Leroy Huizenga ("Matt 1:1: 'Son of Abraham'") argues that "son of Abraham" as a title covers the scope of the entire Gospel.

2. Abraham's connection to wisdom can be found in the fact that he is declared to be righteous when he believes God's promise (Gen. 15:6). Though I don't have time to develop it here, righteousness and wisdom are correlated in the Scriptures (1 Cor. 1:30). Proverbs 1 brings together wisdom, instruction, and righteousness: "to know wisdom and instruction . . . in righteousness and justice. . . . Let the wise hear and increase in learning" (Prov. 1:2, 3, 5). Proverbs 2 speaks in a similar way: "For the Lord gives wisdom. . . . Then you will understand righteousness" (Prov. 2:6, 9). See also Deut. 16:19; Ps. 37:30; Prov. 9:9; 10:31; Eccles. 7:16; 9:1;

David's name is associated with kingdom hopes, and Moses is linked to the new exodus, but Abraham is defined by familial metaphors.[3] Matthew follows the Jewish tradition of employing Abraham as the father of "many nations." There are familial elements in almost every Matthean text associated with Abraham. As with the previous chapters, though, it is not sufficient merely to examine the texts that explicitly mention Abraham. My aim will be to trace the development of Matthew's presentation of Jesus as the new Abraham. The theme and narrative as a whole are more important than the individual uses of the name. As I proceed, I will attempt to answer questions such as these: How does Matthew conceive of the family of God with the arrival of Jesus? What is the relationship between Jews, gentiles, and the church in the First Gospel? How do we understand the relationship of Jesus's mission to Israel (10:5–6) and then his mission to all nations (28:18–20)?[4]

A brief preview of my argument might be helpful. Matthew, through portraying Jesus as the new Abraham, reveals that the people of God are redefined. The new people of God, the church (ἐκκλησία), are those who have faith (πίστις), both Jews and gentiles. Thus, not only those who are ethnically Abraham's children are Abraham's progeny; Abraham's seed are those who have Abraham's faith and who "do the will of [his] Father in heaven" (Matt. 12:50). This includes Israel, but also more than Israel. The new people of God are those from the east and west who recline at Abraham's table (8:11) and those who produce fruit consistent with repentance (3:8). But this mission to all nations is not presented in a flat or imprecise manner; there is narrative development.[5]

10:2; Jer. 23:5. Wisdom 10:5 also speaks of wisdom recognizing the righteous man (referring to Abraham) and preserving him as blameless before God.

3. Kingdom and exodus themes are also associated with Abraham, but the familial metaphors rise to the surface. What is a kingdom or an exodus without a people? Abraham fills out our picture of "who" composes the people of God in this kingdom and who is a part of this exodus. I use the word "familial" to summarize the terms offspring, seed, etc. Readers should not import modern notions of "family" into this terminology.

4. The relationship between Israel and the church has been a contentious issue in the study of the NT. I will limit my discussion to Matthew here, although certainly other texts in the NT canon need to be taken into consideration.

5. One of my main interlocutors for this chapter will be Matthias Konradt (*Israel, Church, and the Gentiles*), who has written a significant book on the relationship of Israel, gentiles, and the church in the First Gospel that some are hailing as a new perspective on Matthew. See Donald Senior's comments in *RBL* (April 23, 2013) about the German edition (2007). Konradt proposes that the seemingly contradictory texts of 10:6 and 28:18–20 actually point to a sequence of the two commissions integral to how Matthew unfolds his Christology. The Christology of Jesus as the son of David (to the Jews) and the Son of God (to the gentiles) is key to understanding the narrative.

In the First Gospel, the mission to the gentiles is spurred on by Israel's rejection of Jesus; however, not all of Israel rejects Jesus. While the religious leaders and scribes are condemned as false shepherds, the crowd and the disciples are sometimes portrayed in a more positive light. Therefore, Jesus weeps over Jerusalem because they will not allow their messiah to gather them under the shadow of his wings (23:37). If Israel does not produce fruit, their tree will be cut down (3:10), their temple will be destroyed (cf. 21:12–13), and their fig tree will be left barren (21:18–22).[6] Israel's hardening thus leads to an *expansion* of the people of God.[7] The expansion is both "new" and "old." It is "old" because Abraham's family was always meant to be a blessing to the whole world; here the role of Israel is not downplayed or superseded but fulfilled. Jesus fulfills the role that Israel could never attain and is *the* light to the nations. The expansion of the family of God is also "new" because Jesus stands at the apocalyptic shift of the ages. His death and resurrection function as the means by which he is installed as the universal Lord of all creation, who then calls all nations to come and be his disciples.

I will trace Matthew's understanding of the family of God by looking first at the introduction and then the conclusion of the Gospel. The way an author begins a work sets up how readers are to understand the narrative development. In the same way, a conclusion usually brings the threads together that appeared at the start and helps readers grasp the significance and meaning of the body. Therefore, after I have dealt with how Matthew begins and how he concludes, I will examine the development of the family-of-God theme, showing how Abraham is key to understanding Matthew's presentation of Jesus and his followers. However, before all of this, it is important to establish

---

6. I take the cleansing of the temple to imply the destruction of the temple. This is made clear by Jesus's action being paired with his fig tree condemnation. One has to wonder if Paul was reflecting on the Jesus traditions as he wrote Rom. 9–11. Paul says that the inclusion of the gentiles is based not on Israel's restoration but on Israel's rejection of Jesus. The inclusion of gentiles is made possible by Israel's "stumbling," "defeat," and "rejection." This stumbling creates "riches for the Gentiles" (Rom. 11:12) and reconciliation for the whole world (9:15). Paul states that this hardening is temporary, and it will lead to an even further inclusion of Israel, but the pattern is still set. The stumbling of Israel leads to riches for the gentiles, which leads to greater inclusion of Israel: Stumbling of Israel → Riches for gentiles → Greater inclusion of Israel.

7. There is much to commend in Konradt's work, and a good portion of it will align with my work here. However, Konradt's work takes a method different from mine, and therefore our conclusions differ slightly. Konradt seems to take 10:5–6 and 28:18b–20 as equal texts. Rather than reading the whole Gospel in light of the mission at the end, Konradt seeks to read it through 10:5–6. I will argue that Matthew wrote with the Great Commission always in his mind, since it had already happened. To put this more succinctly, the question is not how 28:18b–20 fits into the mission of 10:5–6, but how 10:5–6 fits into the mission of 28:18b–20.

from the Jewish Scriptures themselves that Abraham should be associated with familial metaphors.

Abraham in the Hebrew Bible

Not only Matthew's narrative supports viewing Abraham under the lens of *family, offspring, or seed*. The Jewish Scriptures and other extant Jewish literature also maintain this inclination. Three foundational pillars support the idea that Matthew draws on the key OT descriptions of Abraham and informs his readers about Jesus's new family by drawing on Abrahamic imagery.

First, when Abraham initially shows up in the Scriptures, the promises are all family related. In Gen. 12:1 Abraham is called to go from his country, kindred, and father's house. The three descriptions narrow in focus: country is the largest category, kindred is intermediate, and father's house is the most specific. In the ANE, people and place were linked concepts. Where you were from defined who you were. When Abraham is called to go from his country, it naturally follows that he will leave his kindred and his father's house. If this is the case, then when Abraham is told to leave these three things and "go to the land" (singular), the implication is that he leaves all those other things behind. Go from "country, kindred, father's house" to "*the land*." The tension is found in the emptiness of the request. He leaves what is known and goes to the unknown. Yahweh asks him to "go" from the familiar to the unfamiliar. The unknown land is not his country and does not contain his people or his father's house.

> **Go from**
>> country
>>> kindred
>>> father's house
>
> **To**
>> land

But Yahweh promises to provide a double portion of what he asks Abraham to leave. The family and people he forsakes will be returned in abundance. In Gen. 12:2 Yahweh promises him that if he leaves these things, he will (1) make Abraham into a great nation, (2) bless him, (3) make his name great, and (4) and make him a blessing.

Go from

> country
>> kindred
>> father's house

To

> land

Promises

> great nation
> blessings
> great name
> he will be a blessing

Genesis 17 fills out this promise by saying that Abraham's offspring will be multiplied greatly (17:2). His name is even changed from Abram to Abraham, because Yahweh makes him "the father of a multitude of nations" (17:4–5). Yahweh says, "I will make you exceedingly fruitful, and I will make you into nations, and kings shall come from you" (17:6). The blessings that Abraham receives reverse what he lost by leaving his own land and family. A key theme is introduced here that Matthew will develop: *the leaving of his family leads to double familial blessings.*[8]

God promises Abraham a new family, a new nation, in return for his obedience, but this blessing does not terminate upon just his own people. The purpose of God's blessing is "so that you will be a blessing" (Gen. 12:2). Verse 3 makes the recipient of the Abrahamic blessings apparent: "In you all the families of the earth shall be blessed." Abraham is called from his family and promised that he will be a great nation, but the aim is so that the whole world will be blessed. Already, before the time of Matthew, the rejection of his own family (leaving) leads to another family being established. The universal (all families) will be blessed through the particular (Abraham's family). The universal dimension emerges from the particular.

Yet there is a condition for the blessings. Those who bless Abraham will be blessed, and those who curse Abraham will be cursed (Gen. 12:3). Since Jesus is the son of Abraham, as Matthew asserts, then those who bless Jesus will be blessed, and those who curse Jesus will be cursed. Those who follow

---

8. It is still Abraham's family, but his family is redefined and expanded.

and accept Jesus's message will be welcomed into the family. Those who do not will be cast out. As in Genesis, it is not based on ethnicity but on God's favor. Those who plot against Jesus will find only curses in their path. How people respond to them determines whether these blessings will flow freely or be impeded. Therefore, in the first pillar, the central concept is the familial promises God makes with Abraham. The covenant with Abraham is about his future family.

The second pillar demonstrating the prominence of familial themes with Abraham is the flurry of "seed" texts. The fulfillment of the promise made to Abraham, and indeed the entire Abrahamic narrative, revolves around his progeny. In Gen. 15 Abraham questions God's covenant with him "for I continue childless, and the heir of my house is Eliezer of Damascus" (15:2). God takes him outside, shows him the stars, and says, "So shall your offspring be" (15:5). The next chapter in Genesis is about Abraham producing offspring, not through Sarai but through Hagar. Genesis 17 recounts how Yahweh appears to Abraham and says that he will multiply him greatly (17:2). Abraham will be "the father of a multitude of nations" (17:4).[9] Abraham is promised that he will be exceedingly fruitful, and kings will come from him. The covenant that God makes with Abraham is also for his offspring (17:7). God promises to give Sarah a son (17:16). Genesis 18 then fulfills this promise when three men come to visit Abraham and promise that she will bear a son (18:10). The promise made to Abraham in Gen. 12 is repeated (18:18), showing that through a child, a son, Abraham will be "a great and mighty nation, and all the nations of the earth shall be blessed in him." Then in Gen. 21 the Lord

---

9. Note that Abraham is specifically called *father*.

visits Sarah, who conceives and bears a son, Isaac (Gen. 21:1–3). The entire narrative from Gen. 12 onward concerns Abraham's lack of, desire for, or attainment of a child. It is the promise of the "seed" that drives the narrative forward.

The third pillar that confirms the familial theme in Abraham's life comes through later biblical reflections on the significance of Abraham. Consistently, when Abraham's name appears, he is associated with children. Thus Ps. 105:6 says, "O offspring of Abraham, his servant, children of Jacob, his chosen ones!" Also Isa. 41:8 addresses, "You, Israel, my servant, Jacob, whom I have chosen, the offspring of Abraham, my friend." Isaiah 51:2 counsels, "Look to Abraham your father and Sarah who bore you; for he was but one when I called him, that I might bless him and multiply him." In this last text, we get a little commentary on the promises to Abraham. What is important for our purposes is that the "blessings" are put in parallel to the children of Abraham. Paul also reflects on the significance of Abraham, saying that the blessing was not only for the circumcised but also for the uncircumcised (Rom. 4:9). Later Paul says that Abraham became the father not only of the circumcised but also of those who walk in the footsteps of faith (Rom. 4:12). Galatians supports this point when Paul says that those of faith are "sons of Abraham" (Gal. 3:7). A few verses later Paul says that the blessing of Abraham comes to gentiles (3:14), and he mentions the "seed" of Abraham, tying this seed to Christ.[10] As later biblical writers reflect on Abraham, their sine qua non for thinking about Abraham can be described through the imagery of family, offspring, seed.

These three points: the covenant made with Abraham, the wide-angle focus on the Abraham narrative, and later biblical commentaries on Abraham support familial, offspring, and seed themes as central. Matthew, as we will see, writes within this tradition and directs his gaze upon the same leitmotif. But now that the apocalyptic messiah has come, Matthew not only follows the OT tradition but also rethinks what the "family of God" means. Matthew rereads the Jewish Scriptures in light of his rabbi's life, death, and resurrection.

The Introduction to Matthew's Gospel

One of the best ways to see the role that Abraham plays in Matthew is by looking at both his introduction and his conclusion. The introduction sets

---

10. The Galatians text does not undermine my point about the "offspring" but supports it, because Jesus becomes the seed who creates the new family.

the terms for what to look for in the narrative, and the conclusion brings the theme to its climax. While proposals for the structure of Matthew continue to abound, I take the first two chapters as the introduction to the Gospel, and the last three chapters as the conclusion. This division fits the narrative/ discourse pattern outlined in the Gospel.[11] Though this is not the only way to conceive of the introduction and the conclusion, it does provide a place to begin.[12] My focus will be on the true introduction (the genealogy) and the true conclusion (the Great Commission), while using a few other texts in the larger introduction and conclusion to support the points found in the genealogy and Great Commission.

The Genealogy

In the first verse Matthew declares that Jesus is the son of Abraham (1:1). The genealogy is therefore wrapped not only around David's name, but also around the promises to Abraham. Jesus is the son of Abraham who establishes the new people of God.[13] Three points about the genealogy inform how Matthew conceives of the new family of God and Jesus as the fulfillment of the promises to Abraham. First, Matthew begins with a family tree (a genealogy), demonstrating from the start that he has his eye on the "offspring/ family" theme. Second, through Matthew's list we learn about the nature of the family of Abraham. Third, the use of "the son of Abraham" indicates the family is established by an Isaac-type death.

FAMILY TREE

Matthew and Mark have quite a bit of similar material, but Matthew waits until chapter 3 to take up Mark's story. He chooses to write his own introduction. As Morna Hooker comments about Matthew's opening, "If listening to Mark makes us imagine we are in a theatre, then turning to Matthew may well make us feel we are back in school."[14] The first lesson he hands out to his students is a Jewish family tree, which becomes the key to understanding his entire course. Matthew begins his narrative with a list of names that remarkably foreshadows nearly every theme his Gospel is later going to draw out. The messiah is born (present) from the line of David and Abraham (past) and begins his rule and new family (future).

---

11. See chap. 7, on Israel, for a short defense of this structure.
12. Altering the introduction or conclusion slightly (by either expanding it or reducing it) does not have much effect on the argument I make here.
13. For a study on the annotations in Matthew's genealogy, see Hood, *Messiah*.
14. Hooker, *Beginnings*, 23.

Matthew most likely begins with a genealogy because he draws on a rich tradition of genealogical texts. Genealogies are important in the *Tanak* (an acronym for the Hebrew Bible's three main divisions: Torah, Nevi'im, and *Ketuvim*). Genesis, the first book of the *Tanak*—the beginning of the beginnings—is structured around ten genealogies. In the well-attested traditional Jewish canonical order, Chronicles is the last book of the *Tanak* and also begins with nine genealogies.[15] The formal similarities between Genesis and Chronicles are hard to miss. Both are virtually the only books in the Hebrew Bible filled with genealogies. Chronicles commences with Adam and rapidly moves through human history until arriving at David. Genesis also begins with Adam but moves quickly until Abraham comes on the scene. Most of the book of Genesis follows Abraham's descendants. Matthew seems to have detected the "offspring" theme not only in the specific words but also in the specific genre of the bookends of the Jewish canon. The Jewish hopes revolved around a child who was from the family of Israel.

Genealogies served a variety of purposes, yet the most foundational purpose is found in Gen. 3:15, the *protevangelium*. God promises Eve that she will have a child who will be at war with the serpent but ultimately crush him. The rest of the OT traces the line of this seed through the genealogies. This is why the Hebrew Bible begins and ends with genealogies. These genealogies provide historical information, but they are much more than historical information. They provide a metanarrative perspective on how the promises of God progress. The genealogies give the rise and fall of the seed, focusing on God's faithfulness to preserve the seed of the woman through many dangers, toils, and snares. When Matthew opens his Gospel with a genealogy, the form recalls all the hopes and dreams of the Israelite nation. After four hundred years of deafening silence, people are wondering what has happened to God's promises. Matthew breaks the stillness with the opening proclamation that Jesus is the son of David and the son of Abraham.

The hope for resurrection life began with the promises to Abraham when God covenanted with him, telling Abraham that he would give him a new land and a new family. Matthew thus indicates the fulfillment of the promises to Abraham by beginning his Gospel with a family tree. Jesus is identified as the son of Abraham in the title of the genealogy. Matthew points his readers beyond David to God's covenant with Abraham. Jesus, the son of Abraham, will enjoy God's blessing, he will be the agent through whom God will bless all nations and families on the earth, and he will be the founder of a great

---

15. In some canon lists, Chronicles is placed after Kings and sometimes at the head of the Wisdom literature. See Gallagher and Meade, *Biblical Canon Lists*.

nation. Matthew begins with a family tree that points to the promises made to Abraham.

THE COMPLETED FAMILY

Although it is evident that Abraham's family is important to Matthew because he (1) begins his Gospel with a genealogy and (2) explicitly mentions that Jesus is the son of Abraham (1:1), we have not examined what exactly we learn about Abraham's family from this opening. Two related lessons are given about the family of Abraham through Matthew's genealogy. First, Jesus is the fulfillment of Abraham's family (Jewish particularism). Second, the family plan was always to include all nations (gentile inclusion).

First, Jesus fulfills the promises made to Abraham's family. Matthew states that Jesus is "the son of Abraham" (1:1). Matthew believes that Jewish history is unified and fulfilled in the person of Jesus. The arrival of Jesus is the apocalyptic satisfaction of the covenant made with Abraham. Though Abraham had other children, Jesus is his child par excellence (Gal. 3:16). When Jesus is born, he completes the family of Abraham and fulfills the hopes of the Jewish people. Matthew could have traced the genealogy back to Adam, as Luke does, but instead he compiles a markedly Jewish list. The First Gospel, as many have noted, has a distinctively Jewish focus.

Second, Jesus is not only a particular messiah but also one that welcomes all nations to his side. These two things should not be in combat with each other; they come in tandem. The particularity of Jesus as a Jew paves the way for the inclusion of all nations. Universality emerges from particularity as the promise stated in Gen. 12. While it is true that most of this family tree is composed of "Jewish" names, a few persons outside Israel are included. The five women named in the genealogy are usually explained in one of three ways: (1) all are regarded as sinners, (2) all represent a certain irregularity in their unions, and (3) all except Mary are foreigners. Though it is only explicit that Rahab and Ruth are non-Israelites, a good case can also be made for Tamar and Bathsheba. Bathsheba is not actually mentioned by name, but Matthew alludes to her as "the wife of Uriah" (1:6). This could be read in reference to David's wrongdoing, but more likely Matthew includes her by referring to her husband because it makes her gentile status explicit because Uriah was a Hittite (2 Sam. 11:3, 6).

Tamar is also not explicitly identified as a gentile in the OT, but a tradition in Jewish literature asserts she was a proselyte. Philo (*Virt.* 220–22) presents Tamar as from Palestinian Syria and a convert to Judaism. Thus, all the evidence taken together—Tamar and Rahab were Canaanites, Ruth a Moabite, and Bathsheba was the wife of a Hittite—anticipates the universal dimension of the family of Abraham. The community of salvation has always been open to non-Jews; now with salvation history turning, the universality is made explicit. Hays is right to also point out that three of these women (Tamar, Rahab, and Ruth) are characterized by their tenacious fidelity.[16] Jesus will welcome those who are fiercely loyal to him. The family of Abraham is both old and new.[17] Though the other options for the inclusion of women are certainly valid, the gentile inclusion is part of the picture. This inclusion is especially striking since the matriarchs of the faith are left out: Sarah, Rebekah, and Leah.

Careful readers of the OT should not be surprised at the inclusion of gentiles. Abraham was not merely the ancestor of Israel but also the ancestor of a "multitude of nations" (Gen. 17:4–5). Even in his opening verses, Matthew's eye is focused both on Israel's past (the old) and on how Israel is still to become God's chosen vessel to bring salvation to the entire earth (the new). But as Konradt notes, "If Matthew makes a reference to the universality of salvation with the words 'son of Abraham,' this need not be set as an exclusive alternative against Abraham's significance as *Israel's* patriarch. Rather, the two aspects can be positively interconnected: precisely as the patriarch of Israel, Abraham is at the same time the bearer of the promise for the nations."[18] Thus Matthew includes Abraham in his opening introduction to point to the fulfillment of God's promises that he will bless the entire world through the offspring who stands at the end of this lineage. Jesus is the king, the seed promised in Gen. 3:15, the offspring of Abraham, and his family includes all nations.

Isaac-Like Death

We have seen how the *form* of Matthew's opening (a genealogy) directs our gaze to family themes, and the *names* themselves also point toward a universal family through a particular family. Yet the genealogy also leaves some questions unanswered. The genealogy traces the decline of the people of Israel.[19] A key juncture in the genealogy is the exile (1:11), the only event named in the whole list of people. The family of Abraham is in disarray as Jesus steps onto the scene. While Matthew opens his Gospel by indicating

---

16. Hays, *Echoes of Scripture in the Gospels*, 112.

17. France (*Gospel of Matthew*, 37) admits that their sexual past might link the women together, but he acknowledges that this suggestion is weakened by the fact that embarrassment over their sexual activities is primarily a modern phenomenon. In Jewish tradition, Tamar, Rahab, and Ruth are heroes. It is also David who is castigated for adultery, not Bathsheba.

18. Konradt, *Israel, Church, and the Gentiles*, 267–68.

19. It also traces the steadfast hand and covenant love of God in preserving his people.

that the return from exile is taking place, he doesn't explicitly identify *how*. But he does so implicitly.

Jesus is the son of Abraham in the ultimate sense, but Isaac is also the son of promise. Leroy Huizenga's work reveals a rich tradition in Jewish literature of viewing Isaac as a willing sacrifice.[20] He argues that "son of Abraham" is as significant christologically as the title "son of David" (Matt. 1:1). If son of David points to the kingdom the wise king will establish, then "son of Abraham" points to Jesus as an Isaac-type figure. Matthew therefore indicates that Abraham's family derives from a willing sacrifice. The establishment of the family of Abraham, the return from exile, and the new exodus will come only through blood.

Huizenga notes that Isaac's near death develops along several lines in early Judaism, including as an etiology of Passover (Jub. 18.18–19) and depicting Isaac as a willing sacrifice (4Q225). Philo also depicts Isaac as being perfectly virtuous and the "son of God." Philo asserts that many traditions have stories in which persons offer themselves or their child for a cause they believe in, yet Abraham's sacrifice is unprecedented in that he is governed not by custom, honor, or fear but solely by the love of God (*Abr.* 177–99). Pseudo-Philo's *Liber antiquitatum biblicarum* depicts Isaac as a willing sacrifice. In rabbinic literature, the binding of Isaac is spoken of as the prototype of readiness for martyrdom.

The tradition on which all of these stories are based is in Gen. 22. Abraham is tested and told to sacrifice his son Isaac (22:1). Isaac is confused about where the lamb for the burnt offering is to be found (22:7). Abraham says, "God will provide for himself the lamb for a burnt offering, my son" (22:8). When they come to the place, Abraham places Isaac on the altar and takes out his knife to slaughter his son, but the Lord intervenes and provides a ram. Because Abraham does this, God swears to him, "I will surely bless you, and I will surely multiply your offspring as the stars of the heaven and as the sand that is on the seashore, . . . and in your offspring shall all the nations of the earth be blessed" (22:17–18). This text explicitly links Abraham's willingness, and *implicitly* Isaac's willingness, to the promise of a multitude of offspring.[21] We can draw a line from this text to the sacrificial willingness of the son of Abraham (in continuity with both Abraham and Isaac) as the means of salvation for a multitude of nations.

Huizenga cites two further possible points of evidence indicating that Matthew may be drawing on this tradition. First, in Jubilees, Isaac is sacrificed in

---

20. Huizenga, *New Isaac*.
21. Admittedly, the biblical text is formally silent on Isaac's willingness. However, the text also does not present Isaac as unwilling, and Jewish tradition supports his willingness.

the forty-second jubilee year. Not surprisingly, there are forty-two generations between Abraham and Jesus (14 × 3). This may point to the forty-two jubilees completed with the binding of Isaac. Second, Huizenga notes that the "beloved son" term in Jewish tradition constitutes an allusion to Isaac. In Jesus's baptism, a voice declares from heaven, "This is my beloved Son" (Matt. 3:17; cf. Gen. 22:2), and both the Isaac story and the baptism of Jesus have a divine intervention from heaven (cf. Gen. 22:11, 15). As Daniel Kirk says, "In light of the active place that Isaac played in the imagination of early Jewish idealized martyr figures, the allusive force of the voice from heaven seems to disclose, to the attentive reader, that the Christological title secretly bestowed upon Jesus [in the baptism] entails . . . a particular task of submitting to death."[22]

There seems to be enough evidence in the Jewish tradition and in the Gospel of Matthew to view "the son of Abraham" in the new-Isaac tradition. Jesus is the king and messiah, but he is also the father of a multitude of nations. Yet both of these come only through a sacrificial death. The offspring of Abraham is accomplished only by a willing death, as in the Isaac story.

Summary

The genealogy is a storehouse of riches from which Matthew draws out treasures both new and old. Matthew begins his Gospel by signaling the nature and composition of the new people of God and pointing to Jesus as the true son of Abraham. He does this by both explicitly naming Jesus "the son of Abraham" and through the form of his opening, a Jewish family tree. For Matthew, the particular Jewish nature of Jesus is the means for blessings going out to the whole world. Jesus is the son of Abraham and the father of a multitude of nations. Matthew includes four gentile women to let readers know that the line of the messiah includes all nations. The family *from* which Jesus comes reveals the family *for* which he comes. Yet the path to this expansion can be traced only by reading the rest of the Gospel. Jesus ends up going to his death, a willing death, like the willing death of Isaac, the son of Abraham.

Other Indications of Universal Salvation in the Introduction

The rest of Matthew's introduction also includes other indications of the particularity and universality of Abraham's family. Richard Erickson has pointed out that the birth narrative in Matt. 1:18–25 reflects the story of Abraham in Gen. 12–17, and so we should read this text in an Abrahamic

22. Kirk, *Man Attested by God*, 190.

way.[23] An Abrahamic reading of the birth narrative points again to both particularity and universalism, for the "son of Abraham" is to save "his people from their sins" (Matt. 1:1, 21). Although there is much debate about who "his people" are, it seems that, reading this in the context of the whole Gospel, "his people" are those who do the will of his father, and this is not limited to the nation of Israel. The term "his people" thus includes Israel but is also broader than Israel.[24] Jesus is also to be "Immanuel, . . . God with" all those receiving salvation, all who follow Jesus and seek God (1:23); those receiving judgment are all who turn away from Jesus.

The particular and universal nature of salvation for the family of God is also highlighted in chapter 2, where pagan astrologers seek the newborn king of the Jews to worship him. King Herod and all Jerusalem are troubled that another "king of the Jews" is on the scene, but the wise men follow the star and fall down and worship Jesus (Matt. 2:2, 11). For our purposes, it is important to see that the first "worshipers" of Jesus come from outside Israel.[25] Yet this must be paired with the reality that they are worshiping Jesus as "the king of the Jews." Outsiders recognize that the Jewish king is to be worshiped by more than only Jews. As in the genealogy, readers are presented with a particular king (Jewish) who is worshiped by non-Jews. The particularity is not erased, but it fuels the inclusion of all nations.

Also, in chapter 2 Matthew tells his readers that, to protect the child, Joseph takes Jesus and flees from Judea to Egypt. This move is similar to Israel/Jacob and his family going to Egypt to be saved from the famine. But what is different is that Jesus is fleeing from Herod, the king of the Jews. The escape into Egypt allows for the christological fulfillment of Hosea 11:1, "Out of Egypt I called my son" (Matt. 2:15). This scene plays not only into Moses and Israel typology, but also into Abrahamic intertextuality. As the sons of Abraham had to flee into Egypt to preserve their family, so too Jesus must flee to Egypt to preserve his life so that he can become the father of a multitude of nations.

Matthew's introduction is rich with Abrahamic hues. More specifically, it opens the door on a major theme of the First Gospel: the new family of God. In one sense, all of what Matthew presents is "old": Abraham was promised that he would become the father of a multitude of nations and that through

---

23. Erickson, "Joseph and the Birth of Isaac." This point will be developed in the chapter on Israel.

24. Alternatively, one could argue that Jesus needs to save Israel from their sins so that the gospel can then go to the nations.

25. Leithart (*Jesus as Israel*, 70) says, "The magi are much more like Israel herself. . . . [They] are not merely Gentile God-fearers, but the beginning of a new Israel, which is going to consist of Jews and Gentiles."

him the whole world would be blessed. Yet, in another sense, this is new. The apocalyptic arrival of Jesus brings to the forefront the "new" nature of this family. It is not that Jesus rejects Israel (as I will show later in this chapter), but rather that the new family emerges from Israel itself. The new family is not one of replacement but of growth and extension. Universality is birthed from particularity. Abraham's significance as Israel's founder and the universality of salvation are not at odds. "Matthean universalism is grounded in Israel."[26] Though the climactic change has not yet occurred, there is enough in the introduction to assert that the shift has commenced.

The Conclusion to Matthew's Gospel

We have seen how the introduction to the First Gospel prepares readers for the nature of Abraham's new family. Now I turn to the conclusion of the Gospel (chaps. 26–28) and more specifically the Great Commission (28:16–20) to examine how this theme is resolved. What readers find is that the hints of a universal family found in the introduction are confirmed as the mission to the nations is formally launched. The "to all nations" theme comes to a culmination in the Great Commission. Although we find gentile inclusion in the introduction, Jesus's mission in the Gospel is still to Israel (Matt. 10:6; 15:24). Yet after the death and resurrection of Jesus, the mission expands in a more official sense.

The Great Commission

The Great Commission confirms the universal nature of Abraham's family, which was foreshadowed in the introduction.[27] Although this theme has been implicit from the first verse of the Gospel, not until the last verses of the Gospel is the theme cemented. There is a reason for this; only after the death and resurrection of Jesus does the new mission begin in full. All authority is Jesus's in a unique sense after his atoning sacrifice. This section will walk

---

26. Konradt, *Israel, Church, and the Gentiles*, 268.

27. While Konradt proposes a clean break in the Great Commission and provides a nice narrative development, the constitution of the new people of God in the First Gospel is more untidy and progressive than Konradt suggests. This is most likely because Matthew writes a historical account and attempts to communicate the messiness of the development that Matthew has experienced in Jesus's ministry and was still experiencing in the early church. The new people of God is not an easy thing to understand or even live into, as the rest of the NT evidences. Konradt is right that an overall rejection of Israel does not occur, but there is a prophetic condemnation. The temple is cleansed (21:12–13), their leaders are castigated (23:23), and their fig tree is left barren (21:18–19). The king of the Jews has arrived, and Jerusalem does not recognize him, so they crucify him, thereby installing him as the universal Lord of all creation.

slowly through the Great Commission, noting the universal and particular aspects of Jesus's command and tying it to Jesus's fulfillment of the promises to Abraham. Although Abraham is not mentioned in the Great Commission, it would be a mistake to overlook this text in our analysis of the Abrahamic family theme. Just because the name is missing does not mean the theme is absent. I will examine the location of the command, recipients of the command, basis of the command, and the command itself.

LOCATION OF THE COMMAND (28:16)

Jesus gives the command to "make disciples of all nations" on a mountain in Galilee. Both the mountain imagery and the Galilee location are significant for Matthew.[28] First, there are six important mountain passages in Matthew (4:8; 5:1; 15:29; 17:1; 24:3; 28:16). In Jewish literature mountains are common for their theological significance; therefore, it is unlikely that Matthew's mountain references are merely geographical markers. The final mountain scene in the First Gospel is the climax of the mountain imagery and therefore probably encompasses a variety of fulfillments.[29] The Great Commission mountain is *revelatory*: on it Jesus announces who the new people of God are: all nations can become his disciples. It is also a *covenantal* mountain: it fulfills the promise to Abraham in a unique sense. Likewise it is also a *cosmic* mountain: Jesus tells his disciples to go to all nations. Finally, the mountain is *eschatological*: it is a decisive turning point of the ages. The Jewish particularism and gentile inclusion that have been running under the surface for all of Matthew's Gospel come to a head here.[30]

This mountain is also in Galilee.[31] In Matt. 4:15 the First Gospel writer indicates that Jesus performs most of his ministry in Galilee. Matthew calls it "Galilee of the Gentiles" (4:15), and therefore the place where light shone

28. France (*Gospel of Matthew*, 1107) also makes much of the location markers. Davies and Allison (*Matthew*, 3:679) point to the Mosaic imagery, since Moses ended his earthly ministry on a mountain.

29. Donaldson, *Jesus on the Mountain*. According to Donaldson, in Jewish history mountains revolve around four themes. There are covenant mountains, cosmic mountains, mountains of revelation, and eschatological mountains.

30. Donaldson argues that the mountain scene here is a christological reinterpretation of Zion eschatology. The exalted Jesus is now the gathering point for the people of God, not Mount Zion. Jesus is now the presence of God to the people of God, as confirmed by the words "I am with you always, to the end of the age."

31. Carson ("Matthew" [2010], 663) says the association with Galilee not only has nuances with Jesus's humble background and the theme of the gentile mission but also ensures that the risen Christ's ministry is continuous with Jesus's previous ministry. Yet there is also a shift here that should be noted. Turner says that Galilee is fitting because the disciples are Galileans and would have returned home after the Passover in Jerusalem. Yet Turner (*Matthew*, 688)

now becomes the point of departure for ministry to the nations. In Acts, the mission to the world goes through Galilee. In Matthew, Jesus commissions his disciples not in Jerusalem but from a "northern" mountain, thus bringing unity to the north and the south again. As Abraham was called from a foreign land, so too Jesus sends out his disciples into foreign lands from a mountain in northern Israel, launching them into the world.

RECIPIENTS OF THE COMMAND (28:17)

Jesus gives the command (to make disciples of all nations) not to the crowd or the religious leaders but to the eleven disciples (28:17). Jesus called twelve disciples in order to mirror the twelve tribes of Israel, but Judas has fallen away.[32] The command is given to the eleven disciples not just because they are Jesus's followers, but because they represent Israel. In other words, the messengers taking the gospel to all nations are Israel. Israelites are to share the message that Jesus is the king. The particular dimension we noted in the introduction is still at play here. Salvation comes through Abraham's seed, and they are the ones to spread the message, but the universal aspect also arises in this passage because it is to all nations.

This might point to the nations becoming the "twelfth" discile in Matthew's narrative.[33] While some might object because of the account in Acts of Matthias being chosen to replace Judas as the twelfth disciple (Acts 1:21–26), we need to remember that Luke provides a part 2 of his narrative, where another disciple is chosen, but Matthew does not have this luxury. He explicitly notes that there are "eleven disciples," and he tells them to go out and "make disciples," thereby implying that the nations now constitute the new people of God, the new Israel of God. This again means not that the nations replace Israel but rather that they are enfolded into Israel. Or to use Paul's analogy, they are grafted into the tree that already stands (Rom. 11:17–18).

BASIS OF THE COMMAND (28:18)

The main command of Matt. 28:16–20 is "make disciples of all nations." However, this is grounded (οὖν, "therefore," v. 19) in the authority given to

---

also notes that because Galilee has previously been associated with gentiles, it is fitting that the mandate occurs here.

32. Matthew's modifying the count of disciples to eleven does not occur elsewhere in this Gospel; only recently has Judas fallen away, so we would not expect it to occur much.

33. Alternatively, one could argue that Jesus is the twelfth disciple and completes Israel, but I find this less likely since it would be odd for him to be labeled as a disciple of himself. Rather, he stands at the head of Israel.

Jesus: "All authority in heaven and on earth has been given to me." Universal lordship means universal mission. A few things should be noted about this authority. First, it is given to Jesus. The emphasis here is on Jesus receiving the authority from the Father because of his unique relationship to God. Jesus is not only the son of Abraham or the son of David but also the Son of God. These titles actually go together, for David and Abraham are uniquely sons of God. Therefore, the authority given to Jesus is in some sense related to the authority that Adam and Eve were to have in the garden as son and daughter of God (Gen. 2). Yet an aspect of this authority was forfeited by them (Gen. 3), and Abraham's seed is to regain this authority.[34] Jesus was offered authority during the temptation (4:8–10), but he refused, leading to his receiving far more authority than Satan could offer.

Second, Matthew's Gospel associates this authority with teaching and healing. Matthew 7:29 says Jesus "was teaching . . . as one who had authority." In Matt. 10:1 Jesus calls his twelve disciples and gives them authority over unclean spirits. Both teaching and healing are tied to the proclamation of the gospel of the kingdom in Matthew (as in 4:23). So the authority Jesus has received is kingdom authority. This kingdom authority proclaims and invites people into the kingdom; this "authority" is the basis of the command "Make disciples of all nations." The authority is a proclaiming authority, and Jesus has authority that is universal: all authority in heaven and on earth. Because of Jesus's death and resurrection, he is now the universal Lord, exalted to the right hand of God, so he possesses all authority to send his disciples into all nations. This authority is not new, as if he did not have it before; rather, this is the *confirmation* of that authority.

Third, the command to all nations relates to "all authority in heaven and on earth." The other Synoptic Gospels use ἡ βασιλεία τοῦ θεοῦ, while Matthew regularly uses ἡ βασιλεία τῶν οὐρανῶν. N. T. Wright and most modern textbooks argue that the phrase ἡ βασιλεία τῶν οὐρανῶν has long been misunderstood by Christians to mean a place. He asserts that for Jesus it is "a Jewish way of talking about Israel's god becoming king."[35] But Wright and others have not sufficiently reflected on Matthew's use of οὐρανός. Jonathan Pennington has done the most extensive work on this theme in Matthew.[36] As Pennington argues, "To deny a spatial sense of ἡ βασιλεία τῶν οὐρανῶν would require interpreting οὐρανός in this phrase as bearing no relation to the rest of the spatial uses of οὐρανός throughout

34. The language also echoes Dan. 7:14.
35. Wright, *Jesus and the Victory of God*, 202–3.
36. Much of the material that follows comes from Pennington, *Heaven and Earth*. Gerhard Schneider ("Studien zum Matthäusevangelium," 287–89) has also done work on this theme.

Matthew."[37] He maintains that this phrase should be interpreted in light of the tension between heaven and earth. In the Great Commission, Jesus has united these spaces in his death. Jesus is the king of heaven, and by occupying the space of the earth, is in the process of overhauling it for his own purposes.[38] This is interconnected to the command concerning "all nations." Jesus, the son of Abraham, can send his disciples into all nations because he has received authority over all spaces. The mission to all spaces is built upon Jesus's authority in all spaces. The theological link is confirmed when one considers the reference to Dan. 7:13–14. Matthew 28:18b, "All authority is given to me" (ἐδόθη μοι πᾶσα ἐξουσία) is most likely inspired by "He gave him authority" (ἐδόθη αὐτῷ ἐξουσία) in Dan. 7:14. In Dan. 7 the purpose of this authority is explicitly so that "all peoples, nations, and languages should serve him" (7:14). The universal Lord is the basis of the universal command.

THE COMMAND (28:19–20)

The location, recipients, and basis anchor the command "Make disciples of all nations." The main imperative (μαθητεύσατε, make disciples) is the same root as the word used in Matthew's description of the "discipled scribe" (γραμματεὺς μαθητευθείς, 13:52). Three participles revolve around this: *go, baptize,* and *teach.*[39] The command itself "Make disciples" means make followers or pupils of someone. In this case, the charge is to make disciples of Jesus, the son of Abraham. According to BDAG, this word is regularly connected to teaching and instruction. The disciples' task is to teach about Jesus, the universal Lord, and grow his family.[40]

Though the direct object of the command, "all nations" (μαθητεύσατε πάντα τὰ ἔθνη), initially seems clear, the meaning of the noun is debated.[41] However, the point is that the mission expands; the command to witness to Israel (10:6; 15:24) is not revoked, but added to.[42] The family of Abraham, as a

37. Pennington, *Heaven and Earth,* 297. Pennington ("Heaven, Earth, and a New Genesis," 29) categorizes heaven references into three primary uses: (1) the portions of the visible creation distinguished from earth; (2) combined with γῆ as a merism to refer to the whole world; and (3) the invisible, transcendent place(s) above, where God dwells along with his angels and the righteous dead. When heaven modifies kingdom, the third use is likely in view.

38. See my book on this theme (*Body of Jesus*) for an expanded view of this statement.

39. "Go" (πορευθέντες) is most likely giving the attendant circumstance, while "baptizing" and "teaching" tell the means by which the disciple-making is to happen.

40. Growing Jesus's family is precisely what Matthew is doing by writing the Gospel.

41. Konradt, *Israel, Church, and the Gentiles,* 316.

42. France (*Gospel of Matthew,* 1114) agrees, saying that nothing in the text indicates that it means gentiles as opposed to Jews.

particular family, was always meant to bless all nations. The son of Abraham (1:1) extends the universality of salvation in a climactic way in this passage although it has been hinted at from the beginning. Matthew opens his narrative with hints of the universality of salvation, but this is positively allied with the election of Israel from the start. Now gentiles are children of Abraham if they become disciples of Jesus. Matthew is the "discipled scribe," teaching his readers how to become disciples of this Jewish rabbi.

The hoped-for gathering of all nations on Mount Zion is replaced with a call to make disciples out of all nations. Two texts in Isaiah connect the gathering to Mount Zion with an explicit mention of all nations (Isa. 2:2; 56:7). Jesus thus seems to be fulfilling this idea and transforming it. "It is Christ who has replaced Zion as the center of eschatological fulfillment, and the mount motif in Matthew acts as a vehicle by which Zion expectations are transferred to Christ."[43] The shift to the universal mission is based on the comprehensive authority of Jesus, founded upon his death and resurrection. He now is the new mountain to which the nations will stream, but the disciples must "go" to make this happen.

Gentiles are disciples through baptism into the trinitarian name of God and with instruction about Jesus's commandments. What is not mentioned here is circumcision, or even following Jewish customs. Yet they are to follow the one who did say he came not to abolish the law but to fulfill it. So once again, Matthew pairs this universal dimension with a particular dimension. That is because Jesus is a *particular* messiah. He is of the seed of Abraham, and he came to fulfill the promises made to Abraham about a new family.

Other Indications of Universal Salvation in the Conclusion

While the Great Commission contains the most explicit data concerning the universal dimension of salvation in the conclusion, there are also a few other indications in Matt. 26–28.[44] The Great Commission is predicated on the narrative preceding it. But to look for the universal dimensions only here is misguided; as I have been arguing, the universal dimension emerges from the particular. This is seen especially with regard to the use of the titles "King of the Jews" and "the Son of God" in the passion. In Matt. 27 Jesus affirms

43. Donaldson, *Jesus on the Mountain*, 184.
44. Huizenga ("Obedience unto Death") asserts that the arrest sequence in the garden of Gethsemane has Aqedah themes and thus presents Jesus as the new Isaac who willingly faces sacrifice and thereby continues and expands Abraham's family. Rosenberg ("Jesus, Isaac, and the 'Suffering Servant,'") ties Isaac to the suffering servant from Isaiah.

before Pilate that he is the "King of the Jews" (27:11). In Gen. 17:6, Abraham is promised, "Kings shall come from you." Here Jesus indicates that he is the true king from the line of Abraham. The soldiers then mock Jesus as the "King of the Jews" (Matt. 27:29) and put a sign above his head, which reads: "This is Jesus, the King of the Jews" (27:37). Readers should notice that this phrase occurs three times in this chapter (27:11, 29, 37). Jesus is crucified on the charge that he is "the King of the Jews."

Yet readers should also note that three times Jesus is mocked or described also as the "Son of God" (27:40, 43, 54). The rebels who are crucified with Jesus hurl insults at him, saying, "If you are the Son of God, come down from the cross" (27:40; Ps. 2:7, 12). A few verses later they say, "He trusts in God. Let God rescue him now if he wants him, for he said, 'I am the Son of God'" (Matt. 27:43 NIV). After Jesus's death the centurion also declares, "Surely he was the Son of God!" (27:54 NIV).

Konradt has argued that these two titles (king of the Jews and son of God) represent a narrative development for Matthew.[45] The king of the Jews is the son of David and the son of Abraham. And in Jesus's earthly ministry, this correlates with Jesus's ministry to Israel. But Jesus is also born "by the Holy Spirit" and therefore is the Son of God.[46] The inclusion of the nations is on the basis of the Son of God's death and his installation as the Son of God and the universal Lord.[47] The extension of salvation to the nations intersects with his title "the Son of God."

The universal lordship of the Son of God is hinted at when the centurion confesses that Jesus is "the Son of God." As in chapter 2, it is not the Jewish people or leaders who recognize and worship Jesus, but rather a centurion (27:54). Pairing the centurion's confession with that of the magi can help us see the development of the universal and particular dimensions of Jesus's ministry. The magi recognize Jesus as "king of the Jews" (2:2), but in Matt. 27, only after Jesus is on the cross or dead, do people recognize him as "the Son of God." The rebels mock him as the Son of God, and the centurion confesses Jesus as "the Son of God" after his death.[48]

---

45. Yigal Levin ("Jesus, 'Son of God' and 'Son of David'") argues that Jesus is the Son of God and adopted into the royal line of Israel following Roman traditions.

46. Wisdom 9:17 identifies the holy spirit with wisdom.

47. Konradt, *Israel, Church, and the Gentiles*, 324.

48. Throughout Matthew it is mainly the devil and demons who declare that Jesus is the Son of God (4:3, 6; 8:29). Yet there are also two texts in which the disciples or Peter recognize Jesus as the Son of God. After Jesus walks on water and calms the storm, they declare that Jesus is the Son of God (14:33). At Caesarea Philippi, Peter also declares that Jesus is "the Christ, the Son of the living God" (16:16). Finally, the high priest asks Jesus if he is "the Christ, the Son of God" (26:63).

Matthew has generally reserved the title "Son of God" for unique circumstances (either supernatural beings, revelatory events for the disciples, or the trial of Jesus). This might be because, although the reader knows that Jesus is the Son of God because he is born from the Holy Spirit, the title is not confirmed until after his death on the cross. Jesus is *declared* to be the Son of God from his birth, but he is not *appointed* as the Son of God until his death and resurrection. The confession of the centurion therefore begins to close the narrative loop that began in the introduction (1:18–25, "born from the Holy Spirit"). Jesus is both the King of the Jews and the Son of God, but these titles correlate with the focus on Israel and the focus on the nations, respectively.

As the son of Abraham and the son of David, Jesus is the king of the Jews. But he is also the Son of God with universal authority. Although we as readers know this from the beginning, and the rest of the NT shows us how these two titles are inseparable, the original witnesses to Jesus needed to have this revealed to them. Jesus turned from being a national figure to a universal figure. Matthew is the discipled scribe who reveals the nature of Jesus and his mission to both Israel and to all nations. Jesus establishes Abraham's new family as the son of Abraham. All people and all nations are welcomed into a particular family.

Summary

Both the introduction and the conclusion of Matthew indicate that Jesus is the new Abraham, who establishes the new family of God, which includes both Jews and gentiles. Although the title "Abraham" does not appear in the conclusion, the universal dimension begun in 1:1 comes to a climax. The genealogy and the magi worshiping Jesus indicate that the apocalyptic son of Abraham is on the scene; the conclusion brings this theme to a culmination. In the Great Commission, Jesus declares that he has authority over all spaces, and therefore he sends his disciples into all the world. This is based on the fact that Jesus is now *appointed* as the Son of God. This King of the Jews has become, by virtue of his sacrifice, the Son of God. Neither Jewish particularism nor gentile inclusion is diminished. Rather, the two interweave, and the gentile inclusion emerges from the Jewish particularism.

Development of Abraham's New Family

We have examined the introduction and conclusion to Matthew's Gospel, focusing on the genealogy and the Great Commission. In some ways, the focus has been on the universal dimension, for Abraham was promised that he would be the father of many nations and that through him the world would be blessed. But it is also true that Abraham is known not only as the father of many nations but also as the founder of the Jewish nation. Therefore, although the introduction and conclusion indicate that "all nations" will be included, Jesus's mission as the son of Abraham is also to the "lost sheep of the house of Israel" (10:6; 15:24). He is sent to deal with Israel first. What we find in Matthew is that the mission to Israel has both positive and negative results. While the crowds and disciples are presented more positively in the First Gospel than in Mark, the religious leaders (and sometimes the nation as a whole) are condemned in Matthew. Therefore, the developing theme of God's new family in the middle of the Gospel includes three themes that at first seem contradictory but actually fit together.

These themes are not given in order; they weave their way throughout the Gospel, many times making it difficult for interpreters to know where to focus.[49] First, before the cross and resurrection, the disciples' and Jesus's mission is primarily to Israel. Second, this mission to Israel results in a prophetic condemnation and the formation of an alternate school. Third, Matthew indicates that the family of Abraham is now open to all (not excluding Israel but including them). In Matthew, Israel as a nation is not rejected but is judged because of their jealousy. As in the OT, the words of Jesus and his followers serve as a confirmation of judgment on those who do not follow Jesus. But like the prophets, hope arises out of judgment. Only through judgment will Israel be saved; the warning and condemnation function as the means by which true Israel is saved. In other words, there is a genealogical participation in Abraham's family by faith, and this comes on the heels of the condemnation of Israel.

49. Andries van Aarde ("Jesus' Mission") argues for two levels in Matthew's narrative. Level 1 is pre-Easter narration, and level 2 is post-Easter narration.

The middle section of the First Gospel (Matt. 3–25) explores these themes, and although the lines do not run entirely straight, there is progression. The family of Abraham is open to all but only because of the condemnation on those in Israel who will not accept the message. Like Paul, Jesus goes first to those of Israel, but when they reject his message, the way becomes open to the gentiles.

John the Baptist's Declaration concerning Abraham's Family (Matt. 3)

The open nature of Abraham's family is anticipated and prefigured even before Jesus begins his ministry. John the Baptist's words give readers an early clue to what to look for in the rest of Matthew's narrative. John the Baptist comes as the last OT prophet and in the clothing of a prophet (Matt. 3:4). The text says that Jerusalem, Judea, and the region of Jordan are "going out to him" and being "baptized, . . . confessing their sins" (3:5–6). Matthew therefore implies that there are positive movements from within the nation of Israel, and some of Israel will walk through the desert with this new Abraham figure. But when John the Baptist sees the Pharisees and Sadducees coming to his baptism, he calls them "offspring of serpents" (γεννήματα ἐχιδνῶν, AT).[50] Though the people are repenting, the Pharisees and Sadducees are not "bear[ing] fruit in keeping with repentance" (3:8). Then John mentions Abraham in his words to the religious leaders: "Do not presume to say to yourselves, 'We have Abraham as our father,' for I tell you, God is able from these stones to raise up children for Abraham. Even now the axe is laid to the root of the trees. Every tree therefore that does not bear good fruit is cut down and thrown into the fire" (3:9–10). John warns them not to base their acceptance on their ethnic identity. Interestingly, he uses both *familial* and *founder* imagery. Abraham is their "father," which communicates both genealogical and authoritative relations. The familial imagery continues as John says, "God is able from these stones to raise up *children* for Abraham" (emphasis added).

The Baptizer claims that ethnic identity is not determinative for who is part of the family; rather, it is fruit in keeping with repentance that regulates the family boundary. At the same time, the importance of the family of Abraham is highlighted. The stones that God is able to raise up become children of Abraham. John doesn't downplay Abraham's family but redefines it based on faith and repentance. Abraham's family is not rejected; John clarifies the nature of the family and its founder. In a way, he also expands the family by

---

50. Michael Knowles ("Serpents, Scribes, and Pharisees") argues that it is possible there is a wordplay between "serpent," "scribe," and "Pharisees."

saying that stones can become children. John tells them that one is coming who will baptize them with the Holy Spirit and fire, indicating both salvation and judgment. He will clear the threshing floor and gather the wheat but burn the chaff. Judgment will come upon those who do not follow the way of the Lord through the wilderness. In sum, the doorway to being a child of Abraham is repentance. If there is no repentance, then an unquenchable fire awaits. The founder still stands, but the family is redefined. Not all of Israel is judged, but their leaders are rebuked.

Jesus's Mission to Israel First (Matt. 4:12; 10:5–6; 15:24)

As John's ministry was to Israel, so too Jesus goes to Israel first. In Matt. 4:12 readers hear that Jesus retreats into Galilee; for a good portion of the rest of the Gospel, he performs his ministry in Galilee (in 16:21 he heads toward Jerusalem; in 21:10 he arrives in that city). Matthew claims that this movement of Jesus fulfills the geographical statement from Isa. 9:1–2.

> The land of Zebulun and the land of Naphtali, the way of the sea, beyond the Jordan, Galilee of the Gentiles—the people dwelling in darkness have seen a great light, and for those dwelling in the region and shadow of death, on them a light has dawned. (Matt. 4:15–16)

This quotation must be paired with Jesus's and his disciples' mission to "Israel first" (10:5–6; 15:24). In going to Galilee, he still goes to Israel, but to northern Israel, attempting to establish his rule over *all* Israel.[51] Zebulun and Naphtali were the first two tribes to go into exile (2 Kings 15:29), and therefore Jesus returns to restore those who were first conquered. Yet as Isaiah also predicts, whenever Jesus goes through the land of Israel, there is impact on the nations (the gentiles), as we saw in the genealogy. The people of Israel (even despite their failings) serve as a vehicle to bless the nations (Tamar, Ruth, Rahab, Uriah). So although Galilee has a mixed population of Jews and gentiles, Jesus's mission is first to the lost sheep of Israel.

Two other texts in Matthew confirm this Israel-first idea. In Matt. 10:5b–6 Jesus instructs his disciples to limit their mission to the "lost sheep of the house of Israel."[52] He tells them to go nowhere on roads that lead to gentiles or even any Samaritan towns.[53] As they go, they are to declare the same mes-

---

51. Galilee of the Gentiles is a pejorative way to describe those who live in northern Israel. Those in Jerusalem must have thought that Galileans had been coopted into a Gentile way of life.

52. Willitts, *Matthew's Messianic Shepherd-King*.

53. Levine examines the command to go nowhere among the gentiles along a temporal and social axis. Levine (*Social and Ethnic Dimensions*) concludes on the social axis that the

sage Jesus has announced: "The kingdom of heaven has come near" (10:7 NIV). Their ministry should mirror the messianic ministry of the shepherd of Israel by healing the sick and proclaiming the good news of the kingdom. This mission to Israel seems connected to the restoration of the twelve tribes, since the commission to the disciples comes immediately after 10:1–4, where Matthew introduces the twelve disciples for the first time.

The limitation on the disciples' mission has confused many Gospel readers. Readers wonder how this fits with the gentile-inclusion theme that has tracked its way through the pages of the First Gospel. There are two errors to avoid when approaching this text. First, sometimes when people speak of the new family of God in Matthew, they completely ignore or at least downplay the mission of Jesus and his disciples to Israel. It is easy to do this because the gentile inclusion seems so prominent that it is confusing to introduce a singular mission. The other error is to emphasize the mission to Israel at the expense of the mission to the nations.

At least partial clarity comes in reading these singular mission statements not as isolated proclamations, but through the narrative as a whole. If the mission to Israel is a reality in the Gospel, the question becomes, What happens to Israel in light of this mission?[54] The parallel passage in Matthew, where Jesus speaks of his own mission "to the lost sheep of the house of Israel," is clarifying (15:24). Justification for jumping here can be found in that this phrase "the lost sheep of the house of Israel" appears in only these two texts (10:6; 15:24).[55]

In Matt. 15 Jesus withdraws to Tyre and Sidon (gentile territories), and a Canaanite woman comes out crying to Jesus as the "Son of David" (15:21–22). Jesus does not answer her and says to the disciples, "I was sent only to the lost sheep of the house of Israel." But the Canaanite woman persists, and Jesus says, "It is not right to take the children's bread and throw it to the dogs." She replies, "Yes, Lord, yet even the dogs eat the crumbs that fall from their masters' table." Jesus responds by speaking of her great faith and heals her daughter (15:28). Two things are worth mentioning about this text in light of the disciples' and Jesus's mission to the lost sheep of the house of Israel.

First, Jesus confirms that his mission is to Israel. He does not respond to the Canaanite woman at first but explicitly says that he is sent to Israel. He

---

Matthean community transcends the traditional ethnic and religious distinctions between Jews and gentiles.

54. The answer will come not only in this section but also in the following ones.

55. The narrative with Jesus and the Canaanite woman in chap. 15 is more enlightening because it is not a commissioning text but a text where Jesus is in the midst of his mission and explains why he is acting in such a way.

describes his message to Israel as "the children's bread" and likens the gentiles to "dogs."[56] But second, we see that the same text that elucidates the mission to Israel also speaks to the inclusion of gentiles. The question is *How do they relate?* The metaphor that Jesus and the woman toss back and forth is instructive in this regard. The analogy concerns a table.[57] On the table is the children's bread. Most likely it is Jesus's message to Israel that they are to partake of.[58] Jesus says it is not right to take this message and throw it to dogs (gentiles). Jesus confirms that the bread is a metaphor for the message, and the bread is for Israel first. The woman replies by continuing the metaphor. Even the dogs eat the crumbs falling from their masters' table. The crumbs are the leftovers of the message, and Jesus is the master. She affirms Jesus's mission to Israel, but she says that as Israel eats the message, some of the crumbs fall to the ground for the dogs to eat.

The point is that though the mission is to Israel primarily, a secondary mission to gentiles follows as crumbs fall. While an order and a priority exists, this order does not exclude others. Although Jesus tells his disciples, "Do not go anywhere among the gentiles" (Matt. 10:5 AT), which sounds exclusive, it also can be interpreted merely in terms of priority. This is what Jesus confirms in Matt. 15. We can even go further and say that the order is part of the means of including the gentiles. When the children eat the bread, some *will* fall, and then dogs can also eat from their masters' table. Israel's eating of the bread is the means by which gentiles receive crumbs.[59] While we don't want to press the metaphor too far, it is hard not to think of the falling crumbs as a picture of Israel not eating the bread as they should. They are not paying attention to *The Bread* given to them.[60]

When exploring the family of Abraham in Matthew, readers should neither overemphasize nor underemphasize the singular mission to Israel. Rather, we should see the two factors as part of an interplay. The message goes first to Israel, because Israel must be offered their messiah first, but crumbs will fall

56. Whatever one does with the new-family-of-God theme in Matthew, one must provide an explanation for this.

57. In Matt. 8:11 Jesus has already spoken of the table of Abraham.

58. If we expand our view theologically, we could even say that the bread is Jesus's own body, as John speaks of the bread in John 6.

59. This observation may be confirmed by the context of the commission in Matt. 10. The metaphor of the harvest (9:35–38) immediately precedes that commission. Harvest is a frequent metaphor for judgment in the OT; judgment can be punishment but can also relate to the gathering of the righteous (Isa. 27:12).

60. Alternatively, one could take the crumbs falling to the ground in a more innocent way. There is nothing wrong with Israel eating the bread, but it is natural that some crumbs will fall from the table.

to the ground. Both Jesus and John the Baptist affirm that the true sons of Abraham are those who follow *the son of Abraham* in repentance. The mission is to Israel first, but this does not exclude gentiles; it merely speaks to a divinely ordained order. In the same way, when the mission to the gentiles is confirmed in the Great Commission, this does not exclude Israel but includes them, since the mission to Israel has already been authorized.

Crumbs from the Table (Matt. 8:5–13; 12:38–42; 15:21–28)

Throughout his Gospel, Matthew indicates crumbs *do* fall from the table. In Matt. 4:15–16 Matthew quotes from Isa. 9:1–2 because he knows Jesus's mission to Israel will bless the nations. As Isaiah predicted, a great light is coming to the gentiles through the son of Abraham and Israel's king. That is precisely what we find in the narrative (see Matt. 8:5–13; 12:38–42; 15:21–28). The son of Abraham blesses all nations through his ministry to Israel. By going to the lost sheep of the house of Israel and unifying Israel again, gentiles are sanctified. The vocation of the messiah is to Israel first, but as we have already seen in the introduction and conclusion, this "Israel first" is not exclusive. Gentiles are blessed through "Israel first." The following texts support gentile inclusion.

In Matt. 8, in the midst of a string of miracles, a centurion (a non-Israelite) approaches Jesus, asking him to heal his servant. Jesus says he will come, but the centurion replies that he too is a man under authority, and if Jesus only says the word, his servant will be healed (8:8). Jesus affirms the faith of the centurion: "Truly, I tell you, with no one in Israel have I found such faith. I tell you, many will come from east and west and recline at table with Abraham, Isaac, and Jacob in the kingdom of heaven, while the sons of the kingdom will be thrown into the outer darkness. In that place there will weeping and gnashing of teeth" (Matt. 8:10b–12). There are many similarities between this passage and what we have seen with John the Baptist, especially in relation to the themes of judgment and hope. As God is able to raise up children for Abraham from stones, many will come from the east and west and recline at the table with Abraham. But there is also judgment. As trees that do not bear fruit are thrown into the fire in chapter 3, so too the sons of the kingdom of heaven are thrown into the outer darkness. Abraham is portrayed as a founding figure and with familial imagery. It is the table of Abraham, Isaac, and Jacob—thereby implying that they are the founders. But it is also an open table, a place where new fellowship occurs.

The question remains as to whether both of these texts (Matt. 3 and 8) imply a rejection of Israel. On the surface, it may seem so. The Pharisees and

Sadducees are not to presume on their father being Abraham, and the sons of the kingdom are thrown into outer darkness. Yet we can be more precise. Jesus does not reject Israel but rather warns the leaders and redefines the family of Abraham. A redefinition does not necessarily imply rejection. As the Great Commission has already taught us, it can indicate growth. The many who come from the east and the west are gentiles, but these are most likely in addition to the remnant of Israel who has believed. It is not that only the many will come, for some are already there.

Although this is not complete rejection, there is a warning: "The sons of the kingdom will be thrown into the outer darkness" (Matt. 8:12).[61] Readers must pair this "addition" of the gentiles with the warning to "the sons of the kingdom." In some mysterious way, the two go together. The warning and even the reality of the sons of the kingdom being thrown into the outer darkness makes room for the gentiles at the table. Just as Abraham had to clear out from his old family to establish a new family, so too there will be some in the outer darkness, and these make room for the many from the east and the west. The First Gospel writer uses Abrahamic imagery to clarify who belongs to the people of God.

The Result of the Mission to Israel (Matt. 11–13)

Matthew 10 speaks of the disciples' singular mission to Israel, but in Matt. 11–13 readers learn of the *result* of the mission of both Jesus and his disciples to Israel. The reactions to Jesus's ministry are not positive as Jesus castigates "this generation."[62] Abraham's family will grow, but the crumbs need to fall from the table of Israel before this will happen. Jesus and John are both sent to

---

61. Konradt (*Israel, Church, and the Gentiles*, 206) again argues that "sons of the kingdom" refers not simply to Jews but to Christ believers: "The 'sons of the kingdom' are 'fruits' of the ministry of the Son of Man." But Konradt seems to be stretching the data. The context of this passage again is about a centurion's faith, and Jesus notes how he has not seen such faith in Israel. Therefore "sons of the kingdom" more likely refers to Jews. But it does not have to follow that *all* the sons of the kingdom are thrown into outer darkness. Rather, this functions as a warning to the sons of the kingdom who may become jealous of the centurion's faith and the gathering of the nations to Abraham's table.

62. France (*Gospel of Matthew*, 417–18) and others call chaps. 11–12 "varying responses" to Jesus for the following reasons: (1) John the Baptist wants to believe, (2) the children are able to discern the truth (11:25–27), and (3) Jesus's true family is composed of those who do the will of God (12:46–50). France argues that the varying responses in chap. 13 support the idea of chaps. 11–12 not being primarily negative. Yet if these positive responses are read in light of the narrative flow, then they seem to contrast with the large-scale rejection presented. The local towns reject Jesus (11:20–24), the religious leaders demand a sign (12:38–42), they claim that Jesus is in league with the devil (12:22–32), and they begin to threaten his life (12:14). In addition, the section is tied together by references to "this generation," which is not a congratulatory phrase.

Israel, but readers learn that the reaction has been antagonistic. The disciples have been warned that they will be persecuted for this message, so they should not be surprised. Yet Jesus still indicts "this generation" for being unresponsive. Their guilt lies on their own heads. The people have rejected John and rejected Jesus, so Jesus proceeds to denounce the towns where his miracles have been performed. "Woe to you, Chorizin! Woe to you, Bethsaida! For if the mighty works done in you had been done in Tyre and Sidon, they would have repented long ago in sackcloth and ashes. . . . And you Capernaum, will you be exalted to heaven? You will be brought down to Hades. . . . But I tell you that it will be more tolerable on the day of judgment for the land of Sodom than for you" (Matt. 11:21–24). This text needs to be put in parallel with Matt. 4:12–17. The towns in which Jesus does his ministry are the same ones condemned. The natural conclusion from this is that Jesus's ministry reveals both hardness of heart and those who show true repentance. Jesus's message, like the message of the prophets, both tears down and builds up (cf. Jer. 1:9–10). In this case, Jesus has indicated that his mission is to Israel, but Israel is hardened to his message, so the message goes out to other towns (Tyre and Sidon).

This reading is confirmed one chapter later with the kingdom parables in Matt. 13. Jesus describes himself as a sower who scatters his words in all different places. Many times the sower's words will be choked out by the cares of this world, the evil one will snatch them away, or there is rocky ground. Not all, in fact few, will respond rightly to Jesus's words. Only the good ground produces fruit. This language of generating fruit should cause one to recall the imagery that John the Baptist uses to describe the new family of Abraham. But even more specificity can be garnered from this passage. The disciples ask Jesus why he speaks to the crowds in parables. Jesus answers, "The secrets of the kingdom of heaven have been given to you to know, but it has not been given to them. . . . That is why I speak to them in parables, because looking they do not see, and hearing they do not listen or understand" (Matt. 13:11–14 AT).

The parables are the vehicles confirming the hard hearts of the crowds. The parables are meant not to enlighten but to ratify the condemnation of the people. Matthew then says that this is to fulfill what the prophet Isaiah (6:9–10) says to the people of Israel: "'You will indeed hear but never understand, and you will indeed see but never perceive.' For this people's heart has grown dull, and with their ears they can barely hear, and their eyes they have closed, lest they should see with their eyes and hear with their ears and understand with their heart and turn, and I would heal them" (Matt. 13:14–15). Matthew applies the words of Isaiah to Jesus's context. The crowd and religious leaders have seen, but they will not perceive. Their hearts have grown dull. The disciples are given the secrets of the kingdom in the parables, but some in Israel are kept from it.[63]

The indication in Matthew's narrative is that the mission to Israel can at least partially be described as a mission of hardening. Jesus condemns the towns he has been ministering in, and he speaks in parables so that the people will not turn and be healed. If we compare this with the rest of the passages we have already surveyed, then it seems that the mission to Israel leads to condemnation on Israel (in part), and then this leads further to an expansion of the people of God. The gentiles are welcomed into Abraham's family if they have faith in the messiah. The new requirement of the people of God is not ethnicity but repentance and faith.

Jesus Begins to Establish His New People (Matt. 14–18)

Matthew 13 is a turning point, confirming a mixed reaction to Jesus's kingdom message, and then in chapters 14–18 Jesus begins to establish the new people of God. Though there are many texts we could go to, two passages demonstrate this theme most clearly. In Matt. 14–18 we see the double theme of Jesus continuing to care for the Israel of faith and welcoming gentiles through the two feasts over which Jesus stands as shepherd.[64] Matthew 14 begins by comparing two different feasts. Herod, the king of the Jews, throws a feast where the center of the meal is John the Baptist's head. Invited to Herod's feast are the leaders of the day. This is a macabre feast with the prominent citizens of the city. It is set in contrast to the feast over which Jesus presides; Jesus provides food for the common people in a deserted place, not in the palace (the feeding of the five thousand). Later there is another occasion when Jesus provides food for the people (the feeding of the four thousand, in Matt. 15).

While we have already examined this text briefly in the Moses chapter, these two feeding stories also relate to Jesus as the new Abraham. Jesus feeds not only the people of Israel (the 5,000) but the gentiles as well (the 4,000). This section contributes to our understanding of Abraham's family because although Jesus does condemn Israel's leaders, there are also hints in his Gospel that the people of Israel are more open to Jesus's message. The message of

---

63. The connection between wisdom and what is secret or hidden is a common theme: Prov. 10:14; Job 15:18; 28:21; Isa 29:14; Sir. 20:30; 41:14.

64. On this see Allison ("Structure, Biographical Impulse, and the *Imitatio Christi*," 140), who argues that in Matt. 14–17 is the establishment of the new people of God. Peter's emergence in this section "correlates with the emergence of the church."

Jesus goes out like seeds sown: some falls on good soil, others on bad soil. Yet in every case, Jesus expands his mission to encompass not only Israel but also the gentiles. At least three arguments indicate that the second feeding, the feeding of the four thousand, is a feeding of gentiles.

First, the literary structure surrounding these two texts supports this. Generally Matt. 13:53–17:27 follows the Markan sequence, indicating that Jesus moves from Jewish to Gentile territory. The transition comes in 15:1–21, where Jesus explains why he and his disciples break the tradition of the elders. The debate with the Pharisees and teachers of the law alerts readers to a turn toward gentile inclusion. The faith of a *Canaanite* women in the next section confirms this switch (15:21–28). Unlike Mark (who calls her a Syrophoenician woman), Matthew unambiguously calls her a Canaanite, the common OT term for Israel's adversaries. What is evident from this survey of the landscape of Matthew's narrative is that he has made a conscious alteration, from Jesus preaching and ministering first to the Jews to his ministering to the gentiles. Many of the same actions are mirrored (such as healings and feedings), but with slight nuances, signaling a similar ministry but a change of audience.

Second, the gentile feeding is supported by the different numbers used in the feeding stories. Jesus breaks seven loaves, and the disciples collect seven baskets of leftovers.[65] The number seven points to the completion and fulfillment of God's purposes, a common theme in Matthew.[66] The number four thousand is symbolic of people coming from the four corners of the earth. Jesus invites all to sit and dine with him, not only the people of Abraham. The gentile crowd participates in a messianic banquet with him, which can explain the disciples' lack of understanding for this second feeding. This does not mean these numbers are nonhistorical; symbolic does not equal ahistorical.

The final argument for this being a gentile feeding concerns the larger OT background to the feeding. Several passages speak to the feeding theme in the OT.[67] In Isa. 25:6–10 the prophet writes of Yahweh spreading a banquet on the mountain, where he makes a feast for "all peoples."[68] Yahweh swallows up

---

65. Both the numbers four and seven were used symbolically in Semitic and other literature. Seven has to do with perfection, and four came to mean completeness because of symbolizing the four corners of the earth. The OT speaks this way of the earth. Ezekiel 37:9 says to the wind, "*Come from the four winds, O breath, and breathe on these slain, that they may live*" (emphasis added). Job 1:19 mentions the same type of idea. For other interesting uses of four in the Bible, see Isa. 11:2; Jer. 15:3; 49:36; Ezek. 1; 10; Zech. 2:6; Rev. 7:1; 9:13–15; and many others.

66. See Kirk, "Conceptualising Fulfilment in Matthew"; Gundry, *Use of the Old Testament*; Stendahl, *School of St. Matthew*; Stanton, "Matthew's Use of the Old Testament."

67. Other significant mountain feeding passages are Jer. 31:10–14 and Ezek. 34:14, 26–27.

68. Donaldson, *Jesus on the Mountain*, 129.

the covering, the veil that is cast over all peoples, over all nations. Moreover, the feast is abundant, with rich food and well-aged wine, as the abundance in Matt. 15 overflows into seven extra baskets. Matthew uses Isaiah extensively in his Gospel, so it is not a stretch to see allusions to Isaiah's promise at the feeding of the four thousand. Jeremiah 31:10–14 also speaks of the nations coming to a great banquet. Yahweh tells the "nations" and those "far away" that they will be "radiant" over the grain, the wine, and the oil, and they will languish no more. There is also the passage in 2 Kings 4:42–44 where Baal-shalishah brings Elisha loaves of barley and ears of grain; although it does not seem like it will be enough, Elisha tells them that the Lord will provide, and they will have some left.

Although Jesus has cared for gentiles as individuals, not until this point does Jesus feed the gentiles as a whole. This is because after Matt. 13 there has been a shift in the narrative. Jesus has performed his ministry (chaps. 5–9) and sent out his disciples with the same mission (chap. 10), yet the response is not positive. Therefore Jesus reiterates the nature of the kingdom (chap. 13) and then establishes his new community, which he later calls "the church" (16:18; 18:17). In Matt. 14–17 he shows that this new community of Abraham consists of both Jews and gentiles. In chapter 18 he instructs them on how they are to treat one another in the community discourse—a sort of pre-instruction manual for Jews and gentiles in the assembly, on which Paul builds his epistles.

The feeding stories are therefore enlightening not just for Mosaic imagery but also for the definition of the family of Christ. Readers need to remember Yahweh's promise to Abraham that he will have his own land, family, and blessing. The OT interprets this blessing in physical terms. Israel will have a kingdom with walls, water, and food. By providing food for the people on the mountain, Jesus as the apocalyptic messiah is fulfilling the promises to Abraham. He feeds Israel as Yahweh did in the wilderness, but he also feeds the gentiles in fulfillment of the prophecies that the gentiles will stream to Zion to eat the banquet with Yahweh. As the son of Abraham, Jesus constitutes the new people of God.

Condemnation and Warnings to Israel's Leaders and Israel (Matt. 19–25)

Although there has been a shift, the tension between the gentiles' inclusion and the Jewish particularity of the family of Abraham continues to grow as Jesus comes nearer to his death. Jesus heals "large crowds" that follow him (Matt. 19:2), indicating that they are not completely hardened. Yet the Pharisees and religious leaders begin to test Jesus to see whether they can catch him in his words. They ask him about divorce (19:3–11), and Jesus warns the people about the dangers of riches (19:16–22). The disciples state that they have left all things to follow Jesus, and he says that they will sit on twelve thrones, judging the twelve tribes of Israel (Jewish particularity). But Jesus also speaks about gentile inclusion: "And *everyone* who has left houses or brothers or sisters or father or mother or children or lands, for my name's sake, will receive a hundredfold and will inherit eternal life. But *many* who are first will be last, and the last first" (Matt. 19:29–30, emphasis added). Jesus not only promises thrones to the disciples but also promises eternal life to "everyone" who follows him. The promises to Israel are not canceled, but Abraham's family is expanded.

When Jesus enters Jerusalem, the jealousy of the Jewish leaders is on full display. The crowds shout, "Son of David!" to Jesus as he enters the city (Matt. 21:9), but those in Jerusalem wonder who this person is (21:10). Even worse, the chief priests and the scribes are "indignant" (21:15). Jesus does not go in to restore the temple, as the messiah was expected to do, but turns over the tables and condemns the temple. He quotes from Jeremiah's temple sermon, where Jeremiah condemns the people of Israel for corrupting the house of the Lord. The curses upon the temple are confirmed as Jesus curses the fig tree (21:18–19). Jesus seems to be condemning the corrupted system. The temple is in disarray, the leaders are mad at the crowd, and Jerusalem doesn't know what to do with this messiah figure. The messiah has come, but Abraham's ethnic children are not ready for him. This text is important because by condemning the temple and cursing the fig tree, Jesus chastises Israel through their main symbol.

The chief priests and the elders of the people come to test Jesus and ask him, "By what authority are you doing these things?" (Matt. 21:23). Jesus counters their question with another question, refuses to answer, and then gives three parables that condemn Israel's leaders for their hard-heartedness. Two of the parables are about a vineyard, a common image for Israel, and one concerns a wedding banquet. First, he tells the parable of the two sons (21:28–32). One of the sons agrees to work but doesn't, and the other says he won't work but ends up going into the vineyard. Jesus says this parable is about "tax collectors and prostitutes . . . entering the kingdom of God ahead of you [religious leaders]" (21:31 NIV). The religious leaders are those who say they will work but don't, while the tax collectors and prostitutes are those who later change their minds. By this parable Jesus indicates that the family of God expands to include tax collectors and prostitutes. Those who do the will of the father are the sons and daughters of Abraham.

The next parable also concerns a vineyard (Matt. 21:33–46). A landowner plants a vineyard and cares for it. He leases it to tenants, and when the time comes for harvest, he first sends his servants to collect the fruit. The tenants beat, kill, and stone the servants. The landowner sends another round of servants, and they do the same. Finally, he sends his son, thinking they will respect him, but they kill him so that they can have his inheritance. Jesus asks the religious leaders what the landowner will do with the tenants. They rightly reply, "He will destroy those terrible men and lease his vineyard to other farmers who will give him his fruit at the harvest" (21:41 AT).

Jesus quotes from Ps. 118:22–23, reinforcing their answer: "The stone that the builders rejected has become the cornerstone; this was the Lord's doing, and it is marvelous in our eyes" (Matt. 21:42). The quote indicates that Jesus's rejection by the leaders of Israel will be the means by which God establishes his purpose and builds the new community of the people of God. A rejected stone becomes the cornerstone. Jesus confirms this by saying that the kingdom of God will be taken away from the religious leaders and given to those producing fruit. Only through the condemnation of Israel is the kingdom open to all. The chief priests and the Pharisees understand that he is speaking about them, and they seek to arrest him. Jesus's words endorse their condemnation and even further it. For without these words they would not be so upset by him and thereby send him to the cross. Jesus's message is the means by which the leaders are condemned, Jesus goes to the cross, and then the family of Abraham expands.[69]

In context, all these parables are about the religious leaders' response to Jesus. *Jesus has come to the house of Israel, but they have not listened to his summons.* They have said they would work, but they never go out into the field. They are planning on destroying the son so that they have the master's inheritance. All of these actions result in the invitation to others. The kingdom of God is taken away from them and given to those who produce fruit. The requirement of the new people of God is producing fruit, not ethnicity. In some sense, these parables form an *inclusio* with John the Baptist's chastisement of Israel's leaders in Matt. 3.

The next few chapters confirm the rejection of Israel's leaders as they are denounced as hypocrites (Matt. 23) and the destruction of the temple is predicted (chap. 24). But Jesus clarifies that his desire is Israel's repentance. "O Jerusalem, Jerusalem, the city that kills the prophets and stones those who are sent to it! How often would I have gathered your children together as a hen gathers her brood under her wings, and you were not willing! See, your house is left to you desolate. For I tell you, you will not see me again, until you say,

---

69. The final parable in response to the religious leaders continues the theme of the first two parables but with different imagery (Matt. 22:1–14).

'Blessed is he who comes in the name of the Lord'" (23:37–39). Jesus longs to gather them and protect them, but they have rejected him as king. Therefore, Israel's house is left desolate. The faithful and wise servants are those who give food at the proper time (24:45). They are the ones ready for the coming of the messiah, have their oil prepared for the bridegroom (25:1–13), invest what is given to them (25:14–30), and produce fruit in keeping with repentance by taking care of "the least of these" (25:40). Matthew's point repeatedly is that the people of God are those who follow the king of the kingdom. Jews and gentiles are a part of Abraham's family.

Conclusion

Matthew is the discipled scribe who has learned wisdom from his teacher. One of the things he understands is that Jesus redefines the family of God under the aegis of Abraham. Matthew's first words identify Jesus as the son of Abraham. This theme develops as the messiah performs his ministry and accomplishes his mission. Jesus's Abrahamic descent directs readers toward familial themes and the constitution of the new people of God. Abraham was promised that he would have a large family and that this family would be a blessing to all nations. In the OT, it was through a particular family that universal blessings would come. The discipled scribe continues this story, which requires an ending. Through the particular, blessing will come to the universal.

Jesus comes from a Jewish heritage. He is born in Israel. His mission is to Israel. He longs to welcome Israel. But the family of Abraham is also expansive. The family tree includes gentiles. The first worshipers of the "king of the Jews" are magi. John the Baptist and Jesus both define their followers not by ethnicity but as those who do the will of the father. Jesus feeds both Jews and gentiles and speaks of the great faith of a centurion and a Canaanite woman. At the end of the Gospel, another centurion confesses that Jesus is "the Son of God," and finally Jesus sends his disciples into all nations. Neither Jewish particularism nor gentile inclusion can be denied.

The question is How do these relate? I have argued that there is an order, a priority, an Israel-first mission for both Jesus and his disciples; but this does not exclude the gentiles. In fact, the mission to Israel leads to condemnation on Israel, the bread crumbs fall under the table, and the gentiles are there to eat them. In a twist of events, the lack of response from Israel leads to the blessing of Abraham being extended to all nations. At the same time, the welcoming of the gentiles leads to Israel's jealousy and rejection of Jesus. Yet this does not mean that all of Israel is excluded; some believe and some doubt (28:17). Israel is therefore not rejected wholesale but excluded insofar as they turn from their messiah.

A back and forth occurs in the First Gospel that sometimes bewilders readers. Part of the reason for this is because this development in history was untidy. It was chaotic, not in terms of the plan of the messiah but in terms of the people's understanding. Matthew as the scribe reflects on the reconstitution of the people of God and displays the messiness of the original situation, but his overall point is clear: Jesus is the son of Abraham, and he fulfills the familial promises to Abraham by establishing the new family of God as defined by faith and repentance.

7

Jesus and Israel's Destiny

Sometimes the hardest things to see are right in front of us, even all around us. It was G. K Chesterton who said, "The whole object of travel is not to set foot on foreign land; it is at last to set foot on one's own country as a foreign land."[1] In a similar way, we have traveled through the life of Jesus through the eyes of the discipled scribe, attempting to see his teacher afresh and with more depth. We have done so in order to put our foot down again in the familiar country of Gospel literature as if we were foreigners again. The mountains begin to look different, as if they have come from a common history; the faces are somehow familiar, as if we have seen them before; their clothes look worn with a rich history, and the lakes and rivers flow from a time past. This chapter returns to the land of Matthew but climbs the mountain peaks of Matthew to take a bird's-eye view of the landscape.

In this chapter my aim is to demonstrate that Jesus is not merely represented as a new individual but that Matthew's plot as a whole completes the story of the nation. Jesus not only embodies and mimics the life of characters but of Israel as a whole. Israel can be viewed through its individual figures, but Israel can also be conceived as a corporate entity. Matthew offers Jesus's life through both of these lenses, and therefore we would be remiss if we didn't follow the scribe in his teaching. More specifically, *I will argue that Matthew sequences his narrative as the plot of Israel, in which Jesus leads the nation*

1. G. K. Chesterton, "Riddle of the Ivy."

out of exile.[2] If David is associated with the kingdom, Moses with the exodus, and Abraham with family, then Israel's narrative can be put under the banner of exile. Matthew reveals Jesus through the curtain of the history of Israel; the story of Jesus is the story of Israel in repeat. Jesus is not merely the son of David, or the son of Abraham, but *the Son* of Yahweh, who perfects the narrative of Israel.

This sequencing of Matthew's narrative should not be surprising for four reasons.

1. The OT shows signs of not only telling history but also of retelling it in familiar forms. The OT authors told not only a linear history but also a cyclical one. Multiple water crossings, feedings, exiles, returns from exile, famines, stories of anti-kings, prophets, and true kings are told in recognizable ways, with key words showing development and associations.[3] The OT sets the pattern that Matthew imitates. Copying and imitating was not as much of a problem in the ancient world; it was a prime way of communicating.[4]

2. Matthew writes a "gospel story." The "good news" of the coming reign of Yahweh through his representative continues here in Matthew's narrative. If Matthew is continuing the gospel narrative, then he would most likely do so by showing how what is "new" relates to what is "old."

3. Matthew is the Gospel about fulfillment. Jesus fulfills the narrative of Israel as a nation, not merely pieces of its history or a few of its leaders. No; this Gospel says the story of Israel is comprehensively complete in Jesus.

4. Matthew shows incredible precision in his structuring. The writer moves things around from Mark's narrative and sets things up in a unique way. The placement of his stories is not haphazard but purposeful.

These four arguments set us off on the trail of attempting to see the history of Israel as a whole in Matthew's portrayal of Jesus. But before we embark, I should clarify what I am and am not arguing. *I am not claiming that all the echoes and resonances follow a chronological sequence; I am arguing that the large narrative blocks point toward this arrangement.* For example, Ps. 22 is used in great detail in Matthew's portrayal of the crucifixion. But this doesn't

2. Peter Leithart (*Jesus as Israel*) has already argued a form of this in his introduction to his Matthew commentary. I will follow him in many ways, add to his discussion, and then depart from him in others. He does not gather the entire movement under the banner of exile.

3. For a good introduction to this method, see Roberts and Wilson, *Echoes of Exodus*.

4. This is not to deny that there were some issues with pseudonymity.

necessarily work against the fact that Matthew employs monarchy themes in chapters 11–12 (David, Solomon, temple, and rest). Matthew can portray Jesus as the suffering and vindicated son of David at the end of his Gospel and at the beginning, while still following a basic narrative development and focusing on the monarchy in chapters 11–12. Therefore pointing out that there are references to Moses or Adam or Abraham at the end of the Gospel does not overturn this sequential argument. The sequence and intermixing of persons and events don't have to be at odds, because the Scriptures intermix people, places, and time.

Narratives function at several levels, and those who search for "one meaning" in narratives are not attending to the richness that lies within. Matthew doesn't have to restrict himself to one point. He can use one narrative to present Jesus as both a Moses-type figure *and* a David-type figure. He can intermix these not only because this is how narratives work, but also because all of Israel's history is unified in Jesus. All of these figures connect not only because they are part of Israel's history but also because they are unified in Christ. Moses, David, and Abraham's lives carry all the way through, yet there is also a sense in which readers can view the transitions of this Gospel from a higher level.

Multiple analyses can stand side by side rather than our needing to argue that only one character or theme predominates in Matthew's account. Readers don't need to choose teams but can end up seeing the varied layers of meaning presented in the text. Jesus can recapitulate the roles of both major individuals and the nation as a whole. In fact, these two should not be opposed, for the role of individuals and the role of the nation itself are tied together. For example, when Jesus is tempted in the wilderness, he is acting as the new Adam, new Israel, and new prophet. When he feeds the people on the mountain, he is providing food both as a new Moses and a new Elisha. When Jesus gives the Great Commission, it is mirroring Cyrus's edict (2 Chron. 36:23), the commission to Moses (Deut. 31:14–15), and the commission to Joshua (Josh. 1:1–9). Matthew can be generous with his intertextual links while also being structured and thoughtful.

The sequential and nonsequential references also don't need to be at odds, because there is a difference between looking at specific texts that speak to fulfillment and examining how Matthew employs the OT in his larger structure. These coincide at times, but they can also be distinguished. In chapter 2 I explained how Matthew uses "shadow stories" that mirror Jewish history. In this chapter I will look not only at the fulfillment quotations but also at how the narrative transitions reflect and repeat the history of Israel.[5] Matthew

5. In this sense, this chapter works against mistakes that regularly occur in the current study of the NT use of the OT. Sometimes these studies restrict themselves to "quotations" and forget

can be very imaginative and resourceful, employing these themes throughout his Gospel while also following a basic chronology. There are enough correspondences in the chief narrative movements to lead us to conclude that Matthew accomplishes something bigger than merely presenting Jesus as the new Moses, or the new David; he retraces the history of Israel through his portrayal of Jesus. Jesus's footsteps fill in the strides of Israel as he leads the people out of exile.

The Story of Israel in the Structure of Matthew

Structure is clearly important to Matthew. Many call Matthew the most structured of all our Gospels.[6] Matthew relates his message largely by how he put things together, like an architect communicating through the construction. How an artist has placed things speaks volumes about what they are trying to say. In the same way, this scribe has constructed his biography of Jesus in what we could call a "fulfillment form." The placement of each piece builds the argument. Yet the reality is that the structure of Matthew continues to be debated. We can boil down the proposals to three large categories.[7]

1. Some follow the *geographic outline*, mainly paying attention to the *where* of Jesus's travels. Many in this camp see some sort of introduction, usually extending to about 4:11. Then Jesus's ministry in Galilee begins. This ministry lasts from 4:12 to 20:34, though most will note that the journey south to Jerusalem begins in 16:21. Finally Jesus nears Jerusalem in 21:1 and then goes to his death and resurrection in chapters 26–28.

2. Others follow a *plot outline*, focusing on Jesus's actions. The presentation of Jesus is given in 1:1–4:16, the proclamation of Jesus is given in 4:17–16:20, and the passion and resurrection of Jesus is given in 16:21–

---

that large narrative movements also have resonances. With the help of C. H. Dodd, scholars are realizing that quotations are reaching back to whole contexts; yet this step is not enough. Even if we work with quotations and their past contextual whole, we may forget to tie these to the current narrative as a whole. In other words, we can atomize on both horizons. In sum, though there has been a narrative turn in the study of the Gospels, it has not turned enough to study *how* the Gospel writers especially have employed the OT.

6. As evidenced by numerous proposals, only a few of which I list here. Allison, "Structure, Biographical Impulse, and the *Imitatio Christi*"; Carter, "Kernels and Narrative Blocks"; Lohr, "Oral Techniques in the Gospel of Matthew"; Matera, "Plot of Matthew's Gospel"; Powell, "Narrative-Critical Understanding of Matthew"; Smith, "Fivefold Structure in the Gospel of Matthew."

7. Yet there are many minor differences within these proposals.

28:20. This outline respects the repeated phrase "from that time Jesus began to" (Ἀπὸ τότε ἤρξατο ὁ Ἰησοῦς) found in 4:17 and 16:21.

3. Others will follow what we can call a *narrative-discourse outline*. This breaks the book into sections alternating between narratives and discourses and having an introduction and conclusion. This outline respects the repeated phrase "and when Jesus had finished these words" (Καὶ ἐγένετο ὅτε ἐτέλεσεν ὁ Ἰησοῦς τοὺς λόγους τούτους), found with some variations in 7:28; 11:1; 13:53; 19:1; and 26:1. As France and others have pointed out, this language stands out in Matthew and clearly intends to provide important transitions in the material. This formula is not only repeated five times, but each time it stands at the end of a major block of Jesus's teaching, or what we could call a discourse.

These outlines don't need to be opposed to one another; they are different ways of looking at Matthew's narrative structure. The geographic outline provides a look at Jesus's travels, highlighting the exile and return of the Davidic king. It also allows readers to see "where" Jesus ministers and helps paint a portrait of the various responses to Jesus. The narrative-plot outline also rightly recognizes major transitions in the life and ministry of Jesus, allowing readers to follow the preparation for ministry, the presentation of Jesus, and the passion of Jesus. The narrative-discourse outline recognizes that Matthew groups his material into blocks and provides clues as to when and where key transitions take place.

I tend to favor the *narrative-discourse outline* for a few reasons. First, it is the most detailed outline. It provides more transitions and allows readers to see how the discourses are related and how the narratives connect to the discourses. Second, it allows us to see Jesus as the teacher and his followers as disciples and scribes. Third, it best enables us to see Jesus repeating the history of Israel as a whole.[8] While some parts are clearer than others, the clarity of the bookends and the center compel readers to begin searching for more connections. Matthew 1:1–17 reflects a Genesis and new-creation intertext, Matt. 26–28 imitates the exile and return from exile, and Matt. 13 centers on a wisdom tradition.

The argument I provide here builds on, at least in part, the work of three other scholars: B. W. Bacon, Dale Allison, and Peter Leithart. Bacon argues that this organization is part of Matthew's attempt to present his Gospel as the new Pentateuch. He suggests that the Gospel was structured by an alternating fivefold pattern of discourses and narratives, which combine to form

8. Largely through the discourses, but the narratives also support this argument.

five "books" of the Torah.[9] Bacon's theory has both defenders and detractors.[10] To label Matt. 1–2 as a prologue and chapters 26–28 as an epilogue seems to give far too little emphasis to these important sections. Also, Bacon's assertion that the Pentateuch alternates between "narrative" and discourse" is not entirely convincing. While it is fair to point out some of these criticisms, Bacon's fundamental insight is on track. Matthew does gather his teaching into large blocks, and there are examples of other Jewish literature that consciously imitate the Pentateuch's five-book structure.[11]

Dale Allison has probably done the most work in noting the connections to Moses in the narrative of Matthew.[12] In my opinion, Allison has solidified the importance of Moses throughout Matthew's Gospel. But it is striking that most of the clear Moses echoes appear in Matt. 1–9. As Leithart says, though Allison's proposal on the large structure for Jesus as new Moses is quite compelling, there is still something lacking. "Half of the strongly Mosaic passages are exhausted by the end of Matthew 7."[13] After that, they seem more spread out.

Peter Leithart has come alongside Bacon and Allison and added some key details.[14] The discourses are not imitating the five-book structure of the Pentateuch, but the fivefold story of Israel as a whole. Jesus recapitulates not only the Pentateuch but also the narrative of the nation itself. Matthew moves not only from the infancy narrative of Moses (Matt. 1–2) to the commissioning of a successor (28:16–20) but also from creation to the end of exile. Therefore Leithart proposes that Matthew moves sequentially through the history of Israel, with the five discourses and the surrounding narrative marking out major periods of Israel's history. Hence we cannot study only the discourses, for the narratives also give us hints that Matthew is following the history of Israel. The discourses certainly stand as large billboards—alerting readers to

9. Bacon, "Five Books of Matthew"; Bacon, *Studies in Matthew*; Enslin, "Bacon on the Gospel of Matthew."

10. For example, Allison (*Studies in Matthew*, 138) says, "Once one abandons the vain attempt to construct a Matthean Pentateuch, what is the rationale for such procedure? What happens when instead one simply evaluates each narrative section and each discourse on its own terms, as a large thought unit? The results, in my judgment, allow both the structure and plot of the First Gospel to emerge clearly." Kingsbury (*Matthew as Story*, 113) flatly denies the Pentateuchal connection: "Contrary to what many scholars have claimed over the years, the great speeches of Jesus do not constitute the climactic feature of Matthew's Gospel nor do they stand apart from the rest of the story being told."

11. See Gundry, *Matthew*, 10–11.

12. Allison, *New Moses*.

13. Leithart, *Jesus as Israel*, 11.

14. Leithart acknowledges that he builds on Allison, Gundry (*Use of the Old Testament*, 210), and Goulder (*Midrash and Lection in Matthew*).

the path one is to follow—but the narratives also supply vital "packaging" that further supports the view that Jesus comes as the new Israel. He walks in Israel's footsteps, completing the strides the nation was never able to accomplish and suffering the fate the people deserved.

Sermon on the Mount (Matt. 5–7)	New Moses
Sending out the Twelve (Matt. 10)	New Joshua
Kingdom parables (Matt. 13)	New Solomon
Community discourse (Matt. 18)	New Elisha
Prophetic discourse (Matt. 23–25)	New Jeremiah

New Creation, New Wisdom, and New Adam in Matthew 1:1–17

For Matthew, the birth of Jesus is the commencement of the new creation. His introduction immediately propels readers back to Genesis. The first words, "the book of the genealogy," could also be translated as "the scroll of origin," "the book of Genesis," or "the scroll of the lineage." The explicit phrase (βίβλος γενέσεως) occurs in the LXX in only two places, Gen. 2:4 and 5:1. Genesis 2:4 is about the origin of heaven and earth (place), while 5:1 concerns the origin of Adam and Eve (people). These first words thus assemble the themes of heaven and earth that track their way throughout the Gospel.[15] Jesus reunites these realms as all authority "in heaven and on earth" are given to him (Matt. 28:18). A cosmic and spatial unifying force appears at the birth of Jesus (1:1).[16]

The genealogy is not only about the new creation but about the new creation with people at the center (Gen. 5:1). Matthew mobilizes his story as a recovery and resuscitation of the people lost by the prophets, priests, and sovereigns of old. He establishes the redemptive-historical context as one of ongoing exile. The one "event" that Matthew names outside of the birth of Jesus is the exile, which acts as a hinge of Matthew's genealogical structure in chapter 1 and provides the perspective for the Gospel as a whole.[17] Matthew views the plot of Israel under the banner of exile and return from exile.[18] The king therefore comes to rescue Israel from exile; he

15. Pennington, *Heaven and Earth*.
16. Schreiner, *Body of Jesus*. Leithart (*Jesus as Israel*, 53–54) also looks to the generations for a new creation theme: "Six weeks of generations are between Abraham and Jesus and that means that Jesus is the first name in the seventh seven, the beginning of a new week, the week of the new creation."
17. Eloff, "Exile, Restoration."
18. Hays, *Echoes of Scripture in the Gospels*, 110–11.

has been sent to the lost sheep of Israel. This exile stretches further back than the Babylonian exile, for the exile actually begins with Adam (Gen. 3).[19] Though the people of God are in exile, hope bursts through the shadows: a child has come. While Gen. 5 is a picture of genealogical death, the ending of Matthew's βίβλος γενέσεως is not death but resurrection life. A child has been born who will never die.[20]

The revelation of Jesus as the new creation also connects with wisdom themes.[21] Wisdom possesses creative and redemptive functions in the Scriptures and other Wisdom literature outside the Bible. Wisdom 9:2 says, "and by your wisdom you have formed humankind," and wisdom "was present when you made the world" (Wis. 9:9). Proverbs 8:22–31 claims:

> The LORD possessed me [wisdom] at the beginning of his work, the first of his acts of old. Ages ago I was set up, at the first, before the beginning of the earth. When there were no depths I was brought forth, when there were no springs abounding with water. Before the mountains had been shaped, before the hills, I was brought forth, before he had made the earth with its fields, or the first of the dust of the world. When he established the heavens, I was there; when he drew a circle on the face of the deep, when he made firm the skies above, when he established the fountains of the deep, when he assigned to the sea its limit, so that the waters might not transgress his command, when he marked out the foundations of the earth, then I was beside him, like a master workman, and I was daily his delight, rejoicing before him always, rejoicing in his inhabited world and delighting in the children of man.

Wisdom thus is the architectonic being who establishes the world.[22] Matthew's genealogy concerns Wisdom taking on flesh.

After four hundred years of deafening silence since Malachi's final prophecy, people are wondering, What has happened to God's promises? Will God lead them out of exile? Will he rescue them? Matthew breaks the stillness with the opening proclamation that Jesus is the new creation, the new genesis, the new beginning, and new wisdom. Matthew launches his Gospel by showing *how* the return from exile will take place. While Solomon's sons have led the people into exile, the birth of Solomon *redivivus*, the wise king, will bring

---

19. Adam has "wisdom" in the garden, but the serpent is "crafty" and tempts Adam and Eve to eat of the tree of "knowledge." Ezekiel 28:12 says, "You were the signet of perfection, full of wisdom and perfect in beauty." If we view the story line from this perspective, returning from exile is regaining wisdom. See Longman, *Fear of the Lord Is Wisdom*, 94–100.

20. The theme of "return from exile" will return with greater clarity in Matt. 26–28.

21. Nolan (*Royal Son of God*, 228–32) briefly develops the theme of Jesus as wisdom since wisdom possesses creative and redemptive functions.

22. Or at least related to the Creator in a personified way.

them back from exile.[23] Therefore, the plausibility of Matthew retracing the footsteps of Israel commences with the explicit lexical references to the beginning of Genesis. Matthew begins by presenting Jesus not only as the new David and the new Abraham but also the new genesis.

New Abraham in Matthew 1:18–25

The genealogy largely echoes Genesis and the start of a new creation, but then Matt. 1:18–25 moves to the birth of the figure who will bring these blessings to all people and lead them back to their home.[24] This mirrors the structure of Gen. 1 and Gen. 2. Genesis 1 gives a broad poetic presentation (cf. Matt. 1:1–17), while Gen. 2 zooms in on the birth of humankind (cf. Matt. 1:18–25). Rather than mirroring the "birth" of Adam, however, Matthew moves on to the next most significant birth in the OT: the birth of Isaac. Richard Erickson argues that the birth narrative in 1:18–25 reflects the story of Abraham and the birth of Isaac in Gen. 12–17.[25] If the people are going to be led back to the presence of God (Immanuel), it will be, as in the OT, through an unnatural birth. Sarah was barren and Mary was a virgin, yet God grants both of them a promised child. Seven features point toward a connection between the Abraham story and the Matthean Joseph story.

1. As the word of the Lord comes to Abram in a vision (Gen. 15:1), so the angel appears to Joseph in a dream (Matt. 1:20).
2. As the Lord tells Abram not to fear (Gen. 15:1), so the angel comforts the dreaming Joseph with the words "Do not fear" (Matt. 1:20).
3. Abraham complains that he has been left childless (Gen. 15:2), and a form of this same verb is used in Matt. 1:19 to refer to Joseph's thought of rejecting Mary.
4. Jesus, like Isaac, is born to a barren woman.

23. The Jews were hoping for a return from exile, a return to their land, an establishment of their kingdom. As Dempster (*Dominion and Dynasty*) has noted, the twin themes of geography (dominion) and genealogy (dynasty) run a straight line through the OT and right into the NT.

24. Leihart and Goulder argue that this section is about Joseph (Gen. 37–50). Goulder points out that the original Joseph ben Jacob has a set of three dreams, and Matthew's Joseph (also ben Jacob, 1:16) has three dreams (1:20; 2:13; 19). Both of the dreams lead them to Egypt but also end up protecting the promised line from destruction. This also works well because in the OT Joseph precedes Moses and the exodus. I don't think these correspondences necessarily need to be pitted against each other, but the lexical connections make the Abraham tie more convincing.

25. Erickson, "Joseph and the Birth of Isaac."

5. Abraham rejects Hagar, but God reverses the rejection (Gen. 16:5–6, 9); Joseph contemplates rejecting Mary, but God has a greater plan for salvation and divine reversal in relation to the birth of Jesus (Matt. 1:20–21).

6. As Joseph is described as "a just man" (1:19), so too Abraham's faith in the Lord is counted to him as righteousness (Gen. 15:6).

7. The actual wording of the angel's announcement to Joseph corresponds almost exactly to the LXX's wording of the promise that God delivers to Abraham in Gen. 17:19:

Matthew 1:21: τέξεται δὲ υἱόν, καὶ καλέσεις τὸ ὄνομα αὐτοῦ Ἰησοῦν.

Matthew 1:23: καὶ τέξεται υἱόν, καὶ καλέσουσιν τὸ ὄνομα αὐτοῦ Ἐμμανουήλ.

Genesis 17:19 LXX: τέξεταί σοι υἱόν, καὶ καλέσεις τὸ ὄνομα αὐτοῦ Ισαακ.

Thus Erickson concludes that we should read Matt. 1:18–25 in an Abrahamic way. As God promised Abraham a child in a miraculous way, so too God promised Adam and Eve and Israel a miracle child. This child will be Immanuel, God with his people, as God will dwell with Abraham's child Isaac. Matthew began his Gospel with the theme of "new creation" from Genesis, and he immediately moves on to the story of Abraham and his children in 1:18–25. The person through whom the whole world would be blessed, who would bring the people back to the presence of God, is Abraham's seed. Jesus's children are the promised ones who will return the people of God from their wanderings and exile. Matthew has structurally moved from Genesis (1:1–17) to the story of Abraham (1:18–25).

New Moses and Israel in Matthew 2–4

In Matt. 2 the scribe then enters into the Exodus story, portraying the early life of Jesus under the banner of the early life of Moses and Israel as a whole. In chapter 5 I covered how Jesus is the new Moses when he is confronted by Herod in 2:1–23, so it need not be repeated here. But readers should note the sequence. After 1:18–25 the story transitions to a king seeking to destroy God's chosen people and a flight "out of Egypt" (2:15). Then Jesus crosses the water (3:13–17) and goes into the wilderness to be tempted for forty days (4:1–11). This foreshadows the escape from exile that Jesus takes his people on.[26]

26. Hays (*Echoes of Scripture in the Gospels*, 140) says, "Jesus saves people from their sins (1:21) by *representatively* overcoming their unfaithfulness—*proleptically* in his baptism (3:15) and wilderness temptation (4:1–11), where he shows himself to be the obedient 'Son of God' in

antagonistic king → flight out of Egypt → through the water → into the wilderness

The movement of Jesus is remarkably similar to the exodus. Israel is sent into Egypt, meets an antagonistic king, comes out of Egypt, goes through the water, and then retreats into the wilderness. Israel's redemption is a fore-taste of the redemption that is to come, just as Jesus's redemption prefigures the exile out of which he will bring the people. Jesus's footsteps follow the beginning of the Torah so far.[27]

Understanding this movement helps one appreciate the fulfillment quota-tions in Matt. 2:15 and 2:18.[28] Mary and Joseph grab Jesus and flee to Egypt because of the threat of King Herod. Matthew says this act is to fulfill what was spoken by the prophet Hosea (11:1), "Out of Egypt I called my son." This verse has been the subject of much debate.[29] Some argue that this is a form of midrash or *pesher* by Matthew. Others think it is typology or *sensus plenior*. Still others think Hosea is predictive prophecy. While most quickly go to the contextual argument, and this partly solves the problem, additional help comes from recognizing what Matthew is doing structurally. If Jesus is viewed as the new Israel, then Jesus's journey out of Egypt and Matthew's use of Hosea 11:1 are not so odd. There is a rich tradition of Israel coming out of Egypt.[30]

The departure from Egypt loomed large for Israel and shaped the people's imaginations in a unique way. This departure theme is confirmed in Matt. 2:18, when he cites from Jer. 31:15 as Rachel mourns for her children who are deported to Babylon (Jer. 40:1). Both places (Ramah and Egypt) and both prophets (Hosea and Jeremiah) declare that God will both send his people into exile and reach out in mercy and bring them back. Thus Matthew is not playing fast and loose with Hosea 11 but reading the movement of Jesus figurally.[31] As Richard Hays says, "The fulfillment of the words can only be

---

a way that Israel had failed to be, and *definitively* in the passion/resurrection narrative. Thus, as Messiah, he brings the exile to an end (1:17)."

27. That Jesus is functioning as both a new Israel and a new Moses need not be put at odds, for it is Moses who is connected to the deliverance from Egypt.

28. Piotrowski (*Matthew's New David*) even argues that Matthew's quotations draw on texts associated with Israel's exile and restoration and therefore evokes the "end-of-exile."

29. Beale, "Use of Hosea 11:1 in Matthew 2:15."

30. In Exod. 13:3 Moses tells the people to "remember this day in which you came out from Egypt, out of the house of slavery, for by a strong hand the LORD brought you out from this place." The Jews even had a feast in which they ate unleavened bread to remind them of the day they came out of the land. Again and again in the Prophets, the people are reminded of the day when they were brought out of the land of Egypt (Hosea 12:13; Amos 2:10; 3:1; Mic. 6:4; 7:15).

31. Since we are products of our modern Western culture, we still tend to read a given OT statement in only a grammatical-historical manner, considering it almost exclusively from the

discerned through the act of the imagination that perceives the typological correspondence between the two stories of the exodus and the Gospel and therefore discerns that Jesus embodies the destiny of Israel."[32] In other words, time collapses in Matthew's view of these two stories.[33] Jewish exegetes kept in mind something we may tend to overlook: from the perspective of God in eternity, the Scriptures are really a "timeless unity in which each and every verse is simultaneous with every other, temporally and semantically."[34] The movement of Jesus mirrors and completes the struggle of Israel as a nation. Not only does Matthew begin echoing Genesis and Abraham, but he also quickly transitions to the early movement of Israel as they come out of Egypt. The new Israel foreshadows a future return from exile in his geographical movements.[35] Jesus not only walks in the footsteps of Israel—he is Israel.

New Moses in Matthew 5–9

After mirroring the redemption from Egypt, in chapters 5–7 Matthew has Jesus ascend the mountain and instruct his people as the new Moses. A number of intertextual connections have already been noted in a previous chapter, but a few more rise to the surface.[36] First, when Jesus begins teaching, Matthew employs the phrase "and opening his mouth" (ἀνοίξας τὸ στόμα αὐτοῦ), using words similar to those employed in Ps. 78:2 LXX, where the speaker says, "I will open my mouth in parables" (ἀνοίξω ἐν παραβολαῖς τὸ στόμα μου).[37] Psalm 78 recounts the time of Moses with the Israelites at Sinai and in the wilderness, and therefore these words from the Psalms also point to Moses

---

perspective of the human author's understanding and point in time. But Christ has bound together the disparate strands of the temporal flow into a unity of essence and meaning. The supernatural has impregnated history so deeply that there must be a further meaning to historical events.

32. Hays, "Matthew: Reconfigured Torah," 174.

33. It seems that the idea Matthew draws out of Hosea was there germinally, but this does not mean Hosea had the messiah in mind when he penned 11:1. "One might accuse Matthew of pulling this verse out of context because the reference in Hosea is clearly to Israel. However, Matthew's point is not to prove a point, but to make a point, namely that we should be reading the life of Christ in light of Israel" (Hays, "Matthew: Reconfigured Torah") and the history of Israel in light (now) of Christ.

34. Stern, *Midrash and Theory*, 108.

35. The exile theme is also hinted at by the use of Jer. 31:15 in Matt. 2:18 and the reference to Ramah, the place where Israel went into exile (Jer. 40:1).

36. In chapter 5, I mentioned some of the connections to Moses: (1) Jesus goes up on the mountain, (2) it is *the* mountain, and finally (3) he sits down. The Beatitudes might also mirror the Ten Commandments in that the first four concern our relationship to God, and the second four concern our relationship to other humans.

37. Pennington, *Sermon on the Mount*, 140–41.

connections. Second, Jesus presents them with the way of blessedness and the way of death in the Sermon on the Mount (like Deuteronomy). Third, the Torah becomes the focal point in the Sermon. In Matt. 5:17–20, the Torah is upheld by Jesus, and he clarifies the intention of the Torah in 5:21–48.

Moses may also be in view in 5:5 when Jesus says, "Blessed are the meek, for they shall inherit the earth" (μακάριοι οἱ πραεῖς, ὅτι αὐτοὶ κληρονομήσουσιν τὴν γῆν). The church fathers made a connection between this text and Num. 12:3.[38] Finally, at the conclusion to the Sermon, Matthew has Jesus coming down the mountain (καταβάντος δὲ αὐτοῦ ἀπὸ τοῦ ὄρους, 8:1). This is similar to the language of Exod. 34:29 (ὡς δὲ κατέβαινεν Μωυσῆς ἐκ τοῦ ὄρους), where Moses comes down the mountain. The phrase forms a bookend to the Sermon as a new Torah, like what Moses received while on Mount Sinai. Jesus has therefore followed the history of Israel all the way to Sinai in Matt. 1–7, and therefore chapters 8–9 recount what it "looks like" to enact the law and reverse the curse.

Jesus enacts the law in chapters 8–9, and thus Matt. 5–9 can be compared to a recounting of Exodus–Deuteronomy.[39] He heals a leper, welcomes an outsider, cures an ailing mother, relieves a paralytic, and brings life from death. These miracles deal with some of the same issues that appear in Leviticus. But Jesus also confronts the demonic forces (8:28–34; 9:32–34), showing that the sin problem is sourced in a deeper cosmic battle that has been raging from the beginning of time. Leithart has also proposed that these ten miracles may mirror the ten rebellions of Israel in the wilderness (Num. 14:22). Chapters 8–9 show that Israel has not been faithful to the covenant, and the ten rebellions take place after Sinai like the ten healings that take place after the Sermon.[40] As Jesus heals a leper first (8:1–4), so one of the first rebellions after Sinai results in Miriam being made leprous and then healed (Num. 12:1–15).

Matthew 5–9 stretches from Sinai to the end of Deuteronomy because both of these narratives center on Moses. Though at times it might feel as though Matthew moves back and forth between Exodus and Deuteronomy, Leviticus through Deuteronomy also does not travel in a straight line. Leviticus zooms in on the laws from Exodus, and Deuteronomy gives a summary

38. Allison, *Studies in Matthew*, 119–20. Allison makes reference to Eusebius and Theodoret of Cyrrhus making these connections.

39. Others have proposed that in chaps. 8–9 there are ten miracles, which mirror the ten plagues that the Lord sends upon Egypt. Chae (*Jesus as the Eschatological Davidic Shepherd*) argues that the sheep and shepherd metaphors (9:36) relate to the restoration of the house of Israel. This lines up with both Mosaic and Davidic themes.

40. Leithart, *Jesus as Israel*, 23–24.

account of how the people are to act. Neither Matthew nor the Pentateuch needs to move in strictly chronological fashion. The narratives pause, zoom in, go backward, and thrust forward at different times, but they still deal with the same large block of time.

The large narrative structure from Matt. 1 to 9 recounts the story from new creation to the end of the Pentateuch. Matthew begins with Gen. 1–2 and the birth of the new creation, then indicates that a return from exile is coming. This new hope will come through one family and one child (Matt. 1:18–25). God preserves his redeemer, brings him out of Egypt, takes him through the water and into the wilderness. Then Jesus ascends the mountain and delivers the new Torah (Matt. 5–9). The law is given so that the people of God can walk rightly before him. Finally, the law is explained and embodied, and warnings are given of what will happen if they don't follow the law. In sum, the narrative from Matt. 1–9 largely follows the narrative of the Pentateuch and prepares readers for the ultimate rescue from exile. It can schematically be portrayed as follows:

Matthew and the Pentateuch

Matthew	Old Testament
1:1: Book of Genesis	Gen. 2:4; 5:1
1:1–17: son of Abraham	Gen. 12–26
1:18–25: son of Abraham; Israel is birthed	Gen. 18
2:13–15: Herod kills children	Exod. 1–2: Pharaoh kills children
2:14: Jesus rescued, flees	Exod. 2: Moses rescued, flees
2:19–23: Jesus returns to Israel	Exod. 3–4: Moses returns to Egypt
3:13–17: Jesus passes through waters	Exod. 14: The exodus
4:1–11: Temptation in the wilderness	Exod. 17–19 or Numbers // Travel to Sinai, or Travel in the wilderness
4:18–22: Jesus calls disciples	Exod. 18: Moses appoints rulers
5–7: Sermon on the Mount	Exod. 18 or Exodus–Deuteronomy // Giving of the Torah
8–9: Healings	Leviticus–Deuteronomy // Blessings of the Torah

Source: This chart is largely adapted from Leithart, *Jesus as Israel*, 15. I've made only minor changes.

Conquest in Matthew 10

Matthew 1–9 recounts the movement of the Pentateuch, and then Matt. 10 begins with the conquest and entry into the land. Just as the Sermon on the Mount was bracketed by Jesus ascending and descending the mountain, the

Mission Discourse is bracketed by an *inclusio* of "his twelve disciples" in 10:1 and 11:1.[41] Matthew 10 mirrors both the sending of the twelve spies into the land and the commissioning of Joshua as Moses's successor. The picture presented by this discourse is one of taking territory for the kingdom of God, similar to the conquest. At the end of Matt. 9 Jesus describes Israel as "harassed and helpless, like a sheep without a shepherd" (9:36). This parallels the text in Num. 27:15–18, where Joshua is appointed because Moses will no longer lead them. "Moses spoke to the LORD, saying, 'Let the LORD, the God of the spirits of all flesh, appoint a man over the congregation who shall go out before them and come in before them, who shall lead them out and bring them in, that the congregation of the LORD may not be as sheep that have no shepherd.' So the LORD said to Moses, 'Take Joshua the son of Nun, a man in whom is the Spirit, and lay your hand on him.'"

In verse 20 the Lord says, "You shall invest him with some of your authority." So Moses "laid his hands on [Joshua] and commissioned him as the LORD directed through Moses" (27:23). In the same way, Jesus calls the Twelve to him and gives them "authority over unclean spirits" (Matt. 10:1). Like Moses, Jesus instructs the heads of Israel of their duties once they enter the land. The apostles are sent out like the twelve spies and like Joshua on a military operation. They are to go into the land (only a certain land) and let their peace fall on houses who welcome them (think Rahab) and who will receive a reward (10:40–42).[42] When they enter the land, they will face persecution, and they may be tempted to be afraid. But they are told not to be anxious (10:19) because their Father cares for them. This is the same language with which Moses instructs his people and specifically Joshua before the conquest (Num. 14:9; 21:34; Deut. 1:21; 3:2, 22; 31:8; Josh. 8:1; 10:8, 25).[43]

Though there seems to be some back and forth between the sending of the twelve spies into the land and the conquest of Joshua, this should not trouble the readers. For in some sense, this is the same event. One recounts

41. Garland, *Reading Matthew*, 110.

42. Allison (*Studies in Matthew*, 120–21) ties Matt. 10 with Exod. 12. Many of the articles of clothing or accessories that Jesus instructs his disciples *not* to take on the journey are the same items the Israelites had with them as they rushed out of Egypt. Furthermore, he points out that according to Deut. 8:4 and 29:5, the Israelites' clothes and sandals did not wear out while in the wilderness, which may be a reason why Jesus's disciples did not need to worry about taking much. The references to Deuteronomy are intriguing, since they take place before the conquest of the land.

43. Two times Jesus tells his disciples "Do not be afraid" (μὴ φοβεῖσθε, Matt. 10:28; 14:27) and once "Don't worry" (10:19). These are similar to the injunctives given by Moses and Joshua (e.g., Num. 14:9; 21:34; Deut. 31:8).

the people's failure to enter the land; the other recounts the success (though partial) of the people entering the land. Thus it is not odd in the least for Matthew to combine these events in his retelling of the sending of the Twelve. The persecution, trouble, and sword they will face also reminds us of the books of the former prophets (Joshua, Judges, Samuel, Kings). Because of the lack of good leadership, persecution and the sword fall on the nation until the true king of Israel arises. Similarly, the Twelve prepare the way for Jesus, the true king. Jesus sends his messengers to recapture the land, but they will need his resurrection life to truly enter the new creation.

Monarchy in Matthew 11–12

As chapter 10 is about the conquest, so chapters 11–12 concern the monarchy. The opening of chapter 11 speaks of the prophet John the Baptist, who prepares the way for Jesus. Like Samuel, who anointed David, John is somewhat confused about the one he anoints, but Jesus confirms that he is the one promised from long ago. John is thus a Samuel-type figure, while Jesus is the new David. As in the time of David, the people of Israel don't always welcome the king. Jesus condemns "this generation" for their response to him (11:16). Yet Jesus offers to give Sabbath rest to the people as God promised to Israel after the conquest (11:25–30) and as David provided for the people by conquering their enemies. "Of the ten uses of the word 'Sabbath' in Matthew, eight are in chapter 12."[44] But the people quarrel about what Jesus is doing on the Sabbath rather than accepting the rest he offers to them.

In this section Jesus is presented not only as the new David, but Jesus also speaks of himself as greater than the temple (12:6), which pushes readers into the latter days of the monarchy. Jesus is also the one who can enter into the temple and eat the bread (12:1–8; 1 Sam. 21). As N. T. Wright has asserted, this assigns to the Pharisees the role of the persecuting Saul or spying Doeg; the disciples are the companions of David, and Jesus is David himself. Just as David flees from Saul, Jesus, knowing the Pharisees' plot against him, withdraws after the encounter with the Pharisees (Matt. 12:14–15).[45] "Like David, Jesus is approved by the crowds, but opposed by the leaders of Israel (1 Sam. 17–18)."[46] Some welcome Jesus, but many reject the king. Even the religious leaders accuse Jesus of possessing a false spirit, as Saul accused

---

44. Leithart, *Jesus as Israel*, 28.
45. Wright, *Jesus and the Victory of God*, 393–94.
46. Leithart, *Jesus as Israel*, 30.

David of deceitful motives. Jesus makes plain in this section that the religious leaders, like Saul, are the ones with the false spirit. They are the unresponsive generation from whom the kingdom will be torn. Jesus is creating his true family (Matt. 12:46–50) around himself, and even the gentiles will hope in him (12:15–21).

One more argument confirms the monarchy theme in chapters 11–12. In the middle of chapter 12, Matthew employs the longest fulfillment quotation in his Gospel:

> Behold, my servant whom I have chosen, my beloved with whom my soul is well pleased. I will put my Spirit upon him, and he will proclaim justice to the gentiles. He will not quarrel or cry aloud, nor will anyone hear his voice in the streets; a bruised reed he will not break, and a smoldering wick he will not quench, until he brings justice to victory; and in his name the Gentiles will hope. (12:18–21)

While this quotation is from Isaiah, the text reaches back to Davidic and monarchal language. The person of whom Isaiah speaks is "a chosen servant, a beloved one, with whom Yahweh is pleased" (cf. Matt. 12:18). This language echoes Davidic and kingly descriptions. David and Solomon are the chosen servants. The Lord does not choose the other sons of Jesse (1 Sam. 16:10), but the Lord chooses David. In Ps. 89:3 Yahweh says, "I have made a covenant with my chosen one; I have sworn to David *my servant*" (emphasis added here and below). The Lord likewise chooses Solomon to build a house for the sanctuary (1 Chron. 28:10). In addition, David is *a servant* of the Lord (1 Sam. 25:31). In a most important text Yahweh calls David his servant: "Go and tell *my servant David* . . ." (2 Sam. 7:5, 8, 20). Then again in Ps. 89:3 Yahweh calls David not only his chosen one but also *his servant*, and this is repeated in Ps. 89:20, 39.

This servant and chosen one is also the one who possesses the Spirit. Both Matthew and Mark attribute the Psalms to David's being in the Sprit (Matt. 22:43; Mark 12:36).[47] So while the Matthean fulfillment quotation is from Isaiah, it speaks of a future deliverer modeled after the life of David. Thus, the longest fulfillment quotation in this section, and even in the whole Gospel, tells of a future king who will be like David. Matthew portrays Jesus as the king who brings Sabbath rest like the chosen servant of the Lord, David. As in the previous narratives, the exile concepts loom large behind these stories.

---

47. The king also proclaims justice, and 2 Sam. 8:15 gives a summary statement of David's reign over Israel, saying that he administers "justice and equity" to all his people.

The Wise King in Matthew 13

We have traveled through the Pentateuch in Matt. 1–9 and into the conquest and monarchy in Matt. 10–12. The third discourse can be put in parallel with the wisdom tradition.[48] Toward the end of chapter 12, Matthew signals that he is moving to the end of the monarchy with his reference to Solomon and wisdom (12:42). In some ways, the heading for chapter 13 could be "Something greater than Solomon is here."[49] In chapter 13 Jesus speaks in parables and in poetic form like David (Psalms) and his son Solomon (Proverbs). Matthew explicitly quotes from the Wisdom literature, saying that these words fulfill the line "I will open my mouth in a parable; I will utter dark sayings from of old" (Ps. 78:2; cf. Matt. 13:34–35). As before, a key fulfillment quotation provides a clue to where readers are in the history of Israel. Two arguments point toward us seeing this quotation as informative for the section and structure of Matthew as a whole.

First, structurally, this fulfillment quotation sits at the center of the parabolic discourse,[50] and therefore it is also structurally at the center of the Gospel as a whole. Often this quotation is passed over with little comment, but Matthew may be alerting his readers to a structural clue with the placement of this text. Second, and related, as I argued in chapter 2, Matthew reduces the number of fulfillment quotations as the narrative continues and begins to drop them in to summarize large sections of his narrative. In the same way, this quotation is inserted to summarize this whole section. All of chapter 13 has Jesus opening his mouth to speak in parables, as in the wisdom tradition.

It is not just the fulfillment quotation that helps readers see the connection with Wisdom literature in chapter 13. The word "parable" is employed twelve times in this chapter, indicating the completeness of the parabolic and *mashal* tradition. The Wisdom literature is thus summed up in this new son of David, who showers the people with wisdom and truth. Matthew even explicitly says that the people are astonished at his "wisdom" (13:54) immediately after Jesus gives his kingdom parables. Apart from this reference to wisdom, the word appears only in 11:19 and 12:42, with the latter being a reference to Solomon, who so impressed the queen of Sheba. In the next section, gentiles come to Jesus (15:21–29), as the queen of Sheba came to Solomon to sit at his feet, while the nation of Israel rejects him, and Jesus declares Israel to be a wicked

---

48. See the first chapter (above) for a more extended argument of Jesus being presented as a teacher of wisdom in Matthew as a whole but especially in chap. 13.

49. Perkins, "'Greater than Solomon.'"

50. If one follows Davies and Allison (*Matthew*, 2:373) in their trifold structure, then there are three subsections in each block.

generation (16:1–12). When the queen of Sheba comes to Solomon, the explicit wisdom referred to is the house he has built, the temple (1 Kings 10:4; chaps. 5–8). As in the past, the tabernacle's construction was made possible by the Spirit of wisdom resting on people (Exod. 31:1–11). Now in Matthew a Solomon *redivivus* constructs the new temple (the new community) by spreading his message of wisdom.

Overall, there are enough correspondences (the fulfillment quotation, the larger context, the form of the chapter, and the references to wisdom) to appropriately label Matt. 13 as mirroring the wisdom tradition in the OT. If the wisdom tradition comes after the monarchy, then it makes sense that Matt. 13 comes after Matt. 11–12. The true king bestows his wisdom about the kingdom to his people. As in the wisdom tradition, we learn that the kingdom is not all that everyone expects. Revelation is needed. The disciples say they understand (13:51), and they too will be called to go into the nations, calling people out of exile, but many will ask, "Where did this man get this wisdom?" (13:54).

The Divided Kingdom in Matthew 14–17

In chapters 14–17 Matthew moves out of the monarchy to the divided kingdom, which Solomon's sons brought about. The rest that David brought to the kingdom was temporary in Israel's history; now life begins to fall apart again for Israel despite the presence of the son of David showing them that the sin problem runs deep in their hearts. The former prophets emerge on the scene as chaos descends on the nation. Compared to chapters 1–13, the structure in Matt. 14–17 is harder to discern, compelling many commentators to claim that Matthew's carefully structured first half takes a different turn.[51] But these arguments are quite unsatisfying. The structure becomes more chaotic at this point because of the disorderly kingdom that followed Solomon's reign.

A careful look at these chapters reveals a broad structure, though a chaotic element exists. Although many Jews reject Jesus, he still holds out the promise of life to them like the prophets and the prophetic literature. There is a remnant left within Israel, though the nation is divided. The prophets give hope to the remnant and warn the Israel of the flesh that the people are headed for destruction and exile. As the Gospel continues, Jesus fulfills the role of the former prophets and even the whole of the prophetic literature. At

51. Davies and Allison (*Matthew*, 2:463) and France (*Gospel of Matthew*, 547) claim that there is no clear structure at this point.

the same time, Jesus turns to the gentiles, provides for them, and welcomes them, because his eye is focused on the new covenant. Amid this chaos, Jesus establishes his new community, built on the confession of Peter (16:16), which points to the hope of the future.

Chapter 14 begins with the story of John's death at the hands of Herod (14:1–12). We can see what Matthew is doing by reading both backward and forward. The narrative aligns Herod with Ahab, and John the Baptist with prophets of old. Herod is a prototypical anti-king, so here he functions as an Ahab-like figure. Herod attacks and kills the prophet of God; similarly, Ahab allows the murder of prophets (1 Kings 18:4). And "like Ahab, Herod is egged on to attack the prophet by his bloodthirsty wife (Matt. 14:6–8; 1 Kings 18:4; 19:1–2)."[52] Yet this section also introduces what *is* to happen to God's chosen prophets.[53] Thus this opening episode (14:1–12) continues the tradition of an anti-king killing the prophet of God, foreshadowing what will happen to Jesus the prophet.

Anti-King	Prophet	Fate
Ahab	Elijah	Attempted death, but life
Herod	John the Baptist	Death
Pilate	Jesus	Death, but life

The narrative also alerts readers to a key transition: the end of one prophet and the start of another. First, Jesus explicitly links John the Baptist to Elijah (17:12–13). Second, Jesus also specifically references John the Baptist as the "Elijah who is to come" (Matt. 11:14). Third, the Baptist's clothing was earlier described in detail and mirrors the apparel of Elijah (Matt. 3:4; 2 Kings 1:8). Matthew therefore has told the story of John the Baptist's death in a way that mirrors the life of Elijah. The Baptist, like Elijah, is an eclectic prophet who challenges Israel's leaders and therefore suffers under their wrath.

And when Elijah dies, Elisha must take up the prophetic mantle. Matthew largely follows this chronology in chapters 14–17. As John the Baptist (Elijah) dies, Jesus (Elisha) steps onto the scene. The prophetic period has commenced. The negative response to Jesus does not diminish Jesus's care for his people, as the prophets in the divided kingdom still exercised watchfulness for the

---

52. Leithart, *Jesus as Israel*, 32.
53. In the same way, Pilate acts as an "anti-king," who, as Herod did with John the Baptist, seizes Jesus (Matt. 26:4; cf. 14:3), binds him (27:2; cf. 14:3), and does not initially want to put him to death because he fears the people (21:46; cf. 14:5). Pilate's hand is forced, despite his wife's involvement, but he is sorry (27:11–26; cf. 14:6–12). After Jesus dies, his disciples come, take his body, and bury it, as John's disciples did for him (27:51–61; cf. 14:12).

people of Israel. Jesus still feeds Israel, though his hometown rejects him and though he knows he is going to his death at the hands of the Jewish religious leaders. The feeding of Israel (the five thousand) mirrors a story from the life of Elisha (2 Kings 4:42–44).[54]

Matthew then recounts the water-crossing miracle (14:22–33). Most tie this to Moses/Joshua, who feeds the people in the wilderness and then brings them into the promised land. This is not wrong, but there is more. For when the transition from Elijah to Elisha takes place (2 Kings 2:12–14), Elisha takes up the cloak of Elijah and strikes the water, which parts, and Elisha crosses over.[55] The sons of the prophets announce, "The spirit of Elijah rests on Elisha" (2 Kings 2:15), just as the disciples recognize, after Jesus walks across the water, that he is "the Son of God" (Matt. 14:33). Already Matthew has tied the Spirit's anointing on Jesus with the title of Son at Jesus's baptism (3:16–17). The point again is that Jesus is not only the new Moses but also the new Elisha, because he stands in the prophetic stream. Interpreters don't need to choose one theme over another; the prophetic tradition couples them.

Jesus turns to the nations, and the gentiles respond rightly (symbolized by the Canaanite woman in 15:21–28; see Isa. 57:19). This is unlike what we see in 2 Kings, for Jehoshaphat comes to Elisha, asking if he should go and destroy the Moabites, and Elisha says the Moabites will be given into his hand (2 Kings 3:18). Yet it also mirrors Elisha's ministry, since as Jesus heals the Canaanite woman's daughter, so too Elisha raises the Shunammite's son (2 Kings 4:8–37).[56] Both healings have food as central to the story, in both the disciples of the prophets try to keep the women away (Matt. 15:23; 2 Kings 4:27), and in both it is followed by a healing on or near a mountain (Matt. 15:29–31; 2 Kings 4:27–37). Feeding accounts also follow these stories (feeding

---

54. The emphasis on bread holds this section together. Herod throws a feast for his birthday (14:1–12), Jesus feeds the five thousand (14:13–21), the Pharisees and scribes from Jerusalem ask about washing hands before eating (15:1–9), Jesus speaks to the Canaanite woman about bread (15:21–28), he feeds the four thousand (15:32–39), and he warns the disciples about the leaven of the Pharisees and Sadducees (16:5–12). This *bread* then is most likely tied to Elisha, whose ministry also has food as a central theme. Elisha's ministry revolves around the gift of food: he heals Jericho's waters (2 Kings 2:19–22), provides food for the sons of the prophets (4:38–41), multiplies loaves to feed the multitude (4:42–44), gives bread to Aramean (Syrian) soldiers (6:20–23), and prophesies the end of the famine after the siege of Samaria (7:1, 18–20). Therefore, as the new Elijah dies, the new Elisha steps onto the scene.

55. Leithart (*Jesus as Israel*, 36) ties the rescue of Peter from the water with Elisha making the axe head float (2 Kings 6:1–7). I am not sure that this connection works as well.

56. Or one could tie this story to 1 Kings 17:8–24, which is also a possibility. Elisha also faces a woman seeking help, a woman who throws herself at his feet at Mount Carmel (2 Kings 4:25, 27). Though this does not continue the chronology, Matthew does not need to follow it exactly. Here he seems more concerned with presenting Jesus largely as the new prophet in the divided kingdom.

of the four thousand in Matt. 15:5–12; feeding of the prophets in 2 Kings 4:38–44), and there is leftover bread (Matt. 15:37; 2 Kings 4:44).

Peter's confession introduces the hope of a new community amid a divided kingdom (Matt. 16:13–20), and Jesus also instructs his new community on how to act (chaps. 18–20). Though Peter recognizes who Jesus is, he misunderstands the path to Jesus's enthronement. Therefore Jesus reveals his glory to Peter, James, and John on the Mount of Transfiguration, where the two prophets par excellence (Moses and Elijah) show up beside Jesus (17:1–8). The transfiguration of Jesus, like the baptism and the fulfillment quotations, are hot spots for what Matthew is doing with his narrative. It might even mirror Elijah's ascension in a whirlwind (2 Kings 2), or the glory of angels that surround Elisha (2 Kings 6:15–17). "Of the nine uses of the name of Elijah, six are in chapters 16–17."[57] Like Elisha, Jesus tells his disciples to "have no fear" (Matt. 17:7; 2 Kings 6:16).[58] The cluster of explicit or implicit references to Elijah and Elisha places us in a divided-kingdom context, which naturally flows from what we have seen earlier with the two different responses to Jesus from Israel and the gentiles (chaps. 14–17). Yet Jesus creates his new community in the midst of this divided kingdom. Though he feeds the people, the religious leaders are angry at him. Though his hometown rejects him as a prophet, and some ask for signs, no sign will be given except the sign of the prophet Jonah. The strain of hope will not be snuffed out because God preserves his people amid chaos. He will establish his new community and bring them into their land.

Prophetic Hope and Judgment in Matthew 18–25

Prophetic Hope in Matthew 18–20

Chapters 18–20 continue the prophetic theme and center on the new people of God, which the prophets predicted (Isa. 49:3–6; 66:18–21; Zech. 2:11; Ezek. 47:21–23). Through the visionary words of Jesus, he establishes and teaches his ἐκκλησία (church).[59] This is both in contrast to and in continuity with the "assembly of Israel" (cf. Deut. 4:10). The new community even has its own structures of authority and the presence of God uniquely to enforce

57. Leithart, *Jesus as Israel*, 33.
58. I am indebted to Leithart (*Jesus as Israel*, 36) for these observations.
59. Leithart (*Jesus as Israel*, 34) ties this to Elisha, who is unlike Elijah in being constantly surrounded by his disciples. Though readers have already been introduced to the community in Matt. 16, Jesus does uniquely form his new community in chaps. 18–20. This teaching has already been foreshadowed in Matt. 16, where Jesus instructs his disciples to take up their crosses.

standards (Matt. 18:15–20). The people of God, like Israel of old, are to remember the Torah and the instructions about humbling themselves before God and caring for the down-and-outs (18:1–14). They are to become like children in humility (18:1–6) and care for little ones (18:10–14). Likewise, they are instructed to be peacemakers (18:15–35) and care for one another, seeking out reconciliation. In short, Jesus forms a remnant in the midst of a hardened people and instructs them on how to live in the new kingdom he is establishing. The disciples and followers of Jesus represent an Israel within Israel, those who will follow the teachings of the true prophet. This is just as Elijah and Elisha did during the false dynasty under which they lived.

Chapters 19–20 provide the ethics of this new community as Jesus begins to travel south. Now Jesus heads to Judea and Jerusalem (the southern kingdom). As he does so, he turns to his disciples to train them in the way of the covenant, as a prophet would. On the way, Jesus also welcomes the children, reversing the curse on the children who have rebelled against Yahweh. Isaiah said: "Hear, O heavens, and give ear, O earth; for the LORD has spoken: Children have I reared and brought up, but they have rebelled against me. . . . Ah, sinful nation, a people laden with iniquity, offspring of evildoers, children who deal corruptly! They have forsaken the LORD, they have despised the Holy One of Israel, they are utterly estranged" (Isa. 1:2, 4). But Jesus calls to his estranged children and welcomes them to his side, "for to such belongs the kingdom of heaven" (Matt. 19:14).[60] Jesus establishes his new community and redeems the children who have rebelled against him (see Isa. 45:11; 49:25; 54:1, 13; 60:9), thus launching his new community.

Like the prophets, Jesus instructs his community to keep the commandments given in the covenant, but he also says they must follow him and give up what is most precious to them (Matt. 19:16–26). They must not demand to be first but must understand that the kingdom of Jesus is one where status consciousness has no place. They must remember that Yahweh dwells "in the high and holy place," yet he also dwells with "him who is of a contrite and lowly spirit, to revive the spirit of the lowly, and to revive the heart of the contrite" (Isa. 57:15). God will look on the humble, those who tremble at his word (66:2). The new community must become a servant of all, a servant to the nations, so that all can come and drink from the wealth of the king. Matthew 18–20 thus constitutes the "hope" and instruction that the prophets hold out to the community willing to come back to Yahweh as their true king and thus release them from exile.

60. Though some might balk at this simple connection, the rest of the correspondences we have seen give it more weight.

Prophetic Judgment in Matthew 21–25

Matthew 21 marks a definite shift. Though Jesus has given hope to his community in Matt. 18–20, from here onward Jesus is the "judging prophet." He enters the city of Jerusalem on a colt. This comes in fulfillment of Zech. 9:9, which speaks of the king coming in a humble way. "Though the entry certainly has royal overtones, the crowds announce that the prophet has arrived (21:11)."[61] In the Zechariah context, the prophet assures Israel that they will be saved by a coming king; Matthew shows that not all Israel is true Israel, and they are not ready to receive their king. Rather than coming into the city as the conquering messiah, Jesus acts as the condemning prophet by three related temple acts. First, he confronts the temple system. Second, he castigates the leaders of Israel (especially the scribes) in the temple. Third, he foretells the destruction of the temple. For Israel, the destruction of the temple and exile went hand in hand.

Jesus first enters the temple and confronts the current regime. Jeremiah also prophesied against the temple in his so-called temple sermons (Jer. 7; 26). Jesus's language even mirrors Jeremiah's as he calls the temple a "den of robbers" (Matt. 21:13; Jer. 7:11). The temple is not a place where the poor can come and find solace; rather, it has become like a cave, where robbers lie in wait for the poor who would travel along the road. The condemnation of the temple is confirmed when the prophet-king curses the fig tree (Matt. 21:18–22). The cursing of the fig tree builds on Jeremiah and Isaiah's vineyard parable (Jer. 12:10–11; Isa. 5), where these prophets speak of Israel as grapevines or fig trees; when the Lord tries to gather fruit, "there are no grapes on the vine, no figs on the fig tree; even the leaves are withered" (Jer. 8:13). Therefore, the nation will be overthrown.[62]

Second, Jesus condemns the religious leaders in Matt. 23–25, which matches the condemnation by the prophets, especially Jeremiah, Ezekiel, and Isaiah. As

61. Leithart, *Jesus as Israel*, 38. The entry could even have resonances with the story of Elisha anointing Jehu as king (2 Kings 9). "Then in haste every man of them took his garment and put it under him on the bare steps, and they blew the trumpet and proclaimed, 'Jehu is king'" (9:13). Yet Jehu must battle with Joram, as Jesus battles with the current leadership when he enters the city.

62. The vineyard theme continues as Jesus tells two parables about vineyard owners (Matt. 20:1–16; 21:33–44) and another about a father who sends his sons to work in the vineyard (21:28–32). As with the prophets (Isa. 3:14; Jer. 12:10; Hosea 2:12), the vineyard is a metaphor for Israel. The Lord has cared for it diligently, but it fails to produce fruits and rejects the prophets, so the Lord will give it over to other nations and let it be destroyed and chopped down. Jeremiah specifically speaks against the shepherds who have destroyed his vineyard: "They have trampled down my portion; they have made my pleasant portion a desolate wilderness. . . . They shall be ashamed of their harvest because of the fierce anger of the LORD" (Jer. 12:10, 13).

Leithart says, "Jesus is the last and greatest of the Prophets. He is *the* Prophet that Moses predicted (Deut. 18). That means He gives the final word, brings the blueprints for the final temple, speaks the final world into existence, and has complete and permanent access to the divine court, where He can offer a defense for His people. Everything prophets have done, Jesus does, and more."[63] Though the setting of chapter 23 is not made explicit by Matthew, it seems that Jesus is most likely still in the temple. This again establishes strong connections to the temple sermons of Jer. 7 and 26. Jeremiah's declaration sounds like a perfect summary of Jesus's message: "Amend your ways and your deeds, and I will let you dwell in this place" (Jer. 7:3). Jesus himself laments that Jerusalem is "the city that kills the prophets" (Matt. 23:37), and he says, "See, your house is left to you desolate" (23:38; cf. Jer. 22:5).

Significantly, Jesus tells the religious leaders that he has sent them prophets, wise men, and scribes, but they have rejected all of them. God has sent them these prophets (and Jesus himself) so that "the blood of righteous Abel to the blood of Zechariah" might come on them (Matt. 23:34–35). He links Abel and Zechariah through righteous blood being shed, which reveals Matthew's awareness of the larger story line of the Hebrew Bible. Abel is the first in the Hebrew Bible whose blood is spilled (Gen. 4:10), and Zechariah is the last prophet whose violent death is reported (2 Chron. 24:21). In essence Matthew is saying that the blood speaks from "cover to cover," from Genesis through Chronicles.[64] The major point here is that Matthew is aware and tracing themes from beginning to end. In the last discourse, he reveals he is cognizant of the trajectory of the OT.

Finally, Matthew 24–25 then rightly presents the eschatological discourse, describing both the end of the temple period and the end of the world in apocalyptic terms—exile is coming. The discourse begins with Jesus looking at the temple and predicting its destruction (24:1–2). The glory of the Lord is leaving the temple, as Ezekiel prophesied. Ezekiel is brought into the court and told to go and see the vile abominations being committed in the temple. Engraved on the wall are creeping things, loathsome beasts, and idols (8:10). Ezekiel even calls it a great abomination (Ezek. 8:13; Matt. 24:15). Decisively, the glory of the Lord goes out from the threshold of the house and stands over the cherubim. And the cherubim lift up their wings and go out (Ezek. 10:18–19). For Jesus, the glory of the Lord is not only leaving the temple; the temple must also be destroyed.

63. Leithart, "Least of These."
64. Yet there is some question of whether the OT canon was closed at this point. See Peels, "Blood 'from Abel to Zechariah.'"

The apocalyptic language employed in this fifth discourse is eerily similar to Isaiah's prophetic apocalyptic condemnation of Babylon in Isa. 13. Jerusalem has become Babylon—so the city will be left desolate. Isaiah speaks of a coming battle. People are coming from distant lands. The day of the Lord is near, and "all hands will be feeble" (13:7). The land will become a desolation. "For the stars of the heavens and their constellations will not give their light; the sun will be dark at its rising, and the moon will not shed its light" (13:10). Yahweh will make the heavens tremble, and the earth will shake out of its place. Jesus similarly speaks of coming wars (Matt. 24:6–7); he says that tribulation is coming, and the people should flee (24:16). After the tribulation "the sun will be darkened, and the moon will not give its light, and the stars will fall from heaven, and the powers of the heavens will be shaken" (24:29).

The apocalypse and exile come together when Jesus tells his disciples that when the Son of Man appears, coming with the clouds of heaven, "he will send out his angels with *a great trumpet*, and they will gather his elect from the four winds, from one end of heaven to the other (24:30–31). Matthew's addition of the phrase "a great trumpet" alludes to the climactic sentences of Isaiah's apocalypse in Isa. 24–27.

> And in that day *a great trumpet* will be blown, and those who were lost in the land of Assyria and those who were driven out to the land of Egypt will come and worship the LORD on the holy mountain at Jerusalem. (Isa. 27:13, emphasis added)

Though much of Matthew's discourse is focused on condemnation and the end of the temple period, the allusion also shows that in the midst of destruction there is hope. Matthew's allusion proves that Jesus prophesies not only the end of an era, but the end of exile and the final regathering of the people of Israel.[65]

Although Matt. 18–20 mirrors the prophets' hope that is held out to the people, Matt. 21–25 reflects the prophetic judgment that Jesus, as the true prophet, announces on the nations that will not heed his words. Matthew has therefore moved all the way from Genesis into the prophetic literature and right up to the edge of the exile. The sequence we have seen so far can be summarized with the following chart:[66]

---

65. This paragraph is largely dependent on Hays, *Echoes of Scripture in the Gospels*, 137.

66. Noticeably, the sections covered get progressively longer. This should not be a stumbling block, since Matthew also bunches his fulfillment quotations in the first part of his narrative and then in the latter half lets them stand over large blocks of the narrative.

Matthew	Section Title	Old Testament Theme
1:1–17	Genealogy	Genesis, new creation, Adam
1:18–25	Birth of Jesus	Abraham
2:1–23	Travel narrative	Israel's travels
3–4	Beginning of ministry	Exodus begins
5–7	Sermon on the Mount	Mount Sinai: Exodus–Deuteronomy
8–9	Healings	Law enacted: Exodus–Deuteronomy
10	Sending of the Twelve	Conquest
11–12	Reactions to the king	Monarchy
13	Kingdom parables	Wisdom tradition
14–17	Divided reactions to Jesus	Divided kingdom: Elijah and Elisha
18–20	Instruction for the church	Prophets' hope: Establishment of a new community
21–25	Clash of the kingdoms	Prophetic condemnation: Castigation of current leadership

Exile and Return from Exile in Matthew 26–28

If Matthew is following the history of the OT, the next thing that should happen is the destruction of the temple and the exile. Jesus had already affirmed that his body was the temple and that it would be destroyed but rebuilt in three days (Matt. 26:61). Blood should fill this section as the people of Israel are attacked and destroyed by their enemies. But a twist occurs in the passion. The blood of Israel *is* spilled, but it is innocent blood.[67] Blood turns out to be not only the cue to the exile and destruction of the temple but also the prompt for the rebuilding of the temple and the return from exile. Blood is both the curse and the blessing, and it lies at the center of Israel's future. Through the dust of the fallen temple, a ray of light will be seen.

Matthew, as the narrator, laces prophetic texts to locate Jesus at the end of Israel's history. Jesus is Jeremiah, the lamenter, who mourns the sin and exile of the people Israel. But he is also the Jeremiah who declares that a new covenant has come through blood. He is Zechariah, the chastiser of the religious leaders, and he is the one who speaks of the rejected Davidic shepherd. Finally, Jesus is the new Cyrus, who declares that the people shall return from exile, rebuild their kingdom and their temple, and reestablish their family.

67. The blood in the OT is tainted by sin; Jesus's blood is pure.

Blood and Exile in Lamentations

Blood is everywhere in Matt. 26–28 and ends up being central to both the exile and the return from exile.[68] David Moffitt argues that, to portray Jesus's death as an act of righteous bloodshed, Matthew draws on Lamentations in his account of the events leading to the crucifixion.[69] This comes at the hands of the religious authorities and ultimately results in the destruction of Jerusalem and the temple. Matthew draws on Lamentations because laments were key cultural frameworks for the Jewish community during the exile. Lamentations expresses grief at the destruction of the temple and the hope of return from exile. Matthew consistently interweaves Lamentations at the end of his Gospel, thus portraying Jesus as the one who also laments the plight of the people, yet speaks of the hope of a return from exile.

One of the clearest allusions to Lamentations comes at the end of Matt. 23: "So that on you may come all *the righteous blood* shed on earth, *from the blood of righteous* Abel to the blood of Zechariah the son of Barachiah, whom you murdered between the sanctuary and the altar" (23:35, emphasis added). Though we have already looked at this text, and it comes in the preceding section, it sets up how we are to read Matthew's passion.[70] The phrase from this verse "all the righteous blood" echoes Joel 3:19; Jon. 1:14; and also Lam. 4:13, which is specifically dealing with the destruction of Jerusalem and saying that it happened "because" its prophets and unrighteous priests "have shed righteous blood in their land."

In 27:39 Matthew describes the people who pass by as "wagging their heads" at Jesus, thereby mocking him. Though this is probably an allusion to Ps. 22:7, it also reflects Lam. 2:15: "All who pass along the way clap their hands at you; they hiss and wag their heads at the daughter of Jerusalem: 'Is this the city that was called the perfection of beauty, the joy of all the earth?'" The context of Lam. 2 is the destruction of the temple (see 2:7). Therefore, those who pass by and wag their heads at Jesus's death fulfill the role of those who shake their heads at the destroyed temple (Jesus's body). Hays asserts that the text "subliminally suggests that the crucified Jesus paradoxically has become the embodiment of the scorned and destroyed city of Jerusalem."[71] On the cross Jesus is also offered gall, which mirrors the bitterness and wormwood of Lam. 3:19. Matthew therefore interweaves the themes of the exile,

---

68. Gore is not a major emphasis in Matthew's cross scene. Yet out of the eleven references to "blood" in Matthew's Gospel, six of them do occur in chaps. 26–28, and only one before Matt. 23.

69. Moffitt, "Righteous Bloodshed," 300.

70. In one sense, the divisions I have created are artificial, for all of Matt. 21–28 is of one piece.

71. Hays, *Echoes of Scripture in the Gospels*, 142.

the destruction of the temple, mocking, and bloodshed into the final days of Jesus, showing that it is by his blood that return from exile occurs. As Moffit says in his conclusion,

> Matthew alludes to Lamentations three times in chs. 23 and 27 of his Gospel (23:35; 27:34; and 27:39). The fact that these allusions come from chs. 2, 3, and 4 of Lamentations, that the allusion to Lamentations 4:13 resonates throughout the scenes that immediately precede the crucifixion (see Matt. 27:19, 24–25), and that the allusion to Lamentations 2:15 is so closely related thematically to the way Matthew uses Lamentations 4:13, all suggest that Matthew has employed Lamentations as a significant intertext. The allusions to Lamentations function as scriptural warrant for interpreting certain historical events theologically and polemically—namely, for understanding Jesus' crucifixion as the act of righteous bloodshed par excellence that directly results in the destruction of Jerusalem and the temple.[72]

The final chapters of Matthew display that Jesus acts as Israel as he experiences the exile and restoration in his death and resurrection.[73] Jesus submits himself to exile in his death and burial, but then at his resurrection he returns from exile. The bones that were once dead are brought again to life (Ezek. 37), and the bones of those in the city also awake for a time to show the power of Christ's work.

Blood, Zechariah, and the Rejected Shepherd

The story of blood continues from Lamentations to Zechariah (see Matt. 23:35). Four more references to blood appear in Matt. 27. First, in 27:4 Judas claims that he has sinned by betraying "innocent blood" (αἷμα ἀθῷον).[74] Second, Pilate's wife urges him in 27:19 to "have nothing to do with [Jesus,] that righteous man." Third, Pilate in 27:24 washes his hands and declares himself "innocent of this man's blood."[75] Fourth, in 27:25 the people call for Jesus's "blood [to] be on us and upon our children!" These four references point back to 23:35 to show Jesus as following in the tradition of Abel and Zechariah. He will die at the hands of the people, thereby bringing about the destruction of the temple and the exile. In fact, Jewish interpretive traditions

---

72. Moffitt, "Righteous Bloodshed," 319.
73. Leithart, *Jesus as Israel*, 41.
74. See Deut. 27:25; 1 Sam. 19:5.
75. See Hays (*Echoes of Scripture in the Gospels*, 132), who argues that Pilate's image inverts Deut. 21:7–8 and puts a Gentile ruler in the place of Israel when Jerusalem calls for his blood to be upon their heads.

link the story of the murder of Zechariah with the destruction of the temple and Jerusalem.[76]

Ham also argues that Matthew has employed Zechariah (the post-exilic prophet) in his portrayal of Jesus and his mission. In particular, Matthew has the dual related themes of Jesus as coming king and rejected shepherd—themes that come right from Zechariah's predominant messianic image.[77] The *rejected-shepherd theme* comes to the forefront when Judas recants of his betrayal in 27:3–10, and Matthew says that this episode fulfills Jeremiah the prophet. "And they took the thirty pieces of silver, the price of him on whom a price had been set by some of the sons of Israel, and they gave them for the potter's field, as the Lord directed me" (27:9). Jeremiah and Zechariah come into unity here.[78] Only Matthew among the Gospel writers provides the details of Judas asking the chief priests and elders how much they will give him, followed by their payment to him.

Matthew 26:16 says that they weigh out for Judas thirty silver coins. A similar expression appears in Zech. 11:12, where the people weigh out thirty pieces of silver to the shepherd, who loses his temper and breaks his covenant with them. In its canonical setting, the payment of the silver to Zechariah reflects a negative evaluation of his shepherding by leaders of Israel. In the Matthew scene, when Judas asks for the leaders of Israel to set a price on Jesus's head, they weigh out the same amount. In both texts, Israel's leaders reject the shepherd, and in both stories the coins are thrown back into the temple. Both Zechariah and Jesus are the rejected shepherds, whose worth is estimated by their enemies at thirty pieces of silver—the compensation for a slave (Exod. 21:32). Judas and the leaders of Israel thereby devalue and reject Jesus's shepherding ministry. Innocent blood is betrayed at a truncated price, a price that is later used to buy a field. Matthew therefore links the corrupted

---

76. See Moffitt, "Righteous Bloodshed," 306–8. C. Hamilton (*Death of Jesus*) argues that innocent blood signals the end of exile.

77. Three times in this section Matthew alludes to Zechariah (Matt. 21:4–5 = Zech. 9:9–10; Matt. 24:30 = Zech. 12:10–14; Matt. 26:31 = Zech. 13:7). Jesus is thus the shepherd messianic king, whose coming leads to his death. Ham shows how eleven times Zechariah is cited (3×) or alluded to (8×) in Matt. 21–27, including two of Matthew's fulfillment quotations (Matt. 21:5; 27:9–10) coming from Zechariah, thus framing the Zechariah references. It is not difficult to see how the theology of Zechariah has influenced the theology of Matthew. See Ham, *Coming King*; Foster, "Use of Zechariah"; Moss, *Zechariah Tradition*.

78. Matthew attributes this text to Jeremiah because the text is a mosaic of scriptural texts, some of which come from Jeremiah. Matthew most likely says it is from Jeremiah because Jeremiah is the one most commonly associated with potters and the buying of a field. In fact, Matthew seems to be taking the motifs of both coins and a potter's jug and picking up various texts as a magnet picks up paper clips as it goes by (Jer. 18:1–11; 19:1–13; 32:14; Zech. 11:13). Yet Judas knows that he has betrayed "innocent blood" (Matt. 27:4, 24; Jer. 26:15).

leaders of Israel in Zechariah's scene to the leaders of Israel in Jesus's day via the low price paid to worthless shepherds.[79]

Destruction of the Temple and Return from Exile

The temple theme that started in Matt. 21 therefore comes to a climax in the passion of Jesus. Of the twenty references to the temple in Matthew, fourteen of them occur in chapters 21–28. Readers find that at Jesus's trial the charge centers on the temple; they claim that he said he "is able to destroy the temple . . . and to rebuild it in three days" (26:61). While Jesus hangs on the cross, those who pass by mock him: "You who would destroy the temple and rebuild it in three days . . ." (27:40). Then when Jesus dies, the temple curtain is torn in two (27:51), signifying the end of the temple period.[80] While chapters 24–25 predict the destruction of the temple, in 26–28 we see the temple era end.

The temple and exile themes are held together by the above conglomeration of references to blood. The messiah undergoes exile himself as he is rejected and cast out of the city by his own nation. He suffers the death of a criminal at the demand of Israel's leaders. Regularly in the Prophets, the nation is condemned because of a lack of leadership, and the people suffer because of "worthless shepherds" (Ezek. 34; Zech. 11:17). In an intensified way, Jesus suffers at the hands of the worthless shepherds of Israel, who end up giving him over to the judgment of the nations. Ironically, though, the judgment that falls on Jesus becomes both the "end" of Israel and the "salvation" of Israel.

At the tearing of the temple curtain, the new exile begins; at the resurrection, it ends. The temple is destroyed and then rebuilt. In Jewish history, the destruction of the temple signaled the inauguration of exile, but by leaving the temple, Jesus indicates that a new age has come (24:1–2). The time of the temple is over, and the time of Jesus is here. This is confirmed at Jesus's

---

79. See Moss, *Zechariah Tradition*, 174:

> The *chief priests* and the *elders of the people* take counsel to arrest Jesus by stealth (Mt 26.1–4). After the costly anointing of Jesus by the unnamed woman (Mt 26.6ff), Judas approaches the *chief priests,* who pay him a paltry *thirty pieces of silver* to deliver Jesus to them (26.14–15). Following the supper at which Jesus has revealed his betrayer is one of the Twelve, Judas leads the arresting party from the *chief priests* and *elders of the people* to Jesus and betrays him with a kiss (26.47–50). Jesus is led to Caiaphas the high priest, where the scribes and *elders* have gathered (26.57). When Judas sees that Jesus has been condemned, he returns the *thirty pieces of silver* to the *chief priests* and the *elders,* in remorse over his sin of betraying *innocent blood* (27.3–4a). Although they refuse to absolve Judas of his bloodguilt, they are left with the *pieces of silver,* for Judas has thrown the *money* down in the temple before departing to hang himself (27.4b–5). The *chief priests,* knowing they cannot put such *blood money* in the temple treasury, use the *silver coins* to buy a potter's field for use as a burial ground (Mt 27.6–8).

80. Gurtner, *Torn Veil.*

resurrection, where he bursts forth from the tomb, declaring that the era of darkness is over—the epoch of light has come. Though he suffered exile by submitting himself to the wrath of the religious leaders and becoming the rejected shepherd, death cannot contain him. At the center of each shadow story that Matthew tells stands the cross and the resurrection. To miss the climax is to miss the story itself.

Go! Rebuild and Expand the Temple

Matthew closes his narrative with Jesus's commission to go and bring people out of exile by spreading his temple presence (28:16–20). Second Chronicles, the last book of the OT according to the Hebrew ordering, also ends with an eschatological note about the restoration project looming in the future—a restoration project that concerns Israel's kingdom. Cyrus gives a command, a commission, for Israel to go up to Jerusalem to rebuild the temple. Cyrus, the king of Persia, says, "The LORD, the God of heaven, has given me all the kingdoms of the earth, and he has charged me to build him a house at Jerusalem, which is in Judah. Whoever is among you of all his people, may the LORD his God be with him. Let him go up" (2 Chron. 36:23). Cyrus speaks of his universal authority, the source of his authority, and his commission to "go." Jesus lists the same three elements. He has all authority in heaven and on earth, given to him by his Father, and in light of that authority he tells his disciples to "go."

Both Matthew and 2 Chronicles end with a construction project. The new temple will expand, a new home will be provided, a new people will be born.[81] The "servant of Yahweh" has commanded the people to "go out," and he can do so because all authority has been given to him. They are to gather people into this new kingdom because, as the Genesis story has set things up, God is going to rule this earth through his vice-regents. His people are to spread the news of this king—the embodiment of Wisdom—to the whole world. At the center of this story stands Jesus—the new Israel—the teacher of wisdom, who brings blessings to all nations through his life-giving monarchy. Jesus promises his people his presence, he has given his blood, and he has conquered death by his resurrection; he will be with them to the end of the age.

Conclusion

The discipled scribe demonstrates the wisdom he learned from his teacher in a variety of ways. We can follow him down into the valleys and watch

---

81. Scribes in the ancient world regularly work in temples. See van der Toorn, *Scribal Culture*.

how he shifts OT quotations to make a point, or we can track him up to the mountain and watch as he looks out over the life of Jesus as a whole. As we stand at the peak, we can see that Jesus is the new Adam, Abraham, Moses, Joshua, David, Solomon, Elijah, and Jeremiah, but Matthew also has Jesus recapitulate a broad chronological structure of the history of Israel, and therefore Jesus stands as the new Israel, who leads his people out of exile.

All of these figures are contested in different ways. Adam is challenged by the devil, Moses is resisted by Pharaoh, David has to flee from his own nation, and Elijah must be wary of the Israelite kings above him. In the story of Israel, the resistance comes not only from the outside but also from the inside. The people of God have corrupt hearts, as the prophets long ago declared. Therefore, Israel needs to be saved not primarily from foreign armies or tyrannical kings but from their own twisted desires. The resistance comes from *within*, and therefore Jesus must change their hearts. In one sense the future of Israel is grim in Matthew. From the opening pages, the leadership rejects Jesus. Jesus laments their attitude, but he knows that this has been the plan all along. The leaders end up bringing him to his death.

In an ironic twist, the grim hope for Israel leads to a bright future. For Israel to have hope, it must undergo death. Matthew's sequencing of Israel's history through his narrative reveals that where Israel has failed, Jesus succeeds. Israel was called to be a light to the nations, but Jesus ends up being the one who calls the centurion and the Canaanite woman to himself. Israel was meant to crown an everlasting king, but Jesus becomes that king as he is enthroned on the cross by gentiles. Israel was supposed to welcome the prophets and listen to them, but Jesus becomes the prophet whom they must now obey. Israel should have welcomed their messiah and paved the way for him, but Jesus must chart his own path.

Through his structure the scribe has Jesus completing the whole history of Israel by sequencing the life of Jesus in the mold of Israel's history. Matthew traces his story from Genesis to the end of Chronicles (the first and last books in the Jewish canonical order). Though he did not do so in a wooden fashion, there are enough clues in his Gospel to reveal that underneath the narrative there is a frame: an infrastructure pointing readers to Jesus as Israel's hope. This is the wisdom Matthew absorbed from his teacher of wisdom and wrote down for future generations (Matt. 13:52; 28:18–20) as he was discipled by his rabbi in the secrets of the kingdom of heaven (13:11). From his *teacher* he learned Jesus himself is the faithful Son, who completes the mission of Israel. Jesus pursues his Father's will and becomes a sacrifice not only for Israel but also for the nations. He thereby fulfills the mission of Adam, Abraham, Moses, David, Jeremiah, Elijah and many more. He is Israel, but the better Israel.

Conclusion

Review

My argument has been that Matthew is the "discipled scribe" referred to in 13:52, who learns wisdom from his teacher. This wisdom more specifically concerns how the "new" relates to the "old"—or as Jesus puts it, the secrets of the kingdom of heaven (13:11).[1] The best way for Matthew to disciple and teach future generations is to tell the story of Jesus, because in this story the new and the old clatter together. He therefore tells shadow stories—stories that echo the previous narrative of Israel. Matthew's wisdom is thus embedded in his form. His conviction is that the story of Israel is fulfilled in this Solomon-like sage, who taught him how to integrate what is new with the old. The old in fact predicts that the new will come bearing wisdom: someone from Jesse, a new David, a righteous branch, who will have a spirit of wisdom and understanding (Isa. 11:1; 52:13; Jer. 23:5; 2 Chron. 1:10).

We therefore began by exploring how Matthew paints Jesus as the son of David. This son of David is the heir of the throne and the kingdom because he is a wise king, who reunites the north and the south. Yet the people of Matthew's day were probably tempted to have questions about Jesus's claim to kingship because of the seeming failure of his mission. Matthew reminds his readers that as David's path to kingship was filled with conflict, so Jesus himself must endure exile. In addition, if they look to Jesus's life, Matthew's readers can see how Jesus is the living embodiment of the law (à la wisdom). He shepherds and heals his people. He is the king that the prophets foretold—the wise suffering servant.

---

1. As noted earlier in the book, what is secret or hidden is regularly connected to wisdom.

Matthew also styles Jesus as the new Moses. Moses's prophetic role, mediation, healing, and redeeming acts all revolved around the exodus. Moses, though flawed, was a wise leader who brought his people out of Egypt and to the brink of the promised land. Jesus is like Moses but better. Jesus not only leads his people on the new exodus through his death on the cross, but he also tells them to go into the land, spreading the teaching of Jesus.

Jesus is also the son of Abraham. Abraham was promised that he would have a family who would be a great nation. Abraham wisely believed God and followed God's will, but he and his children also turned their backs on God and tried to make families in their own power. Jesus rests in the will of his Father and knows that it is precisely in an act of death that Abraham's family expands.

Finally, Jesus is the new Israel. Because of Israel's sin, Israel was conquered by foreign armies. But Jesus, as the true Israel, submits himself to the armies of sin and darkness, offering his innocent blood on behalf of the nation. The messiah retraces the footsteps of Israel and brings them home from exile by his sacrifice.

Character	Concept/Event
David	kingdom
Moses	exodus
Abraham	family
Israel	exile

Though for the purpose of closer examination, I have separated these characters (David, Moses, Abraham, Israel) and concepts/events (kingdom, exodus, family, exile), they interweave in the narrative. When Jesus commands the disciples to go out into the nations, he instructs them as the king, the new Moses, the new Abraham, and the new Israel. In the command he instructs them to go up out of exile and on the new exodus, to build their kingdom and establish their new family. The new exodus has the kingdom as its goal. The return from exile is a new exodus. The new family of God inherits the kingdom.

Therefore, while lines can be drawn, Matthew ties these hopes together under the banner of fulfillment. The life of Jesus is where the new and the old meet—an understanding Matthew has gained through becoming a disciple of his teacher of wisdom. If Matthew is the discipled scribe, who learned the law of the Lord, thereby making him wise (Ps. 19:7), then he defines his activity not only by a positive portrayal but by negative pictures of foolish scribes. Through looking at the antithesis to scribes, we can draw some conclusions about what it means to be a true disciple and scribe.

The Foolish Scribes

Wise teachers instruct by negation and comparison. Light is opposed to darkness, health is contrasted with sickness, and sheep are distinguished from goats. Both Matthew and Jesus teach in this way. They oppose blessings and woes, worthless shepherds with caring shepherds, and positive instruction with negative denouncement. This new and old alternation—explanation by comparison or negation—is pervasive in the wisdom tradition.

> The fear of the LORD is the beginning of knowledge, but fools despise wisdom and instruction. (Prov. 1:7)

> Let not the wise boast of their wisdom or the strong boast of their strength or the rich boast of their riches, but let the one who boasts boast about this: that they have the understanding to know me. (Jer. 9:23–35 NIV)

> The righteous are like a tree; the wicked are like chaff. (cf. Ps. 1)

> The kings of the earth conspire against the Christ, but the wise kiss the Son. (cf. Ps. 2)

It is therefore appropriate to end this examination of Matthew as the discipled scribe with the negative corollary: foolish or unwise scribes.[2] If Matthew and the other disciples are an alternative scribal school, they must represent an alternative to something. Matthew does not merely define what it means to be a discipled scribe; he also illustrates the opposite of a trained scribe. This serves as both a warning and clarifying instruction about what it means to be a pupil of the teacher. The false scribes, the non-discipled scribes, the adversaries to Jesus in the Gospel—these are the religious leaders, the teachers of the law, the Pharisees, the "kings" of Israel, and finally Judas is revealed as the ultimate false disciple.[3] This conclusion briefly explores the tradition against which Jesus contends.

Matthew 23 is unique to Matthew and bolsters my thesis that Jesus in Matthew is creating an alternate scribal school. Jesus vociferously denounces the actions of the scribes (γραμματέων) and Pharisees: they impose heavy burdens, do their deeds to be seen by others, love the place of honor, and like

---

2. Not all of my examples will pertain specifically to scribes but apply more generally to those who oppose Jesus and his ministry.

3. Matthew uses the phrase "their synagogue(s)" five times (4:23; 9:35; 10:17; 12:9; 13:54) and "your synagogue" once (23:34) to emphasize the distance between Jesus and the current synagogue community.

to be called "Rabbi." So Jesus turns and says to his disciples, "*But you* are not to be called rabbi [ῥαββί], . . . and call no man your father, . . . neither be called instructors [καθηγητής]" (Matt. 23:8–10, emphasis added). Readers should be asking what these false scribes teach us about what it means to be students of Jesus.

Three things come to the forefront in Matthew's presentation of the foolish scribes. (1) They don't recognize Jesus as their teacher of wisdom, (2) they are unreliable interpreters because they don't understand the relationship between the new and the old, and (3) they lack righteousness. Put another way, they lack wisdom theologically, practically, and ethically.[4] They walk down the path of folly. Psalms 1 and 2 therefore loom large over this section. The introduction to the Psalter contrasts the righteous with the wicked—the wise with the foolish. The wise are those who meditate on the Torah, who follow the messiah. The foolish are those who have no future, who plot in vain, and set themselves up against the messiah. Therefore, Yahweh looks at the kings of the earth and calls them to understanding—to wisdom. The wise gain understanding by learning and listening. The foolish travel their own path.

Theological Folly

Foolish disciples and scribes are at their core contrasted with discipled scribes because they don't accept Jesus as their messiah and teacher of wisdom, and so lack *theological* wisdom. If all wisdom is from the Lord (Sir. 1:1), then all folly comes from rejecting him. The foolish scribes claim that Jesus blasphemes (Matt. 9:3), ask him for a sign (12:38), and wonder why Jesus's disciples break the traditions of the elders (15:1–2). Most importantly, the scribes condemn Jesus to death and mock him on the cross (20:18; 27:41). In Proverbs the author claims that the fear of the Lord is the beginning of wisdom (Prov. 9:10). "This fear is not the fear that makes us run, but it is the fear that makes us pay attention and listen. Fear of the Lord makes us humble, a wisdom trait."[5] One can almost hear Jesus saying, "He who has ears to hear, let him hear" (Matt. 11:15; 13:9, 43; Sir. 1:14).

In the Sermon, Jesus forms his alternative scribal school through his teaching, but in another sense, he pleads with the scribes of the day to understand

---

4. Longman (*Fear of the Lord Is Wisdom*, chaps. 1–3) argues that although wisdom has been portrayed as mainly practical in the past, it is theological, ethical, and practical. Though these three realities can be distinguished, they ultimately interweave. The foolish scribes lack righteousness and wisdom because they are not following their messiah. They are twisted interpreters because they are hypocrites, and they can't rightly interpret the new and the old because they don't accept Jesus as the embodiment of wisdom.

5. Longman, *Fear of the Lord Is Wisdom*, 13.

who he is. They don't understand that Jesus is the one of whom the Prophets spoke. Jesus claims this school of scribes has rejected him, and now he must "suffer many things from the elders and chief priests and scribes, and be killed, and on the third day be raised" (Matt. 16:21; 20:18). Foolish scribes are essentially those who have rejected the true teacher of wisdom.

Practical Folly

Second, Matthew continually has the false scribes "searching the Scriptures," but they cannot find life in them for they are impoverished interpreters, lacking *practical* wisdom. They don't recognize that all of the Scriptures point to Jesus. If the new is not accepted, then the old will be left in obscurity. We can see this illustrated in Matt. 2. King Herod assembles all the chief priests and scribes of the people (γραμματεῖς τοῦ λαοῦ) and inquires where the Christ is to be born (Matt. 2:4). The chief priests and the scribes quote a Jewish text to Herod, and it is the correct text (Mic. 5:2), but they seem to miss the point entirely or reject Jesus as the referent. Matthew demonstrates that because they have missed the new, they understand neither the new nor the old. The old makes sense only in light of the new. They have not interpreted the law rightly because they don't know to whom it points.

Similarly, Jesus responds to the indignation of the chief priests and the scribes (Matt. 21:15) by saying, "Have you never read in the Scriptures?" (21:42). He goes on to quote a verse from Ps. 118:22. They certainly had read this text, but again they could not understand it because Jesus is the cornerstone. Later Jesus says to them, "You are wrong, because you know neither the Scriptures nor the power of God" (Matt. 22:29). The false scribes are *foolish* precisely because they do not know the Scriptures, but Jesus creates a new class of scribes who understand his words (13:51). The chief priests and the scribes don't fulfill their role because they don't recognize to whom the Scriptures point. Jeremiah speaks prophetically when he condemns the people, saying, "How can you say, 'We are wise, and the law of the Lord is with us'? But behold, the lying pen of the scribes has made it into a lie" (Jer. 8:8; Ps. 19:7).

Ethical Folly

Finally, the foolish scribes are hypocrites and lack righteousness, and so lack *ethical* wisdom.[6] Throughout Proverbs and other literature, righteousness and

---

6. Dave Bland (*Proverbs and the Formation of Character*) has argued that the proverbs lead to a change of character that reshapes the inner person.

wisdom become connected terms.[7] The false scribes cannot see the ancient texts' true interpretation, partially because they lack righteousness. As C. S. Lewis says, "What you see and what you hear depends a great deal on where you are standing. It also depends on what sort of person you are."[8] Jesus's new scribal school must learn not only how to interpret but also how to embody the life of their teacher. "Unless your righteousness exceeds that of the scribes and Pharisees, you will never enter the kingdom of heaven" (Matt. 5:20).

Though Jesus says that the scribes and Pharisees sit on Moses's seat (23:2), the disciples should do and observe what they say but not the works they do (23:3). They do the opposite of what Jesus says in the Sermon: they impose heavy burdens, do their deeds in order to be seen, enjoy being called rabbi, and boast in their accomplishments (23:4–12). Therefore, Jesus pronounces woes instead of blessings on the scribes and Pharisees because they are hypocrites (23:13–39). He has rejected this scribal school because they refuse to be tutored by him, to interpret the old in light of him, and to practice the righteousness of the Torah.

Judas as a Foolish Disciple

Maybe the most tragic example of a false disciple is Judas. Matthew devotes more lines to Judas than any of the other Gospel writers. He provides clues in his narrative, displaying Judas as *the* foolish disciple: in two tragic texts Judas ironically refers to Jesus as rabbi. When Jesus predicts Judas's betrayal, Judas seals his own fate by asking, "Is it I, Rabbi?" Jesus says to him, "You have said so" (Matt. 26:24–25). Then in a final meeting between Jesus and his betrayer, when Judas comes to the garden, he says, "Greetings, Rabbi!" And he kisses him (26:49). Twice Matthew has Judas paradoxically call Jesus his rabbi as he plans to betray Jesus. Judas has been following his teacher, but he has not accepted his teaching, nor will he pass on his teaching except through a negative example (Matt. 7:21–23). Judas ends up following the allure of riches rather than listening to his teacher's instruction. "Wisdom will not enter a deceitful soul, or dwell in a body enslaved to sin. . . . The ungodly by their words and deeds summoned death" (Wis. 1:4, 16).

Jesus warned his scribal school of the dangers of money, but Judas did not listen. In the Sermon, Jesus says that if the eye is healthy or generous, then the whole body will be full of light (Matt. 6:22). He follows this with claiming that no one can serve two "masters." "You cannot serve God and money" (6:24). The disciples are not to be concerned about their life, for

---

7. Deut. 16:19; Ps. 37:30; Prov. 1:3; 9:9; 10:31; Eccles. 7:16; 9:1; 10:2; Jer. 23:5; 1 Cor. 1:30.
8. Lewis, *Magician's Nephew*, 51.

life is more than money. They are to "seek first the kingdom of God and his righteousness, and all these things will be added to [them]" (6:33). He tells his disciples to "acquire no gold or silver or copper for [their] belts" (10:9). Later in the Gospel a man comes up to Jesus, calling him "Teacher" and asking him what he "must do to inherit eternal life" (19:16). Jesus tells the man that if he wants to be "whole," he must sell everything he possesses and give to the poor, and he will have treasure in heaven (19:21 AT). Finally, Jesus calls his disciples to invest their money well, so that when he returns, they may receive a reward (25:27).

But this teaching does not penetrate Judas's heart. Judas does not follow the teachings of his rabbi.[9] He asks the chief priests what they will give him if he delivers Jesus over to them. They pay him thirty pieces of silver (26:15). Matthew brings up this silver four more times to emphasize the negative effect it has on Judas (27:3, 5, 6, 9). Job affirms wisdom cannot be bought with gold or silver (Job 28:15). Though Judas changes his mind, it is too late. He has betrayed his rabbi and goes out and hangs himself. Judas did not listen when Jesus said, "No one can serve two masters" (Matt. 6:24). The chief priests ironically try to do what is lawful with the silver pieces, saying, "It is not lawful to put them into the treasury, since it is blood money" (27:6). But like Judas, they are neglecting "the weightier matters of the law: justice and mercy and faithfulness" (23:23). Jesus told them that if they attempt to save their life, they will lose it (16:25). Judas's fate led him to a field of blood; the disciples are promised that they will "sit on twelve thrones" (19:28). Judas is therefore the antithesis to Matthew. While Judas dies in a field, Matthew will be commissioned on the mountain in Galilee to spread the teaching of Jesus.

To Be a Discipled Scribe

Through these negative portraits, we can draw a few conclusions about what it means to be a discipled scribe. As Brown has argued, part of the purpose of Matthew's Gospel is to communicate a vision of discipleship.[10] The disciples are ultimately to be like their teacher and become teachers themselves who transmit the message of Jesus to future generations; they are to go out, making disciples by teaching and baptizing (Matt. 28:19–20). Byrskog notes that pupils of a teacher in the ANE and in the first century would acknowledge the

---

9. "For those who despise wisdom and instruction are miserable. Their hope is in vain, their labors are unprofitable, and their works useless" (Wis. 3:11).
10. J. Brown, *Disciples in Narrative Perspective*, 145.

authority of their teacher and transmit their teachings to future generations.[11] Jesus creates an alternate scribal school to pass his wisdom on. The disciples therefore are not merely pupils; they are also future scribes/teachers.[12] According to Matthew, to be a discipled scribe is to fear God by recognizing and submitting to the teacher of wisdom (theological), interpret the law rightly (practical), and practice the law (ethical).

Theological Wisdom

The book of Job asks, "Where shall wisdom be found?" (Job 28:12). Matthew learns that the answer is as Ecclesiastes has said: to be wise is to "fear God and keep his commands, for this is the whole duty of [humanity]" (Eccles. 12:13). Fearing God means accepting the one God has attested—the wise messiah—and following him as he fulfills the law. To fear God means first that one has recognized Jesus as the teacher and embodiment of wisdom (theological). Jesus is God's final word of wisdom, to which all the Law and the Prophets point. He is the king of wisdom, for wisdom sits by his throne (Wis. 9:4). Wisdom involves divine communication, but this communication must be accepted. "For the LORD gives wisdom" (Prov. 2:6). "The beginning of wisdom is this: Get wisdom" (4:7). Jesus thanks God that he has hidden "these things from the wise and understanding and revealed them to little children" (Matt. 11:25). The "wise and understanding" in context seems to refer to the scribes and Pharisees (12:2, 14, 24, 38).[13] The "little children" (νηπίοις), on the other hand, are the disciples and followers of Jesus.[14] Deprivation, oppression, and humiliation characterize the disciples. Ulrich Luz describes the "little children" as the women, the Galileans, the poor people of the land, who have neither the time nor the possibility of going to the school of the "wise."[15] But they become wise as they sit at the feet of *the* wise one.

Matthew himself was a tax collector who gathered money from his own people for the Roman government, and Jesus calls him to repentance. When Jesus sees Matthew sitting at the tax booth, he calls to him and says, "Follow

---

11. He gives the examples of Elijah and Elisha, Elisha and the sons of the prophets, Isaiah and his disciples, Jeremiah and his followers, Ezekiel and his followers, Jesus ben Sira and his "sons," the righteous teacher and the Qumran community, and the rabbis and their pupils. Byrskog, *Jesus the Only Teacher*, 36–53.

12. Byrskog presents a whole chapter arguing that Matthew's presentation of Jesus reflects didactic motives of transmission. Byrskog, *Jesus the Only Teacher*, 237–308.

13. The reference could also more generally refer to Jews in Chorazin and Bethsaida who have rejected him (11:21).

14. Deutsch, *Hidden Wisdom*, 32; Betz, "Logion of the Easy Yoke."

15. Luz, *Matthew*, 163.

me." Matthew rises and follows him (Matt. 9:9), thus acknowledging his deprivation. This Greek word for "follow" (ἀκολουθέω) means to go in the same direction, to obey, comply with. Matthew becomes a pupil of Jesus. A discipled scribe is first and foremost someone who has heard the call of Jesus and risen from his tax booth and followed Jesus. Barton concludes his chapter on wisdom in Matthew by rightly stating: "Jesus the wisdom of God teaches the way of wisdom, authorizes the way of wisdom, and gives access to it both by his invitation to the 'weary and heavy-laden' and by exemplifying it in the humble servanthood of his own life."[16] As Paul argues, Christ is our God-given wisdom (1 Cor. 1:30). For Matthew and a few other scribes, this also means that they remember and pass down the sayings and deeds of Jesus. They inscribe them for generations to come.[17]

Practical Wisdom

Second, a discipled scribe is a true interpreter of the law who understands the relationship between the new and the old (practical). They realize that they can only understand if wisdom is revealed to them. So they pray for understanding and call on God for a spirit of wisdom (Wis. 7:7); they ask God for daily bread, forgiveness, and deliverance from evil (Matt. 6:11–13). "The beginning of wisdom is the most sincere desire for instruction" (Wis. 6:7). In Matthew, the crowds don't understand Jesus's teaching (13:13–15), and the opponents are blind leaders (15:14; 23:16, 24), but they ask questions not to understand but to trap Jesus. Though the Pharisees and Sadducees search the Scriptures, they don't find life in them because they don't understand that Jesus fulfills the Law and the Prophets.

However, a trained scribe is one who realizes that Jesus brings forth treasures both new and old, for they now understand the secrets of the kingdom of heaven (13:11, 51–52). They appreciate that the kingdom spreads slowly, it is carried along by words, and there will be evil in its midst. They know that Jesus fulfills the law, his yoke is easy, he has come to welcome all those who have faith in him, he is the new Moses who brings them on the new

16. Barton, "Gospel Wisdom," 98.

17. Overman (*Matthew's Gospel*, 135–36) argues that Matthew idealizes the disciples. While his case is overstated, there is some truth to his argument. "In his idealizing of the disciples and their emergence in the Gospel as followers who truly learn, understand, and now teach others, Matthew provides a model for the life and behavior of the community member. While Jesus is the hero and agent of God in Matthew's story, it is really the life and ministry of the disciples, centering as it does on learning, understanding, and instruction, which constitutes the primary focus of the member's own ministry in the present. The community members are to identify and emulate the disciples of Jesus as they are portrayed in the Gospel."

exodus, and he must be the rejected king who is strung up on a cross. They understand that the presence of Jesus is the presence of the kingdom, but most of all they realize that Jesus has conquered death by his resurrection. A new exodus and return from exile has come through following this rabbi. The messiah unifies all of the Jewish ancient texts because he is the one to whom they pointed all along. True disciples let Jesus complete the Torah and then live into the Torah by the power of the Spirit. A discipled scribe understands, interprets, and communicates the relationship between the new and the old through the lens of Jesus.

Ethical Wisdom

Third, a discipled scribe is someone who practices justice and mercy—not hypocrisy (ethical). They don't merely rightly interpret the law but rightly live it; this is wisdom. In a text parallel to Matt. 13:52, Jesus says, "The good person out of his good treasure brings forth good, and the evil person out of his evil treasure brings forth evil" (12:35; cf. 7:15–23). The good person has a good treasure, while an evil person has an evil treasure. Those who don't know Jesus are workers of lawlessness (Matt. 7:22–23). Sirach says, "If you desire wisdom, keep the commandments, and the Lord will lavish her upon you. . . . Do not be a hypocrite before others. . . . Do not exalt yourself" (Sir. 1:26, 29, 30). The scribes who follow Jesus are not hypocrites, like Judas, who sought the riches of the earth rather than the treasures of the kingdom of heaven.

The trained scribes perform their righteousness, not to receive praise from others, but to receive a reward from their Father in heaven. They don't neglect "the weightier matters of the law: justice and mercy and faithfulness" (Matt. 23:23). As Luz asserts, the definition of discipleship in Matthew can be summed up in the phrase "doing the will of God" (cf. 12:50).[18] Jesus called his disciples to pray that God's will would be done (6:10). Disciples are to take Jesus's yoke because he is meek and humble (11:29). To understand requires more than merely intellectual effort; understanding involves the heart. "This people's heart has grown dull, and with their ears they can barely hear" (13:15a), yet it is with the heart that people understand (13:15b). The one who understands is also the one who brings forth fruit (13:23). Understanding therefore means doing—or as Jesus summarizes, it means being *whole* (τέλειος, cf. 5:48). This is the wholeness that Jesus calls his disciples to in the Sermon on the Mount. The purpose of wisdom is to impart "righteousness, justice, and virtue" (Prov. 1:3b AT).

18. Luz, "Disciples in the Gospel," 123.

Forming the Nations

I began the book by saying that the purpose of scribal training is the formation of a certain type of community, a certain type of individual.[19] Scribes were the teacher-king's representatives, who shaped ideal humanity after the image of the king.[20] They would copy the king's texts and thereby train others as they transmitted the εὐαγγέλιον (good news) of the king. They would therefore (1) learn, (2) write/interpret, (3) distribute, and (4) teach. Andrew Lincoln argues that in Matthew the disciples are models for teachers.[21] "Matthew's gospel should be read as a story for would-be teachers. The implied author is in effect saying to the implied reader, 'So you want to be a teacher? Let me tell you a story.'"[22]

As Philip Davies notes, "The scribal duties embraced a range of activities, amounting to a good deal of ideological control."[23] Their tasks naturally concerned the past, present, and future: "archiving (possession and control of the present), historiography (possession and control of the past), didactic writing (maintenance of social values among the elite), predictive writing (possession and control of the future)."[24] This may be why Matthew portrays his task as a scribe with respect to the new and the old (13:52). If the scribes' task necessarily related to the future, what did Matthew learn about the future? One way to explore this is to juxtapose Matthew's learning with the frustration expressed by the Qohelet in Ecclesiastes. The Qohelet says that everything is meaningless because of injustice, death, and time. Even wisdom becomes meaningless because of death.

> But I also understand that the same fate awaits both of them. I said to myself, "Even I will meet the same fate as the fool, why then have I become so wise?" So I said to myself, "This too is meaningless." For the memory of neither the wise nor the fool endures forever. The days arrive only too soon when both will be forgotten. How will the wise person die? Like a fool! (Eccles. 2:14b–16 AT)

Matthew's teacher of wisdom also died like a fool. But death was not the last word. While death has always rendered wisdom lifeless, through Jesus's

---

19. Bird (*Gospel of the Lord*, 64–66) is right to note that the Jesus tradition belonged not to individuals but to communities, and thus acting as custodian of the Jesus tradition was a community effort. One should also look to the "social memory" school on this point: Tom Thatcher, Jens Schröter, Alan Kirk, Chris Keith, Anthony Le Donne, and Rafael Rodríguez.

20. Hannan (*Nature and Demands of the Sovereign Rule of God*) asserts that Matthew's Gospel becomes a manual of instruction on the nature and demands of God's sovereignty.

21. Minear (*Good News*) argues similarly that Matthew's Gospel is a training manual.

22. Lincoln, "Matthew," 124–25.

23. P. Davies, *Scribes and Schools*, 75.

24. P. Davies, *Scribes and Schools*, 75.

resurrection, wisdom was vindicated. Matthew learned from his sage that the future of wisdom is life because life and wisdom come only by enduring and bearing death, not bypassing it.

Though scribes molded and interpreted the content to suit their purposes, they were not always the originators of the content, and boundaries were in place to make sure they would faithfully communicate the message of the king or sage. They were essentially mediators between the people and the ruler, and so is Matthew. That is why in Matt. 23:34 Jesus says, "*I send you* prophets and wise men and scribes" (emphasis added).[25] In this passage Jesus looks back on the history of Israel, but in Matthew's Gospel the statement also points to the present and future, where Jesus will also send his "prophets and wise men and scribes."[26] First Enoch 12.4 says, "Enoch, scribe of righteousness, go and make known." Likewise, the commission given to Matthew is to teach righteousness on the basis of the revelation of the secrets of his sage (13:11). The message of Matthew can be partly understood by drawing a line under the following three Greek words:[27]

μάθετε ἀπ' ἐμοῦ
Learn from me. (11:29)

πᾶς γραμματεὺς μαθητευθεὶς . . . ἐκβάλλει ἐκ τοῦ θησαυροῦ
Every discipled scribe . . . brings out treasure. (13:52 AT)

πορευθέντες οὖν μαθητεύσατε πάντα τὰ ἔθνη
Go therefore and make disciples of all nations. (28:19)

Matthew stood in the gap between his teacher and the nations of whom Jesus had commanded Matthew to make disciples.[28] As the scribe Ben Sira said,

> How different the one who devotes himself
>   to the study of the law of the Most High!

25. Patte (*Gospel according to Matthew*, 199) even claims that Matthew's entire Gospel is aimed at training scribes for the kingdom, though Patte overstates his case if he means it in a technical sense. My perspective is more that Matthew provides a portrait of wisdom through his presentation of Jesus that trains others in how to become disciples.

26. Juce ("Wisdom in Matthew," 135) ties the three offices (prophets, wise men, and scribes) to the threefold division of the Hebrew Scriptures. I am not entirely convinced, though it is an intriguing suggestion.

27. I copied this helpful chart from Jeff Blair, "Cultivating a Culture of Wisdom," 99.

28. Justification for linking Matt. 13:52 with 28:18–20 comes not only conceptually but also linguistically. Matthew uses the verbal form μαθητεύω only in 13:52; 27:57; and 28:19.

> He seeks out the wisdom of all the ancients,
> > and is concerned with prophecies;
> he preserves the sayings of the famous
> > and penetrates the subtleties of parables.
> . . . .
> If the great Lord is willing,
> > he will be filled with the spirit of understanding;
> he will pour forth words of wisdom of his own.
>
> > > > > (Sir. 38:34b–39:2, 6)

It is hard to imagine that Matthew did not see himself fulfilling the command to make disciples by the writing of his ancient biography laced with the Hebrew Scriptures so that other followers of Jesus might also gain wisdom.

Bibliography

Alexander, Loveday. "What Is a Gospel?" Pages 13–33 in Barton, *The Cambridge Companion to the Gospels*.

Alkier, Stefan. "Intertextuality and the Semiotics of Biblical Texts." Pages 3–22 in Hays et al., *Reading the Bible Intertextually*.

———. "New Testament Studies on the Basis of Categorical Semiotics." Pages 223–48 in Hays et al., *Reading the Bible Intertextually*.

Allison, Dale. *Constructing Jesus: Memory, Imagination, and History*. Grand Rapids: Baker Academic, 2010.

———. "Matthew's First Two Words (Matt. 1:1)." Pages 157–62 in *Studies in Matthew*. Grand Rapids: Baker Academic, 2005.

———. *The New Moses: A Matthean Typology*. Eugene, OR: Wipf & Stock, 2013.

———. "The Son of God as Israel: A Note on Matthean Christology." *IBS* 9 (1987): 74–81.

———. "Structure, Biographical Impulse, and the *Imitatio Christi*." Pages 135–56 in *Studies in Matthew*. Grand Rapids: Baker Academic, 2005.

———. *Studies in Matthew: Interpretation Past and Present*. Grand Rapids: Baker Academic, 2005.

Ashby, Chad. "Magi, Wise Men, or Kings? It's Complicated." *Christianity Today*, December 16, 2016. http://www.christianitytoday.com/history/holidays/christmas/magi-wise-men-or-kings-its-complicated.html.

Aune, David. "Oral Tradition and the Aphorisms of Jesus." Pages 211–65 in *Jesus and the Oral Gospel Tradition*. Edited by Henry Wansbrough. JSNTSup 64. Sheffield: Sheffield Academic, 1991.

Bacon, B. W. "The Five Books of Matthew against the Jews." *ExpTim* 15 (1918): 56–66.

———. *Studies in Matthew*. New York: Holt, 1930.

Bakhtin, M. M. *The Dialogic Imagination: Four Essays*. Edited by Michael Holquist. Translated by Caryl Emerson. Austin: University of Texas Press, 1982.

Balthasar, Hans Urs von. *Seeing the Form*. Vol. 1 of *The Glory of the Lord: A Theological Aesthetics*. Translated by

Erasmo Leiva-Merikakis. San Francisco: Ignatius Press, 1983.

Banks, R. J. *Jesus and the Law in the Synoptic Tradition*. Cambridge: Cambridge University Press, 1975.

Barber, Michael. "The Historical Jesus and Cultic Restoration Eschatology: The New Temple, the New Priesthood, and the New Cult." PhD diss., Fuller Theological Seminary, 2010.

Barth, Gerhard. "Matthew's Understanding of the Law." Pages 58–164 in Bornkamm et al., *Tradition and Interpretation in Matthew*.

Barton, Stephen C. "The Gospel of Matthew." Pages 121–38 in Barton, *The Cambridge Companion to the Gospels*.

———. "Gospel Wisdom." Pages 93–110 in Barton, *Where Shall Wisdom Be Found?*

Barton, Stephen C., ed. *The Cambridge Companion to the Gospels*. Cambridge: Cambridge University Press, 2006.

———, ed. *Where Shall Wisdom Be Found? Wisdom in the Bible, the Church and the Contemporary World*. Edinburgh: T&T Clark, 1999.

Bauckham, Richard. *James: Wisdom of James, Disciple of Jesus the Sage*. London: Routledge, 1999.

Baxter, Wayne S. "Healing and the 'Son of David': Matthew's Warrant." *NovT* 48, no. 1 (2006): 36–50.

———. "Mosaic Imagery in the Gospel of Matthew." *TJ* 20.1 (1999): 69–83.

Beale, G. K. *A New Testament Biblical Theology: The Unfolding of the Old Testament in the New*. Grand Rapids: Baker Academic, 2011.

———. "The Use of Hosea 11:1 in Matthew 2:15: One More Time." *JETS* 55, no. 4 (2012): 697–715.

Beale, G. K., and D. A. Carson, eds. *Commentary on the New Testament Use of the Old Testament*. Grand Rapids: Baker Academic, 2007.

Beaton, Richard. *Isaiah's Christ in Matthew's Gospel*. Cambridge: Cambridge University Press, 2007.

Betz, Hans Dieter. "Logion of the Easy Yoke and of Rest (Matt. 11:28–30)." *JBL* 86, no. 1 (1967): 10–24.

Billings, J. Todd. *The Word of God for the People of God: An Entryway to the Theological Interpretation of Scripture*. Grand Rapids: Eerdmans, 2010.

Bird, Michael F. *The Gospel of the Lord: How the Early Church Wrote the Story of Jesus*. Grand Rapids: Eerdmans, 2014.

Blair, Jeff. "Cultivating a Culture of Wisdom at the Locust Grove Free Will Baptist Church." Thesis, Northern Baptist Theological Seminary, 2018.

Bland, Dave. *Proverbs and the Formation of Character*. Eugene, OR: Cascade Books, 2015.

Blomberg, Craig. *Matthew*. NAC 22. Nashville: Broadman, 1992.

———. "Matthew." Pages 1–109 in Beale and Carson, *Commentary on the New Testament Use of the Old Testament*.

Boersma, Hans, and Matthew Levering. "Spiritual Interpretation and Realigned Temporality." *Modern Theology* 28, no. 4 (2012): 587–96.

Bornkamm, Günther, Gerhard Barth, and Heinz Held. *Tradition and Interpretation in Matthew*. Translated by Percy Scott. Philadelphia: Westminster, 1963.

Brown, Daniel James. *The Boys in the Boat: Nine Americans and Their Epic Quest for Gold at the 1936 Berlin*

Olympics. New York: Penguin Books, 2014.

Brown, Jeannine K. *The Disciples in Narrative Perspective: The Portrayal and Function of the Matthean Disciples*. Atlanta: Society of Biblical Literature, 2002.

Brown, Raymond E. *The Birth of the Messiah: A Commentary on the Infancy Narratives in the Gospels of Matthew and Luke*. Updated ed. New Haven: Yale University Press, 1999.

Bruner, F. D. *The Christbook: Matthew 1–12*. Vol. 1 of *Matthew: A Commentary*. Grand Rapids: Eerdmans, 2007.

———. *The Churchbook: Matthew 13–28*. Vol. 2 of *Matthew: A Commentary*. Grand Rapids: Eerdmans, 2004.

Bultmann, Rudolf. *Theology of the New Testament*. Vol. 1. New York: Charles Scribner's Sons, 1951.

Burridge, Richard. *What Are the Gospels? A Comparison with Graeco-Roman Biography*. 2nd ed. Grand Rapids: Eerdmans, 2004.

Byrskog, Samuel. *Jesus the Only Teacher: Didactic Authority and Transmission in Ancient Israel, Ancient Judaism and the Matthean Community*. Stockholm: Almqvist & Wiksell International, 1994.

Calvin, John. *Commentary on a Harmony of the Evangelists Matthew, Mark, and Luke*. Translated by William Pringle. Vol. 1. Edinburgh: Calvin Translation Society, 1845.

Carlson, Stephen C. "The Davidic Key for Counting the Generations in Matthew 1:17." *CBQ* 76.4 (2014): 665–83.

Carr, David M. *Writing on the Tablet of the Heart: Origins of Scripture and Literature*. Oxford: Oxford University Press, 2008.

Carson, D. A. "Christological Ambiguities in the Gospel of Matthew." Pages 97–114 in *Christ the Lord: Studies in Christology Presented to Donald Guthrie*. Edited by Harold H. Rowdon. Leicester, UK: Inter-Varsity, 1982.

———. "Matthew" Pages 1–599 in vol. 8 of *The Expositor's Bible Commentary*. Edited by Frank E. Gaebelein. Grand Rapids: Zondervan, 1984.

———. "Matthew." Pages 25–670 in vol. 9 of *The Expositor's Bible Commentary*. Edited by Tremper Longman III and David E. Garland. Rev. ed. Grand Rapids: Zondervan, 2010.

———. "Systematic Theology and Biblical Theology." Pages 89–104 in *New Dictionary of Biblical Theology*. Edited by T. D. Alexander and Brian S. Rosner. Downers Grove, IL: Inter-Varsity, 2000.

Carter, Warren. "Kernels and Narrative Blocks: The Structure of Matthew's Gospel." *CBQ* 54, no. 3 (1992): 463–81.

———. *Matthew: Storyteller, Interpreter, Evangelist*. Peabody, MA: Hendrickson, 1996.

Chae, Young S. *Jesus as the Eschatological Davidic Shepherd: Studies in the Old Testament, Second Temple Judaism, and in the Gospel of Matthew*. Tübingen: Mohr Siebeck, 2006.

Charlesworth, James H. "From Messianology to Christology: Problems and Prospects." Pages 3–35 in *The Messiah: Developments in Earliest Judaism and Christianity*. Edited by James H. Charlesworth. Minneapolis: Augsburg Fortress, 2010.

Charlesworth, Scott. *Early Christian Gospels: Their Production and Transmission*. Papyrologica Florentina 47. Florence: Edizioni Gonnelli, 2016.

Chesterton, G. K. "The Riddle of the Ivy." Pages 244–51 in *Tremendous*

Trifles. New York: Dodd, Mead, and Co., 1909.

Clowney, Edmund P. *The Church*. Downers Grove, IL: InterVarsity, 1995.

Collins, John J. *The Scepter and the Star: Messianism in Light of the Dead Sea Scrolls*. 2nd ed. Grand Rapids: Eerdmans, 2010.

Crenshaw, James L. "The Acquisition of Knowledge in Israelite Wisdom Literature." *Word & World* 7, no. 3 (1987): 245–52.

Cribiore, Raffaella. *Gymnastics of the Mind: Greek Education in Hellenistic and Roman Egypt*. Princeton: Princeton University Press, 2005.

Crisp, Oliver D. *The Word Enfleshed: Exploring the Person and Work of Christ*. Grand Rapids: Baker Academic, 2016.

Crowe, Brandon D. "Fulfillment in Matthew as Eschatological Reversal." *WTJ* 75, no. 1 (2013): 111–27.

———. "The Song of Moses and Divine Begetting in Matt 1,20." *Bib* 90.1 (2009): 47–58.

Davies, Philip R. *Scribes and Schools: The Canonization of the Hebrew Scriptures*. Louisville: Westminster John Knox, 1998.

Davies, W. D. "The Jewish Sources of Matthew's Messianism." Pages 494–511 in *The Messiah: Developments in Earliest Judaism and Christianity*. Edited by James H. Charlesworth. Minneapolis: Augsburg Fortress, 2009.

———. *The Sermon on the Mount*. Cambridge: Cambridge University Press, 1966.

Davies, W. D., and Dale Allison. *Matthew*. 3 vols. ICC. London: T&T Clark, 1988–97.

Day, Adam Warner. "Eating before the Lord: A Theology of Food according to Deuteronomy." *JETS* 57, no. 1 (2014): 85–97.

Dempster, Stephen. *Dominion and Dynasty: A Theology of the Hebrew Bible*. NSBT 15. Downers Grove, IL: IVP Academic, 2003.

Derrett, J. Duncan M. "Matt 23:8–10: A Midrash on Isa 54:13 and Jer 31:33–34." *Bib* 62.3 (1981): 372–86.

Deutsch, Celia M. *Hidden Wisdom and the Easy Yoke: Wisdom, Torah and Discipleship in Matthew 11:25–30*. Sheffield, UK: Continuum, 1987.

———. *Lady Wisdom, Jesus, and the Sages: Metaphor and Social Context in Matthew's Gospel*. Valley Forge, PA: Trinity Press International, 1996.

———. "Wisdom in Matthew: Transformation of a Symbol." *NovT* 32.1 (1990): 13–47.

Dodd, C. H. *According to the Scriptures: The Sub-structure of New Testament Theology*. London: Fontana, 1952.

Donaldson, Terence. *Jesus on the Mountain: A Study in Matthean Theology*. Sheffield, UK: JSOT Press, 1985.

Dryden, Jeff de Wahl. *A Hermeneutic of Wisdom: Recovering the Formative Agency of Scripture*. Grand Rapids: Baker Academic, 2018.

Duling, Dennis C. *A Marginal Scribe: Studies in the Gospel of Matthew in a Social-Scientific Perspective*. Eugene, OR: Wipf & Stock, 2011.

———. "Solomon, Exorcism, and the Son of David." *HTR* 68.3–4 (1975): 235–52.

Dunn, James D. G. *Christology in the Making: A New Testament Inquiry into the Origins of the Doctrine of the Incarnation*. Philadelphia: Westminster, 1980.

———. "Jesus: Teacher of Wisdom or Wisdom Incarnate?" Pages 75–92 in Barton, *Where Shall Wisdom Be Found?*

Edwards, Richard A. *Matthew's Narrative Portrait of Disciples.* Valley Forge, PA: Trinity Press International, 1997.

———. "Uncertain Faith: Matthew's Portrait of the Disciples." Pages 47–61 in *Discipleship in the New Testament.* Edited by Fernando F. Segovia. Philadelphia: Fortress, 1985.

Eloff, Mervyn. "Exile, Restoration and Matthew's Genealogy of Jesus Ὁ Χριστός." *Neot* 38.1 (2004): 75–87.

Enslin, Morton Scott. "'The Five Books of Matthew': Bacon on the Gospel of Matthew." *HTR* 24, no. 2 (1931): 67–97.

Erickson, Richard J. "Joseph and the Birth of Isaac in Matthew 1." *BBR* 10, no. 1 (2000): 35–51.

Ferda, Tucker S. "Matthew's Titulus and Psalm 2's King on Mount Zion." *JBL* 133.3 (2014): 561–81.

———. "The Soldiers' Inscription and the Angel's Word: The Significance of 'Jesus' in Matthew's Titulus." *NovT* 55.3 (2013): 221–31.

Fishbane, Michael A. *Biblical Interpretation in Ancient Israel.* Oxford: Clarendon, 1989.

———. "Revelation and Tradition: Aspects of Inner-Biblical Exegesis." *JBL* 99, no. 3 (1980): 343–61.

Fisher, Fred L. "New and Greater Exodus: The Exodus Pattern in the New Testament." *SJT* 20, no. 1 (1977): 69–79.

Foster, Paul. "The Use of Zechariah in Matthew's Gospel." Pages 65–85 in *The Book of Zechariah and Its Influence.* Edited by C. M. Tuckett. Burlington, VT: Ashgate, 2003.

France, R. T. "The Formula-Quotations of Matthew 2 and the Problem of Communication." *NTS* 27 (1981): 233–51.

———. *The Gospel of Matthew.* NICNT. Grand Rapids: Eerdmans, 2007.

———. *Matthew: Evangelist and Teacher.* Eugene, OR: Wipf & Stock, 2004.

Frye, Northrop. *The Great Code: The Bible and Literature.* New York: Harcourt Brace Jovanovich, 1982.

Fuller, R. H. *The New Testament in Current Study.* New York: Charles Scribner's Sons, 1962.

Gallagher, Edmon L., and John D. Meade. *The Biblical Canon Lists from Early Christianity: Texts and Analysis.* Oxford: Oxford University Press, 2018.

Garland, David E. *Reading Matthew: A Literary and Theological Commentary.* Macon, GA: Smyth & Helwys, 2013.

Gathercole, Simon J. "The Earliest Manuscript Title of Matthew's Gospel (BnF Suppl. Gr. 1120 Ii 3 / P4 [Black Letter])." *NovT* 54, no. 3 (2012): 209–35.

———. *The Gospel of Judas: Rewriting Early Christianity.* Oxford: Oxford University Press, 2007.

———. *The Preexistent Son: Recovering the Christologies of Matthew, Mark, and Luke.* Grand Rapids: Eerdmans, 2006.

Gench, Frances Taylor. *Wisdom in the Christology of Matthew.* Lanham, MD: University Press of America, 1997.

Gerhardsson, Birger. *Memory and Manuscript with Tradition and Transmission in Early Christianity.* Translated by Eric J. Sharpe. Grand Rapids: Eerdmans, 1998.

Gibbs, James M. "Purpose and Pattern in Matthew's Use of the Title 'Son of David.'" *NTS* 10.4 (1964): 446–64.

Goodenough, E. R. "The Political Philosophy of Hellenistic Kingship." Yale Classical Studies 1 (1928): 55–102.

Goulder, M. D. Midrash and Lection in Matthew. Repr., Eugene, OR: Wipf & Stock, 2004.

Gowler, David. Host, Guest, Enemy, and Friend: Portraits of the Pharisees in Luke and Acts. Eugene, OR: Wipf & Stock, 2008.

Gundry, Robert H. Matthew: A Commentary on His Literary and Theological Art. Grand Rapids: Eerdmans, 1982.

———. "On True and False Disciples in Matthew 8:18–22." NTS 40, no. 3 (1994): 433–41.

———. The Use of the Old Testament in St. Matthew's Gospel: With Special Reference to the Messianic Hope. NovTSup 18. Leiden: Brill, 1967.

Gurtner, Daniel. The Torn Veil: Matthew's Exposition of the Death of Jesus. SNTSMS 139. Cambridge: Cambridge University Press, 2007.

Hagner, Donald A. "Apocalyptic Motifs in the Gospel of Matthew: Continuity and Discontinuity." HBT 7, no. 2 (1985): 53–82.

———. "Balancing the Old and the New: The Law of Moses in Matthew and Paul." Int 51, no. 1 (1997): 20–30.

———. How New Is the New Testament? First Century Judaism and the Emergence of Christianity. Grand Rapids: Baker Academic, 2018.

———. Matthew 1–13. WBC 33a. Nashville: Nelson, 2003.

Ham, Clay Alan. The Coming King and the Rejected Shepherd: Matthew's Reading of Zechariah's Messianic Hope. Sheffield: Sheffield Phoenix, 2006.

Hamilton, Catherine Sider. The Death of Jesus in Matthew: Innocent Blood and the End of Exile. New York: Cambridge University Press, 2017.

Hamilton, James. "'The Virgin Will Conceive': Typological Fulfillment in Matthew 1:18–23." Pages 228–47 in Built upon the Rock: Studies in the Gospel of Matthew. Edited by Daniel M. Gurtner and John Nolland. Grand Rapids: Eerdmans, 2008.

Hannan, Margaret. The Nature and Demands of the Sovereign Rule of God in the Gospel of Matthew. LNTS 308. London: T&T Clark, 2006.

Harrington, Daniel J. The Gospel of Matthew. Sacra Pagina. Collegeville, MN: Michael Glazier, 2007.

Hay, David M. "Moses through New Testament Spectacles." Int 44, no. 3 (1990): 240–52.

Hays, Richard B. "The Canonical Matrix of the Gospels." Pages 53–75 in Barton, The Cambridge Companion to the Gospels.

———. Echoes of Scripture in the Gospels. Waco: Baylor University Press, 2016.

———. Echoes of Scripture in the Letters of Paul. New Haven: Yale University Press, 1989.

———. "The Gospel of Matthew: Reconfigured Torah." HTS Theological Studies 61.1–2 (2005): 165–90.

———. Reading Backwards: Figural Christology and the Fourfold Gospel Witness. Waco: Baylor University Press, 2014.

Hays, Richard B., Stefan Alkier, and Leroy A. Huizenga, eds. Reading the Bible Intertextually. Waco: Baylor University Press, 2009.

Hedrick, Terry J. "Jesus as Shepherd in the Gospel of Matthew." PhD diss., Durham University, 2007.

Heil, John Paul. "Ezekiel 34 and the Narrative Strategy of the Shepherd

and Sheep Metaphor in Matthew."
CBQ 55.4 (1993): 698–708.

Held, H. J. "Matthew as Interpreter of
the Miracle Stories." Pages 165–299
in Bornkamm et al., *Tradition and
Interpretation in Matthew*.

Hood, Jason B. *Imitating God in Christ:
Recapturing a Biblical Pattern.*
Downers Grove, IL: IVP Academic,
2013.

———. *The Messiah, His Brothers, and
the Nations: Matthew 1:1–17.* LNTS
441. New York: T&T Clark, 2012.

Hooker, Morna. *Beginnings: Keys That
Open the Gospels.* Eugene, OR: Wipf
& Stock, 1997.

Horsley, Richard A. *Scribes, Visionaries,
and the Politics of Second Temple
Judea.* Louisville: Westminster John
Knox, 2007.

Huizenga, Leroy. "The Incarnation of the
Servant: The 'Suffering Servant' and
Matthean Christology." *HBT* 27.1
(2005): 25–58.

———. "Matt 1:1: 'Son of Abraham' as
a Christological Category." *HBT* 30.2
(2008): 103–13.

———. *The New Isaac: Tradition and
Intertextuality in the Gospel of Matthew.* Leiden: Brill, 2012.

———. "Obedience unto Death: The
Matthean Gethsemane and Arrest
Sequence and the Aqedah." *CBQ* 71.3
(2009): 507–26.

Hunziker-Rodewald, Regine. *Hirt
und Herde: Ein Beitrag zum alttes-
tamentlichen Gottesverstandnis.*
BWANT 155. Stuttgart: Kohlham-
mer, 2001.

Jenson, Robert. "Scripture's Authority in
the Church." Pages 27–37 in *The Art
of Reading Scripture.* Edited by Richard B. Hays and Ellen F. Davis. Grand
Rapids: Eerdmans, 2003.

Jipp, Joshua W. *Christ Is King: Paul's
Royal Ideology.* Minneapolis: Fortress, 2015.

Johnson, Marshall D. "Reflections on
a Wisdom Approach to Matthew's
Christology." *CBQ* 36.1 (1974):
44–64.

Johnson, Nathan C. "The Passion according to David: Matthew's Arrest
Narrative, the Absalom Revolt, and
Militant Messianism." *CBQ* 80.2
(2018): 247–72.

———. "Rendering David a Servant in
Psalm of Solomon 17.21," *JSP* 26.3
(2017): 235–50.

Juce, Esther. "Wisdom in Matthew:
Tripartite Fulfillment." *St Vladimir's
Theological Quarterly* 55.2 (2011):
125–39.

Kaiser, Walter. "The Lord's Anointed:
Interpretation of Old Testament
Messianic Texts." *JETS* 42, no. 1
(1999): 99–102.

Keener, Craig S. *The Gospel of Matthew: A Socio-Rhetorical Commentary.* Grand Rapids: Eerdmans, 2009.

———. *The Historical Jesus of the Gospels.* Grand Rapids: Eerdmans, 2009.

Keith, Chris. *Jesus against the Scribal
Elite: The Origins of the Conflict.*
Grand Rapids: Baker Academic, 2014.

———. *Jesus' Literacy: Scribal Culture
and the Teacher from Galilee.* LNTS
413. New York: T&T Clark, 2011.

Kennedy, George A., trans. *Progymnasmata: Greek Textbooks of Prose
Composition and Rhetoric.* Writings
from the Greco-Roman World 10.
Leiden: Brill, 2003.

Kingsbury, Jack Dean. *Matthew as
Story.* Philadelphia: Fortress, 1986.

———. *Matthew: Structure, Christology, Kingdom.* Minneapolis: Augsburg Books, 1991.

———. "The Title 'Son of David' in Matthew's Gospel." *JBL* 95.4 (1976): 591–602.

———. "The Title 'Son of God' in Matthew's Gospel." *BTB* 5.1 (1975): 3–31.

———. "The Title 'Son of Man' in Matthew's Gospel." *CBQ* 37.2 (1975): 193–202.

Kirk, J. R. Daniel. "Conceptualising Fulfilment in Matthew." *TynBul* 59, no. 1 (2008): 77–98.

———. *A Man Attested by God: The Human Jesus of the Synoptic Gospels.* Grand Rapids: Eerdmans, 2016.

Klink, Edward W., III, and Darian R. Lockett. *Understanding Biblical Theology: A Comparison of Theory and Practice.* Grand Rapids: Zondervan, 2012.

Knowles, Michael P. "Scripture, History, Messiah: Scriptural Fulfillment and the Fullness of Time in Matthew's Gospel." Pages 59–82 in *Hearing the Old Testament in the New Testament.* Edited by Stanley E. Porter. Grand Rapids: Eerdmans, 2006.

———. "Serpents, Scribes, and Pharisees." *JBL* 133.1 (2014): 165–78.

Konradt, Matthias. *Israel, Church, and the Gentiles in the Gospel of Matthew.* Edited by Wayne Coppins and Simon Gathercole. Translated by Kathleen Ess. Waco: Baylor University Press, 2014.

Kristeva, Julia. *Desire in Language: A Semiotic Approach to Literature and Art.* Edited by Leon Roudiez. Translated by Thomas Gora, Alice Jardine, and Leon Roudiez. New York: Columbia University Press, 1980.

Kristeva, Julia, and Leon S. Roudiez. *Revolution in Poetic Language.* Translated by Margaret Waller. New York: Columbia University Press, 1984.

Kynes, Will. *An Obituary for "Wisdom Literature."* Oxford: Oxford University Press, 2018.

Leeman, Jonathan. *Political Church: The Local Assembly as Embassy of Christ's Rule.* Downers Grove, IL: IVP Academic, 2016.

Leithart, Peter J. *Jesus as Israel.* Vol. 1 of *The Gospel of Matthew through New Eyes.* Monroe, LA: Athanasius Press, 2018.

———. "The Least of These." *Theopolis Institute.* September 17, 2014. https://theopolisinstitute.com/article/the-least-of-these/.

Levering, Matthew. *Participatory Biblical Exegesis: A Theology of Biblical Interpretation.* Notre Dame, IN: University of Notre Dame Press, 2008.

Levin, Yigal. "Jesus, 'Son of God' and 'Son of David': The 'Adoption' of Jesus into the Davidic Line." *JSNT* 28.4 (2006): 415–42.

Levine, Amy-Jill. *The Social and Ethnic Dimensions of Matthean Salvation History.* Studies in the Bible and Early Christianity 14. Lewiston, NY: Edwin Mellen, 1988.

Lewis, C. S. *The Magician's Nephew.* The Complete Chronicles of Narnia 1. New York: HarperCollins, 1998.

Lincoln, Andrew T. "Matthew—a Story for Teachers?" Pages 103–26 in *The Bible in Three Dimensions: Essays in Celebration of Forty Years of Biblical Studies in the University of Sheffield.* Edited by David Clines, Stephen Fowl, and Stanley Porter. JSOTSup 87. Sheffield: Sheffield Academic, 1990.

Loader, William. *Jesus' Attitude towards the Law: A Study of the Gospels.* Grand Rapids: Eerdmans, 2002.

———. "Son of David, Blindness, Possession, and Duality in Matthew." *CBQ* 44.4 (1982): 570–85.

Lohr, Charles H. "Oral Techniques in the Gospel of Matthew." *CBQ* 23.4 (1961): 403–35.

Longman, Tremper, III. *The Fear of the Lord Is Wisdom: A Theological Introduction to Wisdom in Israel*. Grand Rapids: Baker Academic, 2017.

Luz, Ulrich. "The Disciples in the Gospel according to Matthew." Pages 115–48 in *The Interpretation of Matthew*. Edited by Graham N. Stanton. 2nd ed. Edinburgh: T&T Clark, 1995.

———. *Matthew 8–20: A Commentary on the Gospel of Matthew*. Translated by James E. Crouch. Hermeneia. Minneapolis: Fortress, 2001.

———. "The Son of Man in Matthew: Heavenly Judge or Human Christ." *JSNT* 15.48 (1992): 3–21.

Macaskill, Grant. *Revealed Wisdom and Inaugurated Eschatology in Ancient Judaism and Early Christianity*. Leiden: Brill, 2007.

Matera, Frank J. "The Plot of Matthew's Gospel." *CBQ* 49, no. 2 (1987): 233–53.

Mauser, Ulrich W. "'Heaven' in the World View of the New Testament." *HBT* 9, no. 2 (1987): 31–51.

McKane, William. *Prophets and Wise Men*. SBT 44. Naperville, IL: Allenson, 1965.

Meier, John P. *Law and History in Matthew's Gospel*. Rome: Biblical Institute Press, 1976.

Menken, M. J. J. "Messianic Interpretations of Greek Old Testament Passages in Matthew's Fulfillment Quotations." Pages 457–86 in *Septuagint and Messianism*. Edited by Michael A. Knibb. BETL 195. Leuven: Leuven University Press; Peeters, 2006.

Michel, Otto. "The Conclusion of Matthew's Gospel." Pages 30–41 in *The Interpretation of Matthew*. Edited

by Graham N. Stanton. Philadelphia: Fortress, 1983.

Millard, Alan. *Reading and Writing in the Time of Jesus*. New York: New York University Press, 2000.

Minear, Paul S. *The Good News according to Matthew: A Training Manual for Prophets*. St. Louis: Chalice, 2000.

Moffitt, David M. "Righteous Bloodshed, Matthew's Passion Narrative, and the Temple's Destruction: Lamentations as a Matthean Intertext." *JBL* 125.2 (2006): 299–320.

Moo, Douglas J. "Jesus and the Authority of the Mosaic Law." *JSNT* 6.20 (1984): 3–49.

Moo, Douglas J., and Andrew David Naselli. "The Problem of the New Testament's Use of the Old Testament." Pages 702–46 in *The Enduring Authority of the Christian Scriptures*. Edited by D. A. Carson. Grand Rapids: Eerdmans, 2016.

Morris, Leon. *The Gospel according to Matthew*. PNTC. Grand Rapids: Eerdmans, 1992.

Moss, Charlene McAfee. *The Zechariah Tradition and the Gospel of Matthew*. Berlin: de Gruyter, 2008.

Moule, C. F. D. "Fulfilment-Words in the New Testament: Use and Abuse." *NTS* 14, no. 3 (1968): 293–320.

Murphy, Roland E. *Wisdom Literature*. FOTL 13. Grand Rapids: Eerdmans, 1981.

Nickelsburg, George. *Resurrection, Immortality, and Eternal Life in Intertestamental Judaism*. Cambridge, MA: Harvard University Press, 1973.

Nolan, Brian M. *The Royal Son of God: The Christology of Matthew 1–2 in the Setting of the Gospel*. OBO 23. Göttingen: Vandenhoeck & Ruprecht, 1979.

Nolland, John. *The Gospel of Matthew*. NIGTC. Grand Rapids: Eerdmans, 2005.

Novakovic, Lidija. "Jesus as the Davidic Messiah in Matthew." *HBT* 19.2 (1997): 148–91.

———. *Messiah, the Healer of the Sick: A Study of Jesus as the Son of David in the Gospel of Matthew*. Tübingen: Mohr Siebeck, 2003.

Orton, David. *The Understanding Scribe: Matthew and the Apocalyptic Ideal*. London: Bloomsbury T&T Clark, 2004.

Overman, J. Andrew. *Matthew's Gospel and Formative Judaism: The Social World of the Matthean Community*. Minneapolis: Fortress, 1990.

Paffenroth, Kim. "Jesus as Anointed and Healing Son of David in the Gospel of Matthew." *Bib* 80.4 (1999): 547–54.

Pamment, Margaret. "The Son of Man in the First Gospel." *NTS* 29.1 (1983): 116–29.

Patte, Daniel. *The Gospel according to Matthew: A Structural Commentary on Matthew's Faith*. Philadelphia: Fortress, 1987.

Peels, H. G. L. "The Blood 'from Abel to Zechariah' (Matthew 23:35; Luke 11:50f.) and the Canon of the Old Testament." *ZAW* 113, no. 4 (2001): 583–601.

Pemberton, Glenn. *A Life That Is Good: The Message of Proverbs in a World Wanting Wisdom*. Grand Rapids: Eerdmans, 2018.

Penner, Peter. "The New Testament Scribe in the Perspective of the Gospel of Matthew." *Journal of European Baptist Studies* 2, no. 1 (2001): 5–19.

Pennington, Jonathan T. "Heaven, Earth, and a New Genesis: Theological Cosmology in Matthew." Pages 28–44 in *Cosmology and New Testament Theology*. Edited by Jonathan T. Pennington and Sean M. McDonough. LNTS 355. London: T&T Clark, 2008.

———. *Heaven and Earth in the Gospel of Matthew*. Grand Rapids: Baker Academic, 2007.

———. *Reading the Gospels Wisely: A Narrative and Theological Introduction*. Grand Rapids: Baker Academic, 2012.

———. Review of *Hidden but Now Revealed: A Biblical Theology of Divine Mystery*, by G. K. Beale and Benjamin Gladd. Paper presented at the Sixty-Seventh Annual Meeting of the Evangelical Theological Society, Atlanta, November 2015.

———. *The Sermon on the Mount and Human Flourishing: A Theological Commentary*. Grand Rapids: Baker Academic, 2017.

Perkins, Larry. "'Greater than Solomon' (Matt 12:42)." *TJ* 19.2 (1998): 207–17.

Phillips, Peter M. "Casting Out the Treasure: A New Reading of Matthew 13.52." *JSNT* 31.1 (2008): 3–24.

Philpot, Joshua. "The Shining Face of Moses: The Interpretation of Exodus 34:39–35 and Its Use in the Old and New Testaments." PhD diss., Southern Baptist Theological Seminary, 2013.

Piotrowski, Nicholas G. *Matthew's New David at the End of Exile: A Socio-Rhetorical Study of Scriptural Quotations*. Leiden: Brill, 2016.

Pitre, Brant. *Jesus and the Last Supper*. Grand Rapids: Eerdmans, 2015.

Powell, Mark Allan. "The Magi as Wise Men: Re-examining a Basic Supposition." *NTS* 46.1 (2000): 1–20.

———. "Toward a Narrative-Critical Understanding of Matthew." *Int* 46, no. 4 (1992): 341–46.

Quarles, Charles L. *A Theology of Matthew: Jesus Revealed as Deliverer, King, and Incarnate Creator*. Phillipsburg, NJ: P&R, 2013.

Richardson, Alan. *An Introduction to the Theology of the New Testament*. New York: Harper & Bros., 1958.

Ricoeur, Paul, and Ted Klein. *Interpretation Theory: Discourse and the Surplus of Meaning*. Fort Worth: Texas Christian University Press, 1976.

Ridderbos, Herman. *The Coming Kingdom*. Phillipsburg, NJ: P&R, 1962.

Riesner, Rainer. "Jesus as Preacher and Teacher." Pages 185–210 in *Jesus and the Oral Tradition*. Edited by Henry Wansbrough. JSNTSup 64. Sheffield: Sheffield Academic, 1991.

Roberts, Alastair J., and Andrew Wilson. *Echoes of Exodus: Tracing Themes of Redemption through Scripture*. Wheaton: Crossway, 2018.

Robertson, A. T. *The General Epistles and the Revelation of John*. Vol. 6 of *Word Pictures in the New Testament*. Nashville: Broadman, 1933.

Rollston, Christopher A. *Writing and Literacy in the World of Ancient Israel: Epigraphic Evidence from the Iron Age*. Atlanta: Society of Biblical Literature, 2010.

Rosenberg, Roy A. "Jesus, Isaac, and the 'Suffering Servant.'" *JBL* 84.4 (1965): 381–88.

Sailhamer, John H. "The Messiah and the Hebrew Bible." *JETS* 44, no. 1 (2001): 5–23.

———. *The Pentateuch as Narrative: A Biblical-Theological Commentary*. Grand Rapids: Zondervan, 1995.

Sanders, E. P. *Judaism: Practice and Belief, 63 BCE–66 CE*. Minneapolis: Fortress, 2016.

Schneider, Gerhard. "Studien zum Matthäusevangelium: Festschrift für Wilhelm Pesch." Pages 285–97 in *"Im Himmel–auf Erden": Eine Perspektive Matthäischer Theologie*. Edited by Ludger Schenke. Stuttgart: Katholisches Bibelwerk, 1988.

Schreiner, Patrick. *The Body of Jesus: A Spatial Analysis of the Kingdom in Matthew*. LNTS 555. London: Bloomsbury T&T Clark, 2016.

Senior, Donald. "The Lure of the Formula Quotations: Re-assessing Matthew's Use of the Old Testament with the Passion Narrative as a Test-Case." Pages 89–115 in *The Scriptures in the Gospels*. Edited by Christopher Mark Tuckett. BETL 131. Leuven: Leuven University Press, 1997.

———. "Matthew's Special Material in the Passion Story: The Evangelist's Redactional Technique and Theological Perspective." *ETL* 63.4 (1987): 272–94.

———. Review of *Israel, Kirche und die Völker im Matthäusevangelium*, by Matthias Konradt. *RBL*, April 23, 2013.

Sequeira, Aubrey. "The Hermeneutics of Eschatological Fulfillment in Christ: Biblical-Theological Exegesis in the Epistle to the Hebrews." PhD diss., Southern Baptist Theological Seminary, 2016.

Sharbaugh, Patricia. "The Light Burden of Discipleship: Embodying the New Moses and Personified Wisdom in the Gospel of Matthew." *JMT* 2.1 (2013): 46–63.

Sheridan, Mark. "Disciples and Discipleship in Matthew and Luke." *BTB* (1973): 235–55.

Singsa, Thathathanai. "Matthew's Wisdom Christology in Its Jewish and Early Christian Contexts." PhD diss., Australian Catholic University, 2011.

Smith, Christopher R. "Literary Evidences of a Fivefold Structure in the Gospel of Matthew." *NTS* 43, no. 4 (1997): 540–51.

Sneed, Mark R. "Is the 'Wisdom Tradition' a Tradition?" *CBQ* 73, no. 1 (2011): 50–71.

Spellman, Chad. "The Scribe Who Has Become a Disciple: Identifying and Becoming the Ideal Reader of the Biblical Canon." *Them* 41.1 (2016): 37–51.

Stanton, Graham N. *A Gospel for a New People: Studies in Matthew*. Louisville: Westminster/John Knox, 1993.

———. "Matthew as a Creative Interpreter of the Sayings of Jesus." Pages 273–87 in *Evangelium und die Evangelien: Vorträge vom Tübinger Symposium 1982*. Tübingen: Mohr Siebeck, 1983.

———. "Matthew's Use of the Old Testament." Pages 346–63 in *A Gospel for a New People: Studies in Matthew*. Louisville: Westminster/John Knox, 1993.

Stendahl, Krister. *The School of St. Matthew and Its Use of the Old Testament*. Philadelphia: Fortress, 1968.

Stern, David. *Midrash and Theory: Ancient Jewish Exegesis and Contemporary Literary Studies*. Chicago: Northwestern University Press, 1996.

Strecker, Georg. *Der Weg der Gerechtigkeit: Untersuchungen zur Theologie des Matthäus*. Gottingen: Vandenhoeck & Ruprecht, 1971.

Suggs, M. Jack. *Wisdom, Christology, and Law in Matthew's Gospel*. Cambridge, MA: Harvard University Press, 1970.

Teeple, Howard M. *The Mosaic Eschatological Prophet*. Atlanta: Society of Biblical Literature, 1957.

Theissen, Gerd, and Annette Merz. *The Historical Jesus: A Comprehensive Guide*. Minneapolis: Fortress, 1998.

Thesleff, Holger. *The Pythagorean Texts of the Hellenistic Period*. Acta Academiae Aboensis: Series A, Humaniora 30.1. Åbo: Åbo Akademi, 1965.

Tov, Emmanuel. *Scribal Practices and Approaches Reflected in the Texts Found in the Judean Desert*. STDJ 54. Atlanta: Society of Biblical Literature, 2009.

Treat, Jeremy R. *The Crucified King: Atonement and Kingdom in Biblical and Systematic Theology*. Grand Rapids: Zondervan, 2014.

Turner, David L. *Matthew*. BECNT. Grand Rapids: Baker Academic, 2008.

van Aarde, Andries G. "Jesus' Mission to All of Israel Emplotted in Matthew's Story." *Neot* 41.2 (2007): 416–36.

van der Toorn, Karel. *Scribal Culture and the Making of the Hebrew Bible*. Cambridge, MA: Harvard University Press, 2009.

Van Egmond, Richard. "The Messianic 'Son of David' in Matthew." *JGRChJ* 3 (2006): 41–71.

Van Leeuwen, Raymond. "Wisdom Literature." Pages 847–50 in *Dictionary for Theological Interpretation of the Bible*. Edited by Kevin J. Vanhoozer. Grand Rapids: Baker Academic, 2005.

Verseput, Donald. "The Davidic Messiah and Matthew's Jewish Christianity." Pages 102–16 in *1995 Seminar Papers: One Hundred Thirty-First Annual Meeting, November 18–21, 1995, Philadelphia Marriott and Pennsylvania Convention Center, Philadelphia, Pennsylvania*. Edited by Eugene H. Lovering Jr. SBLSP 34. Atlanta: Scholars Press, 1995.

———. "The Faith of the Reader and the Narrative of Matthew 13:53–16:20." *JSNT* 46 (1992): 3–24.

Vos, Geerhardus. "The Idea of Biblical Theology as a Science and as a

Theological Discipline." Pages 3–24 in *Redemptive History and Biblical Interpretation: The Shorter Writings of Geerhardus Vos*. Phillipsburg, NJ: P&R, 2001.

Wainwright, Elaine Mary. *Shall We Look for Another? A Feminist Reading of the Matthean Jesus*. Maryknoll, NY: Orbis Books, 1998.

Watts, Rikki E. "Messianic Servant or the End of Israel's Exilic Curses? Isaiah 53.4 in Matthew 8.17." *JSNT* 38.1 (2015): 81–95.

Wenham, David. "The Structure of Matthew 13." *NTS* 25.4 (1979): 516–22.

Westerholm, Stephen. *Jesus and Scribal Authority*. ConBNT 10. Lund: Gleerup, 1978.

Wilkins, Michael. *Discipleship in the Ancient World and Matthew's Gospel*. 2nd ed. Grand Rapids: Baker, 1995.

Willitts, Joel. *Matthew's Messianic Shepherd-King: In Search of "The Lost Sheep of the House of Israel."* New York: de Gruyter, 2007.

Wilson, Walter T. "Works of Wisdom (Matt 9,9–17; 11,16–19)." *ZNW* 106.1 (2015): 1–20.

Winsbury, Rex. *The Roman Book: Books, Publishing and Performance in Classical Rome*. London: Duckworth, 2009.

Winter, Bruce W. "The Messiah as the Tutor: The Meaning of καθηγητής in Matthew 23:10." *TynBul* 42.1 (1991): 152–57.

Witherington, Ben, III. *The Christology of Jesus*. Minneapolis: Fortress, 1990.

———. *The Jesus Quest: The Third Search for the Jew of Nazareth*. 2nd ed. Downers Grove, IL: IVP Academic, 1997.

———. *Jesus the Sage: The Pilgrimage of Wisdom*. Minneapolis: Fortress, 1994.

Wright, N. T. *Jesus and the Victory of God*. Minneapolis: Fortress, 1996.

———. *The New Testament and the People of God*. Minneapolis: Fortress, 1992.

———. *The Resurrection of the Son of God*. Minneapolis: Fortress, 2003.

Yieh, John Yueh-Han. *One Teacher: Jesus' Teaching Role in Matthew's Gospel Report*. 2004. Repr., Berlin: de Gruyter, 2012.

Zacharias, H. Daniel. *Matthew's Presentation of the Son of David*. London: T&T Clark, 2016.

Index of Authors

Alexander, L. 52n47
Alkier, S. 57n62
Allison, D. 2n5, 11n16, 44n21, 56, 56n56, 57n60, 66n2, 107n14, 114, 114n27, 115, 115n28, 121n44, 131n1, 141, 141n26, 151, 151n39, 152n40, 153, 153n45, 165, 165n58, 165n59, 166, 166n61, 184n28, 199n64, 210n6, 211, 212, 212n10, 212n14, 219n38, 221n42, 224n50, 225n51
Aquinas, T. 41n13, 96
Ashby, C. 78n32, 78n33
Aune, D. 19n58

Bacon, B.W. 11, 11n14, 211, 212, 212n9
Bakhtin, M. 54n51
Balthasar, Hans Urs von 9, 9n7
Banks, R. 141n21
Barber, M. 162n55
Barth, G. 12, 12n20
Barton, S. 14, 14n32, 29n96, 249n16
Bauckham, J. 2n2
Baxter, W. 121, 122n46, 131n1
Beale, G. K. 37n1, 217n29
Beaton, R. 85n54
Betz, H. 146n33, 248n14
Billings, T. 59n67
Bird, M. 24n77, 251n19
Blair, J. 252n27
Bland, D. 245n6
Blomberg, C. 11n15, 29n93, 120n40
Boersma, H. 51n43
Bornkamm, G. 12n17
Brown, D. 58, 58n66, 59
Brown, J. 12n17, 17n44, 247, 247n10
Brown, R. 131n1
Bruner, F. 40n7, 60, 60n69

Bultmann, R. 69n10
Burridge, R. 51, 51n44
Byrskog, S. 11n15, 13n22, 16, 16n40, 17n43, 27n88, 248n11, 248n12

Calvin, J. 76n27
Carlson, S. 69n11
Carson, D. A. 8n4, 10n8, 11n15, 37n1, 39n5, 119, 119n38, 152, 152n41, 184n31
Carr, D. 24n77
Carter, W. 17n44, 210n6
Chae, Y. 66n5, 121, 122n46, 219n39
Charlesworth, J. 47n33, 66, 66n3
Charlesworth, S. 24n79
Chesterton, G. K. 207, 207n1
Clowney, E. 8n5
Conzelmann, B. 12n21
Crenshaw, J. 23n73
Cribiore, R. 22n71
Crisp, O. 44n21
Crowe, B. 129n54, 134n10

Davies, P. 251, 251n23, 251n24
Davies, W. 48, 48n35, 48n36, 66, 66n6, 107n14, 114, 114n27, 115, 115n28, 121n44, 141, 141n25, 152n40, 184n28, 224n50, 225n51
Day, A. 159n51
Dempster, S. 215n23
Derrett, J. 15n37
Deutsch, C. 13n25, 15n35, 18n48, 18n50, 19, 19n55, 138n16, 145, 145n31, 146n35, 248n14
Dodd, C. 61, 61n75, 61n76, 210n5
Donaldson, T. 184n29, 184n30, 188n43, 200n68
Dryden, J. 14n30, 46n30, 51n45, 53, 54n50
Duling, D. 21, 21n63, 66n5, 121n44
Dunn, J. 2n3, 13n27, 14n31, 15n34, 18, 18n50

Edwards, R. 12n17
Egmond, V. 86, 86n57, 86n58
Eloff, M. 213n17
Enslin, M. 212n9
Erickson, R. 181, 182n23, 215, 215n25, 216

Ferda, T. 96n76, 97, 97n77
Fishbane, M. 54n51
Fisher, F. 158n50
Foster, P. 236n77
France, R. T. 21n62, 31, 31n103, 31n104, 39n5,
    40n7, 56, 56n58, 57n59, 62, 62n79, 74,
    74n18, 75, 75n21, 75n22, 82, 82n43, 82n44,
    82n45, 140, 140n20, 179n17, 184n28, 187n41,
    197n62, 211, 225n51
Frye, N. 50, 50n42
Fuller, R. 10n12

Gallagher, E. 177n15
Garland, D. 221n41
Gathercole, S. 7n1, 18n50
Gench, F. T. 18n50
Gerhardsson, B. 24n77, 26n86
Gibbs, J. 66n5
Goodenough, E. 106n10
Goulder, M. D. 212n14, 215n24
Gowler, D. 132, 132n5
Gundry, R. 34n116, 91n69, 200n66, 212n11,
    212n14
Gurtner, D. 237n80

Hagner, D. 29n95, 31, 31n103, 45, 45n23,
    74n19
Ham, C. 236, 236n77
Hamilton, J. 39n5
Hannan, M. 251n20
Harrington, D. 11n15
Hay, D. 132n4
Hays, R. 30, 30n101, 31n102, 37n1, 40n8, 40n9,
    40n11, 43n19, 54n51, 56n54, 66n5, 90n67,
    102n2, 117n34, 123n49, 131n1, 146n34,
    147n36, 151n38, 179, 179n16, 213n18, 216,
    217, 218n32, 218n33, 232n65, 234, 234n71,
    235n75
Hedrick, T. 111n20
Heil, J. 114n26, 115n30, 118n35
Held, H. J. 12n17, 85, 85n56
Hood, J. 107n14, 176n13
Hooker, M. 176, 176n14
Horsely, R. 22, 22n70, 22n72, 35n119, 36n120
Huizenga, L. 41n14, 85n51, 169n1, 180, 180n20,
    181, 188n44
Hunziker-Rodewald, R. 110, 110n18

Jenson, R. 49, 50n40
Jipp, J. 104n6, 105, 105n9, 106n10, 108n15
Johnson, M. 20n61
Johnson, N. 83n49, 85n55, 86, 86n59, 87n60,
    88n63, 88n64
Juce, E. 35, 35n118, 38n2, 252n26

Kaiser, W. 58, 58n63
Keener, C. 3n7, 14n28, 33, 33n111, 80, 80n41
Keith, C. 7n1, 15n36, 33, 33n110, 33n113
Kingsbury, J. 12n17, 66n2, 66n5, 83, 83n48,
    94n73, 212n10, 251n19
Kirk, A. 251n19
Kirk, D. 39n5, 133n7, 181, 181n22, 200n66
Klink, E. 8n4
Knowles, M. 62n77, 192n50
Konradt, M. 66n5, 170n5, 171n7, 179, 179n18,
    183n26, 183n27, 187n41, 189, 189n47, 197n61
Kristeva, J. 54n51
Kynes, W. 14n30

Le Donne, A. 251n19
Leeman, J. 27n88
Leithart, P. 56n57, 136n14, 182n25, 208n2,
    211, 212, 212n13, 212n14, 213n16, 215n24,
    219n40, 222n44, 222n46, 226n52, 227n55,
    228n57, 228n58, 228n59, 230n61, 231,
    231n64, 235n73
Lenin, Y. 189n45
Levering, M. 49n39, 51n43
Levine, A.-J. 193n53
Lewis, C. S. 246, 246n8
Lincoln, A. 251, 251n22
Loader, W. 124n50, 141n27
Lockett, D. 8n4
Lohr, C. 210n6
Longman, T. 32n109, 38n3, 77n28, 142n28,
    214n19, 244n4, 244n5
Luther, M. 78
Luz, U. 10n8, 12n17, 94n73, 113n25, 248,
    248n15, 250, 250n18

Macaskill, G. 18n50, 19n54, 44n22
Matera, F. 210n6
McKane, W. 21, 21n65
Meade, J. 177n15
Meier, J. 141, 141n23, 144
Menken, M. J. J. 42, 42n16, 42n17, 43n18
Merz, A. 3n7
Michel, O. 163, 163n57
Millard, A. 24n77
Minear, P. 251n19
Moffitt, D. 234, 234n69, 235, 235n72, 236n76

Moo, D. 25n83, 55n52, 58, 58n65, 140n19
Morris, L. 11n15, 29n97, 105, 105n8
Moss, C. 236n77, 237n79
Moule, C. F. D. 39, 39n6
Murphy, R. 16n42

Naselli, A. 25n83, 55n52, 58, 58n65
Nickelsburg, G. 93n71
Nolan, B. 214n21
Nolland, J. 11n15, 79n39, 91n69, 105n7, 109,
    109n16
Novakovic, L. 66n5, 121n43

Orton, D. 10n8, 10n12, 22n69, 25, 25n83, 31,
    31n105, 32n106, 45, 45n24, 45n25, 57,
    57n61
Overman, A. 35n117, 249n17

Paffenroth, K. 120n41
Pamment, M. 94n73
Patte, D. 17n44, 252n25
Peels, H. 231n64
Pemberton, G. 14n30
Penner, P. 26n87
Pennington, J. 17n45, 30n99, 30n100, 40, 40n10,
    40n12, 52n48, 53n49, 139n17, 140n18, 186,
    186n36, 187n37, 213n15, 218n37
Perkins, L. 224n49
Phillips, P. 10n9, 27n89, 29n97
Philpot, J. 157n48
Piotrowski, N. 66n5, 217n28
Pitre, B. 131n1, 133n8, 152, 152n43, 160,
    160n53, 161, 161n54, 162n55
Powell, M. 76n25, 210n6

Quarles, C. 66n5, 155n46, 165n60

Richardson, A. 66, 66n4
Ricoeur, P. 1n1
Ridderbos, H. 141, 141n22
Riesner, R. 13n23
Roberts, A. 208n3
Robertson, A. T. 78n34
Rodriguez, R. 251n19
Rollston, C. 21n67
Roudiez, L. 54n51

Sailhamer, J. 49n38, 136n12
Sanders, E. P. 21n66
Schneider, G. 186n36
Schreiner, P. 50n41, 187, 213n16
Schroter, J. 251n19
Senior, D. 55n53, 88n65, 170n5
Sequeira, A. 58n64

Sharbaugh, P. 146n33
Sheridan, M. 12n17
Silva, M. 125n52
Singsa, T. 18n50
Smith, C. 210n6
Sneed, M. 16n41, 19n57
Spellman, C. 10n11
Stanton, G. 4, 4n9, 32, 32n107, 32n108, 200n66
Stendahl, K. 11, 11n14, 200n66
Stern, D. 218n34
Strauss, D. 146n33
Strecker, G. 141, 141n24
Suggs, J. 18n47, 18n50, 20n61

Taylor, J. 82n43
Teeple, H. 131n1
Thatcher, T. 251n19
Theissen, G. 3n7,
Thomas Aquinas 41n13, 96
Tov, E. 25, 25n80
Treat, J. 85n52
Turner, D. 39n5, 40n7, 184n31

Ulrich, L. 10n8

Van Aarde, A. 191n49
Van der Toorn, K. 7n1, 19n59, 22n71, 25n81,
    25n82, 27n89, 238n81
Van Leeuwen, R. 14, 14n31
Verseput, D. 66, 66n7
Vos, G. 8n4

Wainwright, E. 18n50
Watts, R. 85n51
Wenham, D. 18n52
Westerholm, S. 25n84
Wilkins, M. 12n17, 12n18, 12n19
Willitts, J. 66n5, 69n10, 84n50, 110, 110n18,
    110n19, 115, 115n31, 116n33, 118n36, 119,
    119n39, 193n52
Wilson, A. 208n3
Wilson, W. 46n28
Winsbury, R. 22n71
Winter, B. 15n37
Witherington, B., III 14n29, 15n33, 16, 16n38,
    17, 17n46, 18n50, 21n64, 23n73, 33n112, 46,
    47, 47n31, 47n32, 70n12, 131n3
Wright, N. T. 47, 48, 48n34, 48n37, 186,
    186n35, 222, 222n45

Yieh, J. 14n28, 28n92, 34n114

Zacharias, D. 66n5

Index of Scripture and Other Ancient Sources

Old Testament

Genesis

1 215
1–2 220
2 186, 215
2:4 45, 213, 220
3 186, 214
3:15 149, 177, 179
3:24 80
4:2 111
4:10 231
4:16 80
5 214
5:1 45, 213, 220
10:15 122n48
12 174, 175, 178
12–17 181, 215
12–26 220
12:1 172
12:2 172, 173
12:3 173
15 174
15:1 215
15:2 174, 215
15:5 174
15:6 169n2, 216
16:5–6 216
16:9 216
17 173, 174
17:2 173, 174
17:4 174
17:4–5 173, 179
17:6 173, 189

17:7 174
17:16 174
17:19 216
18 174, 220
18:10 174
18:18 174
21 174
21:1–3 175
22 180
22:1 180
22:2 181
22:7 180
22:8 180
22:11 180
22:15 180
22:17–18 180
24:10–28 136
29:2–14 136
37–42 93n71
37–50 215n24
41:8 73n17, 77n28
41:10 77n28
41:10–12 77n28
41:40–41 77n28
41:42 77n28
47:3 111
48:15 111
49:10 74
49:24 111

Exodus

1–2 135, 136, 220
1:1–2:10 166
1:8 135

1:15 135
1:16 135
1:17 135
1:18 135
2 220
2:10 150
2:16–19 150
2:17 136
3–4 220
3–14 151
3:1 133n7
4:1 149
4:1–9 150
4:2–5 149
4:6–7 150
4:19 135
4:20 165
7:8–10 165n59
7:11 73n17
7:19–20 150
12 159, 221n42
12:7 160
12:31–51 166
12:37 151
13:3 217n30
13:21–22 149
14 220
14:10–13 166
14:21–29 149
14:26–27 150
14:31 165n59
15–18 155
15:22–25 149
15:23–25 150

16 151
16:1–17:7 166
16:4 151, 165
16:8 151
16:12 151
16:15 151
17–19 220
17:2–6 149
17:6 150
18 220
19:1–23:33 166
19:3 139
21:32 236
23:12 145
24 154, 160, 161, 162
24:1 155, 156
24:1–18 166
24:4 160
24:8 158, 160
24:8–11 162
24:10 161
24:12 155
24:15–18 155
24:16 155, 156
24:18 139
25:30 160
31:1–11 225
31:15 145
32:11–13 158
32:31–32 158
33:1–23 166
34 154
34:2–3 155
34:4 139

34:5 155
34:29 155, 219
34:29–35 156, 166
34:30 155, 156
34:31 155
35:31 28n91
35:35 28n91
36:1 28n91

Leviticus

4:7 160
4:18 160
4:25 160
4:30 160
4:34 160
19:18 144
24:19–21 144

Numbers

6:24–26 157
11 152
11:31 149
12:1–15 219
12:1–16 150
12:3 219
12:5–15 149
14:9 221, 221n43
14:22 219
17:1–10 149
20:7–12 150
21:4–9 149
21:17–18 165
21:34 221, 221n43
22 79n37
22–24 79
24 78, 79
24:17 78, 78n34, 79
27 116
27:15–18 221
27:17 111, 116,
    116n33, 165n59
27:20 221
27:23 221

Deuteronomy

1:21 221
3:2 221
3:22 221
4:5–8 38
4:6 127
4:10 228
8:3 151
8:4 221n42

9:9 140
12:9–10 145
16:19 103, 169n2,
    246n7
17:18–20 106
17:19 105, 127
18 101n1, 231
18:15 155
18:15–18 132
21:7–8 235n75
24:1–4 143
25:19 145n29
27–28 109
27:18 109
27:19 109
27:25 235n74
27:26 109
29:5 221n42
31:7–8 164
31:7–9 166
31:8 221, 221n43
31:14–15 209
32:18 134n10
34:1–4 163
34:6 167

Joshua

1:1–9 166, 209
1:3 164
1:13 145
8:1 221
10:18 221
10:25 221
18:16 122n48
21:44 145n29
22:4 145n29
23:1 145n29

1 Samuel

16 112
16:1–2 103n4
16:1–13 67
16:10 223
16:11 112
16:11–12 133n7
16:13 70
16:18 103n4
16:19 112
17 103
17–18 222
17:1–54 67
17:12 72
17:15 112, 133n7

17:26 103
17:34 112
17:37 103
17:38–40 103
17:40 112
18–20 126
18:6 125
18:6–30 67
18:8–9 125
19:5 119, 235n74
20 67
21 67, 222
21:10 83
22:1–5 67
24:4 88
25:31 223
27:4 67
27:6 67
29:3 67

2 Samuel

1:16 90n67
5:1–2 112
5:2 75, 75n21, 109,
    110, 112, 114
5:3 110
5:7–8 122, 126
7 70, 129
7:5 223
7:5–17 112
7:8 110, 223
7:8–9 112
7:11 66n2, 83, 145n29
7:14 66n2, 83
7:20 223
8 79
8:15 223n47
8:17 21n68, 36
9:6–7 126
11:3 178
11:6 178
15–19 67
15:12–18:18 86
15:14 83
15:23 87
15:30 87
15:31 87
16:5–14 98n78
16:6–7 98n78
16:23 33n112
17:23 87
19:21–23 88
20:25 36
22:44–45 76n24

23:15–17 90n68
24:17 119n37

1 Kings

1:13 94n72
1:17 94n72
1:30 94n72
1:37 94n72
1:47 94n72
2:12 94n72
4:1–19 33n112
4:3 21n68, 36
4:29–34 121
4:34 77, 95n74
5:4 145n29
8:56 145n29
10:1 33n112
10:1–2 77
10:4 225
10:7 77
11:41 21
14:19 21
14:29 21
17:8–24 227n56
18:4 226
19:1–2 226
22:17 116, 116n33

2 Kings

1:8 226
2 228
2:12–14 227
2:15 227
2:19–22 227n54
3:18 227
4:8–37 227
4:25 227n56
4:27 227, 227n56
4:27–37 227
4:38–41 227n54
4:38–44 228
4:42–44 201, 227,
    227n54
4:44 228
6:1–7 227n55
6:15–17 228
6:16 228
6:20–23 227n54
7:1 227n54
7:18–20 227n54
9 230n61
9:13 230n61
12:11 21

15:29 193
18:18 21n68
22 21n68

1 Chronicles

18:16 36
27:32 22
28:10 223

2 Chronicles

1:10 241
1:10–12 15, 28n91
2:12–13 28n91
9:23 77
18:16 116, 116n33
24:11 21
24:21 231
36:23 209, 238

Ezra

7:6 22
7:11 22
7:12 21
7:25 21
7:25–26 138

Nehemiah

8:1–8 22
8:13 22
9:15 151

Job

1:19 200n65
3:21 18
15:18 18, 199n63
21 15
28:12 15, 248
28:15 247
28:20 18n49
28:21 18, 199n63
40–41 23

Psalms

1 76, 243
1:2 105, 127
2 89, 98, 243
2:1–3 95
2:2 73n16
2:6 96
2:7 66n2, 83, 85, 189
2:9 96

2:11 106n12
2:12 189
3:7 89n66
5:7 106n12
6:10 89n66
8 125
8:2 125
9:20 106n12
15:4 106n12
17:9 87
19:7 27, 242, 245
19:9 106n12
22 86, 91, 92, 208
22:1 86, 92
22:7 86, 96, 234
22:7–8 91
22:8 86
22:18 86, 92
22:23 106n12
22:25 106n12
23 111
23:5 87
25:14 106n12
27:6 89n66
27:12 89
31:5 87
31:19 106n12
33:8 106n12
33:18 106n12
34:7 106n12
34:9 106n12
34:11 106n12
36:1 106n12
37:30 103, 169n2,
     246n7
40:3 106n12
41:6–7 87
42 87n62
42:5–6 87
45:1 82n46
45:6 78n35
51:6 28
54 67
55:12–14 88
55:19 106n12
55:20–21 88
56:2 87
60:4 106n12
61:5 106n12
62:1 89
62:5 89
66:16 106n12
67:7 106n12
69 86, 91

69:1–3 91
69:8 91
69:18 91
69:21 86, 90, 91
71:10 87
72:5 106n12
72:10 77
72:16 165
73:13 90
74:10 96
77:20 111
78 112, 218
78:2 18, 42, 218, 224
78:52 111
78:70–71 110
78:70–72 112
80:1 111
85:9 106n12
86:11 106n12
89:3 223
89:20 223
89:27–28 66n2, 83
89:35 71
89:36 71
89:39 96, 223
90:11 106n12
95:11 145n29
102:15 106n12
103:11 106n12
103:13 106n12
103:17 106n12
105:6 175
107:43 28n91
109:2 89
110 94, 95
110:1 94
111:5 106n12
111:10 106n12
115:11 106n12
115:13 106n12
118 125
118:4 106n12
118:6 106n12
118:22 245
118:22–23 203
118:25 124
118:26 125
119:51 96
119:63 106n12
119:74 106n12
119:79 106n12
119:120 106n12
119:176 116n33

120:2 89
135:20 106n12
145:19 106n12
147:11 106n12

Proverbs

1 15, 169n2
1:2 169n2
1:3 103, 169n2,
     246n7, 250
1:5 169n2
1:7 106n12, 243
1:8 38n3
1:20–33 138, 145
1:28 18n49
1:29 106n12
2 169n2
2:1–8 15, 28
2:4 18
2:5 20, 106n12
2:6 169n2, 248
2:9 20, 169n2
3 15
3:7 106n12
3:10 38n3
4:1 38n3
4:7 248
6:18 38n3
6:19 38n3
7:1 28
8 15, 23
8:1–6 145n30
8:9 20
8:13 106n12
8:14–36 18
8:22–31 214
8:35–36 145
9 15
9:1–6 10n10
9:5–6 145n30
9:9 103, 169n2, 246n7
9:10 106n12
10 38n3
10:1 38n3
10:14 18, 199n63
10:18 38n3
10:27 106n12
10:31 103, 169n2
12:17 38n3
12:19 38n3
13:1 38n3
13:14 36
13:20 27

14:26–27 106n12
15:16 106n12
15:33 106n12
16:6 106n12
19:23 106n12
21:11 20, 28n91
21:12 20
21:20 28
21:29 20
22:4 106n12
23:17 106n12
24:21 106n12
25:1 33n112
28:5 20
29:7 20

Ecclesiastes

2:14–16 251
3:14 106n12
5:7 106n12
7:16 103, 169n2, 246n7
8:1 157
9:1 103, 169n2, 246n7
10:2 103, 170n2, 246n7
12:13 140, 248

Isaiah

1–39 85
1:2 229
1:4 229
2:2 188
3:14 230n62
4:2 80
5 230
6:9–10 198
9:1 81
9:1–2 193, 196
9:2 85
9:4 145n30
9:6–7 70 n12
9:7 85
11 81, 81n42
11:1 56, 80, 241
11:1–2 121
11:1–3 85
11:2 15, 81, 145n29,
    200n65
11:10 85
13 232
13:7 232
13:10 232
22:21–23 70n12
24–27 232

25:6–10 200
27:12 195n59
27:13 232
28:12 145n29
29:14 18, 199n63
29:18 27n89
32:3 85
33:6 28n90
33:18 22
35 121
35:5–6 121
35:8–10 121
37:35 85
39:2 78
39:6 78
40–66 52, 53, 53n49
40:1 53n49
40:2 53n49
40:11 53n49
40:29–31 53n49
41:6 53n49
41:8 175
41:10 53n49
41:17 53n49
42:1 85
42:1–4 85
42:6–7 85
42:7 85
42:9–10 53n49
42:13–17 53n49
42:18 53n49
43:5 53n49
43:8–10 53n49
43:15–19 133
43:18–19 53n49
44:22 53n49
45:3 18
45:11 229
45:14 53n49
47:1–15 53n49
48:6 53n49
49:3–6 228
49:8 53n49
49:22–26 53n49
49:25 229
50:6 96
51:2 175
51:5 53n49
52:7 52
52:9 53n49
52:12 53n49
52:13 15, 241
53 92, 119
53–55 85

53:2 85
53:3 88, 91n69
53:4 92, 128
53:4–6 53n49
53:6 116n33
53:7 89
53:9 89, 90
53:10 92
53:10–12 53n49
53:12 158
54:1 229
54:7–8 53n49
54:13 15, 15n37, 229
55:1–2 53n49
55:3 53n49
55:7 53n49
56:7 188
57:15 229
57:19 227
59:21 53n49
60 78
60:3 77
60:6 77
60:9 229
61:2–3 53n49
65:17 53n49
66:1 145n29
66:2 229
66:15–17 53n49
66:18–21 228
66:22 53n49
66:24 53n49

Jeremiah

1:9–10 198
6:16 145
7 230, 231
7:3 231
7:11 230
8:8 82n46, 245
8:13 230
9:23–35 243
12:10 230n62
12:10–11 230
12:13 230n62
15:3 200n65
18:1–11 236n78
19:1–13 236n78
22:5 231
23:1–6 113
23:5 81, 103, 170n2,
    241, 246n7
23:5–6 15, 70n12, 81
23:7 133
26 230, 231

26:15 236n78
31 83n47
31:7 124
31:10–14 200n67, 201
31:15 101n2, 217,
    218n35
31:31 161
31:31–32 161
31:31–34 161
31:33 148
31:33–34 15n37
32:14 236n78
33:15 81
36 21n68
36:2 23n75
36:4 24
36:23 82n46
36:28 23n75
37 21n68
40:1 82, 83n47, 102n2,
    217, 218n35
49:36 200n65
50 117n34
50:6 116n33
50:6–7 117n34

Lamentations

2 234, 235
2:7 234
2:15 234, 235
3 235
3:19 234
4 235
4:13 234, 235

Ezekiel

1 200n65
1:10 200n65
8:10 231
8:13 231
9:2 82n46
9:3 82n46
9:11 82n46
10 200n65
10:18–19 231
16:59–63 161
16:61 161
24:23–25 116n33
28:12 214n19
34 118, 121, 122, 128,
    237
34:2 118, 122
34:3 128

34:4 122
34:4–16 114
34:5 116n33, 122
34:10 118
34:11 118, 122
34:14 200n67
34:15 118
34:17–19 118
34:23–24 113, 116n32,
    122
34:26–27 200n67
34:31 118n36
37 235
37:9 200n65
37:24–25 70n12
47:21–23 228

Daniel

1:4 28n91
1:17 28n91
2 20n60
2:1 77n28
2:2 80
2:10 80
2:14 77n28
2:21 28n91
2:27–28 19n60
2:46 77n28
2:48 77n28
3–6 93n71
5:1–4 78
7 94, 95, 187
7:13–14 187
7:14 186n34, 187

Hosea

2:12 230n62
2:14–15 133
3:5 70n12
11 217
11:1 72n14, 182, 217,
    218n33
12:13 217n30
14:9 28n91

Joel

3:19 234
4:18 165

Amos

2:10 217n30
3:1 217n30
9:11 70n12

Jonah

1:14 234

Micah

5:1 74, 114
5:1–4 113
5:1–9 114
5:2 56, 72n15, 73, 114,
    245
6:4 217n30
7:14–15 133
7:15 217n30

Zechariah

2:6 200n65
2:11 228
6:12 81
9 161
9–12 113n23
9:9 43, 165, 230
9:9–10 236n77
9:11–13 161
9:13 161
11:12 236
11:12–13 57n58
11:13 236n78
11:17 237
12:10 120
12:10–14 236n77
13 120
13:7 116n33, 118,
    118n36, 119, 120,
    236n77
13:7–9 119

New Testament

Matthew

1 75, 82, 114, 213
1–2 41, 67n9, 68, 82,
    84, 94, 133, 136,
    166, 212
1–7 219
1–9 212, 220, 224
1–13 225
1:1 11, 65, 68, 69, 93,
    97, 98, 121n42,
    169, 169n1, 176,
    178, 180, 182, 188,
    190, 213, 220
1:1–4:16 210
1:1–17 211, 213, 215,
    216, 220, 233

1:5–6 69n11
1:6 69, 178
1:11 179
1:11–12 69n11
1:16 215n24
1:17 69, 217n26
1:18–25 181, 190, 215,
    216, 220, 233
1:19 215, 216
1:20 69, 134n10, 215,
    215n24
1:20–21 216
1:21 97, 115, 121n43,
    136, 167, 182, 216,
    216n26
1:22 40
1:23 115, 182, 216
2 56, 56n58, 67n9, 71,
    72, 72n14, 82, 83,
    95, 95n74, 98, 99,
    101n2, 114, 119,
    126, 134, 136, 148,
    182, 189, 209, 216,
    245
2–4 216
2:1 134
2:1–2 76
2:1–6 76n27, 113
2:1–12 18, 72
2:1–23 72, 216, 233
2:2 79, 182, 189
2:3 73n17
2:4 16, 25n84, 96n76,
    245
2:4–6 25n81
2:5 25n81, 89
2:5–6 41n15, 73
2:6 72, 73, 74, 110,
    113, 114, 118, 127,
    137n15
2:11 182
2:13 215n24
2:13–15 101n2, 220
2:14 220
2:15 40, 49, 72n14,
    137n15, 182, 216,
    217
2:17 40
2:18 82, 137n15, 217,
    218n35
2:19 215n24
2:19–23 220
2:20 135
2:22 101n2

2:23 80, 137n15
3 139, 176, 192, 196,
    203
3–4 233
3–20 84, 98
3–25 68, 84, 192
3:1–16:12 41
3:4 192, 226
3:5–6 192
3:8 170, 192
3:9–10 192
3:10 171
3:11–12 139
3:13–17 139, 166, 216,
    220
3:15 103, 108, 216n26
3:16 103, 150
3:16–17 227
3:17 85, 181
4 139
4:1–11 103, 166, 216,
    216n26, 220
4:3 189n48
4:4 103
4:8 108, 184
4:8–10 186
4:10 103, 108
4:11 210
4:12 193
4:12–16:20 43
4:12–17 139, 198
4:12–20:34 210
4:14–16 42, 43
4:15 67n9, 184
4:15–16 145n30, 193,
    196
4:16 42
4:16–16:20 210
4:17 211
4:18–22 34, 220
4:23 17, 53, 67n8, 70,
    103, 104, 108, 120,
    121, 186, 243n3
4:23–24 121
4:24 121
5 105, 139, 216
5–7 16, 104, 108, 138,
    148, 166, 213, 218,
    220, 233
5–9 115, 201, 218,
    219, 220
5–10 115
5–13 115
5:1 139, 184

5:1–7:29 34
5:3 104
5:4 108
5:5 107, 125, 219
5:6 108
5:7 107
5:8 108
5:10 104, 107
5:17 38, 40n11, 60n68
5:17–18 105
5:17–19 29
5:17–20 107, 109, 138,
    140, 141, 142, 219
5:20 16, 108, 246
5:21 142
5:21–22 143
5:21–26 142, 147n36
5:21–48 138, 141, 142,
    167, 219
5:22 17, 142
5:23 143
5:27 142
5:27–30 143
5:28 142, 143
5:31 142
5:31–32 142
5:32 142
5:33 142
5:33–34 143
5:34 17, 142
5:35 104
5:37 107
5:38 142
5:38–42 88, 144
5:39 107, 142, 144
5:43 142, 144
5:44 142, 144
5:48 41n13, 250
6 189n48
6:10 107, 250
6:11–13 249
6:12 147n36
6:14–15 147n36
6:19 17, 107
6:22 246
6:24 246, 247
6:25–30 18
6:26 24
6:33 247
7 176n11, 212
7:6 107
7:15–23 250
7:21–23 246
7:22–23 250

7:24 142
7:28 211
7:29 16, 17, 25n81,
    27, 142, 186
8 196
8–9 42, 107, 108, 115,
    115n28, 123, 148,
    151, 219, 219n39,
    220, 233
8:1 139, 219
8:1–4 150, 219
8:1–9:38 43
8:3 151
8:4 107, 132, 151, 154
8:5–13 196
8:8 196
8:10–12 196
8:11 170, 195n57
8:11–12 117n33
8:12 197
8:16–17 121, 121n45
8:17 42, 43
8:19 3n7, 16, 34, 35
8:19–22 18n49, 35n117
8:20 17, 108
8–20 10n8
8:21 34
8:28–34 219
8:29 189n48
9 124n51, 221
9:3 16, 244
9:9 34, 249
9:10–11 13n23
9:10–13 122
9:11 3n7, 16, 34
9:12 151
9:13 107
9:16–17 60n70
9:17 29
9:27 107, 121n42, 123
9:27–31 123
9:28 123
9:28–29 109
9:30 123
9:31 123
9:32–34 219
9:32–38 113
9:35 53, 67n8, 70, 104,
    115n28, 120, 243n3
9:35–38 115n28,
    165n59, 195n59
9:35–10:4 115
9:36 110, 113, 114,
    118, 127, 128,
    219n39, 221

9:36–38 115
9:37 115
9:38 108
10 115, 115n28, 138,
    195n59, 197, 201,
    213, 220, 221,
    221n42, 222, 233
10–12 224
10:1 20, 34, 186, 221
10:1–4 115n28
10:5 195
10:5–6 170, 171n7, 193
10:6 117, 183, 187,
    191, 194
10:7 67n8, 194
10:9 247
10:17 243n3
10:19 221, 221n43
10:24 3n7, 13n23,
    16, 20
10:24–25 16, 34
10:25 3n7, 10n10, 12,
    13n23, 16
10:26–27 10n10
10:28 221n43
10:40–42 221
11 146n34, 148, 222
11–12 197n62, 209,
    222, 223, 225, 233
11–13 197
11:1 211, 221
11:2 46
11:2–6 121
11:2–13:58 19
11:5 109
11:5–6 127
11:6–9 18
11:13–14 139
11:14 226
11:15 244
11:16 222
11:19 18, 224
11:20–24 46, 197n62
11:21 248n13
11:21–24 198
11:25 46, 248
11:25–27 18, 46,
    197n62
11:25–30 18n48, 19,
    38, 146, 146n33,
    166, 222
11:27 23, 46
11:28–30 138, 144
11:28–29 145

11:28–30 146
11:29 107, 250, 252
11:29–30 17, 145
12 42, 43, 146, 222,
    224
12:1–8 107, 146, 222
12:2 248
12:6 49, 222
12:7 107, 122
12:9 243n3
12:9–14 146
12:10 122
12:14 43, 197n62, 248
12:14–15 222
12:14–28:20 43
12:15–21 165n59, 223
12:17–21 42, 43
12:18 42, 223
12:18–21 223
12:20 10n9
12:22 124n51
12:22–32 197n62
12:23 121n42
12:24 248
12:30 96n76
12:35 10n9, 250
12:38 3n7, 16, 34,
    165n59, 244, 248
12:38–42 196, 197n62
12:41–42 49
12:42 16, 224
12:46–50 197n62, 223
12:50 170, 250
13 12n21, 13, 14, 18,
    18n51, 18n52, 19,
    20, 34, 60, 138,
    197n62, 198, 199,
    201, 211, 213, 224,
    224n48, 225, 233
13:1–58 43
13:9 244
13:11 19, 20, 22, 34,
    239, 241, 249, 252
13:11–14 198
13:13 12n21
13:13–15 19, 249
13:14 12n21
13:14–15 41n15, 198
13:15 12n21, 250
13:19 12n21
13:23 12n21, 250
13:34–35 224
13:35 40, 42, 43, 60
13:43 224

13:44 28
13:51 12n21, 20, 28,
  225, 245
13:51–52 24, 38, 249
13:52 1, 2, 9, 10,
  11n15, 12, 13,
  16, 20, 21, 24n76,
  27, 27n89, 34, 35,
  35n117, 45, 60, 61,
  187, 239, 241, 250,
  251, 252, 252n28
13:53 211
13:53–17:27 200
13:54 224, 225, 243n3
14 150, 199, 226
14–17 199n64, 201,
  225, 226, 228, 233
14–18 199
14:1–12 226, 227n54
14:3 226n53
14:5 226n53
14:6–8 226
14:6–12 226n53
14:12 226n53
14:13–21 151, 167,
  227n54
14:15 151
14:22–33 227
14:27 221n43
14:29 150
14:33 189n48, 227
15 152, 194, 194n55,
  195, 199, 201
15:1 16
15:1–2 244
15:1–9 227n54
15:1–20 107
15:1–21 200
15:2 33
15:5–12 228
15:10 12n21
15:14 122, 249
15:21–22 194
15:21–28 113, 124,
  196, 200, 227,
  227n54
15:21–29 224
15:22 107, 109, 116,
  121n42, 124
15:23 107, 227
15:24 110, 113, 116,
  124, 127, 183, 187,
  191, 193, 194
15:24–28 118

15:28 116, 124, 194
15:29 184
15:29–31 227
15:29–39 151, 167
15:32–39 227n54
15:37 228
16 43, 84, 228n59
16–17 228
16:1–12 225
16:5–12 227n54
16:12 12n21, 28
16:13 94n73
16:13–20 27n88, 228
16:13–28:20 41, 42, 43
16:16 189n48, 226
16:18 36, 201
16:21 16, 42, 73, 86,
  114, 193, 210, 211,
  245
16:21–21:10 43
16:21–28:20 210–11
16:24 108
16:24–27 108
16:25 247
17:1 155, 156, 184
17:1–8 154, 228
17:1–9 166
17:2 155, 156, 167
17:3–4 132
17:5 155, 156
17:6 155, 156
17:7 155
17:7–8 156
17:9 139
17:10 16, 25n81, 27
17:12 86
17:12–13 226
17:13 12n21, 28
17:22–23 86
17:24 3n7, 13n23,
  16, 35
18 138, 201, 213
18–20 228, 228n59,
  229, 230, 232, 233
18–25 228
18:1–6 229
18:1–14 229
18:4 107
18:10–14 229
18:12 110
18:15–20 229
18:15–35 229
18:17 36, 201
19–20 229

19–25 201
19:1 42, 211
19:2 201
19:3–11 202
19:7 33, 132
19:7–8 132
19:8 143
19:14 229
19:16 3n7, 16, 247
19:16–22 202
19:16–26 229
19:17 11n16
9:21 247
19:27–30 108
19:28 114, 247
19:29–30 202
20:1–16 230n62
20:17–18 42
20:18 16, 73, 114, 244,
  245
20:18–19 86
20:25 34
20:26 92
20:29–34 123
20:30 107, 121n42
20:31 121n42
21 230, 237
21–25 230, 232, 233
21–27 236n77
21–28 234n70, 237
21:1 42, 210
21:4 41n15
21:4–5 42, 43, 158n49,
  236n77
21:5 42, 43, 107,
  236n77
21:9 121n42, 122, 202
21:10 42, 202
21:11 81, 230
21:12–13 34, 171,
  183n27
21:13 230
21:14–15 122, 124
21:15 16, 121n42, 125,
  149, 202, 245
21:18–19 183n27, 202
21:18–22 171, 230
21:23 33, 34, 202
21:28–32 202, 230n62
21:31 202
21:33–44 230n62
21:33–46 202
21:41 203
21:42 203, 245

21:46 226n53
22 94
22:1–14 203n69
22:16 3n7, 16, 35
22:23–33 33
22:24 3n7, 16, 132
22:29 126, 245
22:34 96n76
22:36 3n7, 16
22:36–40 107
22:41 96n76
22:41–46 83n48
22:42 94, 121n42
22:43 223
22:45 83
23 16n39, 17, 26, 32,
  73, 203, 231, 234,
  234n68, 235, 243
23–25 16, 138, 213,
  230
23:1–2 107
23:1–36 24
23:2 16, 25n81, 27,
  132, 246
23:3 246
23:4 122
23:4–12 246
23:8 3n7, 13, 13n23, 16
23:8–10 15n37, 244
23:10 15
23:12 107
23:13 16, 33
23:13–39 246
23:14 122
23:15 16, 33
23:16 249
23:16–19 122
23:23 16, 103, 183n27,
  247, 250
23:24 249
23:25 16
23:27 16, 33
23:27–39 204
23:29 16
23:34 16, 26, 35,
  35n117, 243n3,
  252
23:34–35 231
23:35 234, 235
23:37 108, 171, 231
23:38 231
24 203
24–25 231, 235, 237
24:1–2 231, 237

24:1–25:46 117
24:3 184
24:6–7 232
24:15 231
24:16 232
24:29 232
24:30 236n77
24:30–31 117n33, 232
24:45 204
25:1–13 204
25:27 247
25:31 117
25:31–32 108
25:31–46 113, 117
25:32 110
25:34 117
25:40 204
26 16, 118
26–28 68, 84, 98, 99,
    183, 188, 210, 211,
    212, 214n20, 233,
    234, 234n68, 237
26:1 17, 211
26:1–4 237n79
26:3 96n76
26:4 95, 226n53
26:6 237n79
26:14–15 237n79
26:15 247
26:16 236
26:17 161
26:17–18 13n23
26:17–19 159
26:17–30 166
26:18 3n7, 16
26:24–25 246
26:25 3n7
26:26–29 160
26:28 161
26:30–35 113
26:31 110, 113, 118,
    127, 236n77
26:37–44 107
26:38 87
26:47 87
26:47–50 237n79
26:49 3n7, 246
26:50 88
26:51–53 88
26:53–54 158n49
26:56 119, 158n49
26:57 16, 73, 96n76,
    114
26:57–68 89, 94

26:61 233, 237
26:62–64 94
26:63 89, 107, 189n48
26:63–64 94
26:64 94, 94n73, 107
26:67 107
26:71 81
26:73 81
27 43, 119, 188, 189,
    235
27–28 98
27:1 89
27:1–26 89
27:2 226n53
27:3 247
27:3–4 237n79
27:3–10 236
27:4 235, 236n78
27:4–5 89n66, 237n79
27:5 87, 247
27:6 247
27:6–8 120, 237n79
27:9 40, 43, 158n49,
    236, 247
27:9–10 43, 57n58,
    236n77
27:11 89, 95, 189
27:11–14 95
27:11–26 226n53
27:12 89
27:12–14 107
27:17 96n76
27:18 90
27:19 90, 235
27:21–22 90
27:23 107
27:24 90, 235, 236n78
27:25 90n67, 235
27:26 90
27:27 96n76
27:27–31 95
27:28 96
27:29 96, 189
27:30 96, 107
27:31–32 108
27:32–44 96
27:33 96
27:34 86, 90, 235
27:35 86, 90, 92
27:37 96, 189
27:39 86, 234, 235
27:39–40 91
27:40 189, 237
27:41 16, 73, 114, 244
27:42–44 97

27:43 86, 189
27:44 92
27:46 86, 92
27:51 167, 237
27:51–61 226n53
27:54 189
27:57 252n28
27:62 96n76
28 50
28:6 167
28:12 96n76
28:16 184
28:16–20 166, 183,
    185, 212, 238
28:17 12n20, 185, 205
28:18 108, 185, 187,
    213
28:18–20 163, 167,
    170, 170n5, 171n7,
    239, 252n28
28:19 34, 185, 252,
    252n28
28:19–20 187, 247

Mark

1:1 68
2:23–28 66
4:38 3n7
5:35 3n7
6:52 28
7:10 154
8:21 28
9:4 154
9:5 3n7, 17, 38
9:10 28
9:17 3n7
9:32 28
9:38 3n7
10:17 3n7, 20, 35
10:20 3n7
10:35 3n7
10:47 121n42
10:48 121n42
11:21 3n7
12:14 3n7, 19, 32
12:19 3n7
12:25 121n42
12:26 11n16
12:32 3n7
12:36 223
13:1 3n7
14:14 3n7
14:45 3n7

Luke

1:32 121n42
1:78 78n34
3:4 11n16
3:31 121n42
6:40 1, 2, 3n7, 63
6:45 10n9
7:40 3n7
8:49 3n7
9:38 3n7
10:25 3n7
11:45 3n7
12:13 3n7
18:18 3n7
18:38 121n42
18:39 121n42
19:39 3n7
20:21 3n7, 28, 39
20:28 3n7, 154
20:39 3n7
20:42 11n16
21:7 3n7
22:11 3n7
22:37 41n13
24:27 59

John

1:9 78n34
1:38 3n7
1:46 81
3:2 3n7
4:31 3n7
6 195n58
6:25 3n7
8:4 3n7
8:12 78n34
9:2 3n7
11:18 3n7
13:13 3n7
20:16 3n7

Acts

1:20 11n16
1:21–26 185
2:30 133n7
4:13 11n13
7:42 11n16

Romans

3:25 41n13
4:9 175
4:12 175
8:3–4 41n13

9–11 171n6
9:15 171n6
11:12 171n6
11:17–18 185

1 Corinthians

1:20 22
1:30 103, 169n2,
  246n7, 249

2 Corinthians

1:20 49
5:17 60n70

Galatians

3:7 175
3:14 175
3:16 169, 178
4:4 39, 41n13

Colossians

2:3 28

Hebrews

1:3 65
1:8 78n35
7:19 41n13
8:13 60n70

1 Peter

5:12 24n78

2 Peter

1:19 78n34

1 John

2:7 60n70

Revelation

2:28 78n34
7:1 200n65
9:13–15 200n65
20:15 11n16
22:16 78n34

Old Testament Apocrypha

Baruch

3–4 15
3:37–4:1 38n3

2 Esdras

12:37 22

2 Maccabees

7 93n71

Psalm 151

in toto 112
1 112

Sirach

1 15, 29
1:1 244
1:14 244
1:25 28n90
1:26 250
1:29 250
1:30 250
4:24 103n5
5 29
6:18–37 145
6:19–31 17
10 29
18:28–29 13n22
20:30 18, 28n90,
  199n63
23:9 17
23:27 38n3
24 15
24:8–9 17
24:9 17
24:19–22 145n30
24:23 105
27:30–28:7 147n36
28:3–4 17
29:11 17
31:12–32:6 18
38:24–34 22
38:34–39:2 253
39:1 22
39:1–3 21
39:1–11 22, 23
39:4 26
39:6 253
41:14 18, 28n90,
  199n63
51 146n33, 146n34
51:1 146
51:23 33n112
51:23–26 145
51:23–28 146

Wisdom of Solomon

1–9 15
1:4 246
1:16 246
2:12–20 92
2:17–18 92
2:22 20n60
3:11 247n9
6:7 249
6:20 128
6:20–21 70
6:21 128n53
6:22 18, 20n60
7:7 18, 249
8:21 46n29
9:2 214
9:4 248
9:9 38n3, 214
9:17 18, 189n46
9:17–18 32
10:5 170n2
10:9–10 32
10:12 32
10:16 132n6
10:18–11:16 145

Old Testament Pseudepigrapha

2 Baruch

5.3–7 38n3
29.6 153
38.2 38n3
41.3–4 145
44.14 28n90
48 15
51.3 157n48
54.13 157n48
77–86 114
77.16 38n3

1 Enoch

12.4 252
38.4 157n48
42.1–2 17
42.1–3 18n49
42.2 15
42.4 15
46.3 15n33
49.3–4 15n33
51.3 15, 15n33
63.2 15

2 Enoch

34.1 145
48.9 146n32

Ezekiel the Tragedian

68–69 133n7

4 Ezra

5 15
7.97 157n48
13.34–50 114

Jubilees

4.16–18 24
18.18–19 180

Psalms of Solomon

17 114
17.21 70n12, 85n55
17.42–3 15n33
18.4–9 15n33

Sibylline Oracles

5.357 38n3

Testament of Judah

21.1–4 15n33

Testament of Levi

18.2–6 15n33

Testament of Solomon

3.5 121
4.11 121
22.1 121
3 121

New Testament Apocrypha

Acts of Pilate

5.1 149

Rabbinic Literature

Qohelet Rabbah

1.9 165n60

Dead Sea Scrolls

CD

3.2 149
5.1 149
6.11 15n33
7.18 15n33

1QS

IX, 9–11 134n9

1QSb

V, 21–26 81n42
V, 27–28 79n36

4Q161

frags. 2–6 II 27 79n36

4Q225

in toto 180

4Q511

frags. 10, 9 153n44

4QFlor

1.11 15n33

4QpIsaᵃ

frags. 7–10 III, 22–29
    81n42

11QMelch

18–20 15n33

11QPsᵃ

18 15
XXVII 2 65n1

Church Fathers

Augustine

Quaestiones in Heptateuchum
2.73 60n71, 60n72

Chrysostom

Expositiones in Psalmos
[PG 55:103] 87n61

Clement of Alexandria

Stromateis
6.58.1 13n24

Eusebius

Demonstration of the Gospel
3.2 149

Ignatius

To the Ephesians
15.1 13n24

Irenaeus

Adversus haereses
4.9.1 29n93

Justin Martyr

First Apology
4.5 19

Origen

Commentarium in evangelium Matthaei
10.15 11n13
10.15.1 10n9

Selecta in Psalmos
3.1.29 87n61
3.1.36 87n61

Tertullian

Answer to the Jews
11 76n26, 77n30

Classical and Hellenistic Writers

Aelius Theon

Progymnasmata
2.61–62 26n85

Archytas of Tarentum

On Kingship
33.8–13 106n10

Hermogenes

Progymnasmata
8 3n8

Herodotus

Histories
3.62–97 77n29

Homer

Iliad
2.474–77 111n21

Josephus

Jewish Antiquities
2.228 162n56
18.63 13n24

Philo

On Abraham
177–99 180

On the Life of Moses
1.8 135n11
1.10 135n11
1.13 135n11
1.15 135n11
1.40 149
1.42 149
1.46 136n13
1.155–58 133n7
1.276 79n37
2.187 166

On the Special Laws
4.160–64 106n13

On the Virtues
220–22 178

Plutarch

Alexander
1.1–2 51n46

Moralia
780B 106n11

Quintilian

Institutes of Oratory
9.2.100–101 3n8

Xenophon

Memorabilia
2.1–4 111n22

Index of Subjects

Abel 231, 234, 235
Abraham 48, 50, 53, 136, 163,
    169n2, 170–71, 196–97,
    215–16
  covenant with 172–75,
    177–78
  faith 170, 175, 191, 216
  familial metaphors 170,
    172–75, 192, 204–5
  family 178–81, 183–84,
    187–88, 190–93, 195–96,
    198, 199–200, 202–2
  Jesus as son of 7, 11, 48, 68,
    176–78, 180–82, 186–88,
    196, 242
  nations, blessing to 173–75,
    177–78, 196
  new 169–71, 190, 199–200,
    215–16
  promises to 50, 169n2,
    172–75, 189, 191, 201
  seed of 169–70, 172, 174–75,
    185, 186, 188, 216
Absalom 67, 83, 84, 86, 98n78
Adam 53, 96, 136, 177–78,
    186, 214n19, 215, 239
  new 209, 213–15
adultery 142, 143
Ahithophel 86–88
Akkadian texts 35–36
allusions 8–9, 31, 43, 56,
    80–81, 129, 154–56
ancient Near East (ANE) cul-
    ture 159–60, 172, 247–48
  kings 101, 104, 110, 111–12

anger 142–43
antitheses, contrast 16, 35,
    122, 132, 141–43, 243–44
apocalyptic 171, 183
  sage-messiah 37–38, 44–49,
    57, 59, 75, 109, 201
atonement 44, 68, 96–97, 115,
    121n43, 160–62, 183–84,
    216n26
authority 26–27, 185–86
  of Jesus 33–34, 93, 95, 99,
    103, 108, 133, 163–64,
    183–87, 190, 196, 213, 238

Babylonian Empire / Babylon
    78, 82, 217, 232
Balaam 78–79
baptism 163–64, 188, 192–93
  of Jesus 8, 50, 85, 103, 139,
    150, 155, 163–64, 181,
    216–17, 227
Barabbas 90
Baruch 23n75, 24
Bathsheba 178–79
Ben Sira, Jesus 22–23, 25, 26,
    47, 252–53
Bethlehem 56, 72–76, 82, 83,
    97, 134
biblical theology 2–3, 8n4, 45
biographies, ancient 51–52,
    53–54
birth/infancy narrative of
    Jesus 41–42, 43, 71–76, 99,
    114, 181–82, 213
  of Moses and 134–36, 137

blindness 123–26, 128
blood 158, 159, 180, 231,
    233–37
  of the covenant 160–61, 162
The Boys in the Boat (Brown)
    58–59
bread 159, 160–61, 194–95,
    196–97, 222, 228

Canaan 145–46, 147, 162, 164,
    172–73
Canaanite woman 116–17,
    124, 194–95, 199–200,
    227, 239
Capernaum 42
centurion of crucifixion
    189–90, 204
centurion of faith 196–97,
    204, 239
chief priests 93, 128, 149, 245
  Herod the Great and 25n84,
    99, 114, 245
  Jesus and 33, 73, 89, 95, 97,
    124–26, 202–3
  Judas and 119–20, 236–37,
    247
children 124–25, 229, 248
church 36, 170–71, 201
  early 52–53, 59, 219
  comparison 3, 39, 122, 132,
    137, 142, 243
  contrast 16, 35, 122, 132,
    141–43, 243–44
  convictions 37–38, 44–49,
    51, 62

copyists 24–26, 35–36, 208,
    252
creation 18, 45, 125, 149–50
    new 4, 45, 48, 50, 153, 164,
    211, 213–14, 216, 220
creativity 25, 27, 32, 56–57,
    61, 83
crucifixion 8, 44–46, 68,
    90–92, 158–63, 171, 189,
    234–35, 237–38, 251
curse/curses 79, 96, 98n78, 173
    Deuteronomic, reversing 79,
    109, 219, 229
    fig tree 171, 183n27, 202,
    230
Cyrus of Persia 209, 233, 238

Daniel 76–77, 78, 80
David 8, 15, 27, 50, 88, 122,
    177, 239
    Absalom and 67, 83, 84, 86,
    98n78
    Bethlehem 72–73
    contrasts with Jesus 92–93,
    108–9, 119–20, 126–27,
    128–30
    Goliath 67, 103, 112, 123,
    126
    as healer 120–23, 126
    Jesus as son of 16, 23, 32,
    68–69, 76–77, 79, 82–85,
    92–93, 98–99, 116–17,
    241–42
    kingship journey 67–68,
    84–85, 86–87, 129, 222–23
    messiah 48, 53
    new 66–67, 72, 75, 92, 99,
    110, 124, 222–23
    parallels with Jesus 68–69,
    76–77, 79, 82–84, 85–89,
    90–93, 97–99, 101–3,
    119–20, 125, 128–30
    promises to 70–71, 78, 79,
    112, 129
    servant 85, 223
    shepherding 109–10, 111–12
    traditions 66–67, 83–84,
    85–86
Davidic covenant 70, 79, 129
Davidic king 121, 127
    exile 80–82, 83–84, 101–2,
    109–10, 113, 124, 211,
    237–38

Jesus as 65–68, 70–72,
    74–75, 82–83, 94–99, 104,
    125–26, 128–30
    merciful healer 102–4,
    120–23, 125–28
    messiah 66–70, 71–72, 86,
    94, 99, 104, 109, 113,
    119–20
    shepherd 102, 113–20,
    127–28, 233, 236
Dead Sea Scrolls 72, 79, 134,
    153
demonic realm 120–21, 123,
    219
disciples 24, 33–34, 184, 202,
    221
    definition 10–11, 12–13
    following Jesus 34, 145–46,
    202, 229, 248–49
    Great Commission, send-
    ing out 184–86, 187–88,
    221–22
    Israel, mission to 193–94,
    197–98
    as scribes 34–36, 211,
    247–50
    as teachers 34–35, 163–64,
    186, 187
    as undershepherds 115–16
    understanding 12, 27–28
discipleship 4, 12, 247–48, 250
discourses 16–17, 117–18, 133–
    34, 138, 201, 211–13, 219
    Mission Discourse 220–22
divorce 33, 132, 142, 143, 202

Egypt/Egyptian 35–36, 81, 83,
    135, 149
    exodus 49–50, 55, 111, 133,
    160, 164, 167, 216–18, 242
    Jesus and 182, 215n24,
    216–17, 220
    redemption from 158–59,
    161–63, 217
Elijah 25n81, 27, 229, 233,
    248n11
    John the Baptist and 226–27
    new 66, 239
    transfiguration 154, 156–58,
    228
Elisha 201, 226–28, 229,
    230n61, 233, 248n11
    new 209, 213, 227

Emmaus 59
Enoch 15, 24, 252
enthronement on cross 86–87,
    93–98, 99, 228, 239
eschatology/eschatological
    14n28, 25, 41, 114, 119,
    184, 188, 219, 238
    discourse 231–32
    expectations/hope 114, 157
    fulfillment 38–39, 44, 49, 188
    prophet 134, 140, 147
Eve 53, 177, 186, 213–14, 216
exile 53, 70–71, 77–80, 82,
    179–80, 193, 234–35
    of Jesus 80–82, 83–84,
    101–2, 109–10, 113, 124,
    211, 237–38
    return from 83n47, 102n2,
    207–10, 213–15, 220, 232,
    233–38
    temple destruction and
    230–32, 233, 237
exodus 49–50, 55, 111, 133,
    145, 156–57
    from Egypt 49–50, 55, 111,
    133, 160, 164, 167, 216–18,
    242
    new 133–34, 136–37, 145–
    46, 147–48, 153–54, 156–
    58, 165–66, 242, 249–50
    Passover and 159–63, 180
    Pharaoh of 136, 136n13, 220
    redemption 137–38, 158–59
exorcisms 120–21, 123
Ezekiel 113, 230–31, 248n11
    healing messiah 123, 126, 127
    new covenant 116n32, 161
    shepherds 118, 122, 128
Ezra 21, 22

faith 12, 149, 170, 249
    Abraham 170, 175, 191, 216
    of gentiles 116–17, 124, 194,
    196–97, 199–200, 204, 227
    new people of God 170, 175,
    191–92, 199, 205
faithfulness 107, 112, 177,
    204, 247, 250
    Jesus 67, 103, 119, 239
    scribes 25–26, 107, 252
    to Torah 21, 101, 107, 229–30
familial metaphors 170, 172–
    75, 192, 204–5

family of Abraham 178–81, 183–84, 187–88, 190–93, 195–96, 198, 199–200, 202–2
fear of the Lord 15, 28, 244, 248
feedings 151–53, 165, 209
  messianic feast 152–53, 167, 199–201, 227–28
  wilderness 151–52, 153, 167, 201, 227
fig tree 171, 183n27, 202, 230
folly 243–47
freedom 136–37
fulfillment 30–32, 35, 38–44, 59–60, 61–62, 242
  eschatological 38–39, 44, 49, 188
  formulas/quotations 41–44, 55–56, 75, 137n15, 209–10, 217–18, 223–24
  Law and Prophets 105–6, 109, 157–58, 248–49
  of Scripture 30–32, 35, 38–44, 49–51, 59–60, 119, 121, 127, 129, 140–44

Galilee 81–82, 83–84, 98, 184–85
  ministry 41–43, 102–3, 108, 124, 126–27, 193–96, 210
genealogy 7–9, 48, 68–71, 82, 98–99, 149, 176–81, 193, 213–15
gentiles 127, 152, 179
  Canaanite woman 116–17, 124, 194–95, 199–200, 227, 239
  centurions 189–90, 196–97, 204, 239
  inclusion 184–85, 188, 191, 194–98, 199–201, 204–5
  Jesus and 171, 181, 199–201, 224–25, 226
  Jews and 153, 170–71, 188, 201
geographical movement 67, 83–84, 86–87, 98–99, 101–2, 184, 210, 211
gifts 77–78
glory 108
  of God 155, 157–58, 231
  of Jesus 132n4, 157, 167, 228

God 159, 177. See also people/ family of God
  fear of the Lord 15, 28, 244, 248
  glory 155, 157–58, 231
  loving 107, 180
  reign of / kingdom 52–53, 68, 170, 186, 188, 228
  Son of 59, 68, 83, 85, 89, 94, 180, 188–90, 227
  sovereignty 134–35
  will 14n28, 45n25, 103, 107, 109, 157, 197n62, 202, 204, 242, 250
  Word of 157, 167
Goliath 67, 103, 112, 123, 126
Gospels 54, 96–97, 128. See also Mark, Gospel of
  ancient biographies 51–52, 53–54
  John 16, 81, 97
  Luke 16, 38, 59, 110, 121, 138, 185
  Old Testament and 1, 2–3, 7–9, 30–31, 51–54
  Synoptic 17, 31, 154–55, 186
Great Commission 4, 34, 134, 190, 196–97, 209, 238, 242, 252–53
  disciples and 184–86, 187–88
  mountain setting 163–64, 184–85
Greco-Roman culture 8n3, 24n77, 52
  kingship 105–6, 111–12
  philosophy 13, 17

Hagar 174, 216
healing 103–4, 115–16, 120–23, 186, 201–2
  blindness 123–26, 128
  of Davidic king 102–4, 120–24, 125–28
  kingdom of heaven 123, 126–27
  leprosy 150–51, 153–54, 219
  messiah 123, 126, 127
  miracles 123, 150–51
heaven and earth 185–87, 213, 232
Hebrew Bible / Tanak 7n2, 139, 177, 239. See also Old

Testament / Hebrew Bible; Torah
  Matthew's knowledge of 23–24, 69–70, 110, 126, 166, 231
Hellenistic kingship 105–6, 108–9, 127
hermeneutics 3, 14, 60, 62, 166
Herod Antipas 103, 199, 226, 227n54
Herod the Great 83, 101n2, 127, 136n14
  birth of Jesus and 25n84, 73, 76, 114, 245
  king of Jerusalem 72–73, 75–76, 79–80, 92, 119, 134, 184, 216–17
  Pharaoh of exodus and 136, 136n13, 220
Hezekiah 78
Hitler, Adolf 58–59
Holy Spirit 81, 189–90, 223, 227
  of wisdom 15, 46, 85, 225
hopes of Israel/Jews 1, 20, 30, 44n20, 47–48, 53, 92n70, 133, 196, 225
  eschatological 152–53, 157, 239
  exile, return from 83n47, 102n2, 214, 220
  fulfilling 30–31, 37–38, 41, 43
  judgement and 191, 196, 225–26, 228–33
  messianic 7, 15, 47–49, 69–70, 73, 79, 113, 122–23, 126, 177–78
  reign of God / kingdom 52–53, 68, 170, 186, 188, 228
  resurrection life, salvation 177, 191, 214
hosanna 124–25
Hosea 133, 137n15, 217–18
humility 84, 99, 103, 107, 112, 127, 229–30, 249, 250

Immanuel 115, 182, 215, 216
interpretation of Scripture 23–24, 30–31, 32, 74–75, 94–95, 156, 161–62
  by scribes 21–22, 23–24, 25–28, 249

irony 93–94, 97–98, 239
Isaac 136, 175, 179–81, 215–16
Isaiah 15, 42, 46, 78, 79, 133, 193, 198, 201, 232
  Davidic king 121, 127
  suffering servant 85, 89, 92, 96, 223
Israel/Israelites/Jews 1, 50, 109, 182–83, 185. See also exile; exodus; hopes of Israel
  elders 33, 73, 95, 97, 110, 119–20, 161, 202, 236–37
  Judea/southern 81–82, 182, 192, 229
  messianic expectation 15, 47–49, 79, 122–24
  mission of Jesus to 191–96, 197–200, 204–5
  new Israel, Jesus as 209, 212–13, 217–18, 238–39, 242
  northern 81, 84n50, 116, 127, 185, 193
  promised land 145–46, 147, 162, 164, 172–73
  reign of God 52–53, 70–71, 101, 109, 208, 238
  rejection of 196–97
  rejection of Jesus 170–71, 191–92, 197–99, 201–5, 222–27
  remnant 119, 197, 225–26, 229
  reuniting kingdom 67–68, 70–71, 83, 98, 114, 117, 119, 127
  Sanhedrin 89, 94
  shepherding metaphor 116–17
  sin of 53, 147, 182, 225, 233, 239, 242
Israelite history 41, 69, 163–64, 224–25, 233, 252. See also exile; exodus
  conquest of Canaan 220–22
  divided kingdom 68, 114, 214, 225–28
  in Gospel of Matthew 8–9, 25, 30–31, 165, 205, 208–12, 219, 233, 239, 252
  Jesus fulfilling 39, 44, 129, 178–79, 208, 224
  Jesus, life of 207–10, 239
  monarchy 222–25

structure of Matthew 210–13, 224, 233, 239
unification 38, 49–51, 62, 178, 209

Jacob 78–79, 85n53, 111, 112, 136, 163
Jehoshaphat 227
Jeremiah 23n75, 24, 133, 217, 236, 245, 248n11
  new 213, 239
  new covenant 161, 233
  temple 202, 230–31
Jerusalem 76, 80, 84, 125–26, 229
  destruction 231–32, 234–35
  journey to 41, 42–43, 83–85, 98–99, 202, 210
  king of, Herod as 72–73, 75–76, 79–80, 92, 119, 134, 184, 216–17
  Mount of Olives 86–87, 119
  triumphal entry 124–26, 129, 202, 230–31
Jesus Christ 9, 16, 28, 53, 61–62, 88–90, 98–99. See also David; messiah; parables
  Abraham, new 169–71, 190, 199–200, 215–16
  alternate scribal school 32–35, 73, 83–84, 128, 243–45, 248
  apocalyptic sage-messiah 37–38, 44–49, 57, 59, 75, 109, 201
  authority 33–34, 93, 95, 99, 103, 108, 133, 163–64, 183–87, 190, 196, 213, 238
  baptism 8, 50, 85, 103, 139, 150, 155, 163–64, 181, 216–17, 227
  betrayal 85, 86–89
  characterization / portrait of 1, 4, 27, 93
  Davidic king 65–68, 70–72, 74–75, 82–83, 94–98, 98–99, 104, 125–26, 128–30
  death/crucifixion 8, 44–46, 68, 90–92, 158–63, 171, 189, 234–35, 237–38, 251
  enthronement on cross 86–87, 93–98, 99, 228, 239

exile 80–82, 83–84, 101–2, 109–10, 113, 124
fulfillment of Scripture 30–32, 35, 38–44, 49–51, 59–60, 119, 121, 127, 129, 140–44
healing 103–4, 115–16, 120–23, 127–28
Immanuel 115, 182, 215, 216
incarnation 44, 46
innocence 85–86, 89–90, 93
Israel, new 209, 212–13, 217–18, 238–39, 242
justice, enacting 102–3, 108, 120, 123
King of the Jews 89, 95–97, 188–89, 190
law, living 102, 103–9, 120, 127, 241
Law and Prophets 23, 29, 38–39, 138–39, 140–44, 147, 157–58
mission 183–88, 191–96, 197–200, 204–5
mocking of 85, 91–92, 95–97, 98–99, 129, 189, 234–35
Moses, new 55, 65–66, 105, 110, 131–34, 140, 143, 146–52, 162, 212, 216–20
Moses, parallels to 134–35, 137–39, 151–54, 158, 163–67
prophet-teacher 104, 137–39, 141–46, 148, 228–32, 233, 239
redeemer-king 134–38, 147, 165
rejection of 73, 79–82, 84, 119, 124–26, 129, 173–74, 244–45
sacrifice 118–20, 128, 180–82, 183–84, 190
scribal authorities and 32–35, 73, 79–80, 89, 93, 94–95, 114, 125–26, 243–44
shepherd, Davidic 102, 113–20, 127–28, 233, 236
son of Abraham 7, 11, 48, 68, 176, 177–78, 180–82, 186–88, 196, 242

son of David 16, 23, 32,
    68–69, 76–77, 79, 82–85,
    92–93, 98–99, 116–17,
    241–42
Son of God 59, 68, 83, 85,
    89, 94, 180, 188–90, 227
Son of Man 48, 94–95,
    117–18, 232
suffering servant 84–89,
    90–93, 96, 107, 121, 128,
    165n59
as teacher-sage 2–4, 35,
    44–45, 61–62, 103–4, 115–
    16, 120–21, 211, 218–19,
    238–39
temptation 8, 103, 150, 186,
    209, 216
Torah and 138–39, 140–44,
    219–20
trials 89–90, 94–95, 107, 237
reuniting Israel 67–68,
    70–71, 83, 98, 114, 117,
    119, 127
universal Lord 171, 183n27,
    186–87, 189–90
water 150, 153, 163–64, 165
wilderness 162, 166, 209,
    216–17, 220
Wisdom personified 32, 44,
    46–47, 214, 238, 248–49
wisdom teacher 12–16, 20,
    34–35, 70–71, 224–25,
    239, 242
worship of 76–77, 78, 80,
    95, 182, 189
yoke 144–46, 147
Jesus Seminar 14
Jews/Jewish 180–81. See also
    hopes of Israel/Jews;
    Israel/Israelites/Jews
Gentiles and 153, 170–71,
    188, 201
King of the 89, 95–97,
    188–89, 190
literature 165–66, 184, 212
Matthew as 23, 61, 68, 110,
    162
particularism 173, 179,
    181–82, 184, 187–89, 190,
    201–2, 204
tradition 29–30, 35, 47, 152–
    53, 157n48, 170, 179n17,
    180n21, 181, 235–36

Job 15, 247
John, Gospel of 16, 81, 97
John the Baptist 13, 18, 139,
    192, 203, 204
    Abraham's family 192–93,
    196, 197–98
    Elijah and 226–27
    Herod and 199, 226
    Jesus and 46, 103, 121, 222
    prophet, last OT 103, 139,
    192, 222
Jonathan 67, 119
Joseph (husband of Mary)
    69, 80, 97, 101n2, 135,
    182, 217
    Abraham and 215–16
Joseph (son of Jacob) 73n17,
    76–77, 93n71, 111, 135
Joshua 50, 66, 145, 164, 208,
    213, 221, 227
Jubilees, book of 180–81
Judah 72, 136
Judas Iscariot 86–88, 119–20,
    185, 235–36
    foolish disciple 243, 246–47,
    250
Judea 81–82, 182, 192, 229
judgment 108, 150, 191–93,
    196–97, 198, 225–26,
    228–33, 237
    shepherd-judge 117–18
justice 102–3, 107, 108, 120,
    123, 250

kingdom of heaven 18–20,
    126–27, 203–4, 196–97
    authority 185–86
    ethics/wisdom 70–71, 229–
    30, 250–51
    healing 123, 126–27
    inauguration 68, 70
    incarnation 46, 102
    secrets of 21–22, 24, 28, 30,
    34, 198–99
Sermon on the Mount 104,
    123
    treasures 28–29, 31–32
King of the Jews 89, 95–97,
    188–89, 190
kings/kingship 126, 135–36.
    See also Davidic king
    ancient Near Eastern (ANE)
    101, 104, 110, 111–12

Greco-Roman 105–6,
    111–12
Hellenistic 105–6, 108–9,
    127
law and 103–6
salvation 97–98, 127, 129,
    136–37
scribes and 35–36, 251–52
shepherd metaphor 102,
    110, 111–12
Torah 21, 36, 106–7, 113,
    120, 127
wisdom/wise 19, 21, 76–77,
    82, 85–86

Lady Wisdom 138, 145
Lamentations 234–35
Last Supper 87, 134, 153, 154,
    158–63
law 128–29, 148
    kings and 103–6
    living/embodied 102, 103–9,
    120, 127, 241
    scribes of 16–17, 24, 108,
    140, 243–44, 246
Law and Prophets 17, 105–6,
    109, 157–58, 248–49
    Jesus and 23, 29, 38–39,
    138–39, 140–44, 147
Leah 179
leprosy 150–51, 153–54, 219
The Lion King 129–30
Lord, universal 171, 183n27,
    186–87, 189–90
love/loving 107, 142, 144, 180
Luke, Gospel of 16, 38, 59,
    110, 121, 138, 185

magi / wise men 18, 76–80,
    182, 189, 204
Mark, Gospel of 110, 138,
    154, 208
    beginning 11, 52, 68, 176
    exorcisms 120–21
    feedings 152, 200
    Matthew and 25, 38, 88n63,
    191, 208, 223
    son of David 16, 223
    suffering servant 85–86
    understanding in 12, 28
Mary (mother of Jesus) 178,
    215–16
Matthean authorship 7n1

Matthew (apostle) 20, 26–27,
  248–49
  convictions 37–38, 44–49,
    51, 62
  creativity 25, 27, 32, 56–57,
    61, 83
  discipled scribe 2, 4, 9–12,
    21–22, 36, 61–62, 187–88,
    204–5, 207, 238–39, 241–43
  Hebrew Scriptures, knowl-
    edge of 23–24, 69–70, 110,
    126, 166, 231
  interpretation 23–24, 30–31,
    32, 74–75, 94–95, 156,
    161–62
  Jewishness 23, 61, 68, 110,
    162
  subtlety 55–57, 129
  as teacher 1–2, 27, 162, 166,
    241
  wisdom 23–24, 30, 241
Matthew, Gospel of 29–31,
  132–33. See also structure
  of Matthew
  allusions 8–9, 31, 43, 56,
    80–81, 129, 154–56
  birth/infancy narrative
    41–42, 43, 71–76, 99, 114,
    134–36, 181–82, 213
  canonical placement 1, 31
  discourses 16–17, 117–18,
    133–34, 138, 201, 211–13,
    219, 220–22
  Galilean ministry 41, 42, 43,
    102–3, 108, 124, 126–27,
    193–96, 210
  genealogy 7–9, 48, 68–71,
    82, 98–99, 149, 176–81,
    193, 213–15
  Hebrew Scriptures / Old
    Testament 30–32, 54–55,
    57–59, 132–33, 137
  irony 93–94, 97–98, 239
  Jerusalem, journey to 41,
    42–43, 83–85, 98–99, 202,
    210
  methods 8, 9, 10–11, 37–38,
    54–55, 57–60, 61–62,
    129–30
  mission of Jesus 193–96
  Moses traditions 136–37, 212
  narrative 30, 30–31, 47,
    131–32, 208–10

passion narrative 89–96,
    118–19, 158, 188–89,
    237–38
  Psalms parallels 86–88,
    89–92, 94
  shadow stories 8–9, 38,
    49–51, 54–55, 57, 131, 137,
    154–56, 162–63, 164–67,
    241
  shepherding metaphor
    113–20
  spatial perspective 50–51
  scribes and disciples 34–35
  time 49–51, 218
  transfiguration 134, 154–56,
    157–58, 228
  triumphal entry 124–26,
    129, 202, 230–31
Matthias 185
meekness 107–8
mercy 103, 107, 116–17, 250
Mephibosheth 126
messiah 7–8, 47–49, 53
  apocalyptic sage 15–17,
    37–38, 44–49, 57, 59, 75,
    109, 201
  branch 15, 56, 72, 80–81, 82,
    85, 99, 121, 127, 241
  Davidic 66–70, 71–72, 86, 94,
    99, 104, 109, 113, 119–20
  expectation 15, 47–49, 73,
    114, 123–24
  feast 152–53, 167, 199–201,
    227–28
  healing 123, 126, 127
  as shepherd / shepherding
    73, 75–76
  suffering 48, 67, 84–89
messianism 48, 110
metanarrative 30–31, 53, 177
methods 8, 9, 10–11, 37–38,
  54–55, 57–60, 61–62,
  129–30
  fulfilment formulas 41–44,
    55–56, 75, 137n15, 209–10,
    217–18, 223–24
Micah 133
miracles 133–34, 149–51,
  152–54, 219
  healing 123, 150–51
  manna feeding 151–53, 165,
    209, 227

  Moses mediating 148–51,
    152–54
  water 150, 151, 153, 163–64,
    165, 227
Miriam 219
money/riches 107–8, 202,
  246–47
Moses 8, 50, 132, 162–64, 239
  birth/infancy story 134–36,
    137
  Jesus, parallels with 134–35,
    137–39, 151–54, 158,
    163–67
  Joshua and 50, 66, 145, 164,
    208, 213, 221, 227
  as mediator 133, 138, 149,
    154–56
  messiah 48, 55
  miracles 148–51, 152–54
  Mount Sinai and 139–40,
    148, 152, 154–56, 161,
    218–19
  new 55, 65–66, 105, 110,
    131–34, 140, 143, 146–52,
    162, 165–67, 212, 216–20,
    242
  Pharaoh and 135–36, 239
  prophet like 132–34, 152–53,
    155
  serpent 149–50, 153
  shepherding 111, 116,
    165n59
  as teacher-prophet 137–38,
    164
  traditions 136–37, 212
  transfiguration 154–58, 228
  typology 164–67, 182, 201
  water 150, 151, 153
mountain settings
  feeding / messianic feast
    152–53, 167, 199–201,
    227–28
  Great Commission 163–64,
    184–85
  Olives, Mount of 86–87, 119
  Sermon on the Mount 17,
    55, 105, 138–40, 166, 218
  Sinai, Mount 55, 105,
    138–40, 148, 152, 154–56,
    160–61, 218–19
  transfiguration 154–56,
    157–58, 228
  Zion, Mount 188, 201

mourning 108
murder 142–43
mysteries 19–20, 24, 30, 36, 38, 44–45, 46

narrative/narratives 4, 9, 30–31, 47, 60, 131–32, 208–10
echoes 54–55
historical 51–54, 208
metanarrative 30–31, 53, 177
narrative-discourse outline 211–13, 219–20
parallels 28, 30, 54–55, 72–73, 79, 83–85
Nathan (prophet) 112
Nazareth 20, 56, 80–82, 83
Nazarene 56, 72, 80–82, 99
new and old 29–31, 39, 45–46, 49, 128–29, 243
relationship 41, 60, 61
treasures 1–4, 8, 9–10, 20, 23–24, 27–32, 160
new covenant 55, 71, 133–34, 226, 233
old covenant and 80, 147–48, 157, 160–61
prophecies of 116n32, 161, 163, 233
Torah and 140, 147–48, 229–30
New Testament, Old and 1–4, 29–30

oaths 142, 143
old covenant, Mosaic 8–9, 31, 159–60, 162
new covenant and 80, 147–48, 157, 160–61
Old Testament / Hebrew Bible 58–59, 172–73. See also promises, Old Testament; Torah
Gospels and 1, 2–3, 7–9, 30–31, 51–54
Greek 73–74, 80
historical narratives 51–54, 208
kingship 105–6, 108–9, 111–13, 127
messianic expectation 15, 47–49
scribes 21–22, 36

shepherd metaphor 111–13, 116, 118–19
Tanak 7n2, 139, 177, 239
Olives, Mount of 86–87, 119

parables 10, 24, 202–3, 204
kingdom 18–20, 42, 198–99, 213, 224
vineyard 202–3, 230
passion narrative 89–96, 118–19, 158, 188–89, 237–38
crucifixion 8, 44–46, 68, 90–92, 158–63, 171, 189, 234–35, 237–38, 251
trials 85, 89–90, 94–95, 97–98, 107, 237
Paul (apostle) 169, 175, 185, 249
people/family of God 148, 153, 194
new 148, 153, 170–71, 176, 181–85, 190, 199–201, 203, 204–5, 228–29
particularism, Jewish 173, 179, 181–82, 183–84, 187–89, 190, 201–2, 204
universality 173, 178–79, 181–82, 183–84, 190–91, 204
persecution 107, 135, 198, 221–22
Peter (apostle) 27n88, 31, 35, 150, 155, 199n64, 227n55
confession 42, 86, 189n48, 226, 228
Pharaoh of exodus 111, 135–36, 239
Herod the Great and 135–36, 136n13, 220
Pharisees 122, 132, 192, 196–97, 200
Jesus and 32–35, 43, 94, 132, 200, 201–3, 222
scribes of the law 16–17, 24, 108, 140, 243–44, 246
wisdom teachers 13, 17, 26–27, 146, 248–49
Pilate, Pontius 89–90, 95, 107, 149, 189, 235
prayer 107, 249
promised land 145–46, 147, 162, 164, 172–73
promises, Old Testament 60, 164

to Abraham 50, 169n2, 172–75, 189, 191, 201
covenant 39, 132, 137
to David 70–71, 78, 79, 112, 129
to Israel 121–22, 132, 145, 214
Jesus fulfilling 39, 49, 75, 79, 149–50, 163, 176–77
messiah 15, 72, 101
prophecy 21, 217, 225–26, 228–29
messianic 40, 59–60
new covenant 116n32, 161, 163, 233
predictive 38–39, 40–41
scribes and 22, 23, 24, 26, 35, 58–59
shepherd metaphor 112–13
wisdom 13, 15
prophets 139, 198, 237. See also individuals
eschatology 134, 140, 147
Jesus as the Prophet 55, 139, 157, 209, 225–27
John the Baptist as 103, 139, 192, 222
Moses-like 132–34, 152–53, 155
prophet-teacher, Jesus as 104, 137–39, 141–46, 148, 228–32, 233, 239
wisdom 15, 46
prospective reading 58, 60, 135–36, 153
proverbs 16–17
Psalms parallels 86–88, 89–92, 94

quotations of Scripture 41–44, 55–56, 75, 137n15, 209–10, 217–18, 223–24

Rachel 217
Rahab 178–79, 221
Ramah 82, 83, 217
Rebekah 179
reception 57–60
redeemer-king 134–38, 152–53
redemption 133, 148
from Egypt 158–59, 161–63, 217
exodus 137–38, 158–59

redemptive history 4, 8n4,
    148, 213
repentance 192–93, 196,
    198–99, 203–4
resurrection 150–51, 153–54,
    171, 190–91, 210–11, 222,
    250, 251–52
    life 177, 214, 222
    return from exile 234–35,
    237–38, 250
retrospective reading 57–59,
    61, 135–36, 153
revelation 18, 19, 20, 23,
    30–32, 45
    new, of the Son 32, 154–55,
    157
revenge for evil / lex talionis
    142, 144
righteousness 41n13, 45, 108,
    244, 252
    Jesus bringing/fulfilling 67,
    81, 103
    wisdom and 14n30, 38n3,
    78n35, 103, 245–46
Romans 71n31, 95–96, 97, 189
    centurions 189–90, 196–97,
    204, 239
    Pilate, Pontius 89–90, 95,
    107, 149, 189, 235
Ruth 178–79

Sabbath rest 145, 222, 223
sacrifice 118–20, 128, 179–82,
    183–84, 190
Sadducees 33, 192, 196–97, 249
salvation 53, 115, 127, 150,
    180, 185, 193
    age of 133, 166
    kings and 97–98, 127, 129,
    136–37
    new exodus 133–34
    resurrection life 177, 191, 214
    universality 179, 181–83,
    185, 188–90
Samuel 67, 70, 103n4, 112, 222
Sarah 174–75, 179, 215–16
Satan 103, 186, 239
Saul 67, 83, 84, 88, 90n67,
    110, 112, 119, 125, 222–23
scribes 10–12, 24–26
    alternate school of Jesus
    32–35, 73, 83–84, 128,
    243–45, 248

copyists 24–26, 35–36, 208,
    252
discipled 2, 4, 9–12, 21–22,
    36, 61–62, 187–88, 204–5,
    207, 238–39, 241–43
disciples as 34–36, 211,
    247–50
distribution 26–27, 35, 36
faithfulness 25–26, 107, 252
foolish 243–47
interpretation of Scripture
    21–22, 23–24, 25–28, 249
Jesus and 32–35, 73, 79–80,
    89, 93, 94–95, 114, 125–26,
    243–44
kings and 35–36, 251–52
of the law 16–17, 24, 108,
    140, 243–44, 246
learning/knowledge 22–23,
    24, 27–28
Old Testament 21–22, 36
prophecy and 22, 23, 24, 26,
    35, 58–59
revelation, special 20, 23,
    30–32, 45
teaching 27, 251–53
training 19, 22–24, 35–36
wisdom 21–24
scrolls 11–12, 26
seed 149, 169, 177, 179
    of Abraham 169–70, 172,
    174–75, 185, 186, 188, 216
Septuagint (LXX) 73–74,
    213, 216
Sermon on the Mount 8, 125,
    213, 246
    antitheses 141–43
    Jesus as king 104–5, 107–8
    kingdom of heaven 104, 123
    mountain settings 17, 55,
    105, 138–40, 166, 218
    new Moses 139–40, 152,
    218–20
    Torah and 141–44, 145–47,
    219–20
    wisdom 17, 104, 244–45, 250
serpent 149–50, 153, 177,
    214n19
shadow stories 8–9, 38, 49–51,
    54–55, 57, 131, 137, 154–
    56, 162–63, 164–67, 241
Sheba, queen of 18, 77–78,
    224–25

shepherds / shepherding meta-
    phor 112–13, 165n59
    ancient Near East (ANE)
    110, 111–12
    David 109–10, 111–12, 122
    Davidic king 102, 113–20,
    127–28, 233, 236
    false shepherds 112–13,
    118–19, 120, 122, 128
    Jesus as 102, 113–20, 127–
    28, 233, 236
    kings 102, 110, 111–12
    messiah 73, 75–76
    Moses 111, 116, 165n59
    Old Testament 111–13, 116,
    118–20
    undershepherds 111–12,
    115–16
silence of Jesus 85, 86, 89–90,
    94, 107
Simon of Cyrene 96
sin 41n13, 45, 97, 219, 233
    atonement for 44, 68, 96–97,
    115, 121n43, 160–62,
    183–84, 216n26
    forgiveness of 109, 161
    of Israel 53, 147, 182, 225,
    233, 239, 242
    slavery to 138, 153, 167,
    225, 246
Sinai, Mount 55, 105, 138–40,
    148, 152, 154–56, 160–61,
    218–19
Solomon 8, 71, 84, 94n72,
    121, 223
    new 95n74, 213, 214–15
    sons of / Rehoboam 68, 114,
    214, 225
    temple 81, 225
    wisdom 15, 18, 46, 77, 121,
    224–25
son of Abraham 7, 11, 48,
    68, 176, 177–78, 180–82,
    186–88, 196, 242
son of David 16, 23, 32, 68–69,
    76–77, 79, 82–85, 92–93,
    98–99, 116–17, 241–42
Son of God 59, 68, 83, 85, 89,
    94, 180, 188–90, 227
Son of Man 48, 94–95, 117–
    18, 232
sons of the kingdom 196–97
star 78–79, 80
Star Wars 54

structure of Matthew 18–20,
69, 83–84, 115, 138–39,
175–76, 200, 208–13, 217
geographical movement
67, 83–84, 86–87, 98–99,
101–2, 184, 210, 211
history of Israel 210–13,
224, 233, 239
narrative-discourse outline
211–13, 219–20
Pentateuch/Torah and 211–
13, 219–20
subtlety 55–57, 129
suffering servant 84–89, 90–93,
96, 107, 121, 128, 165n59
Sumerian texts 35–36
Synoptic Gospels 17, 31,
154–55, 186

Tabernacles, Feast of 125
Tamar 178–79
Tanak 7n2, 139, 177, 239
teachers/teaching
comparison 3, 39, 122, 132,
137, 142, 243
contrast 16, 35, 122, 132,
141–43, 243–44
disciples as 34–35, 163–64,
186, 187
Matthew as 1–2, 27, 162,
166, 241
Pharisees 13, 17, 26–27, 146,
248–49
prophet-teacher 104, 137–
39, 141–46, 148, 228–32,
233, 239
teacher-sage 2–4, 35, 44–45,
61–62, 103–4, 115–16, 120–
21, 211, 218–19, 238–39
wisdom teacher 12–16, 20,
34–35, 70–71, 224–25,
239, 242
temple 77–79, 81, 202, 203,
222, 230–31
destruction 231–32, 233,
234–36, 237–38
Jesus and 230–31, 233
rebuilding 233, 238
of Solomon 81, 225
temptation of Jesus 8, 103,
150, 186, 209, 216
Testament of Solomon 121
time 49–51, 218

titulus 96–98, 189
Torah 21–22, 211–13, 219–20
faithfulness to 21, 101, 107,
229–30
intention, true 141–44
Jesus and 133–34, 138–39,
140–44, 219–20
kings and 21, 36, 106–7,
113, 120, 127
new covenant 140, 147–48,
229–30
Sermon on the Mount 141–
44, 145–47, 219–20
wisdom 32, 105
traditions
of David 66–67, 83–84,
85–86
of elders 23, 24, 27, 29, 200,
244
Jewish 29–30, 35, 47, 152–
53, 157n48, 170, 179n17,
180n21, 181, 235–36
of Moses 136–37, 212
wisdom 16–19, 25, 27–28,
32, 211, 224–25, 243
transfiguration 134, 154–56,
157–58, 228
treasures 27–28, 250
old and new 1–4, 8, 9–10,
20, 23–24, 27–32, 160
temple 77–79
trials of Jesus 89–90, 94–95,
107, 237
false witnesses/testimony 85,
89–90, 97–98
triumphal entry 124–26, 129,
202, 230–31
truth/truthful 107, 142, 143
Tyre and Sidon 116, 194, 198

understanding 12, 19–20,
22–23, 28, 245, 249, 250
universal/universality
family of Abraham 173,
179, 183–84, 190–91, 204
Lord 171, 183n27, 186–87,
189–90
people/family of God 173,
178–79, 181–82, 183–84,
190–91, 204
salvation availability 181–
83, 185, 188–90

violence 88–90, 144

water 150, 151, 153, 163–64,
165, 227
wilderness 111, 133, 150, 193,
218–19, 221n42
feeding in 151–52, 153, 167,
201, 227
Jesus and 162, 166, 209,
216–17, 220
will of God 14n28, 45n25,
103, 107, 109, 157, 197n62,
202, 204, 242, 250
wisdom 13, 15, 16–19, 24,
27, 70–71, 169n2, 244–47,
251–52
branch 15, 72, 80–81
definition 14–15
Holy Spirit 15, 46, 85, 225
Jesus as personified 32, 44,
46–47, 214, 238, 248–49
kings 19, 21, 82, 85–86
Lady Wisdom 138, 145
literature 14n30, 46, 80,
214, 224
new exodus 145–46
personification 15–16, 17–18,
28, 32, 47, 138, 145, 214
righteousness and 14n30,
38n3, 78n35, 103, 245–46
scribes 21–24
seeking 22–23
Sermon on the Mount 17,
104, 244–45, 250
Solomon 15, 18, 46, 77, 121,
224–25
Torah 32, 105
tradition 16–19, 25, 27–28,
32, 211, 224–25, 243
yoke of Jesus 145–46
Wisdom of Solomon 46
wisdom teachers 13, 17,
26–27, 146, 248–49
Jesus 12–16, 20, 34–35,
70–71, 224–25, 239, 242
wise men / magi 18, 76–80,
182, 189, 204
Word of God 157, 167

yoke of Jesus 144–46, 147

Zechariah 43, 120, 161, 230,
233
death of 231, 234, 235–37
Zion, Mount 188, 201